Praise for *Religion and the Death Penalty:*

"In my many years of experience fighting the injustices of the death penalty, I have worked closely with people who support capital punishment and with those who oppose it. This book thoroughly captures the complexity of this contentious and emotional issue. Its fascinating and compelling essays move the conversation beyond the usual political rhetoric. Through their religious dimension, these essays pose urgent questions that policy experts, legislators, and citizens alike must grapple with. This is essential reading for anyone who cares about justice in our society."

> — Virginia E. Sloan
> *The Constitution Project,*
> *Washington, D.C.*

"Every evangelical in America should read this extraordinary and compelling contribution to the death penalty debate. I recommend this book without reservation. It challenged my own thinking in ways that nothing else has in years."

> — Richard Cizik
> *National Association of Evangelicals*

THE EERDMANS RELIGION, ETHICS, AND PUBLIC LIFE SERIES

Jean Bethke Elshtain and John D. Carlson, Series Editors

This new series aims to explore dilemmas and debates at the intersection of religion, ethics, and public life. Its high-caliber books will include both single- and multi-authored volumes by scholars, public officials, and policy experts discussing the religious and moral meanings of pressing social issues. At a time when people puzzle over the connections between religious belief and civic practice, this series will offer valuable perspectives to a wide range of readers.

RELIGION AND THE DEATH PENALTY

A Call for Reckoning

Edited by

Erik C. Owens, John D. Carlson, and Eric P. Elshtain

William B. Eerdmans Publishing Company
Grand Rapids, Michigan / Cambridge, U.K.

Wm. B. Eerdmans Publishing Co.
255 Jefferson Ave. S.E., Grand Rapids, Michigan 49503 /
P.O. Box 163, Cambridge CB3 9PU U.K.
www.eerdmans.com

Printed in the United States of America

09 08 07 06 05 04   7 6 5 4 3 2 1

Library of Congress Cataloging-in-Publication Data

Religion and the death penalty: a call for reckoning / edited by Erik C. Owens,
    John D. Carlson, and Eric P. Elshtain.
        p.   cm.
    Includes bibliographical references.
    ISBN 0-8028-2172-3 (pbk.: alk. paper)
    1. Capital Punishment — Religious aspects — Congresses.   I. Owens,
    Erik C.   II. Carlson, John D. (John David).   III, Elshtain, Eric P.

    HV8694.C229   2004
    201'.764 — dc22

                                        2004043325

"Imperatives" from the poem cycle "Mysteries of the Incarnation" from *Little Girls
at Church,* by Kathleen Norris, © 1995. Reprinted by permission of University of
Pittsburgh Press.

Contents

Series Foreword

This series explores dilemmas and debates at the intersections of religion, ethics, and public life. At a time when religion pervades the public square, concerned citizens puzzle over the connections between their religious beliefs and the moral practices of civic life. The Eerdmans Religion, Ethics, and Public Life Series delivers high caliber books that reflect on the religious and moral dimensions of politics, culture, and society. The series foregrounds the relationship among theological and philosophical scholarship, practical ethics, and policy studies — all contextualized in light of contemporary themes and issues. It does so by integrating a broad array of perspectives from diverse religious faiths, moral traditions, academic disciplines, political persuasions, and professional vocations. Some of the books in the series bring scholars, public leaders and officials, and policy experts together within one volume to discuss the religious and moral meanings of timely issues and to provide a venue in which their work can be mutually informative. In addition to multiauthored volumes, the series also features monographs which make compelling arguments that enrich ongoing conversations or initiate new ones. Books in the series are intended for a wide readership, including academics, clergy, government officials, journalists, students, policy experts, leaders of public institutions, and interested citizens generally.

As the first book in the series, *Religion and the Death Penalty: A Call for Reckoning* aptly embodies the goals and aspirations set forth above. In tackling head-on one of the most contentious issues in American political life (and one with growing implications for U.S. relations abroad), the contributors to this book do not shy away from controversy. On the contrary, they boldly embrace it by deepening the debate beyond the surface rhetoric that usually overtakes popular opinion and typical media coverage. The book plumbs the richness of various theological traditions and, juxtaposing them with profound insights and experiences relating to the capital justice system, strikes a balance that affords the divergent voices much-needed room to air their views. We hope this book will encourage vigorous, thoughtful debate as it challenges readers to come to terms with this weighty institution.

JEAN BETHKE ELSHTAIN *and* JOHN D. CARLSON
series editors

Foreword

There isn't very much in the writing of political philosopher Jean-Jacques Rousseau with which I agree. But I concur heartily with his conviction that the person who would separate politics from morals fails to understand both politics and morals. Too much of the same territory is claimed by each. Our political and moral lives are unthinkable absent attempts to wrestle with the big questions: What does it mean to live a good human life? What are the bases for order in a body politic? How do we hold people accountable for their deeds? Are people always fully accountable? What is the purpose of justice? Is retributive justice really a form of justice or simply vengeance disguised as something more dignified? What are the occasions that justify putting citizens in harm's way (as in war) or taking a human life (as in capital punishment)?

For some — committed pacifists, for example — the last question in that daunting series of queries is readily answered: there is no occasion that justifies the intentional taking of human life, whether in war (whatever its cause or intent) or in the penal system (however heinous the crime). For the vast majority of us who are not pacifists, however, such a blanket response is hard, if not impossible, to come by. Most of us look at German National Socialism and say that it would have been better had the world responded with force to Adolf Hitler sooner rather than later. But we might also believe that not every threat to the comity of nations or to one's own polity warrants a response with force. One works it out on a case-by-case basis with a set of fundamental principles at hand. This, at least, is the way the Christian just war tradition works when addressing such matters.

In the matter of capital punishment, the great historic theologians, those whose names are virtually synonymous with the Christian tradition — St. Augustine, St. Thomas Aquinas, Martin Luther, John Calvin — all found ways to support or to justify capital punishment with varying degrees of affirmation (although Augustine came very close to opposing it, finally). At the same time, there was always a strand of Christianity that caviled at capital punishment and called it into question. That strand — now called "abolitionism" — is visible and audible in all current debates on the subject and, in some denominations and congregations, has become perhaps the majority position. One of the important developments in recent decades is the seismic shift within Roman Catholicism from its historic position in support of capital punishment for many crimes (including heresy) to the virtual abolition of the death penalty (or, more precisely, the death penalty's justification), in the writings of Pope John Paul II.

The other great Abrahamic religions, Judaism and Islam, have not historically sustained a strong pacifist or abolitionist tradition. Being religions of the law, they encoded support for capital punishment early on, and that support has remained (with varying degrees of enthusiasm) the dominant strand in the tradition, if not the belief of each and every practicing member of the faith.

The complexity to which I have but briefly alluded is wonderfully reflected in the pages of this book. The editors asked leading theologians to explicate their religious traditions' positions on capital punishment, and they asked important public figures to describe how their moral and ethical convictions intersect with their legal and political convictions and responsibilities. This was a serious assignment taken seriously, as the challenging, thoughtful, and at times quite eloquent essays in this volume demonstrate. The overall animating purpose of the Pew Forum on Religion and Public Life — to make more nuanced and forthright our appreciation of the interplay of politics and religion in public life and public policy — is here well-served.

Whatever our positions on capital punishment, the question of its moral status should haunt us. No one should take capital punishment casually or for granted. No one should cheer when a convicted murderer's life is taken. These are occasions of grave solemnity. For some in this volume, such an occasion reminds us of the dignity and irreducible worth of a human life: he or she who takes a life must pay with his or her own, especially if the crime is particularly violent and egregious. The value of human life demands no less. Those who categorically oppose the death penalty insist that the value of human life is such that the state, in the name of all of us, should not take a life, even under the severe provocation of a serial killer or a predator who violates and murders children. To execute a human being, they suggest, is to make law and its enforcement an ultimate measure, when in fact human law can only aspire to the limited and the penultimate. We hear in this opposition an echo of Albert Camus's powerful arguments in his classic essay, "Reflections on the Guillotine."

Camus's position has been my own since I was eighteen years old. Indeed, I argued in *Who Are We? Critical Reflections and Hopeful Possibilities* that we are always tempted to make an idol of the state, as if it were the ultimate giver and taker of life, which is a role reserved only for God.[1] Given the frailty of our minds, the limits of our knowledge, and the need to temper justice with mercy, we should follow Camus, who said, "We know enough to say that this or that major criminal deserves hard labor for life. But we do not know enough to decree that he should be shorn of his future — in other words, of the chance we all have of making amends."[2] But I must say that I was challenged by a number of the essays on the subject that appear in these pages. Certainly it is worth entertaining the possibility that human dignity may cut as much in favor of capital punishment — under certain limited circumstances when there is a moral certainty of the guilt of a person for a particularly horrific crime — as it does in favor of abolition.

Wherever one finally comes out on this issue, the way in which we are obliged to debate the question demonstrates beyond a shadow of doubt that he or she who would understand politics must understand morals, and he or she who would understand morals must understand politics. Because the keepers of our great religious traditions are this society's primary stewards of what we call ethics or morals, debating capital punishment is also, deep down, a debate about the entanglement of religion with public life, citizenship, and public responsibility. This is a good thing, and it works best when we bring our differences to the surface and debate them in an atmosphere of seriousness and good will commensurate with the gravity of the matter at hand.

JEAN BETHKE ELSHTAIN

1. Jean Bethke Elshtain, *Who Are We? Critical Reflections and Hopeful Possibilities* (Grand Rapids, Mich.: Wm. B. Eerdmans, 2000).

2. Albert Camus, "Reflections on the Guillotine," in *Resistance, Rebellion, and Death,* trans. Justin O'Brien (New York: Vintage Books, 1974), p. 230.

Preface

Producing a book on such a grave topic as the death penalty is a sobering process. At the most basic level, deliberation about capital punishment raises mortal concerns: it involves matters of life and death, usually those of our fellow citizens. We ought not lose sight of this reality as we delve into the various philosophical, religious, political, and other conceptual underpinnings of the issue. Yet, there are other high moral and deliberative stakes as well. As with so many other gripping issues that democratic polities face, *what* we think about the death penalty obliges us to dwell deeply upon the very process of *how* we think about it. How can we or should we draw upon religious traditions, past and present, to make sense of a centuries-old practice that faces new challenges, particularly in an era of globalization? Certainly, it makes a difference which political, theological, and philosophical principles are considered and the comparative weight that our society assigns to them as it fashions and implements public policy. Can some consensus possibly emerge among those who vigorously disagree on this issue and the principles underlying it? Our aim in this book has been to provide a spectrum of viewpoints among supporters and opponents of capital punishment, while also uncovering areas of agreement. Ultimately, however, the reader will have to determine for him- or herself how to resolve the crucial questions surrounding this most solemn practice in American political life.

This book reflects the mission and commitments of the Pew Forum on Religion and Public Life, so a few words about the Forum will help to illuminate the scope, methods, and aspirations of the volume. The Pew Forum is a non-profit, non-partisan organization that seeks to promote a deeper under-standing of how religion shapes the ideas and institutions of society. People of faith and the institutions they build play an essential role in the public life of our nation; the Forum explores these contributions while honoring Amer-ica's traditions of religious liberty and pluralism. The Forum takes no posi-tions on legislation or other important issues of the day, including the death penalty. Rather, it is guided by the belief that clarity is found by airing rigor-ous and cogently articulated positions on many sides of an issue. Where pos-sible — and this book is no exception — the Forum strives to identify areas of agreement among previously embattled factions. However, the search for ar-eas of common ground is not an attempt to blur critical distinctions and dif-ferences of opinion that demonstrate the depth or sincerity of representative beliefs. The goal is to facilitate a truly civil forum in which people of goodwill can openly share their views, honestly debate them, and productively reason together about controversial problems in our political life and culture.

Two guiding metaphors encapsulate the Pew Forum's strategies and methods. As a *town hall*, the Forum has sponsored public events that bring together contrasting perspectives from the fields of religion, politics, and journalism to examine the intersections of religion and public affairs. One such example occurred on January 25, 2002, when the Forum sponsored a conference entitled "A Call for Reckoning: Religion and the Death Penalty" at the University of Chicago Divinity School in Chicago, Illinois. This high-profile event, attended by an overflow audience of more than five hundred engaged citizens, made national news as it convened distinguished voices from federal and state governments as well as leading academic institutions. The conference boasted an exceptional array of speakers, placing public offi-cials of the highest levels of government (including a Supreme Court justice, governor, senator, and federal prosecutor) alongside eminent religious lead-ers and scholars. On another occasion, June 3, 2002, the sitting governor of Il-linois—the most prominent battleground state of capital punishment re-form—chose a Pew Forum venue to go public with his religious views on capital punishment and to preview his thoughts on the commutation of all Il-linois capital sentences that would, six months later, shake the foundations of the death penalty debate. The success of such town hall events is a tribute to these participants who generously took time and energy from their demand-ing schedules to discuss how religion informs the shared concerns of our public life.

Through its capacity as a *clearinghouse*, the Pew Forum promotes re-search and makes available important and timely publications about the in-tersections of religious commitments and public life. To this end, this book consolidates edited versions of the talks and papers delivered at the afore-mentioned town hall events. In addition, the editors have commissioned chapters that lend further diversity and insight to the wide range of view-points surrounding the death penalty debate.

As conference organizers and editors, we owe a great debt to The Pew Charitable Trusts for its generous grant that finances and supports the work of the Pew Forum. We extend our deep gratitude to the Trust's President, Rebecca Rimel, and to Luis Lugo, Director of the Trust's Religion Program and Pew Forum Executive Director, for their support of the conference and this publication. Dr. Lugo has been an especially stalwart defender and patron who offered vital encouragement throughout this project. We are grateful to the University of Chicago Divinity School and its dean, Richard Rosengarten, for hosting the conference and providing innumerable logistical details that underlie a public event's success. The Divinity School also provided crucial institutional support during this book's production.

We also wish to thank Forum Co-chair E. J. Dionne Jr. and Melissa Rogers, the Forum's dynamic founding Executive Director, for their assistance in planning the conference and for making the trip to Chicago to ensure its success. We express our special appreciation to Professor and Forum Co-chair Jean Bethke Elshtain, who worked tirelessly to support this project while also affording us the freedom to strike out on our own. She has made innumerable contributions to the vitality of American civic life and to the overlapping realms of religion, political theory, and public affairs. We also thank the splendid company of colleagues at the Forum who helped conceive, plan, and support the conference and who offered their valuable encouragement in the production of this book: Staci Simmons Waldvogel, Sandra Stencel, Kayla Meltzer Drogosz, and Amy Sullivan as well as Kirsten Hunter, Grace McMillan, Heather Morton, and Christina Counselman.

Jon Pott, Gwen Penning, Andrew Hoogheem, and the staff at Eerdmans Publishing were tremendous to work with, and we appreciate their patience and assistance during the publication process.

Finally, we thank our family and friends for their understanding, support, and encouragement when this project seemed—and, at times, was—all-consuming. Many of them joined hundreds of other civic-minded people who attended or closely followed the Forum events that inspired this book. Their vigorous participation and keen interest in this project bode well for the health of the civic life we all cherish.

Contributors

Khaled Abou El Fadl is Professor of Law at the UCLA School of Law. Professor Abou El Fadl is one of the leading authorities in Islamic law in the United States and the world. Raised in Egypt and Kuwait, he trained in Islamic legal sciences in Egypt, Kuwait, and the United States. He is a Commissioner on the United States Commission on International Religious Freedom. In addition, he serves on the board of directors of Human Rights Watch and he is a member of the advisory board for Middle East Watch. Professor Abou El Fadl's recent books include: *Rebellion and Violence in Islamic Law* (2001); *Speaking in God's Name: Islamic Law, Authority and Women* (2001); *Conference of the Books: The Search for Beauty in Islam* (2001); *And God Knows the Soldiers: The Authoritative and Authoritarian in Islamic Discourse* (2001); *The Place of Tolerance in Islam* (2002); and *Islam and the Challenge of Democracy* (2004). He holds degrees from Yale University (B.A.), University of Pennsylvania (J.D.), and Princeton University (Ph.D.). At UCLA he teaches courses in Islamic law, human rights and terrorism, immigration law, and national security law.

Victor Anderson is Associate Professor of Christian Ethics at Vanderbilt Divinity School. He received his B.A. in history and theology from Trinity Christian College, his M.Div. and M.Th. from Calvin Theological Seminary, and his Ph.D. in religion from Princeton University. Professor Anderson teaches and writes about twentieth-century ethics, American pragmatism, religion and morality, and African-American political theology. He is a former pastor in the Christian Reformed Church, and has written two books: *Beyond*

Ontological Blackness: An Essay on African American Religious and Cultural Criticism (1995) and *Pragmatic Theology: Negotiating the Intersections of an American Philosophy of Religion and Public Theology* (1999).

Jeanne Bishop lost her sister Nancy and brother-in-law Richard and their unborn child to murder in 1990. Ms. Bishop is a member of the national board of Murder Victims' Families for Reconciliation, an organization composed of murder victims' family members who oppose the death penalty. She is a past member of the board of directors of the Illinois Coalition against the Death Penalty and is part of the team of persons who successfully worked toward a moratorium on the death penalty in Illinois. A member of the speaker's bureau for Amnesty International, Ms. Bishop has spoken nationally and internationally against the death penalty and has appeared on broadcast media and in print. As an attorney with the Office of the Cook County (Illinois) Public Defender, Ms. Bishop has defended several murder cases, and she has petitioned the Illinois Prison Review Board seeking clemency on behalf of an inmate facing the death penalty. Ms. Bishop left corporate law practice in the wake of her sister's murder. She attended Northwestern and Yale Law Schools and teaches trial advocacy at Northwestern University Law School. Ms. Bishop lives in Winnetka with her husband and young sons, a few blocks away from the townhouse where her sister was murdered.

J. Budziszewski, a political philosopher with special interests in the problem of toleration and in the tradition of natural law, holds joint appointments in the departments of government and philosophy at the University of Texas at Austin. The author of six scholarly books, including *What We Can't Not Know: A Guide* (2003), *The Revenge of Conscience* (1999), *Written on the Heart* (1997), and *True Tolerance* (1992), he has contributed articles and reviews to numerous journals, including the *American Journal of Jurisprudence, First Things, Review of Politics, Public Choice,* and the *American Political Science Review.* His most recent work focuses on the pathologies that are symptomatic of the repression of moral knowledge, that is, of the attempt to convince ourselves that we don't know what we really do know.

John D. Carlson is a doctoral candidate in religious ethics at the University of Chicago Divinity School, and former Project Coordinator for the Chicago office of the Pew Forum on Religion and Public Life. His research interests lie at the intersection of theology and political life, and his dissertation explores how understandings of human nature and transcendence shape our pursuits of justice. He has taught in the College at the University of Chicago and has twelve years of combined active duty and reserve experience as a U.S. naval officer. He is co-editor (with Erik Owens) of *The Sacred and the Sovereign: Religion and International Politics* (2003) and series co-editor (with Jean Bethke Elshtain) of the Eerdmans Religion, Ethics, and Public Life Series.

The Honorable Mario M. Cuomo was Governor of New York from 1983 to 1994, and currently serves as legal counsel in the New York office of law firm Willkie Farr & Gallagher. Cuomo received his undergraduate and law degrees from St. John's University, where he later served as an adjunct professor of law for thirteen years while also working in private practice. He was appointed as New York's Secretary of State in 1975; in 1978 he was elected Lieutenant Governor, a post he held until winning the governorship himself in 1982. Cuomo's reelection in 1986 and 1990 set records for the highest victory margin by any gubernatorial incumbent in state history. He is the author of five books, including *Reason to Believe* (1995), and is the recipient of several honorary degrees and many awards from religious, ethnic, business, and civic associations.

E. J. Dionne Jr. is senior fellow in Governance Studies at the Brookings Institution and University Professor in the Foundations of Democracy and Culture at Georgetown University. He is a syndicated columnist with the Washington Post Writers Group and a co-chair, with Jean Bethke Elshtain, of the Pew Forum on Religon and Public Life. Dionne is the author of *Why Americans Hate Politics, They Only Look Dead,* and *Stand Up, Fight Back.* He is editor and coeditor of several volumes published by the Brookings Institution Press: *Community Works: The Revival of Civil Society in America; What's God Got to Do with the American Experiment?; Bush v. Gore; Sacred Places, Civic Purpose;* and *United We Serve: National Service and the Future of Citizenship.*

Avery Cardinal Dulles, S.J., is the Laurence J. McGinley Professor of Religion and Society at Fordham University, a position he has held since 1988. After graduating from Harvard College in 1940, he spent a year and a half in Harvard Law School before serving in the United States Navy, emerging with the rank of lieutenant. Upon his discharge from the Navy in 1946, he entered the Jesuit Order and was ordained to the priesthood in 1956. He was created a Cardinal of the Catholic Church in Rome on February 21, 2001, by Pope John Paul II. The author of twenty-one books, most recently *Newman* (2002), Cardinal Dulles has also published over 700 articles on theological topics. Past president of both the Catholic Theological Society of America and the American Theological Society, he is presently a consultant for the Committee on Doctrine of the National Conference of Catholic Bishops.

Eric P. Elshtain is a Ph.D. student in the University of Chicago's Committee on the History of Culture. He is writing his dissertation on the "poetics of scientific speculation," concentrating on German and British Romantic science and poetry. His own poetry and reviews have appeared or are forthcoming in *Fence, Denver Quarterly, Salt Hill, Ploughshares, Journal of Religion, Notre Dame Review, New American Writing, McSweeney's,* and other journals. From 2001 to 2002 he served as Research Associate in the Chicago office of the Pew Forum on Religion and Public Life.

Jean Bethke Elshtain is a political philosopher whose work shows the connections between our political and our ethical convictions. She is the Laura Spelman Rockefeller Professor of Social and Political Ethics at the University of Chicago. Professor Elshtain holds nine honorary degrees, and in 1996 she was elected a Fellow of the American Academy of Arts and Sciences. She has published some five hundred essays and authored or edited twenty books including *Just War against Terror* (2003); *Jane Addams and the Dream of American Democracy* (2002); *Augustine and the Limits of Politics* (1996); and *Women and War* (1987).

Richard W. Garnett is Assistant Professor at the University of Notre Dame Law School. Garnett received his B.A. from Duke University and his J.D. from Yale University Law School, where he served as senior editor of the *Yale Law Journal* and as editor of the *Yale Journal of Law and the Humanities*. He clerked for Chief Justice William H. Rehnquist of the United States Supreme Court and Chief Judge Richard S. Arnold of the United States Court of Appeals before taking his post at Notre Dame in 1999. He practiced law for two years at the Washington, D.C., law firm of Miller, Cassidy, Larroca & Lewin, specializing in criminal-defense, religious-liberty, and education-reform matters. At Notre Dame, he teaches courses on criminal law, criminal procedure, First Amendment law, and the death penalty.

Stanley Hauerwas is the Gilbert T. Rowe Professor of Theological Ethics at Duke Divinity School, and holds a joint appointment in the Law School. His work seeks to recover the significance of the virtues in Christian life, in part by emphasizing the importance of the church, as well as narrative, for understanding Christian existence. He holds a B.A. from Southwestern University and a Ph.D. (and B.D., M.A., and M.Phil.) from Yale University. Professor Hauerwas taught for two years at Augustana College in Rock Island, Illinois, before joining the faculty of the University of Notre Dame, where he taught from 1970 to 1984. He joined the Duke faculty in 1984. The author or editor of more than twenty books, he delivered the prestigious Gifford Lectures at the University of St. Andrews, Scotland, in 2001 (later published as *Against the Grain of the Universe*), the same year *Time* magazine named him "America's Best Theologian."

The Honorable Frank Keating was Governor of Oklahoma from 1995 to 2003, and currently serves as CEO of the American Council of Life Insurers. From 2002 to 2003 he served as the first chairman of the National Review Board, created by the U.S. Conference of Catholic Bishops to oversee the church's sexual abuse policies. Keating received his B.A. from Georgetown University and his J.D. from the University of Oklahoma. He began his career in government service as a special agent of the Federal Bureau of Investigation, after which he served as an assistant district attorney in Tulsa. From 1972 to 1981 he served in Oklahoma's House of Representatives and Senate, ultimately as the senate minority leader. He was appointed by President Reagan in 1981 as U.S. Attorney for the Northern District of Oklahoma, and was later elected chairman of all of the U.S. attorneys. From 1985 to 1991 Keating served the Reagan and Bush administrations as Assistant Secretary of the Treasury, Associate Attorney General, and General Counsel and Acting Deputy Secretary at the Department of Housing and Urban Development; in these capacities he oversaw the operations of virtually every federal law enforcement agency. He was elected Governor of Oklahoma in 1994, and took office just three months before the bombing of the Murrah Federal Building in Oklahoma City. He was widely recognized for his leadership during that crisis.

Gilbert Meilaender is the Phyllis and Richard Duesenberg Professor of Christian Ethics at Valparaiso University. After attending Concordia Seminary (St. Louis) and Washington University, Meilaender earned a Ph.D. from Princeton University. He has taught at the University of Virginia and Oberlin College, and currently serves as an associate editor of the *Journal of Religious Ethics* and sits on the editorial board of *First Things*. His work focuses upon theological and medical ethics. His recent books include *Working: Its Meaning and Its Limits* (2000) and *The Taste for the Other: The Social and Ethical Thought of C. S. Lewis* (1998).

David Novak has held the J. Richard and Dorothy Shiff Chair of Jewish Studies at the University of Toronto since 1997 as Professor of the Study of Religion, Professor of Philosophy, and with appointments in University College and the Joint Centre for Bioethics. Professor Novak is a founder, vice president, and coordinator of the Panel of Inquiry on Jewish Law of the Union for

Traditional Judaism. He helped found the Institute for Traditional Judaism in Teaneck, New Jersey, serves as secretary-treasurer of the Institute of Religion and Public Life in New York, and is on the editorial board of its monthly journal *First Things*. He is a Fellow of the American Academy for Jewish Research and the Academy for Jewish Philosophy. During the academic year 1992-93, he was a Fellow of the Woodrow Wilson International Center for Scholars in Washington, D.C. He has lectured throughout North America as well as in Israel, Europe, and South Africa. Professor Novak is the author of eleven books, including *Natural Law in Judaism* (1998) and *Covenantal Rights* (2000). His articles have appeared in numerous scholarly and intellectual journals.

Erik C. Owens is a doctoral candidate in religious ethics at the University of Chicago Divinity School, and former Research Associate at the Pew Forum on Religion and Public Life. His research and writing focuses on ethics, political theory, and the intersection of law and religion; his dissertation examines religion and civic education in American public schools. He is a graduate of Duke University and Harvard Divinity School, and is co-editor (with John Carlson) of *The Sacred and the Sovereign: Religion and International Politics* (2003).

The Honorable George H. Ryan was Governor of Illinois from 1999 to 2003. He was elected the state's thirty-ninth governor on November 3, 1998, continuing a career of public service that included terms as secretary of state (1991-99) and lieutenant governor (1983-91). Ryan also had an accomplished ten-year legislative career (1973-83) in the Illinois House of Representatives. In January 2000, Ryan instituted the nation's first moratorium on state executions, pending a thorough review of the capital judicial process. Two months later, Ryan formed the Governor's Commission on Capital Punishment to conduct a comprehensive evaluation of the state's policy and process of administering the death penalty. In April 2002, the Commission recommended more than eighty changes to the state's capital punishment system — proposed reforms that have prompted many states across the country to reexamine how capital punishment is being carried out. In January 2003, Ryan pardoned or commuted the sentences of all 171 death row inmates in Illinois.

The Honorable Antonin Scalia is an Associate Justice of the United States Supreme Court. He received his A.B. from Georgetown University and the University of Fribourg (Switzerland), and his LL.B from Harvard Law School. He was a Sheldon Fellow of Harvard University from 1960 to 1961, and from 1961 to 1967 he served in private practice in Cleveland, Ohio. He was a professor of law at the University of Virginia (1967-71) and the University of Chicago (1977-82), and visiting professor of law at Georgetown and Stanford Universities. He served the federal government as General Counsel of the Office of Telecommunications Policy from 1971 to 1972, Chairman of the Administrative Conference of the United States from 1972 to 1974, and Assistant Attorney General for the Office of Legal Counsel from 1974 to 1977. He was appointed Judge of the United States Court of Appeals for the District of Columbia Circuit in 1982. President Reagan nominated him as an Associate Justice of the Supreme Court, and he took his seat on September 26, 1986.

Paul Simon (1928-2003) was a U.S. senator and congressman from Illinois. From 1951 to 1953 he served in the in the U.S. Army Counter-Intelligence Corps as a special agent along the Iron Curtain in Europe. Elected to the Illinois House in 1954 and to the Illinois Senate in 1962, he won the Independent Voters of Illinois' "Best Legislator Award" every session of his fourteen-year career in the state legislature. Simon was elected to the U.S. House of Representatives in 1974 and the U.S. Senate in 1984; during his service in Congress, he crafted legislation in a wide range of issue areas including education, disability policy, and foreign affairs. After his retirement from the U.S. Senate in 1996, he taught political science, history, and journalism at Southern Illinois University, where he founded and directed its Public Polity Institute. Simon was tapped for public service again in 2000, when Illinois governor George Ryan appointed him co-chair of the Governor's Commission on Capital Punishment. After two years of research, the blue-ribbon panel recommended more that eighty changes to the state's capital punishment system. Simon was awarded more than fifty honorary degrees in his lifetime, and he wrote twenty-two books (four with co-authors), including *Lovejoy: Martyr to Freedom* (1964); *Lincoln's Preparation for Greatness* (1965); *P.S. The Autobiography of Paul Simon* (1998); *How to Get into Politics — and Why* (with Michael Dukakis, 2000); and, most recently, *Our Culture of Pandering* (2003).

Glen H. Stassen is the Lewis B. Smedes Professor of Christian Ethics at Fuller Theological Seminary. He has over thirty years' teaching experience in the fields of ethics, religion, and philosophy. He holds a B.A. from the University of Virginia, a B.D. from Union Theological Seminary, and a Ph.D. from Duke University. Professor Stassen's most recent works include *Just Peacemaking: Ten Practices for Abolishing War* (1998), *Capital Punishment: A Reader* (1998), and *Christian Ethics as Following Jesus* (2002). He has also been a prolific writer of articles on peacemaking, the death penalty, and ethical foreign policy, among other topics. He is president of the Council of the Societies for the

Study of Religion; he is also a recent president of the National Association of Baptist Professors of Religion and of the Pacific Coast Section of the Society of Christian Ethics. He is co-chair of the Section of Religion and Social Sciences of the American Academy of Religion, and a board member of Peace Action.

Michael L. Westmoreland-White is an independent scholar in Louisville, Kentucky, and outreach coordinator for the nonprofit organization Every Church a Peace Church. He holds a B.A. in religious studies from Palm Beach Atlantic College and an M.Div. and Ph.D. in Christian ethics from Southern Baptist Theological Seminary. At age eighteen he enlisted in the U.S. Army, but during his service he became a pacifist and was later granted a discharge as a conscientious objector. Since then he has been an active member of the interfaith Fellowship of Reconciliation as well as the Baptist Peace Fellowship of North America. Dr. Westmoreland-White has twice served as Visiting Assistant Professor of Christian Ethics at Fuller Theological Seminary, and his work has appeared in numerous journals, including the *Annual of the Society of Christian Ethics, Journal of Church and State, Sojourners,* and *Princeton Theological Review.*

Beth Wilkinson has served as co-chair of the Constitution Project's Death Penalty Initiative. She served as Special Attorney to the United States Attorney General assigned to the prosecution team for the Oklahoma City bombing trials. She worked closely with the survivors and family members of the victims, prepared them for their testimony at trial and the penalty phases, and delivered the closing arguments for the penalty phases in both the McVeigh and Nichols trials. Prior to this, she was the Principal Deputy Chief of the Terrorism and Violent Crime Section for the Department of Justice. As an assistant U.S. attorney for the Eastern District of New York, she prosecuted numerous trials and appeals including the conviction of a narcoterrorist charged with the bombing of a civilian airliner. She began her legal career in the U.S. Army as an assistant to the General Counsel in the Office of the Army General Counsel. She also served as legal advisor to the Secretary of the Army for intelligence and national security matters and as Special Assistant U.S. Attorney for the Southern District of Florida, in which she helped prosecute Manuel Noriega. Ms. Wilkinson is currently a partner in the Washington, D.C., office of the law firm of Latham & Watkins, where she conducts white-collar criminal defense, internal investigations, and complex civil litigation.

Religion and Capital Punishment:
An Introduction

ERIK C. OWENS AND ERIC P. ELSHTAIN

Less than forty-eight hours before leaving office in January 2003, Illinois Governor George Ryan announced a stunning final act to his administration. Declaring the state's capital punishment system "an absolute embarrassment" and "a catastrophic failure," he issued a blanket commutation of every death sentence in Illinois.[1] He reduced 164 death sentences to life in prison and reduced three sentences to forty years in prison; Ryan also pardoned four inmates outright, saying they were innocent of the crimes for which they were convicted.[2] It was a bold act of executive clemency, noteworthy not only for its unprecedented scale,[3] but also for the fact that Ryan had once unequivo-

1. Office of the Governor of Illinois, "Prepared Text of Gov. George Ryan's Remarks at Northwestern University School of Law [Chicago, Ill.], 11 January 2003." Available online at: http://www.law.northwestern.edu/depts/communicate/newspages/spring03/ryanspeech.htm (accessed 17 April 2003). (Hereafter noted as Ryan speech, 11 January 2003.)

2. One of the men Ryan pardoned remained in prison to serve time for an unrelated crime; the other three were immediately released. On the same day, Ryan also pardoned Gary Dotson, who holds the distinction of being the first person in the nation to be exonerated by DNA evidence. Dotson was convicted of rape based on the victim's testimony, but the self-styled victim admitted in 1985 that she had fabricated the story (and had not been raped at all). An Illinois court deemed her recantation incredible, but Governor Jim Thompson released Dotson on parole; newly-available DNA testing performed in 1989 confirmed Dotson's innocence, but he was not pardoned of the conviction until 2003.

3. Ryan was the fourth U.S. governor to empty death row when he departed office, but none of the other commutations reached the same scale: Governor Lee Cruce of Oklahoma spared twenty-two men in 1915, Arkansas Governor Winthrop L. Rockefeller commuted fifteen

1

cally supported Illinois' capital punishment system and had voted as a state legislator in 1977 to reinstate it. It was also an implicit challenge to the nation's governors, legislators, and citizens to consider the justice of the death penalty as it is applied in their states, and to act upon that considered judgment. Ryan issued his commutation two years after he had instituted the nation's first moratorium on executions; the intense public debate about the death penalty during these two years rippled well beyond the Illinois state lines and shows no sign of abating in the wake of the governor's decision.

Indeed, the responses elicited by the commutations illustrate the complexity of the contemporary death penalty debate in the United States. Shock and outrage was the most oft-reported reaction from state prosecutors and victims' families. The brother of one murder victim said Ryan's circumvention of the courts made "a mockery and a farce out of our legal system and our prison system"; the sister of another victim claimed that "what [Ryan did] to all these victims' families, it's like we were murdered again, our family members, that's how bad it is." Richard Devine, the Cook County state's attorney, expressed the frustration of many state prosecutors when he told a reporter: "Yes, the system is broken; the governor broke it today."[4] A profound sense of relief accompanied the decision for most — though not all[5] — of the death row inmates and their families. Those who were pardoned and released finally had their claims of innocence vindicated; though they could not reclaim the years they spent in prison, they were overjoyed by the open vistas that suddenly lay before them.

Religion was woven into the debate about the commutations in complex and sometimes unpredictable ways. Perhaps most importantly, given the unique and virtually unlimited power he held to pardon or commute sentences, Governor Ryan told audiences that his personal religious beliefs deeply influenced his thinking about the injustice of Illinois' death penalty system. He said that he regularly prayed to God for guidance on the issue, and, citing the Bible, that the special legal power of his office brought with it a special obligation to protect the innocent.[6] Ryan also said that in commuting

---

death sentences in 1970, and New Mexico Governor Toney Anaya granted five clemency petitions in 1986. Jodi Wilgoren, "Governor Empties Illinois Death Row," *New York Times,* 12 January 2003, p. A1.

4. All quotes reported in "Reaction to Blanket Clemency for Illinois Death Row Inmates," Associated Press, 11 January 2003. Available online at http://www.sfgate.com/ryan/ (accessed 17 April 2003).

5. Jodi Wilgoren, "Leaving Death Row Is Blessing and Curse," *New York Times,* 17 January 2003.

6. See Chapter Twelve of this book (especially p. 221, where Ryan quotes the book of Exo-

the death sentences, he acted upon his belief that "the Illinois death penalty system is arbitrary and capricious — and therefore immoral."[7] He did not suggest that capital punishment *as such* was immoral, but rather that the lack of fairness and accuracy in administering the death penalty *in Illinois* made its application there immoral. As he said to a rapt audience the day he made his historic commutation announcement, "The facts that I have seen in reviewing each and every one of these cases raised questions not only about the innocence of people on death row, but about the fairness of the death penalty system as a whole. Our capital system [in Illinois] is haunted by the demon of error: error in determining guilt and error in determining who among the guilty deserves to die."[8] It is clear that for Ryan, fairness, justice, innocence, and guilt are moral concepts, informed in part by his personal religious faith.

Of course Governor Ryan was not alone in citing religious faith as a source of guidance on this issue. Participants on all sides of the debate did the same, both before and after he decided to commute the death sentences. Religious leaders and institutions made strenuous efforts to influence Ryan (as well as their congregations and the wider public) in the final nine months before he left office. Among those who lobbied the governor were Pope John Paul II and South African archbishop and Nobel Peace Prize laureate Desmond Tutu, both of whom urged him to commute the death sentences to life imprisonment.[9] Prosecutors, victims' families, legislators, and ordinary citizens also spoke out about how they understood their faith to apply to the public policy of capital punishment.[10]

Illinois is just one of many places where citizens and political leaders are trying to reckon with the teachings of their faith in light of the reality of the capital judicial system. The fierce debate taking place there and elsewhere in the United States illustrates how complex and multifaceted this relationship can be. This book is both a testament to that complexity and an attempt to provide some clarity to the confusion that has inevitably resulted from it.

---

dus), which is adapted from a speech he delivered at the University of Chicago Divinity School on 3 June 2002. See also Cathleen Falsani, "Ryan's Faith a Factor in Death Penalty," *Chicago Sun Times*, 15 March 2002.

7. Ryan speech, 11 January 2003.

8. Ryan speech, 11 January 2003.

9. The governor also received personal appeals from international political leaders such as Mexican president Vincente Fox and former South African president Nelson Mandela.

10. Among the many columns and newspaper articles written about religion and the death penalty since 2000, see Jamie Riley, "Religious Leaders Say Ryan Acted with Mercy," *St. Louis Post-Dispatch*, 12 January 2003, p. A12; Falsani, "Ryan's Faith a Factor in Death Penalty"; and Martin E. Marty, "Ryan's Commute," *Sightings*, 20 January 2003, http://marty-center .uchicago.edu/sightings/archive_2003/0120.shtml (accessed 6 August 2003).

ERIC C. OWENS AND ERIC P. ELSHTAIN

Context and Contours of the Death Penalty Debate

Disagreement over the death penalty in the contemporary debate is often couched in terms of "abolitionist" and "retentionist" positions; the former seek to abolish the death penalty, while the latter seek to retain it. These labels can be useful in ascertaining or stating a policy position on capital punishment, or in aggregating public opinion into simplified categories, but in themselves they say nothing about why, when, or how one thinks the death penalty ought to be abolished or employed. To use these terms without elaboration tends to polarize, even bifurcate, a debate that, in fact, has a much broader spectrum of possible positions. For example, some retentionists support the use of the death penalty in only the most unusual circumstances, such that executions might occur once or twice in a generation rather than once or twice per week, as is the case in the United States today.[11] Such a person is arguably closer to an abolitionist position than many of her retentionist cohorts, but in the simple calculus of "either/or" descriptions, she is a retentionist all the same. In similar fashion, to say a person supports "death penalty reform" (or that his stance is "reformist") says little of substance about his position, because almost everyone agrees that *some* reforms are needed in the way state and federal governments administer capital punishment today. A nuanced understanding of the debate must consider, therefore, not just a particular policy position, but also the complex reasons behind that policy. In this introduction, we provide a brief overview of the most common arguments for the retentionist and abolitionist positions, leaving to the contributors the detailed presentation and critique of these and other arguments.

Retentionists believe that there are at least some circumstances in which the death penalty is the most just or efficacious course of action; they believe the practice to be morally permissible — some might even say morally necessary — and, thus, seek to retain capital punishment as a legal option. Among the most commonly cited reasons to retain the death penalty are its retributive, deterrent, and defensive elements. *Retribution,* or the exacting of punishment by a community in recompense for crime, is the principle at work in the biblical injunction to take "an eye for an eye";[12] retentionists claim that in

11. In the five-year span from 1998 to 2002, an average of seventy-eight inmates per year were executed in the United States, with annual totals ranging from sixty-six to ninety-eight; this is an average of 1.5 executions per week. (Death Penalty Information Center, http://www.deathpenaltyinfo.org.)

12. Exodus 21:12-27; cf. Matthew 5:38-39. The context of the injunction to take "an eye for an eye" remains, however, a matter of heated contention. For a detailed look at this passage in

certain circumstances, death is the only proper retribution for murder. The *deterrent* effect of capital punishment upon potential future criminals — an effect described in the nineteenth century as "counterbalancing temptation by terror, and alarming the vicious by the prospect of misery"[13] — is notoriously difficult to measure, yet its intuitive appeal is often cited as a reason to retain the death penalty. Many retentionists also support the death penalty as a means of *protecting society* against future crimes, since executing a murderer is the only guarantee that he will not kill again. Other important but less frequently cited arguments on behalf of the death penalty include the claim that only the death of the offender can restore the order and common good of a community that has been violated; and that knowledge of impending death encourages sincere repentance among the condemned. As Samuel Johnson famously remarked, "When a man knows he is to be hanged in a fortnight, it concentrates his mind wonderfully."[14]

Abolitionists believe that the death penalty ought to be eliminated as a punishment for any crime under any circumstance. Like many retentionists, they base their policy position upon moral, practical, legal, and theological reasons, or some combination thereof. Among the most commonly cited reasons to abolish the death penalty are reservations about its accuracy, fairness, finality, and severity. Questions about the *accuracy* of the capital justice system stem from the possibility of false convictions and the execution of innocent persons, two issues that have received high-profile media coverage in recent years.[15] *Fairness* is another central concern of abolitionists, who often point to the unequal and seemingly arbitrary application of the death penalty across jurisdictions, among races or between sexes. Abolitionists also often argue that the ultimate nature of the death penalty — its *finality* — is itself problematic, because it eliminates the possibility of correcting a mistaken conviction. This argument is also tied to concerns about penitence and rehabilitation, because executing prisoners ends their opportunity to reform, repent, or otherwise come to terms with their crimes and its victims, with soci-

---

the Hebrew Bible/Old Testament, see the chapter in this book by Michael Westmoreland-White and Glen Stassen.

13. Quoted in Stuart Banner, *The Death Penalty: An American History* (Cambridge: Harvard University Press, 2002), p. 10.

14. Quoted in James Boswell, *Life of Samuel Johnson* (Garden City, N.Y.: Garden City Books, 1945), 19 September 1777 entry.

15. Polls show that Americans are highly attuned to questions of accuracy: in a 2000 Gallup poll, more than nine in ten respondents indicated that they believed that an innocent person had been sent to death row in the past twenty years. We discuss this question, along with similar survey findings, at some length below. See note 24 for more statistics.

ety, and with God. Many people oppose the death penalty for being too *severe,* even barbaric. They ground their belief on a variety of sources, including theological conceptions of mercy; evolving standards of decency and humaneness; international interpretations of human rights; and even the American constitutional proscription in the Eighth Amendment of "cruel and unusual punishment." It should also be noted that abolitionists often argue that the traditional goals of punishment (retribution, deterrence, penitence, and the defense of society) commonly cited by retentionists can be achieved effectively by other, less extreme means than the death penalty.

Notwithstanding the fact that abolitionists and retentionists by definition disagree as to whether capital punishment ought to be a legal option, there remains between them a certain measure of common ground on broad concepts as well as specific policy proposals. We may assume, for example, that no one wants innocent people to be executed, and that everyone believes the state has an obligation to prevent such an occurrence. As a result, common ground can often be found among retentionists who want to reform the capital justice process and abolitionists who are willing to support reform as a step toward abolition. Examples of such proximate reforms include those designed to ensure access to qualified legal defense counsel, improve the accuracy and incidence of forensic testing, and protect the integrity of investigations by videotaping interrogations. Some retentionists also join abolitionists in supporting moratoria on executions while these reforms are studied and implemented.[16]

Underscoring the depth and complexity of the debate over capital punishment is the fact that religious traditions, institutions, and scriptures can lend powerful support to *all* these positions and critiques. Religious perspectives can form the link between the abstract and concrete levels of evaluation that public policymaking requires. Statistics about recidivism, deterrence, racial disparity, or poorly trained public defenders, for example, mean little without a frame of reference by which to measure the value of such claims — and, for many, religion provides just such a frame of reference. Religious understandings of justice, retribution, mercy, reconciliation, and evil (to name but a few of the crucial concepts at work in the death penalty debate) are often inextricably tied to the basic questions that citizens, scholars, and

16. For two prominent examples of how common ground can be found among such divergent opinions, see the Constitution Project's *Mandatory Justice: Eighteen Reforms to the Death Penalty* (Washington, D.C.: Constitution Project, 2001) and "Report of Governor Ryan's Commission on Capital Punishment" (Springfield, Ill.: State of Illinois, 2002), available online at http://www.idoc.state.il.us/ccp/ccp/reports/commission_report/index.html (accessed 20 August 2003).

policymakers face. For example, how do we reconcile the human capacity for evil, which can lead to crime, with the human capacity for error, which can lead to wrongful convictions? What level of error in capital convictions is tolerable, and how can the corresponding level of accuracy be achieved? What are the limits to the kind of punishment a state should inflict upon citizens? Are there any crimes so extreme or criminals so wicked that death is the only just punishment?[17] Does it matter whether capital punishment deters future killers if its central purpose is to exact retribution for an egregious offense against a community or nation?

Opinion surveys confirm that religion continues to be a powerful and variable resource for people of faith as they wrestle with the morality of capital punishment. A 2001 poll conducted by the Pew Forum on Religion and Public Life found that religion is the second most important factor in people's beliefs about the death penalty (the media was slightly more influential by a margin of 2 percent). Curiously, among those who opposed the death penalty for murderers, 42 percent cited religion as their most important influence, while only 15 percent of those who favored the death penalty said the same.[18] Given that the official teachings of the most numerous American religious denominations and traditions tend more toward the abolitionist position (Southern Baptists being the primary exception),[19] this perhaps comes as little surprise.

17. Stuart Banner writes that this "basic moral question" is the root of all philosophical, political, or economic arguments for and against the death penalty (Banner, p. 3).

18. "Faith-Based Funding Backed, But Church-State Doubts Abound," the Pew Forum on Religion and Public Life, and the Pew Research Center for the People and the Press (10 April 2001). Available online at http://people-press.org/reports/display.php3?ReportID=15 (accessed 30 July 2003). The national poll surveyed 2,041 adults in March 2001; it has a 2.5 percent margin of error.

These findings were supplemented by sociologists Michael Welch and Thoroddur Bjarnason, who used data from the 2003 Notre Dame Study of Catholic Parish Life to discover that Catholics are less likely to support the death penalty when their parish priest strongly opposes it. http://www.nd.edu/~ndmag/su2003/deathpenalty.html (accessed 29 January 2004).

19. Among the American church bodies that endorse a retentionist position are the Southern Baptist Convention, Lutheran Church (Missouri Synod), Latter-Day Saints, and Orthodox Judaism, along with the National Association of Evangelicals and large numbers of small conservative denominations. The religious bodies supporting abolition of the death penalty in the United States include the Roman Catholic Church, American Baptist Churches, United Methodist Church, Evangelical Lutheran Church in America, Eastern Orthodox Churches, Reformed Judaism, Presbyterian Church (U.S.A.), Episcopal Church, Reformed Church in America, United Church of Christ, Disciples of Christ, Friends United Meeting (Quakers), Church of the Brethren, Mennonite Church, Moravian Church in America, and the Unitarian Universalist Association. Pentecostal churches are mixed in their support or opposition; no definitive hierarchy exists among American Muslims. For links to official statements

As Ronald Tabak has shown, however, American churchgoers are generally ill-informed regarding their traditions' teachings on the death penalty,[20] so the gap may indicate a greater failure on the part of retentionist groups to explain their position to followers.

Whatever their successes or failures in educating believers about specific theological positions, religious institutions and organizations also wield influence in the death penalty debate by lobbying state and federal politicians on behalf of sometimes huge constituencies. For example, the pontiff and bishops of the Roman Catholic Church (the largest religious body in the United States, with over sixty million members) have levied substantial pressure to reform and/or abolish the death penalty, while the Southern Baptist Convention (the second largest American religious group, with about sixteen million members) has consistently lobbied to retain — and sometimes reform — the death penalty. Other religious organizations such as the Christian Coalition, the Interfaith Alliance, National Association of Evangelicals, and People of Faith against the Death Penalty, to name but a few, also serve as important voices in public policy debates over the death penalty, in large part because they represent constituencies intensely committed to this issue, whether in support or opposition.

In the debate over the death penalty in America, religious beliefs, symbols, institutions, and leaders influence and amplify other factors as well. To provide background information that may prove helpful when reading the chapters that follow, the remainder of this section provides a brief account of recent legal, political, and academic developments in the death penalty debate, with special attention to these religious dimensions. The issue's growing salience is the result of the confluence of several events and trends, including the execution of several high-profile criminals; statistics showing a decrease in violent crime; a series of important court decisions regulating the practice of capital punishment; battles over legislative and executive moratoria on executions in many states; and the ongoing debate over how to punish terrorists in the wake of the 2001 terrorist attacks in the United States. There are many fascinating aspects of the national conversation about the death penalty, but perhaps none so surprising as the willingness among some of the death penalty's traditional supporters — political and religious conservatives — to reconsider the morality and wisdom of the pol-

by church bodies, see http://pewforum.org/deathpenalty/resources/internetresources.php (accessed 6 August 2003).

20. Ronald J. Tabak, "Overview of the Symposium's Background and Purpose," *Rutgers Journal of Law and Religion* 4:1 (2002): para. 1-14.

icy at a time when many liberal politicians vociferously pronounce their *support* for capital punishment.[21]

The 1998 execution of Karla Faye Tucker in Texas was an important catalyst for reconsideration of capital punishment among religious conservatives. Tucker was convicted of brutally murdering two people with a pickaxe, but while in prison she experienced a religious conversion and, by all accounts, a personal transformation upon being "born again." As her execution date neared, both Pat Robertson and Jerry Falwell — who had long expressed their support for capital punishment — appealed (unsuccessfully) for clemency on her behalf and spoke publicly of their growing concerns about the justice of the death penalty as administered in the United States.

Meanwhile, Pope John Paul II renewed his efforts to end the death penalty worldwide during the Jubilee Year 2000, personally appealing to several U.S. state governors for clemency in advance of executions in their states. The Pope also appealed (unsuccessfully) to President Bush for clemency for Timothy McVeigh, who, on June 11, 2001, became the first federal prisoner to be executed in nearly forty years.

The events of September 11, 2001 have transformed the American political landscape in many ways, but at this writing they appear not to have brought about a surge in capital charges against those indicted for terrorist activity. A few months prior to September 11, the terrorists convicted of plotting to bomb American embassies in Africa received life sentences — not the death penalty — because the jury said it did not want to create "martyrs." Since September 11, American civilian juries have heard several terrorism cases, handing down a variety of sentences: Englishman Richard Reid, the infamous "shoe bomber," received life in prison; Frenchman Zacarias Moussaoui could receive the death penalty for his alleged role as "the twentieth hijacker" on September 11, but as of April 2004 his case remains mired in a dispute over access to evidence; and John Walker Lindh, the "American Taliban," received twenty years in prison.

Underlining the importance of "getting it right" in these high-visibility trials was the growing evidence in recent years that innocent people have been sent to death row — and perhaps even executed — for crimes they did not commit. Illinois, for example, released eight death row inmates

---

21. On conservatives' ambivalence about the death penalty, see E. J. Dionne's Afterword in this book, and Thomas C. Berg, "Religious Conservatives and the Death Penalty," *William and Mary Bill of Rights Journal* 9:1 (December 2000): 31-60; on democratic presidential candidates' support for the death penalty, see David Firestone, "Absolutely, Positively for Capital Punishment," *New York Times*, 19 January 2003; and "Candidates on the Issues: Death Penalty," *Chicago Sun-Times*, 14 January 2004.

between 1999 and mid-2003 (seventeen have been released since 1976 — five more persons than it executed in that time); Florida released twenty-three death row inmates between 1973 and 2003. These exonerations were accompanied by admissions that the state had made a mistake. It is not unreasonable to assume that a mistake was made in the conviction of one or more of the 3,503 persons awaiting execution on death row (as of 1 January 2004), or of one or more of the 908 prisoners executed since 1976 (as of 16 April 2004).[22] Still, the continuing dispute as to whether an "actually innocent" person (meaning one who did not commit the crime, as opposed to a "legally innocent" person whose guilt cannot be proven in court) has been executed in the United States is itself a reminder that no irrefutable evidence has yet been uncovered.[23] Notwithstanding a lack of such evidence, the conventional wisdom among abolitionists and retentionists alike holds that if it hasn't already happened, the execution of an "actually innocent" person is likely to occur in the future. Supreme Court Justice Antonin Scalia made this point at a recent conference,[24] and his colleague Sandra Day O'Connor

22. The number of death row inmates cited here accounts for the pardons and commutations in Illinois on 10-11 January 2003. "Death Row Inmates by State," Death Penalty Information Center, http://www.deathpenaltyinfo.org/article.php?scid=9&did=188#state (accessed 16 April 2004). Statistic on the number of executions since 1976 is from "Executions by Year," Death Penalty Information Center, http://www.deathpenaltyinfo.org/article.php?scid=8&did=146 (accessed 16 April 2004).

Thousands more persons were of course executed in the United States before the practice was reestablished 1976, but reliable estimates of the total number of executions are difficult to obtain, especially for the years before 1930. According to Stuart Banner, the best estimate available today was generated by Watt Espy, who in 1998 estimated that 19,248 executions had taken place in the United States and its colonial predecessors (Banner, p. 313).

23. Stuart Banner notes that an innocent person was in fact executed in 1835 for murdering a man in an Alabama tavern, several months before the tavern owner confessed to the crime on his deathbed (Banner, p. 122). Nevertheless, modern estimates of the incidence of incarceration and execution of "actually innocent" people vary widely, and can be difficult to ascertain. For example, according to the Death Penalty Information Center (DPIC), which is respected by abolitionists and retentionists alike despite its anti–death penalty stance, "Since 1973, 108 people in 25 states have been released from death row with evidence of their innocence." ("Innocence and the Death Penalty," Death Penalty Information Center, http://www.deathpenaltyinfo.org/article.php?scid=6&did=110 [accessed 25 May 2003].) The national and international media routinely cite this statistic without noting that DPIC deems "innocent" any person convicted and sentenced to death who subsequently had the conviction overturned or was granted "absolute pardon." (See "Cases of Innocence 1973–Present," Death Penalty Information Center, 21 May 2003, http://www.deathpenaltyinfo.org/article.php?scid=6&did=109 [accessed 25 May 2003].) By this account, persons are "innocent" if they committed a capital crime but were freed from death row because of a so-called legal technicality.

24. In response to a question from the audience at the University of Chicago Divinity

has agreed that "If statistics are any indication, the system may well be allowing some innocent defendants to be executed."[25] Indeed, law professor Franklin Zimring conservatively estimates that five to seven innocent people have been executed in the United States since 1976.[26]

As a result of such concerns, Americans are increasingly ambivalent

---

School in January 2002, Scalia said, "[It] has not been demonstrated that a single person has been wrongfully executed. I'm willing to acknowledge that can happen. I expect it will happen. But it is infrequent enough that those in favor of abolition have not come forward with a single case that demonstrates it." Transcript available online at http://pewforum.org/deathpenalty/resources/transcript3.php3 (accessed 25 May 2003).

25. Associated Press, "O'Connor Questions Death Penalty," *New York Times,* 4 July 2001, p. A9. According to Ronald Tabak, O'Connor told a law school audience six months later that "More often than we want to recognize, some innocent defendants have been convicted and sentenced to death." Ronald J. Tabak, "Afterword on Capital Punishment: Highlights Since the Symposium," *Rutgers Journal of Law and Religion* 4:1 (2002): para. 246. See also Alan Berlow, "A Supreme Court Shocker — Sandra Day O'Connor's Criticisms of the Death Penalty Couldn't Have Come from a More Unlikely Source," *Salon* (4 July 2001), http://archive.salon.com/news/feature/2001/07/04/oconnor/ (accessed 23 May 2003).

Justice Ruth Bader Ginsburg has also expressed support for legislation that would impose a moratorium on executions. As she noted in April 2001, "People who are well represented at trial do not get the death penalty"; "I have yet to see a death case among the dozens coming to the Supreme Court on eve-of-execution stay applications in which the defendant was well represented at trial" (quoted in Tabak, "Afterword," para. 243).

26. Zimring says his estimate is based on a variety of well-reasoned assumptions, but no irrefutable evidence of "actual innocence" of those executed. For an explanation of his method, see "The No-Win 1990s" in Franklin Zimring, *The Contradictions of American Capital Punishment* (New York: Oxford University Press, 2003), pp. 143-78, esp. pp. 163-70. For more statistics on "actual innocence," see the Death Penalty Information Center's list of 108 people in twenty-five states who have been released from death row from 1973 to May 2003 thanks to "evidence of their innocence," posted online at http://www.deathpenaltyinfo.org/article.php?did= 412&scid=6 (accessed 23 May 2003).

It is interesting to note that even proof of "actual innocence" sometimes falls short of the legal grounds for dismissing a case, since the judicial system (it is argued) cannot function if no case is ever "closed" to further scrutiny. Witness this exchange between a Missouri Supreme Court judge and a state prosecutor:

> Judge Laura Denvir Stith seemed not to believe what she was hearing. A prosecutor was trying to block a death row inmate from having his conviction reopened on the basis of new evidence, and Judge Stith, of the Missouri Supreme Court, was getting exasperated. "Are you suggesting," she asked the prosecutor, that "even if we find Mr. Amrine is actually innocent, he should be executed?" Frank A. Jung, an assistant state attorney general, replied, "That's correct, your honor." That exchange was, legal experts say, unusual only for its frankness.

(Adam Liptak, "Prosecutors See Limits to Doubt in Capital Cases," *New York Times,* 24 February 2003.)

about the death penalty. "As a matter of principle," writes Zimring, "the American public believes that death is an appropriate penalty for murder, but the average citizen neither trusts nor supports the system that determines who shall be executed."[27] Indeed, as of mid-year 2003, a large majority of Americans — from 64 percent to 74 percent[28] — continues to support capital punishment in general terms. Yet, in the same year, 73 percent of respondents said they believe an innocent person has been executed within the last five years; 51 percent told pollsters in 2001 that they supported a national moratorium on executions.[29] In a July 2003 poll taken by the Pew Forum on Religion and Public Life, fully 58 percent of Americans said they oppose the death penalty for those who commit murder before the age of eighteen.[30] This ambivalence — support for the death penalty in principle but concern about its application — seems to have shaken the confidence some supporters used to have; those who say they "strongly favor" the death penalty for convicted murderers have decreased in number from 43 percent in 1996 to 28 percent in 2003.[31]

These polling statistics help to explain why the most popular stance among politicians of both parties today is to support death penalty reform but not abolition. Agreeing upon the extent of such reform has proved difficult for state governments. The legislatures of both Nebraska and New Hampshire, for example, passed moratoria (in 1999 and 2000, respectively)

27. Zimring, p. 10.
28. The finding of 64 percent support was published in "Religion and Politics: Contention and Consensus," the Pew Forum on Religion and Public Life, and the Pew Research Center for the People and the Press (27 July 2003). Available online at http://pewforum.org/docs/index.php?DocID=26 (accessed 31 July 2003). The national poll surveyed 2,002 adults in June and July 2003; it has a 3.5 percent margin of error.

The finding of 74 percent support was published in Jeffrey M. Jones, "Support for the Death Penalty Remains High at 74 percent," Gallup News Service, 19 May 2003. http://www.gallup.com/poll/releases/pr030519.asp (accessed 23 May 2003).

A Fox News poll conducted in June 2003 split the difference: it found that 69 percent of Americans favor "the death penalty for persons convicted of premeditated murder." The national poll surveyed 900 adults on 3-4 June 2003; it has a 3 percent margin of error. Rachel Sternfeld, "Poll: Peterson, Rudolph Guilty" (9 June 2003). Available online at http://www.foxnews.com/story/0,2933,88944,00.html (accessed 6 August 2003).

29. More people believe that an innocent person has been *sentenced* to death in the past twenty years (91 percent said this in 2000, 82 percent said so in 1999) than that an innocent person has been *executed* in the past five years (73 percent said this in 2003, 91 percent in 2000, and 82 percent in 1995). These are findings of annual Gallup Polls, available online at http://www.gallup.com. The finding that 51 percent of Americans in 2001 supported a national moratorium on executions is from a Gallup Poll, cited in Zimring, p. 12.

30. The Pew Forum, "Religion and Politics," note 23.
31. The Pew Forum, "Religion and Politics," note 23.

that were vetoed by unsympathetic governors. Several state legislatures debated moratoria bills in 2002 and 2003, but none was passed into law. Maryland Governor Parris Glendening instituted a moratorium by executive order in 2002, but it was quickly rescinded by his successor upon taking office in January 2003.[32] George Ryan's gubernatorial successor in Illinois retained the state's moratorium on executions, but its capital punishment statutes remain in effect, and prosecutors continue to seek the death penalty in new cases.

The U.S. Supreme Court mandated important changes to state death penalty laws as a result of two important decisions in 2002: one that banned the execution of persons with mental retardation and another requiring that a death sentence be determined by a jury, not a judge.[33] In early 2004 the Court agreed to hear a case that challenges the execution of people who were minors when they committed their capital crimes.[34]

With the death penalty's increased scrutiny by legislators and judges has come an increase in media interest on the subject. A number of important books on the topic have been published by academic and "popular" presses alike, many of them offering balanced historical surveys or assessments of arguments for and against the practice.[35] Among the most influential of these

32. The Maryland moratorium was instituted after a finding of racial and geographic bias in the application of the death penalty, not in response to particular cases of innocent men awaiting execution on death row (as in Illinois). For example, defendants with white victims were two to three times more likely to receive a death sentence than those with nonwhite victims; those living in Baltimore County were twenty times more likely to receive the death sentence than those in the city of Baltimore. See Sarah Koenig, "Death Penalty Study Is Reviewed: Author Briefs Lawmakers; Says Crimes' Venue, Race of Killers, Victims Are Factors," *Baltimore Sun*, 10 January 2003, p. 2B.

33. *Atkins v. Virginia*, 122 S. Ct. 2242 (2002), reversing *Penry v. Lynaugh*, 492 U.S. 302 (1989); *Ring v. Arizona* 122 S. Ct. 2428 (2002).

34. The case, *Roper v. Simmons*, likely will be decided in the court's 2004-2005 term.

35. Dozens of books about the death penalty that consider issues of religion or morality have been published in the past five years. Among the most prominent of those published by academic (mostly university) presses are: Franklin Zimring, *The Contradictions of American Capital Punishment* (New York: Oxford University Press, 2003); Cathleen Burnett, *Justice Denied: Clemency Appeals in Death Penalty Cases* (Boston: Northeastern University Press, 2002); Stephen P. Garvey, ed., *Beyond Repair? America's Death Penalty* (Durham, N.C.: Duke University Press, 2002); Stuart Banner, *The Death Penalty: An American History* (Cambridge: Harvard University Press, 2002); Saundra D. Westervelt and John A. Humphrey, eds., *Wrongly Convicted: Perspectives on Failed Justice* (New Brunswick, N.J.: Rutgers University Press, 2001); Austin Sarat, *When the State Kills: Capital Punishment and the American Condition* (Princeton, N.J.: Princeton University Press, 2001); Andrew Skotnicki, *Religion and the Development of the American Penal System* (Lanham, Md.: University Press of America, 2000); Hugo Adam Bedau, ed., *The*

recent works have been James Megivern's weighty 1997 work *The Death Penalty: An Historical and Theological Survey* and Stuart Banner's 2002 book *The Death Penalty: An American History.*[36] In addition, recent academic symposia have focused upon the challenges and contributions religion has made and can make to our thinking about the death penalty.[37]

The renewed scholarly attention to the religious dimensions of the death penalty is a welcome addition to the wider public debate. Religious voices are present (and influential) in politics these days in ever growing numbers, but

---

Death Penalty in America: Current Controversies (New York: Oxford University Press, 1997); William A. Schabas, *The Abolition of the Death Penalty in International Law* (Cambridge: Cambridge University Press, 1997).

Many important books on the topic have also been published by so-called "popular" presses, including: Scott Turow, *Ultimate Punishment: A Lawyer's Reflections on Dealing with the Death Penalty* (New York: Farrar, Straus and Giroux, 2003); J. Michael Martinez, William Richardson, and D. Brandon Hornsby, eds., *The Leviathan's Choice: Capital Punishment in the Twenty-First Century* (Lanham, Md.: Rowman & Littlefield, 2002); Gardner C. Hanks, *Capital Punishment and the Bible* (Scottdale, Pa.: Herald Press, 2002); Stephen Nathanson, *An Eye for an Eye? The Immorality of Punishing by Death,* 2nd ed. (Lanham, Md.: Rowman & Littlefield, 2001); Christopher D. Marshall, *Beyond Retribution: A New Testament Vision for Justice, Crime, and Punishment* (Grand Rapids, Mich.: Eerdmans, 2001); Robert Jay Lifton and Greg Mitchell, *Who Owns Death? Capital Punishment, the American Conscience, and the End of Executions* (New York: William Morrow, 2000); Aharon W. Zorea, *In the Image of God: A Christian Response to Capital Punishment* (Lanham, Md.: Rowman & Littlefield, 2000); T. Richard Snyder, *The Protestant Ethic and the Spirit of Punishment* (Grand Rapids, Mich.: Eerdmans, 2000); Barry Scheck, Peter Neufeld, and Jim Dwyer, *Actual Innocence: Five Days to Execution and Other Dispatches from the Wrongfully Convicted* (New York: Doubleday, 2000); Robert Bohm, *Deathquest: An Introduction to the Theory and Practice of Capital Punishment in the United States* (Cincinnati, Ohio: Anderson Publishers, 1999); Lloyd Steffen, *Executing Justice: The Moral Meaning of the Death Penalty* (New York: Pilgrim Press, 1998); Glen H. Stassen, ed., *Capital Punishment: A Reader* (New York: Pilgrim Press, 1998); Bryan Vila and Cynthia Morris, eds., *Capital Punishment in the United States: A Documentary History* (Westport, Ct.: Greenwood Pub. Group, 1997); Gardner C. Hanks, *Against the Death Penalty: Christian and Secular Arguments against the Death Penalty* (Scottdale, Pa.: Herald Press, 1997); James J. Megivern, *The Death Penalty: An Historical and Theological Survey* (New York: Paulist Press, 1997).

36. Megivern cited in note 35, above; Banner cited in note 13, above.

37. In January 2002 the Pew Forum on Religion and Public Life sponsored a conference entitled "A Call for Reckoning: Religion and the Death Penalty" at the University of Chicago Divinity School; the proceedings of this conference formed the core of this book's chapters. Other influential symposia have included the 1999 conference at William and Mary School of Law, "Religion's Role in the Administration of the Death Penalty," the proceedings of which are published in *William and Mary Bill of Rights Journal* 9:1 (December 2000); and "The Death Penalty, Religion, and the Law: Is Our Legal System's Implementation of Capital Punishment Consistent with Judaism or Christianity?" held at Central Synagogue in New York City in March 2001, the proceedings of which are published in *Rutgers Journal of Law and Religion* 4:1 (2002).

without informed, critical interlocutors, many religious claims remain unexamined, unchallenged, or even ignored. To help deepen our understanding and thereby promote a broader and more informed public discussion, this book brings together twenty-one contributors with vast and varied experience with the issue. They are among the most important and persuasive voices of our day, and we have asked them each to reckon with the ways in which the death penalty intersects with religious belief and political life.

Reckoning with Religion and the Death Penalty

The contributors to this book are a diverse lot by almost any measure — profession, politics, faith, race, gender, ethnicity — yet they are united by a shared belief that the debate over capital punishment cannot be understood properly without careful attention to its religious and/or moral dimensions. For many of the contributors, religion is the essential lens through which the death penalty must be viewed; for others it is one consideration among many; but all agree that religion and politics are inextricably intertwined in the United States, even if "church and state" are not. To highlight this diversity while facilitating thematic interconnections among the chapters, we have divided the book into three parts.

Part One, "Faith Traditions and the Death Penalty," surveys historical and contemporary teachings about capital punishment within Jewish, Christian, and Muslim scriptures and traditions. Its five chapters, written by distinguished scholars of religion, illustrate the richness of contemporary religious thought while illuminating its complicated past as well. In the opening chapter, Avery Cardinal Dulles calls Catholics to "be faithful to both the past and present teaching of the magisterium" as they consider the morality of the death penalty in the United States. In so doing, he argues, Catholics will see that Pope John Paul II's encyclical *Evangelium vitae* neither categorically rejects the death penalty nor breaks from church tradition, as it is often interpreted as doing. In Chapter Two, Rabbi David Novak delves into the complex talmudic legal and theological teachings about capital punishment in the Jewish tradition. Drawing upon the insights of Jewish political philosopher Hannah Arendt in light of the September 11th tragedy, Novak explores the contexts in which a human being may be required "to imitate the divine Judge" by invoking a penalty of death.

In Chapter Three, theologian Gilbert Meilaender considers how the Protestant tradition's conception of the state entails a particular understanding of punishment and justice, and why the death penalty makes little sense without a recognition of God. Stanley Hauerwas, also a theologian, sketches a pacifist theory of punishment in Chapter Four, arguing that "appeals to forgiveness and reconciliation [ought not obscure] the seriousness of punishment and the proper role punishment has, not only for any society but in particular in the church."

Islamic legal scholar Khaled Abou El Fadl completes Part One with a provocative chapter inviting Muslims to rethink their widespread support of the death penalty. Drawing upon the Qur'an and the historical teachings of Muslim jurists, Abou El Fadl sheds new light on the political and theological conditions under which "the killing state" was legitimated, and why such authority ought not be granted to the state. This has important implications especially for the new constitutions of Afghanistan and Iraq.

Part Two, "Theological Reflections on the Death Penalty," presents five in-depth chapters about particular problems or considerations that stem from theological inquiry into capital punishment. In Chapter Six, moral philosopher J. Budziszewski asks why mercy is so highly valued; after all, he writes, "mercy is punishing the criminal less than he deserves, and it seems no more clear at first why not going far enough is better than going too far." Budziszewski explores the concepts of justice and mercy in depth, concluding that the state can indeed be both merciful and just while administering the death penalty. Chapter Seven, by Michael Westmoreland-White and Glen Stassen, homes in on the problem of "proof-texting" among retentionists and abolitionists in the death penalty debate. The two evangelical scholars perform a close reading of key biblical texts, interpreting their meaning "in light of the life, teachings, death and resurrection of Jesus Christ," which is, they say, "the hermeneutical Rosetta Stone for biblical interpretation."

Two chapters in this section consider how a theological understanding of the human person — an area of inquiry sometimes called "moral anthropology" — informs our understanding of capital punishment. Legal scholar Richard Garnett argues in Chapter Eight that a pluralistic society must safeguard the public space for discussions and debates about moral anthropologies, especially when strict boundaries are presumed to exist between matters of private faith and public life. In Chapter Nine, John Carlson explores how views of human nature, in addition to understandings of transcendence, shape and limit our pursuits of justice. Tracing out several Protestant positions on the death penalty, he proposes a casuistry of capital punishment that seeks to appeal to a range of religious believers and unbelievers, too.

In Part Two's concluding chapter, theologian Victor Anderson draws upon the theologies of Karl Barth and H. Richard Niebuhr to present a "stereoscopic view of the Christian moral life" through which we can "reflect clearly on the morality of the death penalty." Anderson deftly contrasts the powerful allure of "dark symbols" such as vengeance with the "deep symbols" of grace and mercy as they relate to the Christian understanding of capital punishment.

Part Three, "Personal Commitments and Public Responsibilities," features seven chapters by distinguished contributors whose roles as legislators, executors, interpreters, and defenders of law have afforded them firsthand experiences with the death penalty and the broader system of criminal justice. Each grapples in his or her own way with how to reconcile personal religious beliefs with the duties of public office. Essays by a trio of former governors — two Republicans and a Democrat, each widely known for his outspoken views on the death penalty — illustrate the unique responsibility (and attendant pressure) placed upon a state's chief executive when a prisoner appeals for mercy. In Chapter Eleven, Frank Keating, the former governor of Oklahoma and prominent Catholic lay leader, explains why and under what conditions he supports capital punishment, and how his view is not as far from the Pope's teaching as some have said. Former Illinois governor George Ryan reflects in Chapter Twelve upon his religious upbringing and beliefs, and how they influenced his decision to impose a moratorium on executions in his state. And in Chapter Fourteen, former New York governor Mario Cuomo, like Keating a Roman Catholic, explains why he has vociferously opposed the death penalty for nearly fifty years, and how this led to his electoral defeat in 1994.

In a provocative essay, Supreme Court Justice Antonin Scalia notes in Chapter Thirteen that his personal opinions about the morality of capital punishment — which diverge sharply from those of the Pope (and of Cardinal Dulles, author of the first chapter) — have "nothing to do with how I vote in capital cases that come before the Supreme Court." With that caveat, he argues that the death penalty is both well-grounded in the Christian tradition and unambiguously supported by the "enduring" Constitution of the United States. In Chapter Fifteen the late Senator Paul Simon, the son of a Lutheran minister, writes that he never let "personal moral questions blur into the public policy decisions" he had to make. Thus, rather than asking whether capital punishment is *moral*, he frames his chapter around the question of its *wisdom* as public policy, given its failings as a form of true justice.

Beth Wilkinson, a federal prosecutor in the Oklahoma City bombing trials, explores in Chapter Sixteen how her religious background influenced her position as a "struggling supporter" of the death penalty. Through her work with the Constitution Project's Death Penalty Initiative, she has shown herself to be just as committed to leading vigorous reform efforts of the crim-

inal justice system as she was to petitioning for the execution of Timothy
McVeigh. In the final chapter of Part Three, Jeanne Bishop, a criminal defender whose pregnant sister and brother-in-law were murdered, explores
how the experience of grief and the Christian message of forgiveness have en-
ergized her calling to work for the abolition of the death penalty.

Jean Bethke Elshtain and E. J. Dionne, the co-chairs of the Pew Forum
on Religion and Public Life, provide bookends to this volume with their fore-
word and afterword, respectively. Elshtain explains why the chapters in this
book have forced her to rethink her long-standing opinion about the death
penalty, while Dionne explores why Americans as a whole have changed their
minds about capital punishment since the 1960s.

*   *   *

An issue as grave as the death penalty demands a careful reckoning among
citizens, which is best accomplished through the presentation of rigorous and
articulate arguments for public scrutiny. The value of this approach lies not
just in the collection of such arguments, persuasive as they may or may not
be, but also in the distinctions and similarities to be found among them. To
wit, a number of important themes connect the chapters across the three sec-
tions of this book.

Almost every chapter in this book considers in some manner how traditional religious teachings — Protestant, Catholic, Jewish, Muslim, or some
subset or combination of these — ought to influence our consideration of
contemporary policy problems like the death penalty. They explore the ways
in which contemporary thinkers can attend to the long history of a religious
community's moral discourse (undertaken, for example, by rabbinic commentators, Christian "church fathers," Qur'anic jurists, and early modern reformers) while also recognizing that a tradition actually encompasses *many*
traditions. A related theme in this book, given special attention by Abou El
Fadl, Westmoreland-White and Stassen, Scalia, and Bishop, is how to reconcile explicit *scriptural* injunctions with contemporary political and legal realities.

Several contributors — especially Dulles, Budziszewski, and Keating —
focus on the purposes of punishment itself: why do we punish people, and
does the death penalty serve these ends better than the alternatives?
Hauerwas, Cuomo, Anderson, Meilaender, Simon, and Bishop focus this
question by asking whether capital punishment harms society by perpetuating violence, or even vengeance. Others, including Abou El Fadl and Carlson,
inquire explicitly whether the death penalty encroaches upon the province of

the divine and how this affects relations among citizens and the state in the wake of violent crime. Broadening the theme, Garnett and Dionne join the contributors to Part Three in exploring the role of personal religious convictions in the creation of public policy and law — should this role be different for ordinary citizens than for legislators, judges, juries, or governors?

We note these few themes by way of introduction, with the hope that they — and many others — will be more fully fleshed out by readers as they consider this book in relation to their own beliefs and religious traditions. Indeed the chapters in this book call each of us to reckon with the death penalty in light of the religious resources informing our conceptions of justice, retribution, forgiveness, and reconciliation.

I Faith Traditions and the Death Penalty

1. Catholic Teaching on the Death Penalty: Has It Changed?

AVERY CARDINAL DULLES, S.J.

Until at least the middle of the twentieth century it was generally agreed in the Catholic Church that the state had the right, and sometimes the duty, to impose the death penalty for certain heinous offenses. This teaching seemed to have an adequate foundation in Scripture and was the common doctrine of the Fathers and Doctors of the Church, including the two great Doctors of the West, Augustine and Thomas Aquinas. Pope Innocent III, early in the thirteenth century, made acceptance of this doctrine a condition of reconciliation with the Church for certain heretics, who denied the doctrine. They were required to subscribe to the following proposition: "The secular power can, without mortal sin, exercise judgment of blood, provided that it punishes with justice, not out of hatred, with prudence, not precipitation." After the Second World War, Pius XII clearly supported the death penalty in addresses to jurists and doctors. The same position was affirmed by the Catechism of the Council of Trent (the Roman Catechism) and many other catechisms, manuals of theology, reference works, and the like. The view that capital punishment was legitimate was clearly dominant.

The death penalty was judged to fulfill the purposes of punishment, which were often enumerated as the following four:

1. *Retribution.* When the justice has been grossly violated, the restoration of due order may require that the offender be deprived of the good of life itself. The primary biblical texts referred to were Genesis 9:5-6 and Romans 13:1-4, both of which emphasize this retributive aspect.

2. *Defense of society against the criminal.* The death of criminals is the surest guarantee that they will not be able to commit further crimes.
3. *Deterrence.* Where administered in a timely fashion and on a regular basis, the death penalty appears to deter others from committing serious crimes.
4. *Rehabilitation.* Although execution does not of course reintegrate offenders into society, it prevents hardened criminals from spiritually harming themselves by further sin. The prospect of imminent execution is a powerful inducement to repentance and reconciliation with God, as many accounts of ministry to convicts on death row attest.

A small but increasing number of Catholic theologians have opposed the death penalty, especially since World War II, perhaps because of the notorious abuses of criminal justice in the death camps of Nazi Germany and Stalinist Russia. Nevertheless the first edition of the *Catechism of the Catholic Church,* published in 1992, reiterated the classical position. It stated:

> ... the traditional teaching of the Church has acknowledged the right and duty of legitimate public authority to punish malefactors by means of penalties commensurate with the gravity of the crime, not excluding, in cases of extreme gravity, the death penalty. (2266)

The next article added a cautionary note:

> If bloodless means are sufficient to defend human lives against an aggressor and to protect public order and the safety of persons, public authority should limit itself to such means, because they better correspond to the concrete conditions of the common good and are more in conformity to the dignity of the human person. (2267)

Pope John Paul II in his encyclical *Evangelium vitae* (1995) expressed a slightly different point of view. After stating that public authority must impose adequate penalties for the purposes of defending public order, ensuring people's safety, and offering the offender an opportunity to be rehabilitated, the Pope added:

> It is clear that, for these purposes to be achieved, the nature and extent of the punishment must be carefully evaluated and decided upon, and ought not to go to the extreme of executing the offender except in cases of absolute necessity; in other words, when it would not be possible otherwise to defend society. Today, however, as a result of steady improvements

in the organization of the penal system, such cases are very rare, if not practically non-existent. (56)

As a result of this statement the *Catechism of the Catholic Church* was revised. Paragraph 2266 was amended in the 1997 edition by omitting the phrase "not excluding . . . the death penalty." The next paragraph was altered to read as follows:

> Assuming that the guilty party's identity and responsibility have been fully determined, the traditional teaching of the Church does not exclude recourse to the death penalty, if this is the only possible way of effectively defending human lives against the unjust aggressor.
>
> If, however, non-lethal means are sufficient to defend and protect people's safety from the aggressor, authority will limit itself to such means, as these are more in keeping with the concrete conditions of the common good and more in conformity with the dignity of the human person.
>
> Today, in fact, as a consequence of the possibilities which the state has for effectively preventing crime, by rendering one who has committed an offense incapable of doing harm — without definitively taking away from him the possibility of redeeming himself — the cases in which the execution of the offender is an absolute necessity "are very rare, if not practically non-existent." (*CCC* 2267, quoting *EV* 56)

On a visit to St. Louis in January 1999, the Pope went even beyond his previous statements by characterizing the death penalty as "both cruel and unnecessary."

In accordance with the Pope's declarations and the new wording of the *Catechism*, the American bishops have published a number of statements advocating a moratorium on, if not the total abolition of, the death penalty. In November 2001, the United States Conference of Catholic Bishops issued a lengthy "Pastoral Plan for Pro-Life Activities," containing three paragraphs against the death penalty, in which a number of quotations were made from *Evangelium vitae* and the *Catechism of the Catholic Church*.[1] Besides making doctrinal pronouncements, the Pope and the U.S. bishops have regularly pleaded for clemency in the case of criminals being executed, including the notorious case of Timothy McVeigh in the spring of 2001.[2]

---

1. USCCB Meeting, "Pastoral Plan for Pro-Life Activities: Campaign in Support of Life," *Origins* 31 (6 December 2001): 433.

2. See the very moderate statement of Archbishop Daniel Buechlein of Indianapolis, published in *Origins* 30 (26 April 2001): 727-28. Statements by Cardinal Bernard Law, Bishop Joseph Fiorenza, Bishop Bernard Schmitt, and Bishop Thomas Daily may be found in *Origins* 31, issues of 17 May and 21 June.

Prima facie, then, it would seem that the Catholic teaching on the death penalty has changed from approval in the past to disapproval in the present. What was previously seen as licit or even mandatory is now seen as forbidden.

The reversal of a doctrine as well established as the legitimacy of capital punishment would raise serious problems regarding the credibility of the magisterium. Consistency with Scripture and long-standing Catholic tradition is important for the grounding of many current teachings of the Catholic Church; for example, those regarding abortion, contraception, the permanence of marriage, and the ineligibility of women for priestly ordination. If the tradition on capital punishment had been reversed, serious questions would be raised regarding other doctrines.

It might be contended that the tradition on capital punishment, unlike some of the other subjects just mentioned, is not infallible and is therefore reversible. Granting but not conceding this point, one might ask what would be needed to reverse it. I believe that competent authority would have to declare that the previous teaching was in error and to show by arguments from reason or revelation why the new doctrine is superior. But Pope John Paul II and the bishops have not said a word against the tradition. In fact, they have appealed to the tradition in proposing their doctrine on capital punishment. From this I conclude that their teaching ought to be understood, if possible, in continuity with the tradition, rather than as a reversal.

If, in fact, the previous teaching had been discarded, doubt would be cast on the current teaching as well. It too would have to be seen as reversible, and in that case, as having no firm hold on people's assent. The new doctrine, based on a recent insight, would be in competition with a magisterial teaching that has endured for two millennia — or even more, if one wishes to count the biblical testimonies. Would not some Catholics be justified in adhering to the earlier teaching on the ground that it has more solid warrants than the new? The faithful would be confronted with the dilemma of having to dissent either from past or from present magisterial teaching.

It may not be necessary, however, to choose between the classical doctrine and the contemporary teaching. In the theological literature, there seem to be at least three interpretations of the current teaching in relation to the tradition. The first school, which may be called abolitionist, maintains that the Church has reversed its earlier teaching, since it now forbids public authorities from ever inflicting the death penalty as a punishment. Commentators of a second school hold that the Pope and the revised *Catechism* are developing and refining Catholic teaching. They admit the power of the state to execute dangerous criminals, but only in cases in which the physical protection of society requires it. A third school of interpretation contends that the encyclical and the *Catechism*, while leaving the traditional doctrine unchanged, express the prudential judgment that it would be better not to practice capital punishment in countries like the United States today, for reasons that I shall later attempt to summarize.

The first school of interpretation is exemplified by E. Christian Brugger, a professor at Loyola University of New Orleans.[3] He declares that the *Catechism* is laying the theoretical ground for a change (not "development" precisely understood) in the Church's teaching.[4] Although the Church previously taught that the state could and even should intentionally inflict death as a punishment, this teaching is now seen to be invalid. The death penalty is acceptable only under the rubric of self-defense. Brugger maintains, in fact, that in defending itself society may not intend to kill the malefactor, but only to render the malefactor incapable of causing harm. On this theory, the death of the aggressor would only be an unintended consequence of self-defensive action. It would not be intended as a punishment.

I personally believe that this is an extreme and erroneous interpretation of the encyclical and the *Catechism*. Neither rules out all intentional killing. The Pope in *Evangelium vitae* lays down the principle: "The direct and voluntary killing of an innocent human being is always gravely immoral" (57). If he had wanted to teach the doctrine proposed by Professor Brugger, he would have omitted the word "innocent" in that sentence. It is also important to distinguish between the object and the motive of an act. One will not find in the teachings of the Pope or the *Catechism* the idea that it is never legitimate to kill another human being intentionally. Whenever capital punishment is warranted, however rarely this may be the case, the intention of the executioner is certainly to kill the criminal, who has lost the right to life.

The second school of doctrinal revisionism proposes a more moderate thesis. It contends that whereas several ends of capital punishment were previously acknowledged, only one end (the physical protection of society against the criminal) is now admissible.[5] The other ends (retribution, deterrence, and rehabilitation) do not by themselves warrant the death penalty. This is indeed a plausible reading of the two documents I have cited but, if

---

3. Brugger is not alone in this position. John F. Kavanaugh in *Who Count as Persons: Human Identity and the Ethics of Killing* (Washington, D.C.: Georgetown University Press, 2001), expounds a "radical personalism" which rules out the direct intentional killing of any human being (p. 119).

4. E. Christian Brugger, letter to the editor, *First Things*, August/September 2001, pp. 7-8.

5. Such is the contention of Charles E. Rice in a letter to the editor, *First Things*, August/September 2001, pp. 8-9. A similar position is taken by Kevin M. Doyle on pp. 11-12 of the same issue.

correct, it would involve a partial reversal. Besides, it may not take sufficient account of the retributive aim of punishment. In *Evangelium vitae* the Pope approvingly quotes the *Catechism* as saying, "The primary purpose of the punishment which society inflicts is to redress the disorder caused by the offense" (*EV* 56, quoting *CCC* 2266). On this basis the Pope asserts: "Public authority must redress the violation of personal and social rights by imposing on the offender adequate punishment for the crime" (*EV* 56). Punishment, he then says, is not adequate unless it defends public order and ensures people's safety, while at the same time offering the offender the opportunity to change for the better.

Since the documents we are examining say that punishment, to be adequate, must defend the public order, it is necessary to inquire what they mean by public order. The *Catechism* answers the question to some extent when it states, in another context, that public order ought not to be conceived in a positivist or naturalist manner as mere physical protection but as including legal principles in conformity with objective justice (*CCC* 2109). A careful interpreter of *Evangelium vitae*, Professor Steven A. Long, draws the conclusion that when the Pope speaks of the protection of society as legitimizing capital punishment, he has in mind much more than the mere physical safety against the criminal's behavior, but includes what Long calls "the somber efficacy of transcendent moral sanctions in social life,"[6] which may require execution as a penalty proportionate to the wickedness of the crime. To interpret the Pope as meaning only defense of the community against bodily harm, according to Long, is a "reductionist reading." Thus the second school of interpretation, as well as the first, may be contested.

Let us turn, therefore, to the third school of interpretation, with which I associate myself. It holds that the Pope and the revised *Catechism*, without rejecting the traditional doctrine, render a prudential judgment that, under present circumstances in countries like the United States, cases in which the death penalty is justified are extremely rare, if not non-existent. But it can be legitimate if required to defend society either physically or morally against the dangers that would arise if capital punishment were not used. Although the classical teaching of the Church was correct, the application of the death penalty is held to be undesirable in a society like our own, because of circumstances that would render the application harmful. As reasons for militating against capital punishment one might list the following:

---

6. Steven A. Long, "*Evangelium Vitae*, St. Thomas Aquinas, and the Death Penalty," *The Thomist* 63 (October 1999): 519.

1. The inequitable application of the death sentence by courts and juries that are prejudiced against blacks and other minorities.
2. The inability of poor and uneducated clients in many cases to obtain adequate legal counsel.
3. The likelihood of miscarriages of justice, which is enhanced by the two considerations just stated. The large number of sentences reversed on appeal, in some cases with the help of DNA evidence, makes it seem likely that some judicial errors have slipped through and that some innocent persons have in fact been unjustly executed.
4. The difficulty of judging the subjective guilt of the defendant. At best this is very difficult, and the difficulty is increased where the defendant is very young, mentally retarded, or psychologically impaired.
5. The tendency of executions to feed an unhealthy appetite for revenge. From a Christian point of view, the administration of justice should never be motivated by anger or vindictiveness.[7]
6. The failure of modern democratic society to perceive the judgment of the state as legitimately embodying a transcendent order of justice. The capacity of the death penalty to manifest the morally unacceptable character of criminal behavior is weakened because the sentence of the court is commonly viewed as an implementation of the will of the people.
7. The urgency of manifesting respect for the value and dignity of human life at a time when assaults on innocent human life through abortion, euthanasia, and violent crime are widely prevalent.

It is not necessary for all seven of the objections I have listed to apply in each particular case. Even in cases when there can be no doubt about the perpetrator of the crime, it would seem that the death sentence may fuel rather than extinguish violence in our society.

The seven objections I have stated, while they do not invalidate the classical doctrine of capital punishment, pose severe limits on its implementation. They favor limiting the application to extremely rare cases, where the safety of persons and the moral order of society would be jeopardized unless the criminal were deprived of life.

This third interpretation, unlike the previous two, does not entail a re-

---

7. In *A Call for Reckoning: A Conference Reader on Religion and the Death Penalty* (Chicago: Pew Forum on Religion and Public Life, 2001), Thomas R. Rourke speaks of the danger of fostering "the evil passion to take delight in vengeance" (p. 22). His words will repay study and reflection.

jection of previously settled Catholic doctrine. Catholics who wish to be faithful to both the past and the present teaching of the magisterium will be inclined to adopt a "hermeneutics of continuity" that reads current magisterial teaching in the light of Scripture and tradition. In terms of such a hermeneutics I propose my interpretation as the best available.

Afterword

For those interested in the practical applications of my analysis, I can make three suggestions:

1. The death penalty should not be abolished. It should remain in law, and its implementation should be a real possibility.
2. The death penalty should be imposed only in cases where the restoration of social order and the moral health of the society strictly require it and where the serious guilt of the perpetrator is certain. Such cases will be extremely rare for the reasons I have given.
3. The judgment of these concrete cases is a prudential one to be made in the actual situation. Those who make the judgment should not be priests but competent secular agents, including judges and juries who are guided by sound principles. By reason of their vocation, priests cannot suitably call for a judgment of blood.

2. Can Capital Punishment Ever Be Justified in the Jewish Tradition?

DAVID NOVAK

The Death Penalty and Moral Responsibility

Debate over the death penalty is of such practical import in our society that it would be irresponsible for me to simply report opinions regarding it in my own tradition. The import of this question requires responsible citizens in our by now heterogeneous society, coming from their respective traditions, be they religious or secular, to at least suggest a judgment *on* the death penalty emerging from their tradition. A question of such immediate moral concern makes a greater and more specific claim on our judgment than any question only motivated by general curiosity. Indeed, merely reporting what one's tradition has said *about* a current moral controversy, like the one concerning the death penalty, usually shows that same moral controversy can be found within his or her own tradition. As such, leaving the discussion at the merely descriptive level allows the reporter to evade responsibility for what the answer *of* his or her tradition ought to be *for* the question at hand here and now. At the descriptive level alone, one can get away with concluding that "some Jewish thinkers are in favor of the death penalty and others are opposed to it."[1] But that is hardly enough. In other words, the political implications of any public discussion of the death penalty are too significant for any such discussion to be left in such an irrelevant academic corner.

1. For a discussion of these views, see D. Novak, *Jewish Social Ethics* (New York: Oxford University Press, 1992), pp. 174-80.

Moreover, even though the Jewish tradition I discuss here is only morally authoritative for us Jews, its wisdom can nonetheless provide guidance, even if only by suggestion, for those of other traditions. This is especially so when they discover analogous patterns of moral reasoning during a process of authentic multicultural dialogue. Out of this process of multilateral guidance could emerge a unilateral conclusion having real governance; that is, a theoretical conclusion leading to real political and even real legal results. Furthermore, in the process of becoming more normatively focused, such specific judgments, only tentative and suggestive at present, should still have some direct relevance to a particular situation or case of deep moral concern. It takes no stretch of the imagination at all to see the death penalty as a matter of such particular concern for us all due to the terrible events of September 11, 2001. Of course, even had these events not occurred, we would have other events on which to focus our particular concern. Nevertheless, the events of September 11 have very much eclipsed them.

How could anyone here or elsewhere, when the death penalty is so much as mentioned, not think of the victims and the victimizers who came together on that by now infamous date of September 11 in a global danse macabre? A death penalty was decreed and enacted, even entailing the suicide of the immediate perpetrators. Yet, some of the victims and some of the less immediate victimizers survived the killing. What are we to do with them? In the case of the victims who survived, our immediate response must be to offer them financial aid and emotional comfort. But, do we not also owe them — both the living and the dead — justice? In relation to the victimizers, who are still living and at large, are we not required, in the oft-stated words of President Bush, "to bring them to justice"? The question is, of course, just what sort of justice we are to bring them to. And, to cite the most important case that could possibly face us, what could we justifiably do if we were to capture Osama bin Laden or one of his close associates in the leadership of al-Qaeda? Could we try him or them in a court of law? Who could sit in such legal judgment of him or them? What could be the maximum punishment meted out to him or them if and when found guilty? In terms of this last question, the question immediately following is: Could we justify executing him or them on moral and legal grounds? What does Judaism say — or better, what could Judaism say — about this? Surely, Jewish pride in having a true teaching (torat emet) requires that Jewish thinkers not remain mute or non-committal, especially when asked for their opinion by others.[2]

Of course, we are assuming that Osama bin Laden and the leadership of

2. Novak, *Jewish Social Ethics*, pp. 225-39.

al-Qaeda are being charged as war criminals. And, of course, there are the precedents of the 1947 Nuremberg trials of the Nazi leaders, and the 1962 trial of Adolf Eichmann in Jerusalem. In both of these cases, the accused were tried in a court of law as opposed to simply being killed upon capture. Thus it was assumed that the accused had violated a law for which they were responsible before the time of their crime *(nulla poena sine lege)* and were thereby responsible for its legal consequences after their crime. And that means that the victors in a war had the right to try those of the vanquished whom they could indict for instigating the crime of killing whole populations. Dealing with this crime is different in kind from the way the victors have often dealt with those who simply killed enemy combatants in what could be seen as a program of conquest. The "crime" of failed conquest, if that is even the right word for it, has more often been "punished" by political and economic sanctions against the offending nation than by legal sanctions, like the death penalty, against its leaders. In both the Nuremberg and Eichmann trials, it was assumed even before it was formally concluded that we may punish such wholesale acts of murder with the death penalty.

The reason for the death penalty in such cases was best expressed, I think, by the late political philosopher Hannah Arendt. Despite her rather ambivalent relationship with her own Jewish heritage, she nevertheless expressed views, as we shall soon see, which have strong foundation in the Jewish tradition, whether she knew it or not. In the epilogue to her still controversial book of 1963, *Eichmann in Jerusalem,* she formulated what she thought should have been the justification for the death sentence against Adolf Eichmann for the crime of genocide. Dramatically speaking in the second person, as if she herself were the presiding judge pronouncing the death sentence against Eichmann, she wrote: "And just as you supported and carried out a policy of not wanting to share the earth with the Jewish people and the people of a number of other nations — as though you and your superiors had any right to determine who should and who should not inhabit the world — we find that no one, that is, no member of the human race, can be expected to share the earth with you. This is the reason, and the only reason, you must hang."[3]

---

3. Hannah Arendt, *Eichmann in Jerusalem,* rev. ed. (New York: Penguin Books, 1965), p. 279.

DAVID NOVAK

The Death Penalty for Ordinary Murder

I would like to place Hannah Arendt's great insight about the death penalty
for the crime of genocide in the context of the exceptionally rich tradition of
moral experience and reflection of the Jewish people, something she herself
did not do. And how she responded to the program of terror implemented by
Adolf Eichmann and those with him is, to a large extent, the way we can respond to the program of terror initiated by Osama bin Laden and those with
him. By so doing, we can develop her insight with greater precision, and we
can better connect it to the moral distinction that needs to be made between
the murder of individual human persons for reasons extraneous to their essential humanity (homicide), and the murder of persons for the sole reason
of removing them, and everyone like them, from humankind itself altogether
(genocide). Making this great moral distinction should lead to even greater
legal differences between homicide and genocide.

Although all Jewish norms can be derived from either specific biblical
commandments or the general biblical mandates warranting legislation by
Jewish authorities, Jewish reflection on the meaning and purpose of these
norms takes place in the Talmud and its related literature. Surely such is the
case with Jewish reflection on the death penalty. All of it comes from the Talmud. And, quite significantly, this reflection takes place during a time when,
according to the Talmud itself (and some other cognate sources), the Jewish
people did not have enough political sovereignty to enforce the death penalty
on anyone.[4] This means that talmudic reflections on the death penalty were
either reflections on what had transpired in previous Jewish history, or what
the rabbis hoped would transpire in future Jewish history with the restoration
of Jewish political sovereignty, or what the rabbis either approved of or disap-
proved of in the surrounding gentile societies, especially those gentile societies under whose rule Jews were living at the time. In the case of these gentile
societies, the rabbis were in effect telling them rabbinic views of their judicial
practices, even though it is quite unlikely these societies were interested in
what the rabbis thought of them and their laws, and were even less interested
in listening to the practical guidance their thoughts about them implied. As
we shall see, though, things today in this area of political consultation might
very well be different.

It is important to note that the legal situation of the Jews today, especially

---

4. See *Palestinian Talmud:* Sanhedrin 1.1/18a and 7.2/24b; *Babylonian Talmud* (hereafter
"B."): Sanhedrin 41a and Shabbat 15a; also, John 18:31; H. H. Cohn, *The Trial and Death of Jesus*
(New York: Ktav, 1977), pp. 31-32, 346-50.

when it comes to our relation to what the tradition mandates concerning the death penalty, has not changed essentially. That is, even though Jewish political sovereignty has been regained in the State of Israel, the State of Israel is not governed by traditional Jewish law, certainly not by traditional Jewish criminal law, by which the death penalty is prescribed. Such is not the case in the Jewish state, and even less so in the worldwide Jewish Diaspora. On the one and only occasion the State of Israel ever judicially executed anybody — and that "anybody" was Adolf Eichmann — it was *not* done according to the governance of Jewish law *(Halakhah)*. Nevertheless, even though we Jews have no jurisdiction for the specific application of the Jewish law of capital punishment, we are able to look to the Talmud more selectively for guidance in how the death penalty should or should not be applied where there is such jurisdiction. That guidance should function in the form of rational persuasion. Moreover, unlike the Jews of the talmudic period, we Jews who live in secular democracies like the United States and Canada are not just offering guidance from our tradition to societies in which we are essentially outsiders. Instead, because of our full citizenship and cultural presence as well, we are in a position to offer some guidance to our own societies in areas of law where we are both subjects and objects of the overall political process of which law is the most authoritative part.

Before we come to the rabbinic speculation on the death penalty that can be most directly applied to the events of September 11, we must see how the rabbis looked at the death penalty in what might be seen as more ordinary circumstances, which are when one private citizen murders another private citizen. Only after looking at what is ordinary can we better appreciate rabbinic speculation on what is clearly much more extraordinary. We must understand the legal reaction to homicide before we can understand the legal reaction to genocide. In some ways they are similar; in others different. By his declaration of a war of extermination on Jews *qua* Jews, Americans *qua* Americans, and Christians *qua* Christians, Osama bin Laden and his close associates have taken responsibility for what is in our eyes — but not in his — the crime of genocide.

In the context of dealing with ordinary homicide, no traditional Jewish thinker could be opposed to capital punishment in principle, since it is clearly mandated by Scripture. To all humankind Scripture mandates, "Whosoever sheds human blood, by humans shall his blood be shed" (Gen. 9:6). To Israel (that is, what came to be solely identified as the Jewish people) Scripture mandates, "Whosoever strikes a man dead, he shall be put to death" (Exod. 21:12), and "Whosoever kills another human being, he shall be put to death. There shall be one penalty for the alien and the native . . ." (Lev. 24:21-22). Nevertheless, there is debate in the rabbinic tradition as to how widely applicable these laws are, especially the laws applying to Jewish murderers in a Jewish polity.

Despite the scriptural mandate for capital punishment, certainly for premeditated murder, there is a great debate regarding the extent to which this mandate could be put into actual practice. Thus two of the most influential sages of the second century of the first millennium, Rabbi Tarfon and Rabbi Akivah, stated that had they been in the Sanhedrin — the Jewish supreme court — when Jews did have the political power to administer capital punishment in their own community, no one would have ever been executed.[5] They would not have been executed because almost none of them *could* be executed according to the law. Clearly, for theological reasons, these rabbis could not justify this opinion by declaring their opposition to the scriptural mandates of capital punishment. Scriptural mandates may never be repealed because the law of God cannot be corrected by humans; it can only correct them.[6] Instead, later sages explained their opinion by arguing that they would have interpreted the laws of evidence so strictly that, in fact, if not in principle, it would never be possible to officially sentence anyone to death.[7] In other words, being stricter as regards the laws of evidence *de jure* enables one to be more lenient regarding the death penalty *de facto*. In effect, then, they would make the mandate for capital punishment a null class, which is a legal fiction. And, if anyone asked why Scripture would mandate what is in effect a null class, they could answer that the purpose of the law is moral instruction about the gravity of the crime of homicide. As was said about another such law, one involving the death penalty for a juvenile delinquent, where some rabbis also argued for a null class, stating "it never was applied and never will be," the purpose of the law is theoretical, namely, that those who study it are to "be rewarded for ethical reflection about it" *(darosh ve-qabbel sekhar).*[8]

It is important to connect the legal views of Rabbi Akivah especially, who was the most prominent of the early rabbis, with his theology. One of the cardinal points of his theology is that the essence of humanness is that humans are created in the "image of God" *(tselem elohim),* which seems to mean that there is a sacred dimension to human life itself: human beings are the objects of particular divine concern or providence.[9] So, even though the victim of homicide is designated by Scripture to be made "in the image of God" (Gen. 9:6), and that is the reason his murderer is to be executed, the murderer

5. *Mishnah* (hereafter "M."): Makkot 1.10.
6. See e.g. B. Kiddushin 29a re Num. 15:23.
7. B. Makkot 7a.
8. B. Sanhedrin 71a.
9. M. Avot 3.14.

too is no less made in the image of God. As such, even the execution of the murderer, to use the words of Rabbi Akivah in another vital context, is "as if one diminished *(k'ilu me'et)* the divine likeness."[10]

Moreover, if Kant's second formulation of the categorical imperative — namely, that a person always be treated as an end-in-himself-or-herself *(Zweck an sich selbst)* — is taken as a secular version of the doctrine of the image of God *(imago Dei)*, then we would certainly have to dispense with the most frequently cited reason for the death penalty.[11] That reason is that by executing one murderer now, we deter many would-be murderers from murdering in the near future. Following the theology of Rabbi Akivah and the philosophy of Kant, we could not execute anyone for this reason inasmuch as it would be taking one human life for the sake of saving other human lives. But that is unacceptable because it means the life of the murderer is being turned into a means for the end of another life. Similar logic is at stake in the rabbinic principle that one is "not to set aside one human life for another" *(ein dohin nefesh mipnei nafesh)*, unless that one life is directly threatening the life of another.[12] And, as another rabbinic text famously put it, "whoever destroys even one other human life *(nefesh ahat)*, Scripture ascribes guilt to him as if *(k'ilu)* he destroyed an entire world *(olam mal'e)*."[13]

The opposing view, enunciated by Rabban Simeon ben Gamliel, argues that if this legal fiction, which makes capital punishment for homicide a null class, were actually in force, the effect would be to "increase murderers in Israel."[14] The usual interpretation of this more stringent view is that it assumes that capital punishment as a real social institution is required for the deterrence of homicide. Thus, what seems be a view consistent with that of Rabban Simeon ben Gamliel, another sage, Rabbi Hanina the vice–High Priest, argued that Jews need to pray for the success of the Roman government. But isn't this the same Roman government that destroyed the Temple, the religious center of the Jewish people, and the same Roman government that squashed Jewish sovereignty by its defeat of the army of Bar Kokhba? His reason, nonetheless, is that without such governmental authority and power, "a

---

10. *Beresheet Rabbah* 34.14, ed. Theodor-Albeck, p. 326. See B. Yevamot 63b. Another version of this idea says that "one indeed destroys *(hareh hu mevatel)* the divine image" (*Tosefta: Yevamot* 8.7). Cf. *Tosefta: Sanhedrin* 9.7 re Deut. 21:23.

11. See Kant, *Groundwork of the Metaphysic of Morals*, trans. H. J. Paton (New York: Harper and Row, 1964), pp. 95-99.

12. M. Ohalot 7.6. Cf. M. Sanhedrin 8.5; Novak, *Jewish Social Ethics*, pp. 168-69.

13. M. Sanhedrin 4.5. See Maimonides, *Mishneh Torah* (hereafter "MT"): Laws of the Sanhedrin, 12.3.

14. M. Makkot 1.10.

person would swallow his fellow person alive."[15] Surely he had the widespread Roman use of the death penalty in mind. And, as is best known from the execution of Jesus of Nazareth, the Roman government often used capital punishment as a way of maintaining political order because of what they believed to be its deterring effects as well as the effect of eliminating those likely to again cause trouble for the Roman authorities.

Conversely, those sages who would have probably been closer to the more lenient views of Rabbi Tarfon and Rabbi Akivah at times expressed their disapproval of how easily, carelessly, and guiltlessly the Romans used the power of capital punishment.[16] Indeed, one could see Jewish revulsion at the prevalence of capital punishment in their society, which they did not control politically. This revulsion was a major factor in their decision to rule quite differently what they hoped would be the future society they would control politically and legally according to more accurate criteria of justice.

For this same reason, the Romans removed the power of capital punishment from their Jewish captives, since, presumably, this power over life and death was inappropriate for a captive people to administer for themselves or for anyone else. All killing was to be done by the Roman rulers alone and for their purposes alone. In fact, when Jews did regain the power of capital punishment for a while from their Christian host society in fourteenth-century northern Spain, they seem to have adopted the view of the political necessity of capital punishment, even dispensing with some of the stricter standards of evidence of the earlier rabbinic tradition.[17] This dispensation was justified on the grounds that the needs of political order required it. One could no longer assume, as much of Jewish tradition did assume, that homicide was extremely rare among the Jewish people. As the rabbis had to admit in another dispensation from a traditional Jewish law pertaining to homicide, "the murderers had increased."[18] Nevertheless, it could also very well be argued that this departure from the tradition of greater caution in capital cases was required by the Christian host society: namely, that Jewish legal practice be consistent with Christian legal practice. If that is the case, then this Jewish departure from the tradition of caution should not be taken as a precedent for what Jews should do when they do not have to conform to the standards of others; that is, when Jews either have a state of their own or are full citizens in a state that is neither Jewish nor Christian but fully secular.

15. M. Avot 3.2.
16. See, e.g., B. Gittin 28b.
17. See Y. Baer, *A History of the Jews in Christian Spain* 1, trans. L. Schoffman (Philadelphia: Jewish Publication Society of America, 1978), pp. 232-33.
18. M. Sotah 9.9.

The main aspect of the Jewish law of homicide that makes capital punishment very rare — something, by the way, never disputed in principle even by seemingly pro–death penalty jurists of the view of Rabban Simeon ben Gamliel — is the practice of *hatra'ah* or "forewarning." This practice assumes that the only way one can assume malice of forethought in the crime of homicide, thus differentiating it from what today we would mostly consider to be manslaughter, is if the criminal had been explicitly forewarned by the same witnesses who witnessed the crime itself.[19] In other words, we need explicit evidence that the fully conscious intention of the criminal had been to violate a law of whose content and consequences he or she was fully aware. This forewarning consists of the witnesses explicitly informing the criminal just about to commit the crime that (1) the act he or she is about to commit is proscribed by the Torah; (2) what is the exact punishment for which he or she will be liable if he performs the proscribed act; (3) the exact status of the would-be victim in a case of a crime of aggression; and (4) the verbal indication by the would-be criminal back to the same would-be witnesses just before committing the crime that he or she intends to commit the crime anyway. Accordingly, the burden of proof is on the accuser, on the prosecutor, to show that the person charged with homicide explicitly demonstrated that he or she was *compos mentis* in the most complete sense possible. Yet it is extraordinarily difficult for this to happen. Even when crimes are actually witnessed by others, the presence of these others is rarely known in advance. In fact, foreknowledge of the presence of witnesses by a would-be criminal would probably deter all but the most foolhardy from actually carrying out criminal intentions.

Whether what might be termed this legal "ritual" was ever actually practiced by the Jews is difficult to say. Nevertheless, its actual practice would be extremely rare for another reason, which is the biblical commandment "You shall not stand idly by the blood of your neighbor" (Lev. 19:16), which the rabbis interpreted to mean a positive obligation to rescue someone from imminent mortal danger.[20] That being so, wouldn't two witnesses who could get close enough to warn a would-be assailant just about to attack his or her would-be victim be in a position to save the would-be victim from homicide — even if that meant killing the would-be assailant rather than wasting precious time warning him or her against committing the crime? As such, could one not assume that the practice of *hatra'ah* might have been invented by those who agreed with Rabbi Tarfon and Rabbi Akivah that the law of the death penalty be, in effect, a null class? Also, since the practice of

19. B. Sanhedrin 40b-41a.
20. B. Sanhedrin 73a.

hatra'ah is not disputed in general — there only being dispute about some of its more specific aspects — it seems that the only difference between those rabbis who seemed to be anti–death penalty and those who seemed to be pro-death penalty is that the pro–death penalty rabbis would interpret the laws of evidence somewhat more leniently than the anti–death penalty rabbis, epitomized by the view of Rabbi Tarfon and Rabbi Akivah as interpreted by later scholars.

Comparing the traditional Jewish law of the penalty for homicide with current American legal practice in this same area, or at least current American legal practice in most states and in federal jurisdictions, indicates that we execute criminals far more easily. Such practices as self-incrimination and the use of circumstantial evidence (that is, the absence of eyewitnesses) to cause a conviction for homicide, which we find in our own society's legal practices, are proscribed by traditional Jewish law.[21] Moreover, this greater stringency of the Jewish law pertaining to the death penalty is even the case with what the rabbis envisioned to be the standards Jews could accept and respect when practiced by gentile societies. Here the rabbis assumed that one could be convicted for homicide on the testimony of one witness rather than two, and without the forewarning of *hatra'ah.*[22] Nevertheless, even here, there would be far less capital punishment than in our society today because the chance for error in judgment would be far less.

Of course, here again, because of the primacy of Scripture (which influenced common law cases until the twentieth century) no one could advocate on traditional Jewish grounds that the death penalty, especially for the crime of homicide, be abolished. But on these same traditional Jewish grounds, one could argue that the law of capital punishment is more symbolic than real. This is especially convincing when one questions whether the death penalty really is a deterrent and that without its active practice, chances increase of a greater number of homicides. Here again, Jews might question the depth of the commitment of our society to the sanctity of human life. This is also at the heart of the rabbinic principle that "when there is any doubt regarding human life *(safeq nefashot),* the benefit of the doubt should be in favor of the human life" — even when that human life is very likely the life of a murderer.[23] That does not mean, though, that we might not devise other ways to protect society from those whose guilt and presumed danger to society is less

21. See A. Kirschenbaum, *Self-Incrimination in Jewish Law* (New York: Burning Bush Press, 1970).

22. See *Beresheet Rabbah* 34.14.

23. B. Shabbat 129a and parallels. See, also, B. Sanhedrin 78a and *Tosafot,* s.v. "be-goses."

than perfectly ascertained. That is, this concern for human life does not rule out the institution of imprisonment, even for a life term.

Public Crimes

The rabbis were also aware of some basic differences between what might be termed "public crime" as distinct from what we have seen as "private crime." By public crime I mean a crime ordered by the leaders of a society — even if that society be a band of pirates, whom one can judge al-Qaeda to be, even when governments who support their operations deny they do so. Indeed, a pirate used to be placed in the category of "enemy of the human race" *(hostis humani generis)*.[24] The crime is even more public if it is ordered after a public declaration of intent by the leaders of a society, and it is most public when it is directed towards the extermination of all the members of another society — that is, *genocide.*

Concerning the ordering of a crime, note the following rabbinic dispute:

> "One who says to another, 'go and kill another person *(ha-nafesh),*' the one who killed is liable *(hayyav),* but the one who sent him is exempt *(patur).* Shammai the Elder in the name of Haggai the prophet says 'the one who sent him is also liable.' This is based on Scripture, 'You killed him with the sword of the Ammonites' (2 Samuel 12:9)."[25]

The killer here is King David who, it will be recalled, ordered his general, Joab, to place his soldier Uriah the Hittite, the husband of the king's paramour Bathsheba, in a battle situation where Uriah was certain to be killed.[26] The king's orders, though, were followed unquestioningly by Joab, who again and again proved that his loyalty to his king took precedence over everything else, even over the divine law of justice.

Subsequent discussion in the Talmud, however, qualifies this dispute by assuming that the first (anonymous) sage is not saying that the one who instigates a murder is totally innocent.[27] Rather, the dispute is over the extent of guilt. Haggai the prophet (as reported by Shammai the Elder) is assumed to assign direct guilt *(dina rabba)* to the instigator of the homicide, whereas the first sage is assumed to assign indirect guilt *(dina zuta)* to him. Furthermore,

---

24. See Arendt, *Eichmann in Jerusalem,* p. 261.
25. B. Kiddushin 43a.
26. 2 Sam. 12:1-24.
27. B. Kiddushin 43a.

there is an attempt to argue that the citation of the charge against King David made by the prophet Nathan is no source of law for other cases because it involved a special case of divine revelation for David alone.[28] Clearly, the editors of the Talmud accepted the principle "there is no agency for sin" *(ein shaliah le-dvar aveirah)*, whose purpose seems to place direct responsibility on the actual perpetrators of a crime, and not allow them to divert responsibility onto those who had been "bad influences" on them.[29] As for these bad influences, the most that they could be guilty of in a human court is the violation of the scriptural norm "You shall not place a stumbling block before the blind" (Lev. 19:14), which the rabbis interpreted to mean leading the morally obtuse astray, but by no means relieving them of their moral responsibility thereby.[30] Here leading someone astray is much less of a crime than the act of the one who chose to be so led astray; that is, one who should have known better. The question is whether or not a king is an ordinary instigator of a crime committed by someone following his orders and over whom the king, as commander-in-chief, has the power of life and death.

The fifteenth-century Jewish statesman and theologian Don Isaac Abravanel, contrary to the drift of the talmudic discussion, considers the prophetically condemned act of King David to be paradigmatic. In fact, he sees another example of such officially ordered, but not directly implemented, murder in the case of the priests of Nob who were murdered according to the order of King David's predecessor, King Saul.[31] Thus he writes, "The reason for this is because he was a king, and no one violates his command. Therefore, it is as if *(k'ilu)* he himself killed him."[32] Kings have the power of life and death over their subjects, and even though later rabbis ruled that one should die rather than kill someone else due to an unjust decree, the fact is that very few people would risk their lives by defying someone as powerful as a king.[33] And, it helps our appreciation of this insight to know that Abravanel was a man who held high state posts in Spain, Portugal, and Venice, and who thus had intimate knowledge of how political power operates in the world. Political power, when unencumbered by moral and legal restraint, frequently operates as terror. Abravanel more than the other Jewish thinkers on these questions certainly knew that from his own experiences of state.

28. B. Kiddushin 43a.
29. B. Kiddushin 42b.
30. B. Pesahim 22b.
31. 1 Sam. 22:9-19.
32. *Commentary on the Earlier Prophets:* II Sam., chap. 12. See Maimonides, MT: Laws of Murder, 4.9.
33. See B. Pesahim 25b; B. Sanhedrin 74a.

What we learn from this is that the essential difference between private and public murder is that in private murder we are to punish the direct perpetrator of the crime far more severely than the instigator of the crime; whereas in public murder, which is the murder ordered by political leaders (however informally the political state or organization might be structured), we are to punish those who ordered the crime at least as severely, and often more severely, than we are to punish the actual perpetrators of the crime. The actual practice of the Nuremberg court, which followed this kind of logic, concretized Abravanel's biblical speculation so as to make it a real precedent in law.

Abravanel is silent on the question of whether the errant kings of Israel, Saul and David, could be tried before a human court, or whether their judgment is to be left to God alone. Since in the biblical account, David was indicted by the prophet Nathan but not by human judges, it would seem that his judgment and those of other kings would have to be left to God's own ways of rendering justice, ways only known and only made knowable by a prophet. Nevertheless, rabbinic opinion is divided on this question. One view is that only God is above the king, so only God can judge him.[34] But another view is that the king is both to "judge and be judged" *(danin oto)*, or as a later sage put it, "if he is not to be judged by others, how can he judge them?!"[35] This latter opinion seems to have been preferred by later theologians.[36]

If we accept the validity of human judgment of a king (or any political potentate), who is justly authorized to judge him? If humans are to judge him, then those humans who can judge him now are to be preferred to those humans who might be able to judge him better but later. Justice delayed is often justice denied. The most effective justice is the justice that can be done at present. Following this logic, it would seem that the optimal judge of such a public criminal would be a court authorized by his own people. In fact, wouldn't their judgment of their own leader restore their national honor, which the terrorist, even genocidal, acts of their leader had so tainted? Thus, if rabbinic tradition permits a king to be judged by his own people when judgment is called for, then isn't this permission in effect a mandate to the people to judge their king? Along these lines, the great medieval Jewish jurist and theologian Maimonides argues that the people of the biblical city of Shechem were guilty for not having judged their crown prince when he openly abducted and raped Dinah, the daughter of the patriarch Jacob (Gen. 34:1).[37] Because of this dereliction of

---

34. *Palestinian Talmud:* Sanhedrin 2.3/20a re Ps. 17:2.
35. B. Sanhedrin 19a re Zeph. 2:1.
36. See Maimonides, MT: Laws of the Sanhedrin, 2.5.
37. MT: Laws of Kings, 9.14.

public duty by the Shechemites, the brothers of the victim were entitled to effect justice themselves. The implication of this interpretation is that if the people of Shechem had done their public duty, the brothers of Dinah would not have been entitled to avenge the crime committed against their sister, which they recognized to be something "not to be done" (Gen. 34:7); that is, not to be done anywhere and to be punished by anyone when the local authorities are either incapable or unwilling to take appropriate judicial action.[38]

Wouldn't a trial of Eichmann — or, optimally, of Hitler — by the German people have provided the world with the most satisfying form of justice? And, wouldn't a trial of Osama bin Laden by an Islamic court, whose law he claims to be following, be the optimal venue for his trial? Wouldn't that be an act of supreme theological and political responsibility? Yet in order for this trial to take place, the criminal would first have to be apprehended by his own people. If they could not or would not apprehend him, then they are in no position politically, and probably legally as well, to try him. The will to justice that the execution of justice requires was not there and is not here. The sad fact is that the Germans did not apprehend Adolf Eichmann in 1961, although that capture would have been easy; and bin Laden has operated with and was protected by the militantly Islamic regime of the Taliban in Afghanistan. Furthermore, no other Islamic regime seems willing to or even interested in apprehending bin Laden and his associates.

That leaves the apprehension of a genocidal war criminal either to an international court or a court of the people targeted for genocide and who have, nonetheless, survived, and in some cases, like that of the Jews, have even become more politically powerful after their survival. The fact that there is no international court (and that includes, it seems to me, the newly constituted International Court of Justice) capable of meting out what most would consider full and swift justice rules out any real hope that such a court could be trusted with a criminal as dangerous as Osama bin Laden. Accordingly, we are only left with a court of the survivors, who seem to be the second best alternative in principle, but the only real alternative in practice.

A good biblical precedent for this judicial alternative is the execution of the Amalekite king Agag by the prophet Samuel. The Amalekites were a people who engaged in what we would today call terrorism. They indiscriminately attacked the "faint and the weary" (Deut. 25:18); that is, they killed noncombatants for no military reason. In fact, later biblical tradition saw the plan of the Persian prime minister Haman to "utterly destroy" *(l'abbdam)* the Jews (Esther 3:9) to be the result of his being a literal and spiritual descendent

---

38. See MT: Laws of the Sanhedrin, 26.7.

of Agag. He was "Haman the Agagite, persecutor of the Jews" (Esther 3:10). Now it seems that optimal justice would have been fulfilled if the Amalekites themselves had executed their terrorist king. In fact, Maimonides, who is the only medieval theologian to fully codify the rabbinic laws pertaining to the conduct of the state, rules that even the Amalekites would be spared mass destruction by the people of Israel if they would repudiate their terrorist tradition and adhere to universally applicable laws.[39] Two of these laws are the rule that every society judge and convict its own criminals *(dinim)*, and that every society prohibit murder *(shefikhut damim)*.[40] Thus, in order for the nation of Amalek to redeem itself, it would have to execute justice against itself in the person of its leader. The fact that they did not do this, and the fact that Saul the king of Israel wanted to compromise with a fellow king, required that the prophet Samuel, who was the judicial leader of the people, try and convict Agag himself, even though this unusual case called for unusual methods of execution. He justified his act by stating to Agag at the time of his execution, "Just as your sword made women childless, so may your mother be made childless" (1 Sam. 15:33). Samuel did to Agag what the Israelis later did to Adolf Eichmann and what the Americans should do to Osama bin Laden — if they ever have the opportunity to do so.

Public Forewarning

The second difference between private and public murder centers on the question of forewarning *(hatra'ah)*. It will be recalled that if a murderer is tried according to traditional Jewish law, then he or she must have been forewarned by the witnesses to the crime, and that he or she must have verbally indicated full awareness of the contents of the forewarning. However, certain rabbinic sources may enable us to see things differently in cases of public murder, especially genocide, and especially when the leaders under consideration have announced their program in public.

The first relevant opinion in the Talmud, albeit an opinion subsequently judged to be a minority opinion, is that a rabbinical scholar, then called a "fellow" *(haver)*, does not require forewarning in order to be convicted of a crime for which premeditation is an essential factor.[41] Premeditation *(mezeed)* can only be assumed when the person about to commit the crime is fully aware of

---

39. MT: Laws of Kings, 6.4. See Novak, *Jewish Social Ethics*, pp. 187-201.
40. B. Sanhedrin 56b.
41. B. Sanhedrin 8b.

(1) the prohibition of the act about to be committed; (2) the legal consequences if the act is committed; (3) that the object of the act — the would-be victim — is the true object of the prohibition (that is, in the case of murder, the witness must inform the would-be assailant who the would-be victim is); and (4) the would-be assailant indicates that he or she knows that the would-be victim is the true object of the prohibition.⁴² Anything less than this full awareness makes the crime subject to the penalties for inadvertence *(shogeg)*, very much akin to what we now call manslaughter, which are always something less than the death penalty. Therefore, in the case of someone who knows the law and is also considered to be quite perceptive, we may assume that such a person has already been forewarned for any prohibited act he or she may be tempted to perform. Surely, the ruler of a society, a maker of public policy, or a political leader falls into this already-forewarned category.

Despite the fact that the view that learned persons do not require forewarning is a minority view in cases of private murder, in cases of crimes of negligence not involving murder, there is a majority opinion that public officials are already forewarned by virtue of their public office *(ke-mutrin v'omdin)*.⁴³ Perhaps one could conclude that the above opinion (that of Rabbi Yose son of Rabbi Judah) was only rejected in the case of a private murder committed by a public official, but that it might apply to a case of a public murder being ordered by a public official. Such a process of contextualization, what some have called casuistry, is very common in the ongoing process of rabbinic jurisprudence.

An even better source, though, is the rabbinic opinion that states that before one can be convicted to be punished by the death penalty, one has to have "permitted himself for death" *(hiteer atsmo le-meetah)*.⁴⁴ What does this rather opaque phrase mean? There are three interpretations: (1) It means that by accepting the forewarning, yet violating its proscription anyway, the would-be criminal has sentenced himself or herself to death.⁴⁵ (2) It means that the forewarning could even be uttered by the would-be victim to the would-be assailant just before the crime is committed.⁴⁶ (This is what some rabbis imagine Abel did just before being murdered by his brother Cain.)⁴⁷

42. Maimonides, MT: Laws of the Sanhedrin, 12.1-2.
43. B. Baba Metsia 109a-b. See Maimonides, MT: Laws of Employment, 10.7 and *Magid Mishneh* thereon.
44. B. Sanhedrin 40b.
45. B. Sanhedrin 40b., Rashi, s.v. "hiteer" thereon. See *Tosefta:* Sanhedrin 11.4.
46. B. Makkot 6b, Rashi, s.v. "mi-pi atsmo" thereon.
47. See Louis Ginzberg, *Legends of the Jews* 1, trans. H. Szold (Philadelphia: Jewish Publication Society of America, 1909), p. 109.

(3) It means that the murderer forewarns him- or herself *(hayah matreh b'atsmo).*⁴⁸ In other words, the would-be murderer defies the law he or she knows, violates the victim whose protected status he or she knows, and takes responsibility for his or her act in advance. Clearly such an act of self-recognition places the would-be murderer in the class of a "defiant rebel" *(mumar le-hakh'ees),* which designates someone who violates the law out of conviction and not just out of appetite or even mindless passion *(mumar le-te'avon).*⁴⁹

Would not a public murderer who, like Hitler or bin Laden (or, to a lesser but still culpable extent, Eichmann), orders public murders out of conviction, and who does so because of a publicly declared ideology — wouldn't such a leader qualify as one who is already forewarned? Don't their very public speeches and publications (Hitler's *Mein Kampf* immediately comes to mind) make any argument about their lack of full awareness ridiculous? Hence, I think a good case can be made for answering yes to this question. In fact, unlike the public murder of a private citizen conducted by King David, in which the king issued his death sentence for Uriah in a secret memorandum, and which was certainly not genocidal, the publicly justified acts of Hitler and bin Laden — with their frightening appeals to a law above what most persons would consider the natural law of God — seem to fit the joint category of publicly initiated murder *and* publicly declared and justified (that is, by the political leader) genocide. In such cases involving enemies of the human race, one could make the strongest possible argument for the death penalty that could come out of the whole Jewish tradition of moral and legal reflection for the sake of immediate justice in the world.

Nevertheless, I cannot in good faith conclude without recalling that one of the greatest sages quoted in the Talmud, Rabbi Meir, taught that God suffers even when the blood of the guilty *(damam shel resha'im)* has to be shed.⁵⁰ Perhaps in order to enable human judges to imitate the divine Judge, Rabbi Meir's teacher, Rabbi Akivah, ruled that human judges have to fast on the day the convicted criminal is being executed.⁵¹ This is, no doubt, meant to be an act of atonement *(kapparah)* like fasting on the Day of Atonement *(yom ha-kippurim).* It is an act of atonement for what is necessary to do for justice, but which is tragic nonetheless.

48. Maimonides, MT: Laws of the Sanhedrin, 12.2, *Kesef Mishneh* thereon.
49. B. Sanhedrin 27a.
50. M. Sanhedrin 6.5.
51. B. Sanhedrin 63a re Lev. 19:26.

3. The Death Penalty: A Protestant Perspective

GILBERT MEILAENDER

I begin with an illustration that gives rise to a puzzle. Suppose the police have tracked down the infamous leader of the Cavendish gang, a man who has boasted of his responsibility for the brutal murders of at least eight innocent people. They have him trapped in a building, and, as he tries to escape out the back door of the building, police sharpshooters gun him down and kill him. I doubt that there would be much public criticism of the police for this action. No criticism despite the fact that Cavendish was never charged with murder, never tried or found guilty in a court of law. Despite the fact that he had been given no chance to have a lawyer argue his case, point to extenuating circumstances, or plead insanity.

Suppose, on the other hand, the police had managed to capture Cavendish as he fled out the back door — and that he had been tried, convicted, sentenced to death, and executed. How much less acceptable this would have been to our contemporary sensibilities, "[s]o great is our horror of that hint of the religious which the cool process of judicial execution contains."[1] Is it not puzzling that we should accept his death in the first instance, a death that occurs without any benefit of judicial proceeding, and that at least some

---

1. Oliver O'Donovan, *Measure for Measure: Justice in Punishment and the Sentence of Death,* Grove Booklets on Ethics No. 19 (Bramcote, U.K.: Grove Books, 1977), p. 21. In this context O'Donovan discusses an actual case that is somewhat like the hypothetical case with which I began. I have, however, altered a number of details to make the hypothetical case suit my purposes.

among us should be appalled by his death in the second instance? This puzzle is worth reflecting on, and I will return to it at the end of this essay.

I need at the outset to emphasize two things about my Protestant position that should probably be obvious. First, I am presenting "a" Protestant perspective — at least if we are speaking descriptively or empirically. From that angle the Protestant world can only appear hopelessly fragmented. From that angle, "the" Protestant perspective does not exist. It is just as important, however, perhaps for a Protestant even more important, to emphasize that one does not do Christian ethics by taking a survey of the opinions of Christians — or, in this case in particular, of Protestant churches. One can speak normatively on behalf of the church only if, in Karl Barth's words, "in all humility" one is willing "to risk being such a Church" in one's own place and as well as one knows how.[2]

Second, it is, I think, a mistake to suppose that there should be some uniquely "Protestant" position on every question that comes along. Protestants are Catholics with a bit of a twist — with some special concerns. But to try to build an entire theological position on those special concerns, to imagine that one could do this without the extensive structure of Catholic faith that underlies the special concerns, is folly. Protestants, therefore, have to recognize that the church has generally taught that duly constituted governments have the right, under certain circumstances, to execute offenders. The death penalty has not been forbidden. This does not mean, of course, that it has been required — or that the church should not ask that mercy temper justice. But the truth has to lie somewhere between a mistaken view that the death penalty is prohibited and a mistaken view that it is required. It is simply permitted.

I have come to believe that the greatest danger in discussions of the death penalty is that we may end up adopting viewpoints which turn out to undercut the very rationale for government, punishment, or justice. If we avoid those dangers, we will be in a position to see what might really concern us about capital punishment. My opening illustration was designed to point to that concern, and I will return to it at the end. First, though, we need to situate our discussion of the death penalty within the larger framework of an understanding of government and punishment generally.

If and when a state inflicts any punishment — and, certainly, the death penalty — on one of its citizens, it is imperative that such action be understood as public, not private, action. For Christians this is because the state, by God's ordinance, is authorized in certain circumstances to serve the common

---

2. Karl Barth, *Church Dogmatics*, I:1 (Edinburgh: T&T Clark, 1936), p. xii.

good even by taking the life of a duly convicted criminal. When God makes his covenant with Noah after the great flood, promising never again to destroy "all flesh," this promise is fulfilled in part through government, which, by executing just punishment, enacts fitting retribution for crimes. "Whoever sheds the blood of man, by man shall his blood be shed, for God made man in his own image," Genesis (9:6, RSV) says, in a passage regularly cited by theologians to depict the institution of government and the authority delegated it by God. The law of retribution articulated here is not the civil law of ancient Israel. It would be better called moral or natural law, specifying, as it does, fundamental truths about human life. There is, to be sure, something paradoxical about this law of retribution and, let us note, about government in general. Retribution is required because the victim bears God's image. But, of course, so does the murderer. It might seem that by punishing the murderer in order to honor the image in the victim, we simultaneously demean the image in the murderer, but that is, of course, the paradox of all governmental retribution. And it is precisely why it is so essential that we understand civil and criminal punishment as public retribution, not private vengeance. In killing his victim, the murderer has demeaned the image of God in one particular way — by means of an act that is private. In executing the murderer, civil government carries out a different kind of act — one that is public.

The other passage that has played a major role in Protestant reflection is Romans (13:4), where St. Paul writes that government bears the sword as "the servant of God to execute his wrath on the wrongdoer." Hence, what none of us is permitted to do as a private citizen on his own authority the state may do — not because it is itself "lord" of life and death, but because it is the authorized agent of the God who is that lord. Thus, for instance, J. M. Reu and Paul Buehring write, in a standard old Lutheran text called, interestingly, *Christian Ethics:* "The punishment of criminals is not to be considered as an act of revenge on the part of the community for the wrong committed, but as a solemn act on the part of the government to uphold the majesty of the law."[3] One might argue, of course, that to think of the matter as settled by teaching drawn from such passages would be to overlook other central theological themes — in particular, Christian teaching about forgiveness. Such a claim is not uncommon among contemporary Protestant thinkers. I offer here two examples and brief comment upon each.

One theologian writes: "Informed as I am by Christian sensibilities about forgiveness, I think that the role of courts is to identify the crime, establish the

---

3. Johann Michael Reu and Paul H. Buehring, *Christian Ethics* (Columbus, Ohio: Lutheran Book Concern, 1935), p. 328.

extent of culpability, and impose punishment, but only for the sake of prevention and restoration, not for the sake of retribution."[4] This is, if I may say so, at least as puzzling as honoring the life of the victim by taking the life of the murderer. Evidently Christian sensibilities about forgiveness do not actually require forgiveness, since something called "punishment" is still permitted. What difference do these Christian sensibilities therefore make? It's not at all clear. The most charitable interpretation is to suppose that the author simply means that when we punish our motive should be something other than revenge — but, as I have already noted, that prohibition against revenge is built into the traditional position on punishment and the death penalty. A less charitable interpretation would be to suppose that the author grounds punishment in prevention and restoration rather than retribution — in which case he is going to face some very old difficulties about why, in fact, only the guilty must be punished, difficulties that I will spell out more fully in a moment.

Perhaps sensing that he has not really taken seriously the spirit of forgiveness to which he has appealed, this author goes on: "Should the advocates of forgiveness and reconciliation pardon persons who have committed atrocities and have publicly been found guilty but in whose case we are sure that they would not repeat their crimes?" That is exactly the right question to put to his view. In such cases neither prevention nor restoration is required, and it would seem that forgiveness ought to end the matter. But it does not. "Simply letting them go," our author writes, "would certainly be wrong; it would be a form of cheap grace and therefore in the end no grace at all."[5] He takes refuge, that is, in a formula that sheds no light whatsoever on our problem.

Here is a second example from another Protestant theologian, who writes:

> Christ takes on our sin, and frees us from it. Some of us may have a more immediate need of rehabilitation, or more need to be prevented from doing harm to others in the short run, but according to Christian faith it makes no sense to think of "distinguishing the innocent from the guilty." Apart from Christ, we are all guilty. In Christ, we can all be found innocent. We may need to be helped, both by being protected from doing further wrong and by being helped to be better, but there is no reason to punish anyone.[6]

4. Miroslav Volf, "How Can You Be Croatian?" *Books and Culture* (January-February 2001), p. 31.

5. Volf, p. 31.

6. William C. Placher, "'You Were in Prison . . . ,'" *Christian Century* 118 (26 September– 3 October 2001): 20.

Now I myself doubt whether there is a theologian alive who, in his capacity as, say, a father, would raise his children in accord with such a theory. Moreover, I would not want to spend much time in the company of children who had actually been raised in such a way, nor in a society that eschewed the idea of punishment. And we should not pass off as theological wisdom a view that we would not actually try to live by.

The difficulties with this second position are several. Even more than my first exemplar, this theologian will face those old difficulties about theories of punishment. If the point is, as he seems to believe, to provide therapy for those who need to be helped or kept from doing harm, there is no need at all to provide this therapy only for those who have actually wronged someone. Nor is there any need to try to make the "punishment/therapy" for those who have done wrong somehow "fit" their wrongful deed. Within a retributive framework it makes sense to claim that a given punishment is disproportionate to the wrong done and, hence, not proper punishment. But with therapy — which, alas, turns out to be just as compulsory as punishment — proportionality makes no sense. Instead, we simply need a treatment that cures, that achieves its aims. It is perfectly reasonable to give someone who kills a pill and to treat for a lifetime within an institution someone who has broken a dish and manifested a proneness to such accidents.[7]

Those who lived through a decent portion of the twentieth century ought to know that a society can achieve more effective and total control through a system of reeducation than through a system of punishment. In fact, looking back on the last century we can say that because a system of punishment is an institution through which "force is used retrospectively, and only retrospectively, against those, and only those, who can be shown to have offended, [it] is a form of control which betrays a high degree of civilised concern to limit the damage of governmental coercion."[8] I would be sorry to see Christian theology put in the service of a more totalitarian/rehabilitative and less civilized and less controlled organization of government's power.

But the problems with the passage from my second exemplar go well beyond such standard philosophical issues; they are also theological. Reinhold Niebuhr distinguished helpfully between the "equality of sin" that we all share before God, and the "inequality of guilt" that is ours in the world we share with our neighbors. It is peculiar to find contemporary theologians (who might think that earlier ages of believers had underappreciated the significance of earthly life in their single-minded devotion to the life to come)

---

7. Herbert Morris, "Persons and Punishment," *The Monist* 52 (October 1968): 483.
8. O'Donovan, p. 13.

themselves seeming to imply that we should think of sin and guilt only in relation to God and not in civic life. Before God, to be sure, we are all equally sinners, but some of our sin brings much greater harm and destruction to others. For that we are guilty and responsible. A failure to make such distinctions will leave us unable to say everything that needs to be said about wrongdoing, punishment, and forgiveness.

Another way to put my point theologically might be as follows: Christians do want to say that in the death of Christ and the penalty visited upon him we see the "end" of the temporal order of human life, sustained, as it is, by governmental power. But Christians also want to say that, until God fully manifests that "end," he wills the continuation of this temporal order toward the kingdom of Christ.[9] How to manage the intricate simultaneities required to say both things is never easy, but it will surely always be insufficient to talk as if, since the death of Christ, Christians could find "no reason to punish anyone." There is, in short, good reason to think that the received Christian wisdom about government and punishment, and about the death penalty, is well grounded. Until the end of history, government exists as God's servant to sustain ordered human life — in part, by fitting punishment of wrongdoers. It is permitted, though not required, that such punishment should, in certain cases, extend even to execution.

Of course, many of our fellow citizens will not understand the work of government in terms grounded in Genesis 9 and Romans 13. As a people we are more likely to think of government in terms the social contract theorists taught us: as founded to stop the injustice that dominates a state of nature, but founded by our own compact. Even in these terms, however, the distinction between public and private action is crucial. A world in which each of us is permitted to judge guilt and execute punishment, in which revenge and blood feuds are permitted, is likely to be the one Hobbes described — in which life is "solitary, poor, nasty, brutish, and short." It will be a world given over to injustice.

When, therefore, the state executes a convicted murderer, it is essential that we not think of this as responding to the desires of family or friends of the murderer's victim or victims. We are all aggrieved when one of our fellow citizens is murdered, and the criminal's punishment (even execution) satisfies not our need for therapeutic closure but our need for a just society. Opponents of the death penalty will rightly note that there is something paradoxical about punishing the taking of one life by taking another, but, of course, the "takings" are not the same. One is done by a private individual

9. O'Donovan, p. 9.

acting simply in his or her own name; the other is done by public authority acting in the name of us all. The force of the objection depends precisely on blurring — or missing — the difference between private and public action. Moreover, this "paradox" — if we are given to such language — is only the paradox of government generally; for through criminal law, government defends freedom by incarcerating lawbreakers and through civil law it defends our property by imposing penalties on those who have harmed that property.[10]

Suppose then that a murder has been committed. Suppose, even, many murders have been committed in terrorist fashion by a Timothy McVeigh. It is, under such circumstances, difficult for me to find the argument that execution is not a permitted, even appropriate, punishment.

I suspect that many opponents of the death penalty find it a little difficult as well. That is why in McVeigh's case the argument turned in other directions — in particular to whether families of the victims should be permitted to view his execution. Why just the families? some have asked. Why not all of us? Shouldn't we see what we are doing and judge whether we really have the stomach for it? This argument — in the mouths of death penalty opponents committed to the sanctity, or at least equal dignity, of every human being — comes perilously close to suggesting that we should use an execution of one of our fellow citizens as a means to desired ends. We should reject even the faintest whiff of that idea.

There is, moreover, no reason to have any confidence that making a media event of an execution will engender clear and careful thought about the meaning of the death penalty. Neither is there good reason to use the occasion of an execution to provide therapy for those who have been terribly — no doubt, irreparably — hurt by the murderer's deed. The intuition that a civil society — which thinks of itself not from above as God's ordinance but from below as a social compact — needs somehow to take responsibility for executing one of its citizens is sound. Equally sound, though, is the intuition that providing therapeutic closure for families begins to lose sight of the crucial fact that we execute because — and only because — our public order has been wronged.

I find myself wondering whether we might not do some justice to the truth of each intuition by requiring at executions a public presence of randomly selected citizens — something like a jury. They would not in their private capacities have been harmed by the convicted murderer. No one could suppose that we were executing a murderer in order to provide them with

10. O'Donovan, p. 23.

some private healing. But their presence as the representatives of us all would bear witness to the fact that an execution is not a claim that some of us are more equal than others, but, rather, that — as a public act of punishment undertaken by a legitimate state — it is a different kind of deed altogether. We do not pull rank when we do it, because we do not act and are not present in our private capacities.

Perhaps there remains one reason why we should never execute — not even execute a terrorist such as McVeigh. We can reflect upon it by recalling the hypothetical illustration with which I began. Why are we — or perhaps, at least, why are some among us — more troubled by the judicial trial and execution of Cavendish, which has, after all, given him all the benefits that our legal system provides a defendant, than we are if he is simply shot by the police while attempting his escape? To think about this drives us toward the most fundamental reason for hesitation about the death penalty. We hesitate to think of any human court of judgment pronouncing "the last word" on another human life, even one as vile as that of my hypothetical Cavendish. There is the hint of something religious here, from which we draw back — perhaps in humility and awe, perhaps in horror and fear.

I had the sense that there was a time when a judge, pronouncing a sentence of death, would say to the condemned, "may God have mercy on your soul." Perhaps that has in fact been done, but, inquiring of several lawyers I was told, "probably only in movies!" Whatever the facts, it directs our attention to something important. Perhaps counterintuitively, and certainly contrary to what many religious folk might suggest, I think the death penalty would be least problematic in a genuinely religious society. Camus suggested — insightfully — that capital punishment could be justified only where there was a socially shared religious belief that the final verdict on any person's life is given by God, not by us. In such a society it would be clear that even in executing one of our fellows we do not pull rank. We would know that our earthly verdict could be overturned at the ultimate tribunal. In such a society it would make good sense, having sentenced a convict to death, to add, "may God have mercy on your soul."

What of a society in which this could make no sense? In it, Camus thought, execution could only mean elimination from the one community acknowledged by all to exist.[11] And, of course, if execution is equivalent to elimination, it is indeed a godlike act. This, at any rate, is the point that really demands our attention. To the degree that in our public life — as a people —

---

11. Albert Camus, *Reflections on the Guillotine: An Essay on Capital Punishment*, trans. Richard Howard (Michigan City, Ind.: Fridtjof-Karla Publications, 1959), pp. 42ff.

we decline to speak of God, it may be that we — as a people — ought not inflict a death sentence. But it will be very unfortunate indeed if, in our debates about the death penalty, we lose the capacity — or are assisted by Protestant theologians to lose the capacity — to articulate clearly the meaning of government, of punishment, and of justice.

4. Punishing Christians: A Pacifist Approach to the Issue of Capital Punishment

STANLEY HAUERWAS

How Not to Begin Thinking about Punishment

John Howard Yoder begins his contribution to a book entitled *The Death Penalty Debate* by observing that "it has not been my privilege to be vocationally involved in ministries of witness related to 'corrections,' nor in the social sciences which study these matters, but my conviction as to the importance of the matter has not diminished."[1] That the question of punishment was never far from Yoder's attention is indicated by his early pamphlet entitled *The Christian and Capital Punishment* as well as the book, *You Have It Coming: Good Punishment — the Legitimate Social Function of Punitive Behavior*, he was preparing when he died.[2] Some may think it strange or odd that Yoder,

---

1. John Howard Yoder, "Against the Death Penalty," in H. Wayne House and John Howard Yoder, *The Death Penalty Debate: Two Opposing Views of Capital Punishment* (Dallas: Word Publishing, 1991), p. 107.

2. John Howard Yoder, *The Christian and Capital Punishment*, Institute of Mennonite Studies Series, no. 1 (Newton, Kans.: Faith and Life Press, 1961) and John Howard Yoder, *You Have It Coming: Good Punishment — the Legitimate Social Function of Punitive Behavior*. Yoder prepared and "published" the latter book for his Internet site in 1995. I have a downloaded copy of the book which indicates that in spite of Yoder's claim that he had not kept up in the social science literature surrounding issues of punishment, in fact he had. He was particularly interested in the work of René Girard.

I am grateful to Alex Sider and Charlie Collier for their criticisms of an earlier draft of this essay. — S.H.

the pacifist, took punishment so seriously; but Yoder rightly thought those committed to Christian nonviolence cannot avoid providing an account — or even more important, alternative practices — of and for punishment.

I suspect one of the reasons many do not think that pacifism deserves serious consideration is not because they think war is a "good thing." Rather they sense that pacifism simply cannot give an account of how our daily lives depend on violent forms of behavior. How could we live if we had no understanding of crime and/or were unwilling to punish those who engage in crime? I began to explore this kind of challenge in an essay entitled, "McInerny Did It; or, Should a Pacifist Read Murder Mysteries?"[3] That essay was written in honor of my friend, Ralph McInerny, a philosopher and writer of murder mysteries. In this essay, which is written to honor another friend, Duncan Forrester, I will try to extend the argument I began in the first essay in the hope I can convince those who think of themselves as almost pacifist to drop the "almost."

It is my hope that the focus on punishment will provide a way to explore what some, including Forrester himself, may think to be differences between us on matters concerning the responsibility of Christians to the societies in which they find themselves. Forrester has graciously expressed appreciation for the kind of questions I have been pressing against Christian accommodation to liberal social arrangements. Yet he is a good Scot; he has worked tirelessly as a representative of the Church of Scotland to help his country be a more just society. Contrary to what some may think I should think as a representative of Christian nonviolence, I applaud him for the work he has done for social reforms in Scotland. For example, he has thought hard about and helped to encourage prison reform there.[4]

The work Forrester and his colleagues have done to reform Scottish prisons is the kind of work Yoder would encourage. For example, Yoder observes that neither Jesus nor Paul rose up against capital punishment. They did not do so because the gospel cannot eliminate such practices "from secular society, since, being non-coercive, the gospel cannot 'rule the world' in

---

3. That essay was originally published in *Recovering Nature: Essays in Natural Philosophy, Ethics, and Metaphysics in Honor of Ralph McInerny,* ed. John O'Callaghan and Thomas Hibbs (Notre Dame: University of Notre Dame Press, 1999), pp. 163-75. It can also be found in my book *A Better Hope: Resources for a Church Confronting Capitalism, Democracy, and Postmodernity* (Grand Rapids, Mich.: Brazos Books, 2000), pp. 201-10.

4. I know of this work primarily through conversations with Duncan, but he discusses the work of the penal policy group in his essay "Priorities for Social Theology Today," in *Vision and Prophecy: The Tasks of Social Theology Today,* ed. Michael Northcott (Edinburgh: Centre for Theology and Public Issues, 1991), pp. 29-31.

that way. Yet, to condone the way things stand is not approval: 'from the beginning it was not so' (Matt. 19:8)."[5] According to Yoder, though Jesus said this about the Mosaic provision for divorce, this is the way early Christians thought about other areas where the world was ruled by pagan powers. Yet the Christians also thought that the new level of love and forgiveness made possible by the Holy Spirit is good news for the "real world" because such love will work as salt and light for those who are not Christians. Yoder continues,

> This should be true anywhere; even more evidently should it be the case in the Anglo-Saxon world, where a large number of citizens claim some kind of Christian sanction for society's values. If Christ is not only prophet and priest but also king, the border between church and the world cannot be impermeable to moral truth. Something of the cross-bearing, forgiving love, and dignity which Jesus' life, death, and resurrection revealed to be the normative way to be human, must be the norm for all humans, whether they know it or not. We cannot *expect* of anyone, not even of believers, that that norm be lived out perfectly. Yet, [there] is the calling of the followers of Jesus to testify that there is no other norm. The one strategy which will not serve that calling, which could not be done in the first century, and cannot be done in our century, is to claim to possess, and to impose on society, a body of civil rules independent of the faith of the persons called to respect them. The alternative is to work with the acceptance of the others' unbelief which is what I call "condoning" the lesser moral level of the civil order.[6]

However, Yoder's understanding of the permeable boundaries between church and world does not in itself suggest how Christians ought to think about punishment in general and/or, in particular, capital punishment. He observes that watching the debate between advocates and opponents of capital punishment over the years has taught him that there is no one right place to begin.[7] That there is no place to begin seems to me to be right, but it is a hard lesson learned. For our temptation is to once again roll out the various theories of punishment — rehabilitation, defense against the criminal (deterrence), retribution — and then to grade the practice of punishment against these theories of punishment.[8]

---

5. Yoder, "Against the Death Penalty," p. 141.
6. Yoder, "Against the Death Penalty," p. 141.
7. Yoder, "Against the Death Penalty," p. 107.
8. The examples of this strategy are legion, but for a recent display of how this kind of analysis works see Avery Cardinal Dulles, "Catholicism and Capital Punishment," *First Things*

The problem is not that these theories are "wrong" (though I think they often give us a false sense that we know what we are talking about when we talk about punishment); but it is by no means clear what work the theories are meant to do. In particular the theories give the impression that how Christians punish is but an instance of a more general practice of punishment shared by all societies. It is that presumption I want to challenge in this essay by calling attention to the way Christians have punished and should punish.

Of course the strategy of beginning with general theories of punishment is often an attempt to show that capital punishment fails to be justified on grounds of this or that theory. For example, it is suggested that capital punishment cannot pass muster if we believe that rehabilitation or the protection of society is the primary purpose of punishment. You certainly cannot rehabilitate someone you have killed, nor does it seem that the use of capital punishment protects society by deterring others from killing. It is often pointed out, for example, that murderers are seldom repeat offenders, unless they are professional killers, so capital punishment does little to deter. Professionals after all will not be deterred exactly because they are professionals.

One response to the attempt to defeat capital punishment by showing it does not deter is to observe that capital punishment is associated with the wrong crime. If we killed people for stock fraud, for example, there is every reason to believe that capital punishment would deter. Erect a gallows or a guillotine on Wall Street, televise the execution of those guilty of stock fraud, and I think there is every reason to believe that stock fraud would be a much less common crime. That most people today recoil against killing people for theft indicates that questions of punishment involve more than the various abstract theories of punishment suggest in and of themselves.

For example, Duncan Forrester reports that the penal policy group that took as their assignment an attempt to understand how the penal system worked and should work in Scotland began by looking at the various theories of punishment. However, he reports it soon became apparent that none of the theories — nor all the theories together — explain what actually happens in the penal system in Scotland. He observes that his group increasingly became convinced "that theories often disguise, mystify, and subtly justify what is really happening."[9] It was only when the group began to go more deeply into

---

112 (April 2001): 30-35. I am not suggesting that the various theories of punishment are not useful ways of exploring the conceptual issues entailed in various claims about punishment. Rather I am calling into question the temptation for the theories to take on a life of their own irrespective of the thick practices that surround punishment in different historical periods and in various cultural locations.

9. Forrester, "Priorities for Social Theology Today," p. 30.

the experience of being and surviving as a prisoner did theological themes begin to emerge to illumine the practice of punishment. Forrester observes:

> We discovered the necessity of hope. We noted that although offense involves *guilt,* this is not today recognized as something with which the penal system can or should engage. And, most important of all, we noted that in the Christian tradition offense, crime, and sin are met with *forgiveness* which wipes away the guilt and the memory, while our society remains highly punitive and former prisoners rarely experience real forgiveness and reconciliation at the hands of their neighbors and colleagues. We concluded that any Christian account of punishment must see it as *discipline* directed to the good of society and of the offender. Most of those working in the system or in academic criminology found the notion of forgiveness a fresh and exciting and challenging idea. In Christian theology it is of course rooted deeply in the understanding of God, and theologians would wish to affirm that it is a universal truth that God is a God who forgives.[10]

I am sure that Forrester and his colleagues are on the right track for helping us think as Christians about punishment. Too often attempts to think through the practice of punishment using the standard theories means theological considerations are absent or used to support positions determined on other grounds. I am sure, moreover, that Forrester and his colleagues are right that the *telos* of punishment must be reconciliation and forgiveness. As he observes, the absence of the hope of forgiveness means "prisons become human warehouses and both offenders and those who operate the criminal justice system have great difficulty in seeing their experience and their work as significant and meaningful."[11]

Yet I am equally sure that we must be careful not to let appeals to forgiveness and reconciliation hide from us the seriousness of punishment and the proper role punishment has, not only for any society but in particular in the church. It is not enough for Christians to say "forgiveness" if they do not exemplify in their own lives why punishment is a necessary practice if the church is to be the church. Appeals to forgiveness are too easy if we have not first made clear why we think it is wrong to execute people for stock fraud. After all the church at one time thought those convicted of heresy should be

---

10. Forrester, "Priorities for Social Theology Today," p. 30. I think it wrong to suggest that the Christian practice of forgiveness "wipes out memory." On the contrary, forgiveness makes memory possible. For an argument along these lines see my *A Better Hope*, pp. 139-54.

11. Forrester, "Priorities for Social Theology Today," p. 30.

killed — a position we may find extreme, but one justified if you believe that heresy is a more serious crime than murder. A murderer only robs us of our life; a heretic robs us of our salvation.

In order to explore the theological issues at the heart of punishment I want to introduce Oliver O'Donovan's compelling justification of capital punishment. His account, moreover, is all the more important because it emerges in the process of his critique of John Paul II's praise in *Evangelium vitae* (1995) for the growing tendency in our time to limit the use of or to abolish capital punishment. O'Donovan, I think, rightly fears that the Pope on this matter may have succumbed to the sentimental humanism of our time. However, before such a judgment can be sustained, I need to attend to the details of O'Donovan's analysis and critique of the Pope's position.

O'Donovan's Analysis of *Evangelium Vitae*

O'Donovan's critique involves a close reading of the passage in *Evangelium vitae* that deals with capital punishment. That passage reads:

> This is the context in which to place the problem of the *death penalty.* On this matter there is a growing tendency, both in the Church and in civil society, to demand that it be applied in a very limited way or even that it be abolished completely. The problem must be viewed in the context of a system of penal justice ever more in line with human dignity and thus, in the end, with God's plan for man and society. The primary purpose of the punishment which society inflicts is "to redress the disorder caused by the offense." Public authority must redress the violation of personal and social rights by imposing on the offender an adequate punishment for the crime, as a condition for the offender to regain the exercise of his or her freedom. In this way authority also fulfills the purpose of defending public order and ensuring people's safety, while at the same time offering an incentive and help to change his or her behavior and be rehabilitated.
>
> It is clear that for these purposes to be achieved, *the nature and extent of the punishment* must be carefully evaluated and decided upon, and ought not go to the extreme of executing the offender except in cases of absolute necessity: in other words, when it would not be possible otherwise to defend society. Today, however, as a result of steady improvements in the organization of the penal system, such cases are very rare, if not practically nonexistent.
>
> In any event, the principle set forth in the new *Catechism of the Catho-*

lic Church remains valid: "If bloodless means are sufficient to defend human lives against an aggressor and to protect public order and the safety of persons, public authority must limit itself to such means, because they better correspond to the concrete conditions of the common good and are more in conformity to the dignity of the human person."[12]

O'Donovan begins his criticism of the Pope's position noting that three points in particular are in need of clarification: (1) what characteristics of a society are presupposed by the "steady improvements" to which the Pope refers? (2) what kind of situation would count as an "absolute necessity"? and (3) why does the Pope justify capital punishment in classical retributive categories, but make the possibility for the lessening use of capital punishment turn on remedial considerations?[13] Though the first two questions of clarification are important, O'Donovan's most important challenge to the Pope's position involves the third.

O'Donovan observes that in the late eighteenth and nineteenth centuries

---

12. I am using the text as it appears (including the italics) in *The Encyclicals of John Paul II,* edited with introductions by J. Michael Miller (Huntington, Ind.: Our Sunday Visitor, 1996), paragraph 56.

John Paul II's claim that "this is the context" to discuss capital punishment is fascinating. Paragraph 55 deals with the "paradox" that occurs when the right to protect one's own life and the duty not to harm someone else's life cannot be reconciled in practice. John Paul II observes that the "intrinsic value of life and the duty to love oneself not less than others are the basis of a *true right* to self-defense." He then notes that the commandment to love the neighbor presupposes love of self as set forth in the great commandment. Therefore, "no one can renounce the right to self-defense out of lack of love for life or for self. This can only be done in virtue of a heroic love which deepens and transfigures the love of self into a radical self-offering, according to the spirit of the Gospel Beatitudes. The sublime example of this self-offering is the Lord Jesus Christ."

I confess I find the Pope's defense of self-love as the basis for self-defense puzzling. If our self-love is to be formed by charity, what could it possibly mean to suggest that Christians have a right to self-defense? Our love for life and self only makes sense if the "self" is shaped by the love of God found in the cross. To suggest that such a love is "heroic" seems to accept the natural, if not sinful, self as normative.

This is extremely important for the issue of capital punishment, for the Pope goes on to suggest that legitimate defense is not only a right but a "grave duty" for those responsible for the common good of the family or the state. Accordingly it happens that there is a need to render an aggressor incapable of causing harm which may even require the taking of the aggressor's life. In such cases the "fatal outcome" is not murder because the loss of life is attributable to the aggressor's action. As we shall see, this justification makes the Pope's judgments about capital punishment the harder to understand.

13. Oliver O'Donovan, "The Death Penalty in *Evangelium Vitae,*" in *Ecumenical Ventures in Ethics: Protestants Engage Pope John Paul II's Moral Encyclicals,* ed. Reinhard Hütter and Theodor Dieter (Grand Rapids, Mich.: Eerdmans, 1998), pp. 220-23.

a consensus developed that retributive appropriateness was the final criteria for means of punishment. (He does not explain how or why this "consensus" developed or whether it is a development Christians should applaud. I should think the "reformative" account of punishment was and is the justification most modern people assume justifies punishment.) Accordingly, the death penalty was required since only life could witness to the sanctity of life. O'Donovan observes that the Pope simply gives no reason why we should believe that rehabilitation should count more than public safety. But even more important, the Pope does not adequately explore what is at stake in his praise for societies that have abandoned retribution as the primary purpose of punishment.

In order to clarify what the Pope needs to say, O'Donovan offers an account of why retribution can never be disavowed by the public authorities. Punishment is an expressive act, according to O'Donovan, just to the extent that "punishment must pronounce judgment on the offense, describing it, disowning it, and refounding the moral basis for the common life which the offense has challenged."[14] Punishment, so to speak, "gives back" the offense, not simply as vengeance, but in the sense that a true statement is made about what has happened. Retribution is the primary end of punishment, which means that that is what punishment *is* in the same way that telling the truth is the primary end of making a statement. Retribution is the alternative to vengeance because vengeance is "private" and, therefore, arbitrary.[15]

So understood, punishment is not a means to some other end, even the end of making the offender good; justice is internal to punishment itself. To

14. O'Donovan, p. 224.

15. I understand the distinction O'Donovan is making between retribution and vengeance, but I confess I find it a bit forced. If vengeance is the symbolic way people gesture that order is deeper than disorder, it seems appropriate that retribution serve to provide the vengeance those directly involved in a crime feel they need. That those who have someone close to them violated so often express the need to have the perpetrator of the violence killed and even to see them executed cannot be easily dismissed as "a primitive attitude." That a "public authority" should perform the execution is important, but the execution remains the working out of vengeance.

Yoder in his early pamphlet "The Christian and Capital Punishment" maintained that vengeance shapes capital punishment. His position in this regard does not necessarily make his view of capital punishment different from O'Donovan's stress on justice — because Yoder also observes that "vengeance is happening; the necessity is that it be controlled. Thus the significance of civil order is that it *limit* vengeance to a level equivalent to the offense. . . . Vengeance was never God's highest intent for men's relations with one another; permitting it within the limits of justice, i.e., of equivalent injury, was never really his purpose" (p. 7). According to Yoder, what God wants to do with evil, what he wants *us* to do with evil, is "to swallow it up, drown it in the bottomless sea of His crucified love" (p. 7). Yoder's account of how the civil order "limits vengeance" has at least resemblance to O'Donovan's understanding of justice.

be sure, there may be secondary goods associated with punishment, but such goods should not qualify that the end of punishment is justice. As O'Donovan puts it, "punishment is a kind of enacted language," reminding us that the equivalence of punishment to crime is a "symbolic construct" that "evolves as the symbolic meaning of certain acts with the context of social expectation changes."[16] Thus it may be, as Montesquieu observed, that in countries with mild laws inhabitants are as much affected by slight penalties as inhabitants of countries with more severe laws.[17] O'Donovan hopes that the Pope's understanding of the "improvements in the penal system" simply means that the influence of the Christian message makes it possible for those in authority to follow Ambrose's message concerning the use of capital punishment — "You will be excused if you use it, admired if you refrain."[18]

Yet O'Donovan fears John Paul II may in fact come close to recommending the abolition of capital punishment in principle. For example, O'Donovan calls attention to paragraph 40 of *Evangelium vitae*, in which the Pope seems to be moving to a position that would not require capital punishment to be considered a necessary part of a humane justice system. In paragraph 40 the Pope, in commenting on the prohibition of murder in the Decalogue, says: "Of course we must recognize that in the Old Testament this sense of the value of life, though already quite marked, does not yet reach the refinement found in the Sermon on the Mount. This is apparent in some aspects of the current [i.e., *then* current] penal legislation, which provided for severe forms of corporal punishment and even the death penalty."[19]

O'Donovan thinks this account of capital punishment breaks the link between public safety and the system of retributive justice. As a result capital punishment becomes but an emergency provision that allegedly is no longer required in modern, economically developed, and well-governed states. Accordingly the coercive powers of the state in criminal justice are derived and justified from a just war perspective of "legitimate defense."[20] From O'Donovan's perspective this is a terrible mistake because

---

16. O'Donovan, p. 225.

17. Montesquieu, *Spirit of the Laws* VI, 12, quoted in O'Donovan, p. 225.

18. O'Donovan, p. 227.

19. O'Donovan, p. 229.

20. I confess I am not quite sure what point O'Donovan is making by suggesting that the Pope is making a mistake when he seemingly justifies capital punishment in just-war terms of "legitimate defense." I assume he must mean that "legitimate defense" is a "last resort" which makes "capital punishment" justified only if the survival of the society is at stake. But that would rob capital punishment of its "normality." In other words capital punishment is not like just war if it is required by justice. That said, I think the relation between just war reflection and

one should never attempt such a thing. The right of the state to impose coercive measures against wrongdoers arises not from its need to defend itself but from its office of *judgment*. . . . For if the death penalty is never at home in ordinary penal practice, then it is never invoked for purposes germane to penology but only to shore up the institution upon which all penal practice depends, that is, the state. The idea of an "emergency provision," whether we meet it in John Paul or in some well-known Protestant exemplars, implies an inevitable drift towards statism; for once the power of the sword is notionally set free from the constraints of justice *in extremis,* there can be no function for the sword but to enforce the state's grip. We should hardly be surprised if the state that is refused the just use of force in ordinary operations but is promised a *carte blanche* in emergency, sets about creating one.[21]

To make capital punishment morally discontinuous from other forms of coercive punishment not only invites a loss of constraint on when states may declare their very existence is at stake, but — even more disturbing —

---

capital punishment has not been sufficiently spelled out either by those who support just war and capital punishment or by those who support neither. In particular I think O'Donovan's analysis opens up the question of what "justice" a just war is meant to serve. This is particularly important if just war is understood not as an exception to non-violence, but rather is required because justice always requires us to defend the neighbor. It is, therefore, wrong to try to rid the world of war if war is a necessity for the realization of justice. If such is the case, then capital punishment and war are analogous but it remains a question in what ways the justice that is the end of each is similar and different.

21. O'Donovan, pp. 231-33. For O'Donovan's extended account of the importance of judgment, see his *The Desire of the Nations: Rediscovering the Roots of Political Theology* (Cambridge: Cambridge University Press, 1996), pp. 37-41, 147-51. O'Donovan explicitly criticizes Yoder's account of Matthew 18:15-20. O'Donovan thinks Yoder, at least in *The Original Revolution,* gives the state a role in judgment. Unfortunately, according to O'Donovan, Yoder did not continue that line of analysis in *The Politics of Jesus.* I am not convinced. O'Donovan, I think, fails to appreciate Yoder's refusal to give a "theory" of state action. For Yoder "vengeance happens"; it does not need a justifying theory.

By some "well-known Protestant exemplars," O'Donovan means Barth. In *Church Dogmatics* III/4, Barth argued that capital punishment "must be put on the far edge of what can be commanded." According to Barth there is a place for killing those "whose existence threatens the state and its stability in such a way that a choice has to be made between their existence and that of the state" (p. 446). Barth thinks, for example, the treasonous giving of secrets to the enemy might be grounds for capital punishment. O'Donovan quite rightly observes that Barth-like justifications put the ordinary operations of penal justice in an idealized light. Such justifications hide from us the coercive character of all punishment which draws its power over us through our mortality. Citations from Karl Barth, *Church Dogmatics,* trans. A. T. Mackay et al. (Edinburgh: T&T Clark, 1961 [1936]).

theologically severs death from God's judgment. According to O'Donovan all Christians have to say that death is not part of God's "original" created order. Death is not just death, but judgment on sin. Without such a view of the linkage between judgment and death Christ becomes but another victim of injustice rather than the one that bore our sins and suffered our death. That is why, as happy as it may be to be rid of the ordinary uses of the death penalty, we "cannot be rid of the symbolic role that the death penalty plays in relating death to judgment. There will always be a death penalty in the mind — if, that is, we are all to learn to 'die with Christ,' understanding our own deaths as a kind of capital punishment."[22]

So runs O'Donovan's justification of capital punishment. I admire his argument because he makes candid the moral and theological presuppositions associated with retributive accounts of punishment. Christological questions are rightly at the center, where O'Donovan puts them. Moreover, he makes clear that capital punishment cannot be separated from why and how we punish in other aspects of our lives. Accordingly, any alternative account to O'Donovan's understanding of punishment requires if not forces us to leave behind the sentimentalities so characteristic of compassionate responses to punishment.

The Christian Practice of Punishment

O'Donovan rightly calls into question the sentimental humanism that currently dominates discussions surrounding capital punishment in liberal social orders. Moreover, O'Donovan helps us see why it is extremely unwise for Christians to identify with the call for an end to capital punishment just to the extent that our understanding of punishment is confused with humanist ideologies and practices. Yet I do want capital punishment to come to an end because I think the end of punishment has been transformed by the cross and resurrection of Christ. Moreover, I think that transformation is a possibility

22. O'Donovan, p. 235. O'Donovan suggests that to the extent John Paul II leaves this understanding of capital punishment behind, he becomes a modernist in spite of his otherwise attack on "the culture of death." O'Donovan notes that at the heart of the "culture of death" rests a culture of life. "Precisely because our brief span must (it seems to us) carry the whole meaning of existence, offering all the reconciliation we can ever hope to find; precisely because death (whether Christ's or ours) is allowed no role in this reconciliation; we become greedy of life, demanding to live each moment to the full, snatching from others" opportunities to live that could compete with our own, making calculated sacrifices of the 'worthless' lives to enrich the 'worthwhile,' and so on" (p. 236).

not only for the practice of the church but for any society and the public authorities (what is sometimes identified as the state) who have responsibilities to serve the goods a society holds in common, which include punishment.

By distinguishing "public authorities" from the "state" I mean to do no more than call into question the assumption that the state *as such* is a known entity. I assume peoples can exist with structures of authority that are not the same as a "state," particularly when "the state" in modernity is identified with the locus of hegemonic power. This may seem an unimportant distinction, but too often "the state" is simply accepted as a given in a manner that makes it impervious to the gospel. For example, Avery Cardinal Dulles observes that while the church can and does punish, she is also indulgent toward offenders. "It would be clearly inappropriate for the Church, as a spiritual society, to execute criminals, but the State is a different type of society. It cannot be expected to act as a Church."[23]

Far be it from me to suggest that a cardinal of the Church of Rome has gone over to the Lutherans, but to claim that something called "the state" exists that has not been transformed by Christ could be interpreted as accepting the Lutheran understanding of the distinction between the orders of creation and redemption. For example, it is quite interesting to contrast Dulles's (and O'Donovan's) understanding of the state with that of John Howard Yoder.[24] Responding to the assumption shared by many that to call for the end of capital punishment is to destroy all government, Yoder observes that for the Christian to accept the question "but where will this lead?" is to distort the whole problem. Of course Christians know the world does not share our

---

23. Avery Cardinal Dulles, "Catholicism and Capital Punishment," p. 34. Dulles, like O'Donovan, thinks that in predominately Christian societies the state can lean toward leniency as long as such leniency does not violate the demands of justice. Dulles, also like O'Donovan, thinks the state must believe in a transcendent order of justice which it has an obligation to protect. Such an order of justice is but a "symbolic anticipation of God's perfect justice" (p. 33). Dulles quite rightly distinguishes this view of the state from the general view in our time that sees the state as but the instrument of the will of the governed in which the death penalty becomes but an expression of the collective anger of the group. When this happens, punishment is no longer an analog of the divine judgment on objective evil but simply the self-assertive act of vengeance. I share Dulles's view of the transformation of the state in modernity, but I wonder why he does not conclude from that change that in such social orders capital punishment should be ended exactly because the end of capital punishment has been lost. I often wonder why the same line of reasoning does not lead advocates of just war, which again is dependent on some account of justice, to call for an end to war. Liberal societies simply lack an account of justice that would make just war intelligible.

24. My suggesting that Dulles and O'Donovan may have a similar view of this matter may be mistaken. O'Donovan may well believe that the church can and should execute criminals.

faith, that the world cannot be expected to live as Christians should live, but that does not mean there is some line drawn in the sand that determines what Christians cannot ask of the societies in which we find ourselves.[25] The resurrection and ascension of Christ means there is no situation in which Christians think nothing can be done.

> The world can be challenged, one point at a time, to take one step in the right direction, to move up one modest notch in approximation of the righteousness of love. To challenge capital punishment no more undermines government than does the rejection of the oath (Matthew 5:33-37, James 5:12) undermine truth telling; no more than does the consent of the governed destroy the authority of the state. The civil order is a fact. That it might be done away with by pushing the critique of love "too far" is inconceivable. Thus the Christian (and any believer in democracy) will be concerned to restrain the violent, vengeful potential of the state. That potential for violence does not need our advocacy; it is already there.[26]

Of course, Dulles and O'Donovan may object that Yoder fails to understand that the issue is not whether the state does or does not exist or have a justification to sustain its legitimacy. The issue is justice. Yet just as he challenges the assumption that there is any one thing called the "state," so Yoder questions the assumption that there is any univocal "concept of justice, having the same meaning in all times and places, consisting in an exact logical or mathematical equivalence of offense and retribution, and that such 'justice' must (or can) be either wholly respected or fundamentally rejected."[27] There is, therefore, no culturally invariant understanding of what equivalent punishment should or does entail. The presumption that "retributive justice" requires the murderer's life in return is not written in stone.[28] For

---

25. This theme is also taken up in David Novak's chapter in this volume.

26. Yoder, "Against the Death Penalty," p. 142. Yoder observes that "anarchy" is a grammatical abstraction with no reality. There are varied forms of government — from tyranny to constitutional democracy, but given the many possibilities there is always authority. Even in cases where authority is functioning too little for the welfare and stability of the society, the reason for such dysfunctioning is never due to Christian love being too effective.

27. Yoder, "Against the Death Penalty," p. 143.

28. Yoder observes that if life for life is required by justice, then there is no reason why the mentally handicapped should be spared the death penalty. The character or "freedom" of the murderer should not be taken into account if all that matters is that justice be served. Yoder rightly uses all the anomalies created by capital punishment — it can result in killing the innocent, it falls disproportionately on the poor and African-American, its infrequency ironically makes it more arbitrary — to call into question its use.

Yoder, justice is a direction, not an achievement. I take this claim to mean no more than what is emphasized in all classical accounts of justice, namely that justice depends on the practices of a people that embodies the hard-won wisdom of the past, tested by the challenges of the present, in the hope of a better future.

Yoder has no reason to deny O'Donovan's account of punishment as an "enacted language." O'Donovan, moreover, rightly suggests that as a language, punishment can and should evolve.[29] Rather Yoder is trying to force questions about the "context of social expectation" that Christ's cross and resurrection have made possible. For Yoder is sure that if it is inappropriate for the church to execute criminals, this is equally the case for the public officials of any society. If the shedding of blood is meant to expose the killer to killing in expiation in the name of justice or the cosmic order, it is Yoder's contention that Christ is the end of expiation.[30] At the very least this means Christians cannot help but challenge accounts of justice that assume the only way to restore the injustice murder names is by taking the life of the murderer.[31]

That Christ is the end of expiation does not mean, however, that Christians do not punish. Yet the Christian understanding of punishment must begin with the recognition that we are not punished for our sins, but sin is our punishment. John Howard Yoder and John Milbank are not usually considered allies, but I believe they share this understanding of sin. In *Theology and Social Theory,* Milbank observes that God does not will to punish sin, because "punishment is not an act of a real nature upon another nature, and God always remains within his nature. Punishment is ontologically 'self-inflicted,' the only punishment is the deleterious effect of sin upon nature, and the torment of knowing reality only in terms of one's estrangement from it."[32]

29. O'Donovan, "The Death Penalty in *Evangelium Vitae*," p. 225.

30. Yoder, "Against the Death Penalty," p. 128.

31. The refusal to kill those who kill can be seen as a kind of cruelty just to the extent such a refusal refuses to allow those that kill to determine their own self-understanding. To kill another human being can be the ultimate act of self-assertion, the claim of ultimate autonomy, and thus an act that creates an extraordinary loneliness. Murder is not an act to be shared. The refusal to kill others is the refusal to let them determine the meaning of their lives. The refusal to kill them is the refusal to let their loneliness determine who they are.

32. John Milbank, *Theology and Social Theory: Beyond Secular Reason* (Oxford: Basil Blackwell, 1990), p. 420. In an extraordinary essay on the book of Job, Herbert Fingarette argues that "the Book of Job shatters, by a combination of challenge and ridicule and ultimately by direct experiential demonstration, the idea that the law known to human beings reflects law rooted in the divine or ultimate nature of being, and the idea that the divine or ultimate nature

According to Milbank the trial and punishment of Jesus judges all other trials and punishments just to the extent the latter cannot help but be "alien." It is, therefore, not adequate to say, as O'Donovan seems to do, that such "alien punishment" is a symbolic language. The tragic necessity of such punishment cannot be a sign of God's justice if God's justice is the cross. So the only

> tolerable, and non-sinful punishment, for Christians, must be the self-punishment inherent in sin. When a person commits an evil act, he cuts himself off from social peace, and this nearly always means that he is visited with social anger. But the aim should be to reduce this anger to a calm fury against the sin, and to offer the sinner nothing but good will, so bringing him to the point of realizing that his isolation is self-imposed.[33]

Milbank's position does not commit him to the absurd position that we know that we are being punished for our sin. Indeed one of the most frightening realities is that we may appear to be quite happy in our unrighteousness — happiness can be a form of punishment. To suffer for our sins is a great gift that makes possible the identification as well as the appropriate penance for our sin. For that is exactly what Christian punishment is — penance that makes possible the reconciliation with God, the neighbor against whom we have sinned, and even ourselves. Milbank is quite right that the effect of sin estranges us from ourselves, creating a loneliness that cannot be overcome. To be punished as a Christian is to be called home so that we may be reunited with the community of forgiven sinners called the church and, thus, reconciled with our own life.

Christian punishment is properly understood to be excommunication, or binding and loosing. To be confronted by our brothers and sisters because of our sin is a call to reconciliation; not to hear the call is to condemn ourselves. To be excommunicated is not to be "thrown out," but rather to be told that we are already "outside." Excommunication is a call to come home by helping us locate how we have alienated ourselves from God and those that gather to worship God. Christian punishment only makes sense against the background of the practice of holiness commensurate

---

of being is in its essences lawlike." Fingarette argues that if God were required to punish us for disobedience to God's law, then we could control God by forcing God to punish us. That is a bargain decisively rejected in Job. See "The Meaning of Law in the Book of Job," in Stanley Hauerwas and Alasdair MacIntyre, eds., *Revisions: Changing Perspectives in Moral Philosophy,* (Notre Dame: University of Notre Dame Press, 1983), pp. 249-86. *The quote comes from p. 269.*

33. Milbank, p. 421.

with the Christian desire to be a people called to witness to the one who alone is able to forgive sins.[34]

The Christian practice of punishment cannot help but resist being confined by the various theories of punishment. What Christians have to offer our non-Christian brothers and sisters is not a better theory, but a practice of punishment that can be imitated. There is always the question, however, whether what we do as Christians can be abstracted from our worship of God, from which all that we do gains its intelligibility. Yoder, for example, reminds us that prisons were once called "penitentiaries" because they were understood as places to repent.[35] Once the background practices that make repentance the *telos* of punishment were missing, prisons could not help but become the hellholes they are today.

Christians are rightly concerned with prison reform. Christians rightly seek to live in societies that no longer use the death penalty. But Christians — particularly Christians committed to nonviolence — fail themselves and their non-Christian neighbors when they act as if punishment is a problem "out there." The world must first see that Christians can form a community that can punish. Only then will the world have an example of what it might mean to be a community that punishes in a manner appropriate for a people who believe that we have been freed by the cross of Christ from the terror of death. I believe that is the kind of community Duncan Forrester has always represented, and in so doing, became for the world the kind of "permeable boundary" God desires.

34. That Christians punish means we must also have practices that make it possible to recognize sins. In other words we need to know how to name actions such as lying, stealing, rape, adultery, killing. A fascinating question that needs exploration is the relation between what Christians call sin and what is understood as crime. Christians that commit crimes may sin; but criminals who are not Christians may not be sinners. Yet Christians no doubt have contributed to current understanding of crime that rightly makes it difficult to distinguish between sin and crime. In social orders as fragile as those in the so-called first world, one of the few places the language of the common good works is in agreements about what constitutes crime. But to recognize a crime requires an account of the positive goods the crime injures. It is not clear liberal social orders can confidently name such goods, which makes their presumed arguments about crime increasingly arbitrary.

35. Yoder, "Against the Death Penalty," p. 130.

5. The Death Penalty, Mercy, and Islam: A Call for Retrospection

KHALED ABOU EL FADL

This chapter offers an Islamically informed and inspired critique of the notion of the killing state[1] — the legitimacy and propriety of the state retaining the ability to terminate human life in order to preserve and protect human life or in order to achieve other desirable goals, whether such goals are social, political, or moral. The very concept of the killing state seems to be premised on the notion that, under certain circumstances, the state can or should be trusted to terminate lives in order to serve and promote certain objectives, and that these objectives are of sufficient moral merit and weight that they, ultimately, could justify the act of terminating a life. From an Islamic perspective, this is an extremely serious affair. As we will see below, when one deals with life, one is necessarily dealing with what is known as the boundaries of God *(hudud Allah)* — one is treading upon divine territory and one does so at great peril to one's soul and ultimate well-being in the hereafter.[2] Islamically, it is believed that when it comes to *hudud Allah,* God is the pos-

---

1. I borrowed the expression "killing state" from an Austin Sarat book of the same name: Austin Sarat, ed., *The Killing State: Capital Punishment in Law, Culture, and Politics* (Oxford: Oxford University Press, 1998).

2. On the rights of God, the rights of human beings, and the category of mixed rights, see Mohammad Hashim Kamali, *Principles of Islamic Jurisprudence* (Cambridge: Islamic Texts Society, 1991), pp. 348-49.

I would like to thank my wife, Grace, and my assistant, Naheed Fakoor, for all their help with this article.

sessor of the exclusive right to forgive or punish transgressions and ultimately it is God who decides whether any authority delegated to human beings has been mishandled or abused. Importantly, as to *hudud Allah* or the territory of God's moral jurisdiction, human beings may adjudicate, or otherwise deal with, acts and behavior that fall within this exclusive divine jurisdiction only pursuant to a delegation of authority directly by and from God *(istikhlaf wa tafwid ilahi)*.[3] In the Islamic tradition, human life, and in fact life in general, is sanctified — life is inviolable and its existence or termination is placed squarely within the boundaries of the divine jurisdiction. Consequently, human life may be extinguished pursuant only to a clear, explicit, unambiguous, and unwavering authorization and delegation of proper authority by the possessor of the ultimate right over human existence — in a word, by God.[4] Any ambiguity, doubt, or lack of certitude as to the existence of proper divine authorization or delegation is known in Islamic theology as *shubha*.[5] The existence of any *shubha* accrues in favor of the preservation, and against the termination, of life.[6] This means that in the paradigms of Islamic theology and law, there is a strong presumption in favor of the continuity of life, and to overcome this presumption, one must have a clear mandate from the divine.[7]

3. On this issue, see Khaled Abou El Fadl, "Unbounded Law of God and Territorial Boundaries," in Allen Buchanan and Margaret Moore, eds., *States, Nations, and Boundaries: The Ethics of Making Boundaries* (Cambridge: Cambridge University Press, 2003), pp. 214-27.

4. On the preservation of human life and its relation to the rights of God *(huquq Allah)*, see Khaled Abou El Fadl, *Speaking in God's Name: Islamic Law, Authority and Women* (Oxford: Oneworld Press, 2001), pp. 196-97; Khaled Abou El Fadl, "Constitutionalism and the Islamic Sunni Legacy," *UCLA Journal of Islamic and Near Eastern Law* 1, no. 1 (Fall/Winter, 2001-02): 86-92.

5. In Islamic jurisprudence, *shubha* refers to the existence of reasonable doubt, which pursuant to a famous prophetic admonition must be resolved in favor of the defendant. Reasonable doubt could be the result of insufficient evidence or could be the byproduct of a procedural irregularity. Whether in Islamic jurisprudence there is a concept similar to the common law doctrine of harmless error is an open question.

6. On the presumption of innocence and granting defendants the benefit of doubt in criminal matters, see Subhi Mahmassani, *The Philosophy of Jurisprudence in Islam,* trans. Farhat Ziadeh (Leiden: E. J. Brill, 1961), pp. 168-89; Mohamed El-Awa, *Punishment in Islamic Law* (Indianapolis: American Trust Publications, 1982), pp. 124-31.

7. In this regard, the story of a mythical figure in the Qur'anic discourse, known as the Khidr, is significant. Khidr might have been a prophet or perhaps a holy man who acted upon special divinely inspired knowledge that was unique to him and unshared by any others. Seeking to learn from him, Moses, the Prophet, accompanies the Khidr for a period of time observing how he executed God's will. Importantly, no one, not even Moses, could understand the wisdom behind al-Khidr's behavior until he chose to reveal the divine purpose, which was revealed to him. Moses was shocked when Khidr murdered a youth, and protested the immorality of Khidr's actions. However, Khidr eventually explained to Moses why he received a divine

If there is any doubt as to the existence of such a mandate, the pro-life presumption is not overcome, and the act of killing someone would necessarily become an immoral and unlawful act.[8] In this context, it is important to emphasize the onerous responsibility set upon the killing state. When a state acts to terminate a life, at least for the purpose of performing this particular act, the state represents and stands in for God. In effect, the state claims that the termination of life in question, in any particular case, is both authorized and desired by God. Islamically speaking, because the question of life is always a divine province, then killing can only be justified if God has admitted and empowered the state within this province. In turn, when the state kills, it does not do so on behalf of the citizenry, the will of the majority, or even in the service of compelling national security interests; rather, ultimately, the state is acting on God's behalf, while purporting to know the divine will and while claiming the ability and competence to faithfully and effectively carry out this divine will.[9] Stated in this way, one cannot help but wonder whether the state

---

mandate to kill the youth. See the Qur'an 18:74-81. It is important to note, however, that the Qur'an emphasizes Khidr's unique and singular status. In addition, even Moses is unable to handle the burden of being privy to the divine knowledge, and ultimately, is forced to part ways with the Khidr. Arguably, this narrative emphasizes the permissibility of terminating human life if there is a divine mandate to do so. But more importantly, it also emphasizes the incapacity and inability of common human beings — even those who, like Moses, are considered prophets in Islam — to discharge the burdens of the divine mandate, even when they believe they are able to do so.

8. For instance, a large number of jurists held that a judge who unlawfully sentences someone to death becomes personally liable for the wrongful death, if the judge knew, or in the opinion of some jurists, reasonably should have known, that either the conviction or sentence was unlawful. Abu Bakr Ahmad b. 'Amr al-Khassaf, *Kitab Adab al-Qadi*, ed. Farhat Ziyadah (Cairo: American University of Cairo Press, 1978), pp. 364-65; Abu al-Hasan 'Ali al-Mawardi, *Adab al-Qadi*, ed. Muhyi Hilal al-Sarhan (Baghdad: Matba'at al-Irshad, 1971), 1:233; Abu al-Qasim 'Ali al-Rahbi al-Simnani, *Rawdat al-Qudah wa Tariq al-Najah* (Beirut: Mu'assasat al-Risalah, 1984), 1:157-58; *al-Fatawa al-Hindiyya* (Beirut: Dar Ihya' al-Turath al-'Arabi, 1986), 6:430; Fakhr al-Din 'Uthman b. 'Ali al-Zayla'i, *Tabyin al-Haqa'iq Sharh Kanz al-Daqa'iq* (Medina: Dar al-Kitab al-Islamiyya, n.d.), 3:240.

9. It is important to note that in classical Islamic law, Muslim jurists disagreed on whether a person may be sentenced to death for violating the Rights of People *(huquq al-'ibad* or *haqq 'adami)*, and not just for violating the Rights of God. Some jurists held that even if a violation implicates the Rights of People, once a charge is made and a court of law takes jurisdiction of the case, the Rights of God become implicated. There is a further layer of complexity that results from the fact that the classical jurists elaborated upon a category of acts and offenses that they described as implicating Mixed Rights (both the Rights of People and God) — *huquq mukhtalita* or *huquq mushtaraka.* See El-Awa, *Punishment in Islamic Law,* pp. 1-2, 21-22, 27. This is not the place to engage this fairly complex field of Islamic jurisprudence. Although grossly understudied and poorly understood, the classical Islamic discourses on the Rights of God, Rights of People,

can ever be secure and confident as to the legitimacy and justness of its decision to act on God's behalf and terminate life. Significantly, Muslim jurists often were willing to assume that the state, in fact, can be entrusted to discharge its obligations under the divine mandate, and thus, the state can and should be entrusted to terminate life upon the occurrence of certain offenses.

In this chapter, I present an Islamic critique of the idea of the killing state. I will argue that, from an Islamic perspective, entrustment of the state to be God's faithful executioner is, to say the least, problematic. Entrusting the state to play this hazardous and often untenable role of carrying out the divine mandate, if one does in fact exist, raises a set of theological and ethical problems that are not adequately addressed by simple reliance on procedural guarantees or by augmenting the integrity of the process that results in the decision to terminate life.[10] At this point, I should make two cautionary remarks that are material to the balance of this exposition. First, I should confess that personally, I am not morally opposed to the death penalty under all conditions and circumstances. Since my sense of morality is strongly informed by what I believe to be Islamic ethics and mores, I am unable to take a principled and unwavering stand against the death penalty in all circumstances and under any possible conditions.[11] Islamically, however, as explained below, I find the death penalty to be an inferior and, under the best of circumstances, a suspect moral choice. More importantly, theologically, the

and Mixed Rights is probably one of the most impressive intellectual products of humankind. For an analysis of the implications of this discourse in the contemporary age, see Khaled Abou El Fadl, "The Human Rights Commitment in Modern Islam," in Joseph Runzo et al., eds., *Human Rights and Responsibilities in World Religions* (Oxford: Oneworld Press, 2003). For the purposes of this essay, my point simply is that life is created by God and is terminated either directly by God or by the use of a medium acting on God's behalf, and that the killing state functions as such a medium. Jurists who argued that a human being may be executed for violating the Rights of Human Beings did not intend to remove the issue of life and death from God's jurisdiction and province. Rather, they presumed that certain violations against human beings trigger a longstanding and immediate divine authorization to respond to such violations by terminating the life of the offenders. Therefore, the issue becomes whether these jurists were correct in presuming the existence of such a divine mandate for terminating human life upon the occurrence of certain violations. The issue is not whether the termination of human life remained, in the view of these jurists, within the jurisdiction and province of the divine.

10. For an effective critique of the death penalty in Islamic law, see Robert Postawko, "Towards an Islamic Critique of Capital Punishment," *UCLA Journal of Islamic and Near Eastern Law* 1:2 (Spring/Summer 2002): 269-320.

11. There is a strong worldwide movement today, however, that considers the death penalty to be a violation of basic human rights. On the topic, see Roger G. Hood, *The Death Penalty: A Worldwide Perspective* (Oxford: Oxford University Press, 2003); William A. Schabas, *The Abolition of the Death Penalty in International Law* (Cambridge: Cambridge University Press, 1997).

very notion of the killing state is highly problematic. At what point the state can claim the ability to discharge the divine mandate without the possibility of error, lest it wrongfully destroy what God magnanimously has created, is something that I dare not presume to guess. What does seem to me to be Islamically necessary and compelling is extreme caution and skepticism about the moral probity and indeed worthiness of a state that is willing to share the seat of judgment with God, and kill. This is all the more so when we consider the moral standing and worthiness of certain Muslim and non-Muslim states, such as Saudi Arabia, Pakistan, and the United States — countries that deal with the issue of the death penalty with what appears to be a certain level of casualness and haphazardness.[12]

Historically speaking, my pronounced skepticism about the justness of the death penalty and my strong distrust of the moral integrity of the killing state are not idiosyncratic concerns. As discussed below, Muslim jurists, and perhaps even God, shared many of the same concerns. Muslim jurists questioned the morality of the death penalty, and also questioned whether the state should be allowed to execute its own citizens. The way Muslim jurists responded to these challenges was to seek refuge in the technicalities of the law. In other words, the juristic response was legalistic and profoundly technical. Working with the micro-details and technicalities of the law, Muslim jurists challenged the discretion of the state and made it difficult for the state to

---

12. On the horrendous way that the death penalty is meted out and executed in some Muslim countries, see Postawko, "Towards an Islamic Critique," pp. 269-70, 308-19. The material on the death penalty in the United States is too numerous to be fairly cited, but a large number of researchers have documented the widespread racial disparity in the imposition of the death sentence in the USA, and also the shocking inconsistencies in its application, not just from one state to another, but also within the federal government and within any particular state that continues to apply the penalty. Although the material defies citation, the most informative and impactful works I have read on the subject are the following: Stuart Banner, *Capital Punishment: An American History* (Cambridge: Harvard University Press, 2002); Michael Foley, *Arbitrary and Capricious: The Supreme Court, the Constitution, and the Death Penalty* (New York: Praeger Publishers, 2003); Michael A. Mello and David Von Drehle, *Dead Wrong: A Death Row Lawyer Speaks Out against Capital Punishment*, rev. ed. (Wisconsin: University of Wisconsin Press, 1998); Greg Mitchell and Robert Jay Lifton, *Who Owns Death? Capital Punishment, the American Conscience, and the End of Death Penalty* (New York: William Morrow Press, 2000); Austin Sarat, *When the State Kills: Capital Punishment and the American Condition* (Princeton: Princeton University Press, 2001); Franklin E. Zimring, *The Contradictions of American Capital Punishment* (Oxford: Oxford University Press, 2003). It is troubling that in the United States the death penalty has had to do less with the crime committed and more with the political and economic conditions prevailing within the country; see Eliza Steelwater, *The Hangman's Knot: Lynching, Legal Execution, and America's Struggle with the Death Penalty* (Boulder, Colo.: Westview Press, 2003).

carry out the death penalty, and also made it difficult for the state to claim that it had complied with all the procedural and evidentiary requirements in its application of this ultimate punishment.

The second cautionary remark has to do with the employment of the word "Islamic." A friend once commented that he has seen Muslims walk down the road, love, live, and die, but he has never seen Islam walk down the road or engage in any activity.[13] His point is that as a socio-anthropological fact, it is Muslims who believe and act, while Islam is defined in accordance with what Muslims claim it to be. To the extent that his comment means that Islam is necessarily ephemeral and evanescent — unconditionally bonded to what human beings say and do — I disagree. Islam is the product of the constant and evolving dynamic between the divine and the temporal — between the scripted text, the unscripted text of creation, and the reader of these texts. So, there is no question that Islam evolves, and refashions and rearticulates itself. But it evolves within the parameters set for the engagement by the primordial and transcendent, as expressed in the scripted and unscripted texts of creation and God. This point is important because if Muslim socio-anthropological and political practice was dispositive in defining what Islam is and what it represents, this essay would have to be simply descriptive and not aspirational. I would have to limit myself to describing what Muslims have said and done about the death penalty to date, and my exposition would be concluded at that. But in fact, I am less interested in Muslim practice to date, and far more concerned with explicating aspirational paradigms that, I believe, would constitute a greater fulfillment of the primordial and transcendent ideals of Islam. Put differently, I am advocating a vision, based on what I understand to be Islamic ethics, which would constitute what I believe to be a truer and more authentic fulfillment of Islamic moral ideals. The moral worth of this vision does not entirely depend on whether it is accepted or supported by other Muslims. As a believer, I cling to the hope of achieving God's pleasure with the vision articulated, and also the anticipation of God's judgment as to whether this vision, in fact, constitutes a more effective and persuasive realization of Islam.

To the extent that there will be an occasion to comment on the historical practices of Muslims, it is important to keep in mind certain facts about the historical practice of Muslim jurisprudence and about the nature of Islamic law in general. It is important to note that, contrary to the claims of Western orientalists, when one speaks of the Islamic law, one does not speak

13. Ebrahim Moosa, a professor at Duke University, made this comment in a lecture given in Washington, D.C.

of an abstract theoretical tradition. Rather, the paradigms of Islamic law and determinations of Islamic law have been enforced to various degrees of effectiveness throughout a long historical period. Consequently, the Islamic legal tradition is complex and diverse, and it often defies all simplistic generalizations and essentialisms. In addition, the Islamic legal practice, especially on the issue of the death penalty, often wavered between obstructionism and accommodation, as Muslim jurists balanced between the perceived need for practicality and functionality on the one hand, and the call of idealism on the other.[14] This reality counsels against assuming that Islamic law is unified, cohesive, and systematic on all material points, for Muslim legal practice exhibits a remarkable, and challenging, range of diversity and richness.

The Sanctity of Human Life

I begin this exposition with the Qur'anic narrative on the story of the sons of Adam — Cain and Abel. Overcome by blinding jealousy, Cain resolved to kill his brother Abel, and according to the Qur'anic narrative, Cain did not conceal his murderous intentions. Cain announced to Abel his intentions by threatening to kill him — a threat that Cain carried out by murdering Abel. In Islam, as in other religious traditions, Cain represents the imbalanced man who has arrogantly strayed away from God's guidance, while Abel represents someone who is truer to God, as well as someone who better reflects worthy human ethics and morality. Abel's conduct, in the Qur'anic narrative, is presented as exemplary and inspirational. This is why Abel's response, upon receiving Cain's deadly threat, is important: "If you [Cain] extend your hands against me to kill me, I shall never extend my hands against you to kill you for I fear God, the Lord of all the worlds" (Qur'an 5:28).[15] There are two points that are noteworthy here: first, Abel refuses to engage in anticipatory or preemptive termination of life in order to preserve his own; and second, Abel seems to reject altogether the idea of preserving his own life at the cost of another's. Arguably, Abel would not have been blameworthy if he responded to

14. On the balance between functionality and idealistic morality, see Khaled Abou El Fadl, "Between Functionalism and Morality: The Juristic Debates on the Conduct of War," in Jonathan E. Brockopp, ed., *Islamic Ethics of Life: Abortion, War, and Euthanasia* (Columbia: University of South Carolina Press, 2003), pp. 103-28.

15. (All translations of the Qur'an in this article are my own from the original Arabic.) In the context of this narrative, the symbolism regarding the contamination of the soil with blood and the purification of the soil, which exists in the Jewish tradition, does not exist in the Islamic tradition.

a clear and immediate danger to his life by killing Cain. However, regardless of whether Abel's killing of Cain in self-defense would have been excusable, Abel chose the morally superior option of not risking the termination of another's life and thus, in effect, speculating upon God's mandate. Abel apparently did not wish to partake in the defilement of existence through murder or to be a participant in the act of what the Qur'an calls "corrupting the earth" *(ifsad fi al-'ard).* The very act of spilling blood, even if for justifiable reasons, destroys the life created by God and, in fact, disassembles and subverts the very logic of creation.

Here, it is important to distinguish between corruption on the earth as an ethical concept and as a technical legal doctrine. In the Qur'anic discourse, the expression "corrupting the earth" is used to identify behavior that is destructive of life, creation, and the order of existence. Therefore, in the Qur'anic discourse, the meaningless destruction of livestock, nature, and human life; the dismantling of places of worship, the undoing of social peace, and the undermining of justice; the spreading of rancor, hatred, fear, and anxiety; oppression as well as war in general — all are categorically designated as acts that cause corruption in the earth *(al-fasad fi al-ard).*[16] In Islamic legal doctrine, corrupting the earth refers specifically to acts of banditry, brigandage, piracy, highway robbery, and the modern crime of terrorism.[17] The Qur'anic notion of corruption on the earth is much broader than the Islamic jurisprudential categorization. In the Qur'an, the corruption of the earth is the by-product of committing acts that, at a minimum, can be described as not beautiful or ugly. It is as if corruption of the earth is the outcome of human behavior that violates the primordial order and logic of existence that has been set in motion by acts of divine grace and magnanimity. This primordial order or logic is signified in the Qur'an by the word *al-mizan* (the primordial balance), and the Qur'anic vision enjoins human beings to guard against upsetting or undermining the very balance that sustains God's miraculous creation — life in all its physical and non-physical forms.[18] In essence, corruption of the earth is an act that generates or perpetuates an imbalance in the logic of creation — a logic that is necessary to signify and express divine beauty — by promoting conditions, such as war, injustice, oppression, and terror, that disrupt the flourishing of the full expression of life (including, for instance, the life of the intellect, the heart, and the soul).

16. For instance, see Qur'an 2:27, 60, 205, 251; 3:25; 5:33, 64; 8:73; 11:85; 28:77, 83; 89:12.

17. For a study on the classical legal concept of corruption in the earth and its implications for the modern world, see Khaled Abou El Fadl, *Rebellion and Violence in Islamic Law* (Cambridge: Cambridge University Press, 2001), esp. pp. 234-94.

18. On the *mizan* in the Qur'an, see 6:152; 42:17; 55:7-9; 57:25.

Seen in this fashion, Abel's decision not to defend himself by rushing to preempt his brother by killing him first makes much more sense. By killing, Abel would be setting a precedent, and would be taking the risk of contributing to an imbalance that could possibly strongly constrain the flourishing of — or even negate and void — divinity. If Abel had killed Cain, Abel would have risked disrupting the very supernal balance that sustains divinity in human existence. Simply put, for the sake of preserving his own life, Abel would be risking contributing to a corruption on the earth that could disrupt or fracture so much else in existence. The equation is not simply that in which one life is given in return for another, and also it is not one in which the preservation of one life could justify extinguishing another. So, for instance, Muslim scholars reflecting upon the story of Abel and Cain concluded that even in the presence of overwhelming coercion or duress, a person should not save his or her own life by sacrificing another. It is one thing, the jurists reasoned, to forgive a person who in the heat of the moment defended himself by murdering an aggressor; but it is quite another to deliberately play God and choose who should live or die. As a further example, take the case of a crowded boat in which the only means for the majority to survive is to throw several passengers overboard to drown; most Muslim jurists held that it would not be permissible to do so. Rather, the passengers, as a collective whole, should protect each other, and take their chances with nature. Similarly, if someone puts a gun to a man's head and commands him either to kill a third person or die, the man under compulsion should not do so, even if the cost is losing his life. Significantly, the rule remains the same even in the case of ten people who are threatened with death if they do not all participate in the murder of one person. Even if by murdering one person ten other people could save themselves, most jurists would have still considered the murder unjustified. In contrast to these examples, however, a whole multitude of illegal acts that fall short of murder (such as eating pork, drinking alcohol, stealing, or even cursing God and the Prophet) can be excused if performed under coercion. In summary, Muslim jurists were extremely reluctant to accept a claim of coercion or compulsion in cases of murder, and also rape. Having said all of that, it should also be noted that in the case of murder due to compulsion, Muslim jurists refused to implement a capital penalty to the crime because the existence of duress acts as an element of doubt *(shubha)* that must be weighed in favor of the defendant.[19]

It bears emphasis here that the moral lesson of the story of Cain and

19. See, on the law of coercion and duress in Islamic law, Khaled Abou El Fadl, "The Common and Islamic Law of Duress" *Arab Law Quarterly* 6, no. 2 (1991): 121-59.

Abel is that human life is too noble and supernal to be the subject of mathematical equations. When people kill, they do not just exterminate a breathing being, but they construct certain meanings and deconstruct others. They affirm values and negate others. In giving life, human beings imitate and promote the model set by the divine in perpetuating and reproducing the act of creation. In eliminating life, exactly the opposite takes place — divine creation is challenged and denied. The mathematical logic that supposes one life is equal to another — that two lives are equivalent — is a degradation of divinity. As argued below, it might be acceptable at an elemental and primitive stage of moral development, but it does not represent the ethical vision to which human beings should aspire.

After narrating the story of Cain and Abel, the Qur'an addresses, among other things, the divine commandments regarding murder, especially in the pre-Islamic era. I believe that the balance of the Qur'anic narrative on the issues related to the story of Cain and Abel offers strong support for the interpretation I proffered above. The Qur'an comments that Cain's sin exceeded by far that which is incurred for killing a single human being: Cain virtually killed all of humanity. The Qur'an goes on to state the following: "For that, We (God) ordained for the Children of Israel that he who kills a human soul, unless it be for killing a soul or for spreading corruption on the earth, it would be as if he slew all of humanity, and he who saves a soul, it would be as if he saved all of humanity. Indeed, Our messengers came to them with clear messages and yet many of them, even after that, continue to exceed the limits on the earth" (5:32). From this verse, the Qur'an proceeds to articulate the most unequivocal condemnation against those who wage war against God and God's Prophet and commit corruption on the earth and goes on to set out very strong earthly penalties for this behavior.[20] The Qur'an, however, leaves the door open, so to speak, for the possibility of repentance and forgiveness by emphasizing that those who repent and reform their conduct, before they are apprehended, ought to be forgiven.[21]

---

20. Qur'an 5:33. This became the pivotal Qur'anic verse for the development of the law of *hiraba* (the crime of banditry, brigandage, highway robbery, piracy, and terrorism). As explained in my book, *Rebellion and Violence in Islamic Law*, early state authorities sought to make the crime of *hiraba* a political crime by contending that political rebels are the true corrupters of earth, and the ones most deserving of the penalties set out in the Qur'an. Muslim jurists, however, resisted this effort; they constructed the legal doctrine under which *hiraba* became a non-political crime, primarily defined by the methods pursued, not the ends sought, by the offenders guilty of the crime.

21. Muslim jurists agreed that it is possible for a criminal guilty of the crime of waging war to repent and be forgiven by God. However, they disagreed on the earthly consequences of

The narrative of Abel and Cain, although setting out and identifying the higher moral plane, ought not obfuscate the fact that the Qur'an clearly accepts that killing might be warranted under a certain set of circumstances. But it is also clear that the Qur'an strictly prohibits any killing except for a just cause, and indeed presumes all killing to be unjustly done unless proven otherwise.[22] In addition, the Qur'an flatly states, "It is not for a believer to kill another believer except that it be by mistake (unintentional and accidental). . . ." The Qur'an also decisively threatens whoever commits murder with "God's wrath and everlasting Hellfire" (4:93). The Qur'anic expression for a just cause that can possibly render a homicide justifiable is the word *haqq*. *Haqq* literally means something that is correct or proper, or one's due or right. Pursuant to the Qur'an, all forms of killing are not excusable unless by mistake or according to a *haqq*. As explained above, the *haqq* involved belongs to God, and any dealing with human life that exceeds the limits set by the possessor of right (God), is susceptible to suffering God's anger and wrath. Equally important, since God is the possessor of the *haqq*, the disposition as to what happens if a human life is terminated also belongs to God.

In the case of accidental death, the Qur'an sets out fairly clear rules. As a form of penance or atonement for the unintentional wasting of human life, Muslims are ordered to free a slave, if they own any,[23] and pay the relatives of the deceased a sum of money in compensation for the wrongful death. If offenders do not have a slave to free then they should fast from sunrise to sundown every day for two months.[24] The symbolism here is striking — by freeing a slave, it is as if the offender has given a life back, but he or she must still pay compensation to the relative of the deceased. Interestingly, in this particular passage, the Qur'an does not say anything about the desirability of forgiveness — the desirability of the relatives of the deceased forgiving the sum of money owed to them by the offender. Additionally, as to the consequences of intentional murder, the Qur'an asserts only that intentional homicide is a

---

repentance. Some jurists argued that repentance does not vitiate the need for earthly punishment, while others argued that as long as the criminal repents and reforms before he or she is apprehended, it is possible for the legal system to pardon his or her crimes, and not impose a penalty.

22. The Qur'an repeatedly reminds human beings of the divine command not to kill except for a just cause. For instance, see Qur'an 6:151; 17:33; 25:68.

23. Often the Qur'an commanded Muslims to free slaves as a form of penitence for a variety of intentional and unintentional offenses.

24. Qur'an 4:92. The sum in compensation is known as *diyya*. The amount of the *diyya* and how and when it should be paid has developed into a fairly complex field of law. If the offender does not have a slave to free and is unable to fast two months then he or she is called upon to feed a certain number of the poor and destitute for a specific duration of time.

crime that warrants God's wrath, but does not elaborate upon how a murderer should be treated. In other contexts, the Qur'an does elaborate upon the principles that ought to guide the treatment of murder, but its treatment, as will be seen, is nuanced and not decisive. In addressing the law given to the Israelites, the Qur'an asserts that God had sent the Torah to Moses, containing guidance and light, and commanded the Israelites to judge by it. The Qur'an then comments that those who do not judge according to what God has revealed are the true unbelievers. The Qur'an goes on to state that God had ordained upon the Israelites the rule of the talion that: "A life for a life, eye for an eye, nose for a nose, tooth for a tooth and as to wounds, their (just) equal. But if anyone forgives retaliation by way of charity, it will be atonement for him (or her). And whosoever does not judge by that which God has revealed, such are the true wrongdoers" (5:44-45).

There are several noteworthy, and controversial, issues regarding the intended meaning and import of this revelation. First, it should be noted that although the Qur'an sets out the principle of strict equality as the basis of justice, it actually favors charity and forgiveness. Those who are concerned about their life in the hereafter would be tempted by the opportunity to perform acts of atonement, instead of seeking vengeance on this earth. Second, there are two ways to look at the effect of this Qur'anic commandment. The Qur'an could be seen as imposing a strict, and possibly harsh, law of equality of an eye for an eye — which, as the common saying goes, could make everyone blind. Alternatively, if taken in context, the Qur'an could be seen as actually imposing a rule of limitation, as a base for minimal justice, but not supernal or superior justice. Put differently, the Qur'an rejects the pre-Islamic customary practices of vengeance in which retribution depended on status and class of the victim and aggressor. In that pre-Islamic paradigm, ten lives from a weak or undistinguished tribe could equal one life from a superior tribe. This reading is supported by many sources in the Islamic tradition that explain that Islam abrogated the tribal practices of class-based justice and replaced it with a principle mandating equality between all the victims of crimes, and also between the victims and offenders.[25]

---

25. 'Abd al-Qadir 'Udah, al-Tashri' al-Jina'i al-Islami (Beirut: Mu'assasat al-Risala, 2000), vol. 1, pp. 25-29. Reportedly, inferior tribes that were disadvantaged by the pre-Islamic law practices that violated the law of talion, upon the coming of the revelation, felt empowered by Islam, and refused to pay the exorbitant sums in blood money that were demanded of them by the superior tribes. Jalal al-Din al-Suyuti, Lubab al-Nuqul fi Asbab al-Nuzul (Beirut: Dar Ihya' al-'Ulum, 1980), 91-92. Unfortunately, the abrogation of class-based justice by Islam did not prevent some jurists, especially from the Hanafi and Hanbali schools of legal thought, from basing their notion of justice on the gender status or religious status of the victim and offender. Ac-

The third point worthy of note, and perhaps the most important, concerns the continuing applicability of the law of an eye for an eye and its validity for Muslims. According to the Qur'an, at one point in time, God decreed the law of an eye for an eye for the Israelites, and the question is: Is this law applicable to Muslims? The larger question is whether this law has universal validity. Reportedly, the occasion in which the "eye for an eye" verse was revealed was in the context of rendering a judgment according to Jewish law in a criminal case.[26] According to these historical reports, the Qur'anic verses on the issue were revealed when the Prophet was called upon to arbitrate, according to the rules of Jewish law, a conflict involving Jews living in Medina.[27] Under the interpretation that I am advancing here, the law of talion was a part of an evolutionary process towards a greater fulfillment of divinity and justice. Furthermore, there is an aspirational element to the law — under certain conditions talion might be a necessary step in the development of moral law. It was a step towards weaning human beings away from strongly ingrained practices of classicism and inequality, but the moral hope is to take further steps towards forgiveness, or towards the supernal moral behavior exhibited by Abel towards Cain. This evolutionary interpretive approach is further solidified by another Qur'anic revelation addressing the issue of *qisas* (punishment, or the law of exaction), in general. The Qur'an states:

> Oh you who believe! The law of *qisas* has been prescribed for you in cases of murder: the free for the free, the slave for the slave, and the woman for a woman. But if there be forgiveness by a brother for his brother then adhere to fairness, and remit any rights with handsome gratitude. This is an alleviation and mercy to you from your Lord. Whoever transgresses after

---

cording to these jurists, the life or injury of a woman or non-Muslim is worth less than the life or injury to a male Muslim. Many jurists, however, rejected this position and argued that the principle of an "eye for an eye" mandated strict equality in matters related to criminal law between all human beings, whether male or female and whether Muslim or non-Muslim. For the various positions in Islamic law, in general, see El-Awa, *Punishment in Islamic Law*, pp. 69-83. For a more detailed treatment of the subject, see Ahmad Fathi Bahnassi, *al-Qisas fi al-Fiqh al-Islami* (Cairo: Dar al-Shuruq, 1982).

26. Abu al-Hasan al-Wahidi al-Naysaburi, *Asbab Nuzul al-Qur'an* (Beirut: Dar Ma'rifa, n.d.), pp. 146-47; al-Suyuti, *Lubab al-Nuqul*, p. 92.

27. Nevertheless, a large number of Muslim jurists held that the law of talion, which was originally decreed upon the Israelites, continued to be valid law for Muslims. They reasoned that the laws of the Israelites continue to be valid for Muslims unless expressly and specifically abrogated by a later revelation. Abu Walid Muhammad Ibn Rushd, *Bidayat al-Mujtahid wa Nihayat al-Muqtasid* (Beirut: Dar al-Fikr, n.d.), vol. 2, p. 300; Ahmad Fathi al-Bahnassi, *al-'Uquba fi al-Fiqh al-Islami* (Cairo: Dar al-Shuruq, 1980), pp. 67-78.

this, he will have a grave penalty (from God). Oh people of reason (and understanding), in *qisas* you will find (the saving of) life, so that you may (learn to) restrain yourselves. (2:178-79)

Although some jurists disagreed, the majority read this revelation to mean human beings are equal.[28] The purpose of this verse is not to say that a man, for instance, cannot be punished for killing a woman. Rather, the verse is intended to affirm the end of status-based justice; therefore, most jurists interpreted the word *qisas* in this context to mean the law of equality. Hence, the Qur'an is demanding that, at a minimum, lives be saved by adhering to the strict limits of the law of talion. Importantly, however, the Qur'an encourages finding alternatives to retaliatory killings by opening the door to financial settlements, demanding restraint and prohibiting transgressions, and favoring forgiveness, kindness, and gratitude.[29]

Two significant points regarding the Qur'anic rhetorical strategy should be noted here. First, although the Qur'an is dealing with the painful subject of murder, it reminds its readers that human beings, even the murderer and the kin of the murdered, are still brothers (and sisters). This affirmation of the bonds of brotherhood and sisterhood among human beings is important to remember, especially in the aftermath of a murder, at a time when the temptation to indulge in rancor and hatred is most pronounced. Second, the Qur'an describes as an alleviation and mercy the acceptance of settlements and the promotion of alternatives that limit bloodshed and further loss of life (an alternative referred to in Islamic law by the phrase *haqn al-damm* — restricting the flow of blood). As the Qur'an itself seems to indicate, the ability to put an end to bloodshed and minimize the destruction of life is indicated as a mercy or as a natural good for humanity. The Qur'an does not explicitly state that the law of talion — which as explained restricted the Israelites to an eye for an eye, instead of many eyes for one important eye — is abrogated or voided. Rather, the Qur'an seems to have a moral trajectory, which it attempts to achieve not simply by ordinance and proclamation, but by working with

28. Cf. Qur'an 5:44-45.
29. Some scholars have wrongly assumed that the effect of paying or accepting blood money in Islamic law is to place a price or a monetary value upon human life. This is incorrect. The pre-Islamic practice of paying blood money was affirmed only as a means to lessen the incentive for inflicting reciprocal injury and the taking of human life. If the survivors of the deceased are inclined to seek vengeance, they are encouraged to accept blood money instead of destroying another human life. On whether the payment of *diyya* or blood money in Islamic criminal law is punitive or compensatory in nature, see 'Awad Ahmad Idris, *al-Diyya Bayn al-'Uquba wa al-Ta'wid fi al-Fiqh al-Islami al-Maqaran* (Beirut: Dar Maktabat al-Hilal, 1986), pp. 548-600.

human beings, within their context-bonded limitations, in order to inspire them to reach greater levels of ethical and moral fulfillment. It is as if God, knowing the human weakness for vengeance and for indulging in behavior that leads to the corruption of the earth, proceeds to engage human beings in an evolutionary and incremental moral education; this process allows human beings to reach higher levels of moral awareness, as they learn to restrain their indulgences and redirect their lust for vengeance.[30] If one reflects on the moral trajectory of the Qur'an, one better understands that the greater the desire for destruction and vengeance, instead of reform and repentance, the greater the risk of causing corruption on the earth, and the further away that human beings drift from divinity. On the other hand, the more human beings are able to generate alternatives to the reciprocal destruction of life, the safer they are from falling into the abyss of corrupting the earth, and in the process, negating divinity.[31]

Should the State Kill?

One of the core concepts of the Qur'an is the sanctity of human life. The Qur'anic expression is the word *haram,* which means to make protected or to render untouchable. The Qur'an persistently states that God has sanctified human life *(harrama Allah)* by proclaiming it inviolable and immune.[32] But even more, beyond sanctifying human life, the Qur'an declares that God has

30. The Qur'an repeatedly emphasizes that God does not burden human beings with more than they are able to bear or handle at a particular time. In the Qur'an, it is clear that God's revelation is evolutionary, rendered in proportion to what human beings are able to handle and deal with at different stages of their moral development. For instance, see Qur'an 2:233; 286; 6:152; 7:42; 23:63. The idea of moral growth and development would mean that human beings can incrementally learn to deal with greater moral responsibilities and achieve higher levels of ethical awareness, and thus, coming closer to reflecting the face of divinity on this earth. In this regard, the incremental and evolutionary extinction of slavery in Islam is instructive. Similar to its discourse on the death penalty, the Qur'an clearly preferred the ending of slavery and opened many venues for Muslims to free their slaves, designating such behavior as a higher moral act and as achieving a state of greater ethical awareness. Eventually, slavery was ended in all Muslim lands, as Muslims strove to fulfill the Qur'anic moral ideal. The death penalty could be the subject of a similar evolutionary process. On the evolution of laws in Islam, see Mahmassani, *The Philosophy of Jurisprudence in Islam,* pp. 105-19.

31. The Qur'an emphasizes that it is possible for human beings to cause corruption on the earth while believing that they are doing good (2:11). In many ways, seeking alternatives to the shedding of more blood is the safest precaution against unwittingly spreading corruption in the earth.

32. For instance, see Qur'an 6:151; 17:33; 25:68.

declared that human life is to be honored and revered.[33] In one of the powerful symbolic narratives in the Qur'an, after the moment of creation, God entrusts human beings with the blessing and burden of free will, rationality, and accountability, and as a way of honoring human beings, God commands the angels to prostrate themselves before Adam. God also informs the angels that human beings are going to be entrusted with the earth, as God's deputies and viceroys. The angels, however, who do not have rational faculties or free will, somewhat prophetically, could not help but wonder why God chose to give the earth to what the angels described as beings who will spread corruption and shed blood. The angels noted that while human beings are capable of spreading corruption, they (the angels) unfailingly supplicate and praise God without the possibility of ever going astray. The divine response was to emphasize that God knows what the angels do not know, and to have Adam prove the merit of human beings by displaying his capacity for learning, comprehension, and thought.[34] Notably, the shedding of blood, something in which Cain ultimately indulges, is equated with the corruption, and perhaps defilement, of the earth. The Qur'an depicts God as often intervening to save human beings from the follies of their actions and to squelch the fires of war and destruction that human beings inflict upon themselves. In fact, the Qur'an asserts that, if not for the divine interventions, human beings would have caused greater corruptions on the earth. And, to paraphrase the Qur'an, but for God's compassionate mediations, human beings would have destroyed many more monasteries, churches, synagogues, and mosques — places where the name of God is frequently mentioned.[35] Ultimately, if human beings persist in forgetting God and God's divine mandate, God will forget them, and will allow them to suffer the full consequences of their actions.[36] Within this compelling paradigm, one cannot sufficiently emphasize the extent to which, according to the Qur'an, injustice and oppression play a central role in spreading corruption in the earth. Despots and oppressors are the quintessential corrupters of the earth because in their arrogance and haughtiness, they are blinded to their own transgressions and the resulting imbalance that they produce in the world.[37] However, contrary to the pessimistic outlook of the angels, the divine outlook seems to be marked by its concern for potentialities, not inevitabilities. It is as if the potentiality of cor-

33. Qur'an 17:70.
34. Qur'an 2:30-32.
35. Qur'an 22:40. Also, see 2:251; 23:71.
36. Qur'an 9:67; 30:41; 59:19.
37. Often, the Qur'an equates despotism and oppression with corruption of the earth. For instance, see Qur'an 11:85; 26:183; 27:34, 48; 28:4, 83; 89:12.

ruption on the earth stands as an ever-present specter that must be vigilantly guarded against. This specter is like the persistent danger of despotism and oppression, or what has been described as the iron law of oligarchy, which constantly threatens any society or political entity with the tendency to drift towards authoritarianism.[38] This is crucially important because of the nature of the death penalty and also the potentialities that are unleashed by this punishment. The nature of the death penalty also obliges us to distinguish between the types of political society — despotic or not — in which it might be used.

The Death Penalty in the Despotic State

The finality of the death penalty presents a serious burden for the potential of achieving justice in any particular case. Since capital punishment deals with death, the danger of it contributing to corruption on the earth is rather markedly high. By succumbing to the death penalty, the state is demonstrating its moral inadequacy because it is presumed that the state has not been able to produce alternatives to the destruction of life. In effect, the state is succumbing to the primitive ethical impulse of seeking vengeance instead of pursuing a course that comes closer to reconciliation, reform, and repentance. More dangerously, the state could be using the death penalty to conceal or cover up its profound moral failures. Put differently, the state could have failed to bring about the kind of socio-economic and political conditions that are more conducive to achieving a higher state of moral awareness. Instead of confronting and dealing with these failures, the state comfortably relegates itself to killing people, rather than improving their conditions for moral advancement. If the death penalty is, in fact, pursued as a distraction and as a method of escaping its own socio-economic and political failures, then this means that the state is also moving closer to becoming an oppressor, i.e., a corrupter of the earth. It is of the utmost significance to note that the converse is also true. By using the death penalty, the state could be transforming itself into an oppressor; but, as well, if the state is already an oppressor, it will naturally gravitate towards using the death penalty.

Because of the absence of accountability and transparency in a despotic system, an oppressive state will find the death penalty extremely attractive at

---

38. On the iron law of oligarchy and the threat of despotism within organizational structures, see Robert Michels, *Political Parties: A Sociological Study of the Oligarchical Tendencies of Modern Democracy* (New York: Free Press, 1962).

many levels. The death penalty provides finality; forecloses the doors of accountability; eliminates actual and potential foes to government; disseminates fear in society while also encouraging a superficial and false sense of security; and resolutely underscores the overwhelming power and resolve of the government — all of which are characteristics that serve a despotic regime very well. Therefore, we find that we have a twofold dynamic: states that rely on the death penalty, in part as an avoidance mechanism, are at a very high risk of transgressing the bounds and, therefore, becoming oppressors; states that are already oppressive will tend to favor the death penalty, not just as a mechanism to avoid confronting their moral failures, but also as a mechanism to further anchor and strengthen their oppressiveness.

The nature of this dynamic cautions that dealing with the death penalty is literally like playing with fire. It is reasonable to assert that, even under the best of circumstances, a despotic state is simply not apt to deal with the death penalty. As explained, an authoritarian or despotic state already suffers from the infamy of being a corrupter on the earth. Lacking even the mechanisms for accountability and transparency that are necessary for the dialectical development of ethical responsibility, it is near certain that a dictatorship will transgress the bounds of *haqq* when applying the death penalty. This will only worsen and further exacerbate the status of such a state as a corrupter on the earth. In addition, it should be remembered that the state, when it implements the death penalty, does so pursuant to a perceived mandate (effectively, a license) by God, and that it must stay within the strict bounds of the mandate. A despotic state commits the grave sin of idolatry when an individual, or a group of individuals, within the state become the self-referential arbitrators of the law. Although despots may claim to rule according to God's law, they hold themselves above human judgment, and in doing so they share an attribute that, in Islamic theology, is reserved only to God. Furthermore, in exclusively occupying the seat of judgment over other human beings, and ruling according to their personal whim, despots constantly run the risk of replacing God altogether, as the ultimate authority and frame of reference.[39] I think it is fair to say that it truly pushes the bounds of absurdity to trust a matter as serious as the death penalty to authoritarians, despots, and tyrants. Human beings, and especially Muslims, should demand that, as a matter of principle, the death penalty should not be a tool available to despots and ty-

---

39. On this issue, see Khaled Abou El Fadl, "Islam and Democracy," in Joshua Cohen, ed., *Islam and Democracy* (Princeton: Princeton University Press, 2003). On authoritarianism in Islam, see Khaled Abou El Fadl, *And God Knows the Soldiers: The Authoritative and Authoritarian in Islamic Discourses* (Lanham, Md.: University Press of America, 2001).

rants. Put in the technical language of Islamic law, despotism and authoritarianism should act as an element of doubt *(shubha)* in a capital offense that automatically eliminates the death penalty as an option in criminal matters.

The Death Penalty in the Non-Despotic State

The next logical question is whether the death penalty should exist in a non-despotic state or a democracy. Assuming that a Muslim democracy exists, would it be justified in applying the death penalty? Admittedly, from an Islamic perspective, the case against the death penalty is much more compelling in the case of an authoritarian or despotic system. The more a system is able to meet the criteria of accountability and transparency, the more capable it is of dealing with the moral responsibility of justice, the more capable it is of upholding the principle of *haqq*, and, finally, the more capable it is of discharging its obligations towards God. Furthermore, the more just the system of governance and law, the less there is a *shubha*, and the less risks there are of transgressing the bounds. Nevertheless, other than the factors already discussed, there are further reasons to avoid the death penalty in every possible way even in a non-despotic system. I will call this additional justification the mercy factor.

As noted above, there is a moral dialectic to human existence and its relationship to the divine. While the Qur'an indicates that revelation to the Israelites established the first principles of justice, justice remains a potentiality that can be attained to a greater degree but that can never be fully realized on this earth. It is a tenet of Islamic theology that perfect justice is realizable only in the hereafter, and that the capability to achieve perfect justice belongs to the divine alone. In the unfolding saga of Abrahamic revelations, the Qur'an revealed another factor that constitutes a further element in the formulation of a comprehensive view of justice. This factor is that of compassion and mercy — a factor that, considering the modern Muslim reality, seems like a cruel irony.[40]

I have already alluded to the factor of mercy in the context of discussing God's alleviation of the strict law of talion. This factor, however, is made much more explicit and pronounced when the Qur'an addresses the fundamental purposes of the Islamic revelation. The Qur'an consistently empha-

---

40. On this subject, see Khaled Abou El Fadl, "The Culture of Ugliness in Modern Islam and Re-engaging Morality," *UCLA Journal of Islamic and Near Eastern Law* 2:1 (Fall/Winter 2002-3): 33-97.

sizes that one of the most basic and fundamental purposes of the revelation was to bestow a mercy upon human beings, and to teach human beings to deal with one another with compassion.[41] The Qur'an asserts that the Prophet Muhammad was sent as a mercy to humanity, and it enjoins human beings to hold steadfast to patience and to disseminate mercy amongst themselves.[42] Like other Qur'anic injunctions, the command is broad, so that it offers possibilities of growth for those who are willing to take it seriously. Mercy and compassion is a state in which people can attain a condition of greater beauty — what the Qur'an calls *ihsan* (beneficence).[43] The Qur'an often equates mercy and compassion with the ability to forgive — to rise above the talion's logic of equality-based petty justice — and describes the rejection of retribution as a frame of mind that brings people closer to piety.[44] In the Qur'an, true piety *(taqwa)* is achieved when a human being avoids rancor and anger and exercises self-restraint through acts of mercy and compassion. *Ihsan* (the one who exercises it is described as a *mushin*) is a word with levels of meaning.[45] It encompasses mercy, compassion, self-restraint, and forgiveness, but it ultimately means a state of goodness and beauty.

In one of the many reports explicating some of the requisites of *ihsan*, a group of believers sought out the Prophet to complain to him about their deep sense of frustration. These individuals objected to the level of tolerance the Prophet showed his foes, which, in their view, made them feel weak and subservient. The group explained that because of the Prophet's policies of self-restraint and tolerance, they felt they had received more respect from others when they were non-Muslims, because before their conversion to Islam, people feared them. The Prophet's response reflected the general thrust of his revelation and message, stating: "But I have been charged with the obligation to forgive." The Prophet went on to advise his visitors to be patient.[46]

41. Qur'an 4:83; 16:89; 28:43; 29:51; 40:7; 45:20. The Qur'an also explains that human beings have been made diverse and different as a form of mercy upon them, and that the challenge that confronts human beings is to come to know one another and also to learn to deal with one another (11:119; 49:13).

42. Qur'an 21:107; 3:159; 90:17.

43. Qur'an 5:13.

44. Qur'an 2:227; 42:40; 64:14.

45. Classical Muslim jurists have long been concerned with the implications of the duty of *ihsan* upon the implementation and enforcement of criminal law. For example, see Muwaffaq al-Din Abu Muhammad Ibn Qudamah, *al-Mughni* (Beirut: Dar al-Kutub al-'Ilmiyya, n.d.), vol. 9, pp. 394-95.

46. Al-Suyuti, *Lubab al-Nuqul*, pp. 74-75. The Qur'an affirms this commandment by explicitly commanding the Prophet to exercise self-restraint and forgiveness (2:109; 3:159; 5:13; 7:199).

The point that I extract from this report, as well as many other similar reports, concerns the relationship of mercy and compassion to power and the ego. The death penalty is an ultimate exercise of power — someone gets to decide whether the other lives. Those who suffer a violent crime and also the next of kin of a murdered relative are bound to feel an overwhelming sense of disempowerment and indeed vulnerability. It is perhaps healing and empowering for the victim of a crime to play a role in deciding the fate of the aggressor. The victim no longer remains a passive and powerless entity that suffers what others choose to inflict upon it. Rather, the victim regains his or her initiative and plays an affirmative role in deciding what is to be done to the person who robbed him or her of all sense of power and dignity in the first place. I think this is exactly why the Qur'an consistently gives the victim of a crime a role, if not the central role, in deciding what ought to happen with the aggressor. As mentioned above, the victim has three choices in the case of an intentional crime: exaction, compensatory settlement, or forgiveness.

The Qur'an is aware that it has delegated a considerable amount of power to the victim of crime, and therefore, it cautions against the abuse of that power. The Qur'an states: "Do not slay the soul that God has made sacred, except for just cause (pursuant to a *haqq*). For those who have been murdered unjustly, We have given their heirs authority and power *(sultana)* in the matter [to demand exaction, compensation, or forgiveness], but let them not exceed the just limits in slaying, for they have been given power *(mansura)*" (17:33). What I find particularly intriguing here is the usage of the words *sultan* (power, authority, or jurisdiction) and *mansur* (someone who is empowered, aided, rendered victorious, or supported). It appears that the Qur'an is addressing the same type of human emotion manifested by the companions of the Prophet who protested his policy of self-restraint and forgiveness, but, of course, in a different context. The companions were addressing an issue of general public policy, while the Qur'an in the verse above addresses a private cause of action. As a matter of addressing private rights — individual feelings of disempowerment and vulnerability, not necessarily the desire for vengeance and revenge — the Qur'an seeks to vindicate the victim by allowing him to regain a sense of control and authority over his own life. The feeling of empowerment, however, comes from the choice — the ability to choose, regardless of the actual choice made. Importantly, however, and this is where the mercy factor ought to come in, the victim of crime is not just exercising a choice over his own life, but also the life of the other. At this point, it is important to take note of a rather obvious fact that has been largely ignored in discourses on Islamic law. According to the Qur'an, the state is left out of the decision-making process. It is as if the state is rendered powerless and ineffective, as far as the ultimate decision and disposition is concerned. It is as if the position of the state is similar to the Prophet's — the state stands ready to forgive and forget, but the will of the state is entirely hinged and contingent on the private individual's exercise of discretion and power.

From a criminal law perspective that is concerned with the public administration of justice, the prevention of crime and the upholding of law and order, the Qur'anic approach makes little or no sense. How could murder be treated as a private matter when, in fact, it affects all of society? Doesn't this Qur'anic system, in effect, provide the dreamland for any rich serial murderer who can go on killing with impunity, as he pays off the heirs of his victims? In fact, it is this aspect of the Qur'anic discourse that has provided orientalist scholars with the opportunity to generate a virtual deluge of criticisms against Islamic law, Islamic justice, and what they perceived as the undeniable failures of Islam when compared to the rational and progressive West.[47] But what many non-Muslim and even Muslim scholars have often overlooked are the powerful moral implications of the Qur'anic discourse. The Qur'an is not engaging in criminal law legislation; it is providing an exemplary and normative moral engagement. In the Qur'an, in the case of murder, as well as in most other cases, the state is not ordered to kill. It is as if God knows the risks and dangers involved in empowering the state to kill and, hence, to corrupt the earth, wittingly or unwittingly; it is as if God takes that power away from the state and deposits it where it belongs — in the conscience of the individual. To my knowledge, no commentator has ever noticed the disempowering of the state by the Qur'an, but I believe that a fair reading of the text makes this conclusion undeniable. I am not arguing that the Qur'an prohibits the state from killing in all and every circumstance. Rather, the state is simply not commanded to kill, and the decision, in the world of Qur'anic moral symbol-

47. Of course, orientalist scholars, whether intentionally or not, ignored the fact that, in the case of intentional crimes and murder, Muslim jurists developed what they called the residual right of the state. Upon the occurrence of an intentional crime, two sets of rights are created, the first private, and the second public. The private party exercises its rights first, by demanding exaction, compensation, or forgiveness, after which the residual right of the state remains. The state has one of two choices: it may forgive or it may punish. Therefore, even when the private party forgives the criminal, the state may still insist on exacting one form of punishment or another in order to protect the public. When, whether and under what circumstances the state may forgive its residual rights has been the subject of intense debates throughout the history of Islamic jurisprudence. See Ibn Rushd, *Bidayat al-Mujtahid,* vol. 2, pp. 302-3; Bahnassi, *al-Uquba fi al-Fiqh,* pp. 77-78; 'Abd al-Qadir 'Udah, *al-Tashri' al-Jina'i,* vol. 1, pp. 251-53, 256-61, 774-78.

ism, is taken out of the state's hands and given to individuals who must struggle with their conscience and responsibilities before the Almighty.[48]

In classical Muslim jurisprudence, the jurists assumed that the state should act as the enforcer of the private individual's decision. In fact, the vast majority of classical jurists strictly prohibited self-help measures, and made any attempt to retaliate without relying on the state to establish guilt and liability, and also to enforce judgment, both a criminal violation and a sin.[49] If the individual decides to retaliate by demanding exaction, the state has two choices: either the state could enforce the retaliation on behalf of the individual, or, if the state believes the retaliatory choice of the individual to be unjust, the state could refuse to enforce the penalty and require the individual to enforce it. However, if the individual, instead of the state, applies the physical punishment, he or she does so at great legal risk. If the physical punishment exceeds the rule of strict equality in injury, the enforcer (i.e. the individual) becomes legally liable for any transgression. The physical exaction of punishment had to be precisely equal in every respect, and, if it was not, the individual could easily find himself or herself in the position of the aggressor and offender, instead of the victim of crime.[50] In Islamic legal practice, if the individual could not get the cooperation of the state, this created a strong incentive to seek financial settlements instead of insisting on retaliation. But in all circumstances, the state still possessed the residual right to impose a discretionary punishment, known as *ta'zir* penalty, against the offender for public policy purposes.[51]

It is fair to say that the history of the Muslim juristic tradition represented a persistent, and often brilliant, effort to realize the moral norms of the Qur'an. As will be discussed further below, it is not correct to assume that the determinations and choices made within this impressive tradition com-

---

48. This does not imply that the state is bound to obey the private individual in his or her disposition. As noted above, the state has to be concerned with criminal law policies that do not necessarily correlate with the victim's preferences. However, at a minimum, the Qur'an seems to require that the preferences of the victims of crime be taken into serious consideration, and not be ignored as entirely irrelevant or unhelpful.

49. Ibn Qudamah, *al-Mughni*, vol. 9, pp. 393-95; Muhammad Abu Zahrah, *al-Jarima wa al-'Uquba fi al-Fiqh al-Islami* (Cairo: Dar al-Fikr al-'Arabi, n.d.), pp. 512-13.

50. Ibn Rushd, *Bidayat al-Mujtahid*, vol. 2, p. 303; Ibn Qudamah, *al-Mughni*, vol. 9, pp. 391-92.

51. Discretionary punishments imposed for public policy reasons could include imprisonment, banishment, lashings, or fines. Most jurists held that a *ta'zir* penalty could not include the death sentence. On *ta'zir* penalties, see Riyad Maydani, "Uqubat: Penal Law," in Majid Khadduri and Herbert J. Liebesny (eds.), *Law in the Middle East: Origins and Development of Islamic Law* (Washington, D.C.: Middle East Institute, 1955), pp. 231-32.

pletely, or even partially, realized the moral vision of the Qur'an. I would even go further and argue that any vision that attempts to realize the divine moral charge is bound to be incomplete and ephemeral, and will invariably eventually need to be reconceived, reimagined, and rearticulated. One idea that emerges from the classical tradition, which is profound, is the notion that seeking retaliation and vengeance is dangerous and risky, and that it can easily and unwittingly transform a victim into a transgressor.[52] However, what is conspicuously absent from the deliberations of the juristic tradition is an effort to explore the moral connotations of the Qur'anic empowerment of private individuals in the case possibly implicating the death penalty. In many ways, it is as if the Qur'an considered the death penalty too serious a matter to be left to the state's discretion. Of course, the state may punish criminal behavior in accordance with the prevailing law at the time, but the Qur'an does not empower the state to execute people.[53] Relegating death to the private individual invokes a moral process that must be permeated with the mercy factor. On this front, the Qur'an engages the individual through a dynamic that for a believer is powerful. The Qur'an counsels human beings that if they deal with kindness and compassion even with their enemy, they are bound to change the hearts of people, and those who were once alienated and resentful will become as kindred spirits.[54] In addition, in this context, God sets out what can be described as a rule of reciprocity, which makes the mercy factor all the more compelling. In calling upon the aggrieved to forgive, the Qur'an poses the following rhetorical challenge, in effect saying: Forgive, for wouldn't you like God to forgive you your sins![55] Moreover, the Qur'an promises those who live in accordance with the mercy factor that God will

52. The Qur'an strongly cautions believers to be on guard when trying to maintain the balance of justice so that anger, hatred, fear, or undue suspicion will not unwittingly tempt them into becoming transgressors. The Qur'an expresses very strong concerns about the ease by which those who have been victimized slip into a state whereupon they become the transgressors. For instance, see Qur'an 2:194; 5:2, 87.

53. As will be shown below, the Qur'an did not specifically mandate the death penalty for any crimes that Muslim jurists considered to be capital offenses. Some capital crimes, such as apostasy and adultery, do not generate private rights — these are quintessential state crimes. But in none of these crimes does the Qur'an, as opposed to Islamic jurisprudence, mandate the death penalty. Furthermore, whenever a right does accrue to a private individual, as in the case of murder, exacting death is never the only choice given by the Qur'an. Arguably, banditry is the only possible exception, but first, the Qur'an does not mandate death as the only choice in the case of banditry. Second, juristic precedents gave the state the power to exact death in the case of banditry. The Qur'an, itself, did not give the state that right.

54. Qur'an 41:34.

55. Qur'an 24:22. Also, see 26:51; 26:82.

compensate them in due time, and reward them with forgiveness as well as what could be described as meaningful replacements.[56]

*   *   *

To this point, I have argued that if one explores the Qur'anic moral paradigms, it would become clear that a despotic or tyrannical state should not apply the death penalty under any circumstance because such a state is already a corrupter of the earth. If a despotic state applies the death penalty, it is violating the exclusive province of God over human life, and, by definition, such a state cannot be the recipient of a divine providence to decide matters of life and death. As to a non-despotic state, the issue is more difficult and challenging. Although I could not conclude that a non-despotic state is prohibited from killing, I did note that the Qur'an does not order the state, in general, to execute human beings. While it is possible that a non-despotic state would feel empowered to execute individuals, it cannot derive such empowerment from the Qur'an itself. If anything, the Qur'an seems to empower private individuals with the decision whether to demand a life for a life or any other paradigm of exaction. However, several factors militate against the exaction of talion by private individuals. There is a high risk that private individuals might become the aggressors if they fail to adhere to strict equality between the harm suffered and the harm exacted. Furthermore, the moral trajectory of the Qur'an is not in favor of exaction or vengeance. The moral trajectory of the Qur'an is strongly in favor of the mercy factor — forgiveness as one waits to be rewarded by God. Forgiveness and self-restraint are closer to piety and divinity. I also argue that fulfilling the mercy factor constitutes a higher realization of the moral vision of the Qur'an and Islam. If an individual seeks to be a truer Muslim and a better human being, he or she would not demand talion or exaction.

The question that remains, however, is: Assuming a non-despotic state, what if private individuals do not seek to fulfill the moral vision of the Qur'an or to become truer Muslims, and they demand that the state takes vengeance for them, should the state, rightly and justly, enforce the death penalty on behalf of those private individuals? Or, alternatively, can a non-despotic state on its own initiative seek the death penalty against a criminal? I think that these two questions have been answered, in part, by saying that this is the Islamically inferior moral position, and unless the state rejects the idea of moral growth, this position is not where an Islamic state ideally would

56. Qur'an 8:70.

want to be. But another part of the response is that in order to progress on the road of moral growth, the state must structure its paradigms and justifications in a manner that is consistent with the mercy factor. Achieving the constituent elements of the mercy factor would allow the state to reach the ultimate goal of a condition of *ihsan*. Mercy and compassion could have many characteristics but none of them seem to be premised on the idea of vengeance. One can even go further by saying that vengeance and retaliation are fundamentally inconsistent with the demand for mercy and compassion. Those who choose to be vengeful and who seek revenge might be interested in achieving a certain level of justice, but they are not being compassionate or merciful.[57] Vengeance and retaliation are not sustainable paradigms in the presence of the imperative of compassion and mercy. Vengeance and retaliation standing alone are insufficient to justify the death penalty in an Islamic state that is non-despotic and that is determined to reach the condition of *ihsan*.

Nevertheless, even if one considers the mercy factor to be compelling, the death penalty could be premised on the logic of deterrence, instead of vengeance and retaliation. Arguably, one can be compassionate and merciful, and at the same time seek to deter criminals from committing capital offenses by imposing the death penalty. In fact, if the mercy factor is compelling, deterrence is arguably the only basis upon which the death penalty can be justified in a non-despotic Islamic state, which considers itself bound by the mercy factor. Deterrence or the lack of it in relation to the death penalty is a difficult empirical question that I cannot appropriately address here. However, there appear to be two important parts to the question of deterrence. One part relies on the dissemination and spread of fear in society — those who are thinking of committing a crime avoid doing so because of the fear of execution. The second part relies on a morally educative role for the state — the state emphasizes the importance of life by reserving the most severe punishment to those who destroy it. Of course, like fighting fire with fire, there is an irony to the notion that the state protects life by destroying it. But to be fair, one should recognize that the point of the death penalty in a moral educative paradigm is to convey a message of extreme intolerance to-

57. One could argue that those who are interested in vengeance are actually seeking to be merciful and compassionate towards victims of crimes in general. Arguably, those who seek the death penalty desire to protect other potential victims who might fall prey to the particular criminal who should have been put to death or to other criminals who could have been deterred by the prospect of the death penalty. This position, which is based on empathy with victims of crime, boils down to a question of deterrence. Therefore, I assume and incorporate this possibility in the ensuing discussion of deterrence.

wards certain criminal elements in society. From an Islamic perspective, both parts of death penalty policy seem problematic. As to the first, it should be recalled that the spreading of fear is a characteristic of those who cause corruption on the earth, and the question then becomes, whether the ends justify the means. As to the second part, if, as we have assumed, the state is committed to the mercy factor, it becomes more compelling that the state affirms the message about the value of life by acts of mercy and compassion, and not by engaging in the termination of life. This moral lesson is powerfully reflected in the Prophet's tradition in which he says: "It is much better that the ruler (of a state) be unjustifiably merciful than that he would be erroneously punitive."[58]

The Death Penalty in the Islamic Tradition

Before concluding, there remains one significant task, and that is to address the juristic tradition in Islam, and examine the way that this tradition dealt with the issue of the death penalty. I have left this task to the end because there is no question that my arguments presented here are challenged by the ready acceptance of the juristic tradition to accept the death penalty as a just recourse in several instances. I should emphasize, however, that although I reach conclusions that are atypical for Islamic law, my arguments, in large part, are inspired by certain trends and orientations within the juristic tradition in Islam. I do not claim that the interpretations and determinations of the juristic tradition unequivocally support the arguments presented here. Nevertheless, I hope to demonstrate that certain elements within that tradition do provide the fertile grounds in which my arguments are rooted.

In classical Islamic law, there were six "capital" offenses (known as the *hudud* crimes), three of which could potentially be punished by execution.[59] The three death penalty eligible crimes were adultery, banditry, and apostasy — the other crimes were punished by less than death.[60] Although murder was

---

58. Abu Zahrah, *al-'Uqubah*, pp. 198-99.

59. The six capital offenses were: (1) adultery or fornication *(zina)*; (2) slander *(qadhf)*; (3) consumption of alcohol *(shurb al-khamr)*; (4) theft *(sariqa)*; (5) brigandage or banditry *(hiraba)*; and (6) apostasy *(ridda)*. Muslim jurists disagreed as to whether rebellion *(baghy)* is among the *hudud* crimes or not. See Postawko, "Towards an Islamic Critique of Capital Punishment," pp. 286-300; Ali Ahmad Mar'i, *al-Qisas wa al-Hudud fi al-Fiqh al-Islami* (Beirut: Dar Iqra', 1982), pp. 55-93.

60. Muslim jurists also disagreed, rather strongly, on whether a crime known as *zandaqa* could be punished by death. *Zandaqa* could be translated as Manichaeism or simply heresy. Be-

considered a capital offense, and it could be punished by death, it was not considered among the *hudud* crimes.[61] As to each of the offenses punishable by death, Muslim jurists believed that there was specific textual support for such a penalty. According to Muslim jurists, the death penalty was imposable only if God had specifically, precisely, and clearly authorized such a punishment; these jurists believed that the support for the death penalty, found in Islamic texts, was clear and unambiguous.[62] This is not the place to provide an extensive exposition on whether the textual support in Islamic sources for the death penalty is as unambiguous as some would like to believe, but what is very clear is that the Qur'an does not explicitly or implicitly mandate the death penalty for either apostasy or adultery.[63] According to classical Islamic law, an adulterer or adulteress is to be stoned to death. However, stoning *(rajm)* is not mentioned in the Qur'an, and in fact, the only punishment for adultery that is mentioned is a physical beating consisting of a certain number of canings or lashings. Likewise, the crime of apostasy is not mentioned in the Qur'an. To the contrary, the Qur'an explicitly states that there ought not be any compulsion in religion, and that people should not be forced into becoming Muslim.[64]

Both penalties, stoning for adultery and execution for apostasy, were derived from non-Qur'anic origins but, rather incredulously, they were nevertheless designated by the classical jurists as Qur'anic punishments. Muslim jurists believed that stoning, as a penalty for adultery, was prescribed in the Torah, and they believed that the Old Testament penalty continued to be valid

---

cause of the strong potential for abuse of power in an accusation of heresy, most Muslim jurists were very reluctant to sanction the death penalty for this crime. Some jurists refused to recognize *zandaqa* as a crime, separate and apart from apostasy. They argued that either the heresy reaches the point of apostasy, and then it is punishable by death, or it does not, and then the state has no recourse. Other jurists maintained that *zandaqa*, if proven according to certain evidentiary standards, should be punishable by less than death. Another group of jurists argued that the only appropriate punishment for heresy is banishment and exile. On *zandaqa*, see Abou El Fadl, *Rebellion and Violence in Islamic Law*, pp. 78-79, 103-4, 134, 139, 205.

61. As noted above, Muslim jurists disagreed on whether the state could still impose the death penalty if the family of the victim chose compensation or forgiveness. Many jurists argued that in the case of murder, the death penalty could be imposed only if the family of the victim demands it; otherwise the state is limited to imposing a penalty less than death.

62. The legal maxim was *la hadd bi la nass* (capital offenses cannot be established without clear divine authority). See Abu Zahrah, *al-'Uquba*, pp. 95-96.

63. The Qur'anic texts addressing banditry and rebellion are complex, and communities of meaning and interpretation that formed around these texts are even more so. For an extensive study on the Qur'anic texts dealing with these issues, see Abou El Fadl, *Rebellion and Violence in Islamic Law*, pp. 32-61.

64. Qur'an 2:256; 10:99.

for Islam.[65] The jurists contended that although the Qur'an said nothing about stoning as a penalty for adultery, stoning was the law of the Israelites, and the Prophet had affirmed the continuing validity of this punishment for Muslims.[66] Apostasy, on the other hand, had an even more ambiguous basis in Islamic law. There is no reliable evidence that the Prophet during his lifetime executed anyone for the crime of apostasy. However, the penalty for apostasy seems to have arisen from a period of time, during the caliphate of Abu Bakr, when Muslims were engulfed in what was known as the wars of apostasy *(hurub al-ridda)*. Although there was a specific historical context that elicited the emergence of the law of apostasy, the doctrinal support for such a penalty remained flimsy at best.[67]

Setting aside for the moment the issue of whether the historical determinations of Muslim jurists regarding adultery and apostasy were well supported by the textual and doctrinal sources, there is another aspect to the practices of Muslim jurists that warrants consideration. Regardless of the crime for which they mandated death, Muslim jurists remained extremely reluctant to actually impose the death sentence in any particular case. Although Muslim jurists sought to emphasize the seriousness and graveness of certain crimes by decreeing the death penalty in principle, they were, at the same time, not willing to implement this ultimate punishment with any degree of zeal. This is verified by the surprisingly few number of incidents of stoning for adultery or execution for apostasy conducted in Islamic history.[68] This was, in part, due to the strenuous evidentiary standards that Muslim jurists demanded in order to enforce the death penalty, and it was also due to the cumulative opportunities offered by Muslim jurists to the de-

---

65. For the juristic debates on lashing, stoning, and banishment as possible penalties for adultery, see Ibn Rushd, *Bidayat al-Mujtahid*, pp. 326-27. Some Muslim sects, like the Khawarij, Mu'tazila, and some Shi'is, rejected stoning as un-Islamic.

66. This doctrinal position continues into the modern age. For instance, see Abu Zahrah, *al-'Uquba*, pp. 101-4. The author, who is a notable contemporary authority from the Azhar in Egypt, reviews the various textual evidences for stoning in Islam. He grudgingly admits that the textual support for stoning is far from stellar but then resolves the matter by asserting that stoning was the law of the Israelites and it continues to be valid for Muslims.

67. For an analysis and critique of the evidence on this issue, see El-Awa, *Punishment in Islamic Law*, pp. 49-64; Mohammad Hashim Kamali, *Freedom of Expression in Islam*, rev. ed. (London: Islamic Texts Society, 1997), pp. 87-107. Also, see Abdullah Saeed and Hassan Saeed, *Freedom of Religion: Apostasy and Islam* (London: Ashgate Publishing Co., 2003); S. A. Rahman, *The Punishment of Apostasy in Islam* (New Delhi: Kitab Bhavan, 1996).

68. Not surprisingly considering the highly politicized nature of the efforts to implement Islamic law in the modern age, there have been more frequent implementations of the stoning penalty in the modern age than in any other time in Islamic history.

fendant to express repentance and, thus, escape death.[69] In the case of adultery, for example, what was required was either a freely given, non-coerced confession, repeated four times on four separate occasions, or four witnesses who saw the intercourse by observing the actual act of vaginal penetration. As a deterrent, false accusations were punished by eighty lashes and public censure. Importantly, if one or more of the four witnesses recanted his testimony or was unable to say that he saw the actual act of penetration (perhaps he just saw the couple lying naked in bed), the other witnesses were punished for slander.[70] Naturally, the point of this was that no one should dare bring such an accusation unless they are absolutely certain about their charges, and the evidence is clear and unequivocal.[71] In the case of apostasy, the evidence indicating that the defendant had abandoned Islam was supposed to be clear, explicit, and unequivocal. In addition, the defendant had to be granted three nights and days to repent and return to Islam; in the opinion of many jurists, as long as there remained a reasonable chance that the defendant would repent, he could not be executed.[72] Moreover, regardless of the evidence against the defendant, if at any time, during or after the criminal proceedings, the defendant affirms the testament of faith, the defendant could not be executed.[73]

Militating against the application of the death penalty was the fact that Muslim jurists developed the idea of presumption of innocence in all criminal matters and argued that the accuser always carries the burden of proof

69. The reluctance of Muslim jurists to impose the death penalty in actual cases serves as the basis for Robert Postawko's critique of capital punishment in Islam. See Postawko, "Towards an Islamic Critique of Capital Punishment."

70. Mar'i, al-Qisas wa al-Hudud fi al-Fiqh al-Islami, pp. 59-72.

71. Muslim jurists disagreed on whether the pregnancy of a married woman, under circumstances in which the father of the child could not possibly be the husband, could be used as evidence of adultery. Most jurists considered pregnancy, whether in the case of fornication or adultery, to be insufficient and unreliable evidence. Relying on the legal principle that in the case of hudud crimes any doubt must be used to void the penalty, most Muslim jurists denied that pregnancy could be a means to establish culpability. Ibn Rushd, Bidayat al-Mujtahid, pp. 328-29; Abu Zahrah, al-'Uquba, pp. 198-251.

72. Some jurists argued that apostates should be imprisoned until they repent, but should not be executed.

73. The testament of faith (shahada) consists of pronouncing the following statement: "I bear witness that there is no God but God and that Muhammad is the Prophet of God." In the classical tradition, anyone who pronounces this statement becomes a Muslim bound by all the applicable duties and rights. On the technical requirements for a charge of apostasy, see 'Abd al-Qadir 'Udah, al-Tashri' al-Jina'i al-Islami, vol. 2, pp. 707-31; Abu Zahrah, al-'Uquba, pp. 172-76; Ahmad Fathi Bahnassi, Madkhal al-Fiqh al-Jina'i al-Islami (Cairo: Dar al-Shuruq, 1980), pp. 95-97; Ibn Rushd, Bidayat al-Mujtahid, pp. 343-44.

(al-bayyina 'ala man idda 'a).[74] Muslim jurists also condemned the use of torture, arguing that the Prophet forbade the use of *muthla* (the use of mutilations) in all situations,[75] and opposed the use of coerced confessions in all legal and political matters. A large number of jurists articulated a principle similar to the American exculpatory doctrine — confessions and evidence obtained under coercion are inadmissible at trial. Relying on the legal principle that, in capital offenses, any doubt acts to nullify the penalty, most Muslim jurists argued that coercion, necessity, and torture presumptively act so as to create doubt sufficient to nullify the death penalty.[76]

74. Jalal al-Din 'Abd al-Rahman al-Suyuti, *al-Ashbah wa al-Naza'ir fi Qawa'id wa Furu' Fiqh al-Shafi'iyya* (Beirut: Daf al-Kutub al-'Ilmiyya, 1983), p. 53; Ahmad b. Muhammad al-Zarqa, *Sharh al-Qawa'id al-Fiqhiyya*, 4th ed. (Damascus: Dar al-Qalam, 1996), pp. 369-89; Mahmasani, *Falsafat al-Tashri'*, p. 294.

75. Muslim jurists, however, did *not* consider the severing of hands or feet as punishment for theft and banditry to be mutilation. Jalal al-Din al-Suyuti, *al-Durr al-Manthur fi al-Tafsir bi al-Ma'thur* (Cairo: Matba'at al-Anwar al-Muhammadiyya, n.d.), 2:305-6; Abu al-Fida' al-Hafiz Ibn Kathir al-Dimashqi, *Tafsir al-Qur'an al-'Azim* (Beirut: Dar al-Khayr, 1990), 2:56-57; Abu Bakr b. 'Ali al-Jassas, *Ahkam al-Qur'an* (Beirut: Dar al-Kitab al-'Arabi, 1986), 2:407-8; 'Imad al-Din b. Muhammad al-Kiya al-Harasi, *Ahkam al-Qur'an* (Beirut: Dar al-Kutub al-'Ilmiyya, 1985), 3:65; Abu Bakr Muhammad b. 'Abd Allah b. al-'Arabi, *Ahkam al-Qur'an*, ed. 'Ali Muhammad al-Bajawi (Beirut: Dar al-Jil, 1987), 2:594; Abd Allah Muhammad b. Ahmad al-Qurtubi, *al-Jami' li Ahkam al-Qur'an* (Cairo: n.p., 1952), 6:149-50; Abu Muhammad b. Ahmad b. Ibn Hazm, *al-Muhalla bi al-Athar*, ed. 'Abd al-Ghaffar Sulayman al-Bandari (Beirut: Dar al-Kutub al-'Ilmiyya, n.d.), 12:285-88; Abou El Fadl, *Rebellion and Violence in Islamic Law*, pp. 32, 50-57, 73-77, 340-41.

76. In classical jurisprudence, several opportunities were offered to the offender so he or she could avoid the punishment for a capital offense. For instance, ignorance of law or fact, a mistaken claim of right or status, or improper process, such as spying or invasion of privacy all served to generate doubt, and thus vitiated the necessity of capital punishment. In the case of adultery or fornication, claims of incomplete penetration, rape and coercion, mistaken identity, or wrongful belief were considered sufficient to nullify capital punishments. Many jurists held that necessity or need in the case of fornication or adultery would also nullify the penalty. These jurists relied on a reported incident involving the second Caliph Umar Ibn al-Khattab in which, during his reign, Umar encountered a woman who confessed to fornication but she claimed that, while traveling in the desert, she became thirsty. She met a Bedouin man who agreed to give her water but only if she succumbed to his sexual desires. Umar ruled that the *hadd* could not be applied to this woman. Umar also dropped the *hadd* punishment for individuals who were caught consuming alcohol because their apprehension was due to illegal spying. Umar also suspended the *hadd* punishment for theft during a year of widespread famine because people were moved by hunger to steal. 'Abd al-Qadir 'Udah, *al-Tashri' al-Jina'i al-Islami*, vol. 2, pp. 359-75; Mahmassani, *The Philosophy of Jurisprudence in Islam*, pp. 110-14; Nagaty Sanad, *The Theory of Crime and Criminal Responsibility in Islamic Law: Shari'a* (Chicago: Office of International Criminal Justice, 1991), pp. 72-74; Ibn Rushd, *Bidayat al-Mujtahid*, pp. 328-29. Abu Zahrah, *al'Uquba*, pp. 198-251, provides a thorough review of the many situations that give rise to doubt and vitiate the need for applying the *hadd*. One should note that the classical positions on doubt

The point is not to assess the sagaciousness of these measures or their effectiveness. The point is that the juristic response was legalistic, technical, and creative. In light of the decisive and grave consequences of the death sentence, Muslim jurists were not willing to accept it without qualifications, and they seemed to have struggled with its implications and impact. As often happens in a legalistic interpretive culture, Muslim jurists did not respond at the conceptualized or broad theory level. Rather, their response was at the micro-level of technical legalities.[77] While they accepted the death penalty in principle, at the level of the process and implementation, they made the infliction of the death penalty difficult. In effect, at the micro-technical level, Muslim jurists closed the doors on the possibility of implementing the death penalty, while they left the doors wide open for lesser discretionary criminal punishments and for repentance and pardon. The moral paradigm that inspired Muslim jurists to endeavor to avoid the death penalty is well represented in an educational message that teachers of Islamic law in the classical age often repeated and emphasized to their students. The message provided was this: It is better to let a thousand heretics go free than to wrongfully punish a single sincere Muslim, and it is always better to save the life of a thousand guilty persons than to unwittingly murder a single innocent person.[78]

Towards the Future

Cold utilitarian logic, rational self-interested deduction, instinct, and perhaps even simple whimsy and self-indulgence, when needed, will always supply human beings with good reasons to kill. Aside from that, the state, any political entity that represents the elite, and often the loudest and most obnoxious elements within a society will often want to possess the power to kill. If power, in general, is intoxicating, this kind of power — the power to kill — will often serve as a sort of hallucinogen, giving whoever possesses it an ultimate sense of control, and a false sense of security. It could even allow

---

and the nullification of the *hadd* contrast rather sharply with the modern-day practices that one finds in countries such as Pakistan, Nigeria, Saudi Arabia, and Afghanistan during the reign of the Taliban.

77. On the technical, micro-level responses of a legal culture, see Khaled Abou El Fadl and Alan Watson, "Fox Hunting, Pheasant Shooting, and Comparative Law," *American Journal of Comparative Law* 48:1 (2000): 1-37.

78. Muhammad b. ʿAli al-Shawkani, *Nayl al-Awtar Sharh Muntaqa al-Akhbar* (Cairo: Dar al-Hadith, n.d.), 7:168; Shihab al-Din Ibn Hajar al-ʿAsqalani, *Fath al-Bari bi Sharh Sahih al-Bukhari* (Beirut: Dar al-Fikr, 1993), 14:308.

those who lost a loved one to overcome a sense of violation and vulnerability by thinking that the execution of the offender will somehow restore balance to their lives and, more importantly, to the life of the murder victim. I think we often treat the victims of murder as if they continue to live, and as if killing the offender will restore some of the life that was unjustly taken away from them.[79] But like so many other short-order fixes and instantaneous solutions, the costs associated with seeking after the immediate and gratifying, turn out in the long term to be oppressively prohibitive. It seems to me, however, that executions are too serious a business to be left to the vagaries of societal whimsies or even logic and rationality. More particularly, the infliction of death is too grave a matter to entrust to the state, especially the authoritarian and despotic state. When confronted with something so laden with meaning and consequence as human life, it seems that what is needed is not logic, rationality, or instinct but magnanimity *(ihsan)*. In the case of Islam, this magnanimity is captured and augmented by what I called the mercy factor. The balance of justice, ethics, and, indeed, existence *(al-mizan)* is restored through the pursuit of the mercy factor — not by enforcing the paradigm of strict retribution, or a life for a life and an eye for an eye. Contrary to the message conveyed by the practices of several predominantly Muslim countries that supply some of the highest rates of executions in the world today, the Islamic vision of justice is not founded on vengeance and retribution. The Islamic vision of justice is premised on mercy, compassion, and the absolute sanctity of human life. Regardless of the moral achievements and failures of the past, the burden is always on Muslims to strive continuously towards a greater fulfillment and attainment of the divine charge, and to achieve new levels of magnanimity and sanctification of human life. It is exactly the magnanimity and sanctimony of human life that perhaps today calls upon us Muslims to reconsider the morality of the killing state.

79. I speak here from personal experience. It is possible, however, that my experience was idiosyncratic and unrepresentative.

II Theological Reflections
on the Death Penalty

6. Categorical Pardon: On the Argument for Abolishing Capital Punishment

J. BUDZISZEWSKI

Justice is giving to each what is due to him: Praise to the doers of good, harm to the doers of wrong. So fundamental is the duty of public authority to requite good and evil that natural law philosophers make it the paramount function of the state, and the New Testament declares that the role is delegated to magistrates by God himself. "For the Lord's sake accept the authority of every human institution," says St. Peter, "whether of the emperor as supreme, or of governors as sent by him to punish those who do wrong and to praise those who do right" (1 Pet. 2:13-14). St. Paul agrees:

> For rulers are not a terror to good conduct, but to bad. Would you have no fear of him who is in authority? Then do what is good, and you will receive his approval, for he is God's servant for your good. But if you do wrong, be afraid, for he does not bear the sword in vain; he is the servant of God to execute his wrath on the wrongdoer. Therefore one must be subject, not only to avoid God's wrath but also for the sake of conscience. (Rom. 13:3-5)

So weighty is the duty of justice that it raises the question whether mercy is permissible at all. By definition, mercy is punishing the criminal less than he deserves, and it seems no more clear at first why not going far enough is better than going too far. We say that both cowardice and rashness miss the mark of courage, and that both stinginess and prodigality miss the mark of generosity; why do we not say that both mercy and harshness miss the mark of justice? Making matters yet more difficult, the argument to abolish capital punishment is an argument to *categorically* extend clemency to *all* those who deserve death for their crimes — for to abolish capital punishment is to give *all* of them less than they deserve.

For clarity, I will focus mainly on the crime of murder, the deliberate taking of innocent human life. The reason for this focus is that the question of mercy arises only on the assumption that some crime does deserve death. Suffice it to say that at least death deserves death, for nothing less is sufficient to convey the gravity of the deed. Scripture agrees: "Whoever sheds the blood of man, by man shall his blood be shed, for in his own image God made mankind" (Gen. 9:6, RSV). Someone may object that the murderer too is made in God's image, and so he is. But this does not lighten the horror of his deed. On the contrary, it heightens it, because it makes him a morally accountable being. Moreover, if even simple murder warrants death, how much more does multiple and compounded murder warrant it? Some criminals seem to deserve death many times over. If we are considering not taking their lives at all, the motive cannot be justice. It must be mercy.

The questions we must address are therefore three: (1) Is it ever permissible for public authority to give the wrongdoer less than he deserves? (2) If it is permissible, then when is it permissible? (3) Is it permissible to grant such mercy categorically?

Is It Ever Permissible for Public Authority to Give the Wrongdoer Less Than He Deserves?

Society is justly ordered when each person receives what is due to him. Crime disturbs this just order, for the criminal takes from people their lives, peace, liberties, and worldly goods in order to give himself undeserved benefits. Deserved punishment restores this just order, making the wrongdoer pay a price equivalent to the harm he has done. This is retribution, not to be confused with revenge, which is guided by a different motive. In retribution the spur is the virtue of indignation, which answers injury with injury for public good. In revenge the spur is the passion of resentment, which answers malice with malice for private satisfaction. We are not concerned here with revenge.

Retribution is the primary purpose of just punishment *as such*. The reasons for saying so are threefold. First, just punishment is not something which might or might not requite evil; requital is simply what it is. Second, without just punishment evil cannot be requited. Third, just punishment requires no warrant beyond requiting evil, for the restoration of justice is good in itself. True, just punishment may bring about other good effects. In particular, it might rehabilitate the criminal, protect society from him, or deter crime in general. Although these might be additional motives for just punishment, they are secondary. In the first place, punishment might not achieve them. In the second place, they can sometimes be partly achieved apart from punishment. Third and most important, they cannot justify punishment by themselves. In other words, we *may not do more* to the criminal than he deserves — not even if more would be needed to rehabilitate him, make him harmless, or discourage others from imitation. For example, if a man punches another man in the nose, we may not keep him in a mental institution forever just because he has not yet become kind in spirit, kill him because we cannot be sure that he will never punch again, or torture him because nothing less would deter other would-be punchers. For these reasons, rehabilitation, protection, and deterrence have a lesser status in punishment than retribution: they are secondary.

Now the argument against capital punishment works like this: True, the purpose of retribution is served by the murderer's death, but under certain circumstances retribution might interfere with other purposes of punishment. It might prematurely put an end to his rehabilitation, it might undermine deterrence by inciting wicked men to greater evils, and it might not be necessary for the safety of others. Therefore, it would be better not to kill him, but to protect society by other means — perhaps to lock him up forever. The difficulty with this argument is that it seems to regard the secondary purposes of punishment as sufficient to overturn its primary purpose. If rehabilitation, protection, and deterrence cannot justify doing more than what retribution demands, then how can they justify doing less?

If this were the end of the story, then clemency would be impossible. The correct response to every appeal for mercy would be *By all means kill the criminal, because death is what he deserves. If you fear that death will prematurely put an end to his rehabilitation, then work harder to rehabilitate him before his death. If you fear that his execution will incite wicked men to yet greater evils, then find other ways to damp their vicious energy. Do not demand that justice be abrogated for the sake of your fears.*

But this is not the end of the story; mercy and justice can be reconciled. First let me first consider a false ending to the story which makes their reconciliation seem simpler than it is. This false ending comes from the utilitarian philosophy that has come to permeate our society and legal culture.

To the question "Is it ever permissible to show mercy?" the utilitarian answers "Yes," but it is a misleading "Yes" because he does not understand what is being asked. A utilitarian says that the only reason to have laws at all is to stop things that make people feel pain and start things that make them feel pleasure. Requiting wrong just because it is wrong will make no sense to him because he does not believe in intrinsic wrong; if someone chides him, "Never do evil that good may result," he is confused, because *what results* is the only measure of evil that he has. He cannot distinguish retribution from revenge, viewing it merely as an emotional venting which makes people feel better. Not that he objects to it on that account, for in his view, feeling good is all that matters. Over time, though, rehabilitation, protection, and deterrence make people feel better too, so the only question is what combination of punishment and remission of punishment makes people feel best. Therefore, the utilitarian might very well do less to the criminal than he deserves — but for the same reason that he might do more to him than he deserves: He does not grasp the concept of "deserves."

To the question "Is it ever permissible to show mercy?" I also answer "Yes," but for a different reason. The faith I hold recognizes a dilemma which utilitarians ignore. Justice is inexorable; evil must be punished. This would seem to make mercy impossible; yet there is mercy. As the psalmist says, "Great is your mercy, O Lord; give me life according to your justice" (Ps. 119:156). Somehow the irreconcilables meet and kiss.

How can this be? There are two parts to the riddle, one on God's side, the other on man's. On the divine side, the reconciliation of justice with mercy lies in the cross. God does not balance mercy and justice; he accomplishes both to the full. The reason he can remit punishment to human beings who repent and turn to him is that Christ, the Lamb of God, has taken the punishment in their place. His death and resurrection become their death and resurrection, because he identifies with them through sacrifice and they identify with him through faith; the judge himself steps forward to pay their debt. Divine mercy, then, means two things. One is the divine atonement which makes God's forgiveness possible. The other is the divine patience with which he waits for us to ask for it.

Yet whom God loves, he disciplines. For our good, not even divine forgiveness means that the consequences of sin *in this life* are fully remitted. Among these consequences is punishment by human magistrates, who act as God's agents whether they know it or not. The sentences of human magistrates cannot be, and are not meant to be, a final requital of unrepented evil; that awaits the great day when Christ returns to judge the quick and the dead. But they foreshadow that final justice, so that something of the retributive purpose is preserved. In the meantime they promote restraint, repentance, and amendment of life. Human magistrates turn out to be not plenary but partial delegates, and not only of God's wrath but of his patience.

All this puts the primary and secondary purposes of punishment more nearly on a level than they would be otherwise — not for God, but for man. Although human magistrates are forbidden to let crimes go unrequited, they do not carry the impossible burden of requiting them to the last degree. For temporal purposes, the retributive purpose of punishment can be moderated by the other three purposes after all. The only purpose which cannot be moderated is the purpose of *symbolizing* that perfect retribution which magistrates themselves do not achieve, for human punishment is a sign of wrath to come.

If It Is Permissible, Then When Is It Permissible?

If criminals in general can sometimes be punished less than they deserve, then perhaps capital criminals can sometimes be punished less than they deserve. The desideratum is when the purposes of punishment can be satisfied better by bloodless means than by bloody ones, so let us consider the four purposes one by one.

Rehabilitation refers to the reconciliation of the criminal with man and God. It may seem at first that capital punishment can never aid in rehabilitation, because when the string of life is cut, the process of rehabilitation is cut off, too. But this is overstated. One part of rehabilitation is cut off, for certainly a dead man is not readmitted to society. But what do the opponents of capital punishment propose as an alternative? For serious crimes and dangerous criminals, they propose life imprisonment, but a man in jail for life does not return to society either. The real question is not what the prospect of death does to a man's prospect of readmission to society, but what it does to his prospect of change of heart. Here the picture is quite different. "Depend upon it, Sir," said Samuel Johnson, "when a man knows he is to be hanged in a fortnight, it concentrates his mind wonderfully."[1] Indeed there may be many criminals for whom nothing else concentrates the mind enough. By contrast, an offender who is confined in jail for life, with no society but that of other criminals, is more likely to be hardened than reformed. We are forced to conclude that in some cases, the death penalty may contribute to rehabilitation rather than hindering it.

Protection refers to the defense of society from the criminal. It may seem at first that although capital punishment might once have been necessary for

1. James Boswell, *Life of Samuel Johnson* (Garden City, N.Y.: Garden City Books, 1945 [1791]), entry of September 19, 1777.

protection, modern improvements in the penal system may make it possible to shield the innocent without killing. Such indeed is the argument of Pope John Paul II, although he states the conclusion in less categorical terms.[2] It is the more categorical form of the conclusion to which I object. What the Pope suggests is that today we *may* be able to sentence a criminal to life imprisonment with the reasonable certainty that he will not be able to escape. I agree that this is a deeply significant change which may ultimately reduce the weight of the safety question in cases where clemency has been proposed. However, I do not agree that it has reduced its weight already. Today, the risk is not so much that dangerous and justly judged criminals will escape from prison, as that we will let them out; it has been long since a "life sentence" meant that the prisoner would stay in prison for the rest of his natural life.

There are several reasons for the erosion of life sentencing, and they tend to compound each other. High crime rates have so swelled the number of inmates that officials find it difficult to feed and house all of them; the pressure to set some free is hard to resist. At the same time, American society finds it increasingly difficult to take right and wrong seriously. Not only does our lax moral attitude contribute further to the high rate of crime, but it also generates further pressure to let criminals out of prison. When we do let them out, they are usually more dangerous than when they entered, because of the tips they have learned, the contacts they have made, and the attitudes they have developed among other criminals. The argument is sometimes made that abolishing capital punishment would foster the virtue of compassion. Conceivably this is so, but in the present moral climate it is more likely to foster that counterfeit compassion which thinks no wrong is very wrong. Should this happen, then society would be even more at risk than it is now.

Suppose the unlikely; suppose that somehow we did nerve ourselves to keep all capital criminals in prison for the duration of their natural lives. Even then the protective purpose of punishment would not be fully satisfied. True, a man behind bars no longer endangers society in general. But he endangers other inmates, and he certainly endangers prison staff. Surely they too deserve consideration. We are forced to conclude that even today, with our modern penal systems, safety is still an issue. Safety must not trump desert; the risk of future harm cannot justify doing *more* to the criminal than he deserves. But in some cases it should keep us from doing *less*.

Deterrence refers to the discouragement of crime in general. This is

2. John Paul II, Encyclical Letter *Evangelium Vitae* ["The Gospel of Life"], March 25, 1995, section 56. The full text of the document is available online at http://www.vatican.va/holy_father/john_paul_ii/encyclicals/documents/hf_jp-ii_enc_25031995_evangelium-vitae_en.html.

where some opponents of capital punishment claim their strongest ground, for the statistical evidence for the deterrent effect of capital punishment is inconsistent and inconclusive. Avery Cardinal Dulles suggests a further dilemma in his 2000 McGinley Lecture at Fordham University. Although grotesque and torturous methods of execution seem most likely to deter, they are incompatible with human dignity. Conversely, those methods of execution which are compatible with human dignity seem unlikely to deter. So for the means of capital punishment which could actually be used, we probably could not count on a deterrent effect.

For those who view deterrence as the primary purpose of punishment, the uncertainty of capital punishment as a deterrent provides the fatal argument against it. For those who view its primary purpose as retribution, however, this uncertainty makes little difference; the mere fact that a deserved punishment does not deter makes it no less richly deserved. But is it possible that high rates of capital punishment would actually undermine deterrence, inciting wicked and resentful men to greater evils? We know that *banning* a favorite vice can have this effect; the prohibition of alcohol, for example, can give drunkenness a certain glamour. But the crimes we class as capital must be prohibited in any case. If there were evidence that punishing criminals *by execution* rather than by bloodless means incited them, that would certainly be an argument for using the bloodless means. To my knowledge, however, no such evidence has turned up. It seems then that the data on deterrence neither strengthen nor weaken the case for capital punishment.

Retribution. We saw earlier that although human punishment does not bear the full burden of requiting good and evil, it *must* hold up requital as an ideal; it must point beyond itself, to that perfect justice of which it is merely a token. Cardinal Dulles agrees, but sees a problem:

> For the symbolism to be authentic, the society must believe in the existence of a transcendent order of justice, which the State has an obligation to protect. This has been true in the past, but in our day the State is generally viewed simply as an instrument of the will of the governed. In this modern perspective, the death penalty expresses not the divine judgment on objective evil but rather the collective anger of the group. The retributive goal of punishment is misconstrued as a self-assertive act of vengeance.[3]

3. Avery Cardinal Dulles, S.J., "The Death Penalty: A Right to Life Issue," Laurence J. McGinley Lecture, Fordham University (October 17, 2000). The full text is available online at http://pewforum.org/deathpenalty/resources/reader/17.php3. See also Avery Cardinal Dulles's chapter in this volume.

The cynicism which Cardinal Dulles describes is a real and grave difficulty. Our rulers no longer believe in those divine decrees of which human decrees are but a hint or shadow, and neither does a large and growing part of the population. More and more our intellectuals agree with the famous statement of Oliver Wendell Holmes that "truth is the majority vote of that nation that could lick all others."[4] But what is the import of these facts? They do not make it *less* important for our courts to appeal to justice; they make it *more*. There is a difference between saying that the ideology people hold no longer gives adequate expression to the law which St. Paul says is "written on their hearts" (Rom. 2:14-15), and saying that it is not in fact written on their hearts. Even now, people retain a dim idea of desert; the idea "A deserves B for doing C" has not simply become meaningless to them. The Roman judges of the first century were no less cynical than the American judges of the twenty-first. Tiberius Caesar would have been quite comfortable with Holmes's maxim; Pontius Pilate washed his hands of justice, using the question "What is truth?" not to begin the interview with his prisoner, but to end it. The apostles knew all these things, yet St. Paul calls the magistrate the servant of God to execute his wrath on the wrongdoer.

I do not know whether our society can be brought back to belief in a transcendent order of justice, but of this I am certain: if we who recognize this standard do not act as though we believe in it, then no one will believe in it. If, just because no one believes in it, we must act as though we do not believe in it either, then we speak as do men without hope. We must not stop singing just because our listeners hear so poorly. We must sing more clearly to help them hear.

The question to ask about the retributive purpose of capital punishment is this: is it possible for punishment to signify the gravity of crimes which deserve death if their perpetrators are *never* visited with execution? This seems unlikely. Consider the deviant who tortures small children to death for his pleasure, or the ideologue who meditates the demise of innocent thousands for the sake of greater terror. Genesis says murderers deserve death *because* life is precious; man is made in the image of God. How convincing is our reverence for life if its mockers are suffered to live?

---

4. Oliver Wendell Holmes, "Natural Law," *Harvard Law Review* 62 (1918): 40. Though the author says he is stating a sentiment of his youth, he states it to endorse it.

Is It Permissible to Grant Such Mercy Categorically?
The Argument So Far

To summarize the argument up to this point, the death penalty fares differently under each of the four purposes of punishment.

1. The prospect of execution may contribute, in a way in which no other punishment can, to one aspect of rehabilitation, the criminal's change of heart. It cannot contribute to the other — his readmission to society — but neither can the alternative, life in prison.
2. Despite modern developments in penology, capital punishment is still often necessary for the protection of society. The problem is not that dangerous men may escape from prison, but that we cannot bring ourselves to keep them in. In some ways imprisonment itself may increase their danger to others, both before their release and afterward. Life in prison will never be as safe as life outside.
3. There is no conclusive evidence that capital punishment deters crime in general. Neither is there evidence that it incites it, and a deterrent effect is not necessary to justify deserved punishment.
4. In order for the system of justice to signify the gravity of crimes which merit death, it is probably not necessary that they always be punished as they deserve. Yet it hardly seems possible to signify their gravity if they never are.

Clemency remains a moral possibility in particular cases. Where death is deserved, it might nevertheless be replaced by life imprisonment for those criminals who are least dangerous, who are likeliest to repent, and whose guilt is least compounded (so far as we can tell) — provided that the punishment is not so weak in comparison to the crime that the symbolism of divine retribution is impaired. Yet the propriety of clemency in particular cases is not a warrant for its categorical extension to *all* capital criminals, regardless of their danger to society, heedless of their hardness of heart, irrespective of the heinousness of their deeds.

Let us consider what might be said against this provisional conclusion.

Objections

The judicious Cardinal Dulles, to whom my discussion is already indebted, finds less to commend capital punishment than I do. Yet even he does not think that a review of the purposes of punishment is sufficient *in itself* to justify abolishing the ultimate penalty. The crux of his published argument is found not there, but in four other common objections to the penalty of death: (1) sometimes innocent people are sentenced to death; (2) capital punishment whets the lust for revenge rather than satisfying the zeal for true justice; moreover, (3) it cheapens the value of life; and (4) it contradicts Christ's teaching to forgive. The cardinal calls the first objection "relatively strong"; to the second and third he concedes "some probable force"; the fourth he considers "relatively weak." Yet he concludes that "taken together, the four may suffice to tip the scale against the death penalty."[5] Let us revisit these four objectives.

Erroneous Convictions

Courts sometimes do mistakenly condemn the innocent. Although erroneous conviction is possible in any case, its gravity increases with the severity and irreversibility of the penalty. It would seem that the proper remedy is to require a higher procedural standard in capital cases, and to root out the sources of corruption in the system of justice. Indeed the cardinal acknowledges the point, approving the suggestion that capital punishment would be justified if the trial were held in an honest court and the accused were found guilty "beyond all shadow of doubt." His point is that this criterion cannot be satisfied, for despite all precautions, errors do sometimes occur.

The difficulty with the argument lies in the notion of guilt "beyond all shadow of doubt." When we say this, do we mean beyond shadow of *any* sort of doubt, or do we mean beyond shadow of *reasonable* doubt? In law, the latter standard rules, and surely this is as it ought to be. Anything *might* be doubted, but it does not follow that doubt is always justified by the facts in evidence. The murderer might have told the grocer, doctor, and cabdriver what he was going to do; he might have been videotaped doing it by a newsman, a passerby, and an automatic security camera; he might have boasted about it afterward to a co-worker, bartender, and next-door neighbor; and he might have confessed, in the presence of his lawyer, to the arresting officer, the investigating officers, and the court. Yet perhaps someone on the jury has been reading the *Meditation* of René Descartes, and is troubled by the possibility that the sensible world is only an illusion caused by an evil demon or by the nature of minds.[6] If

---

5. Dulles, McGinley Lecture.

6. René Descartes, *Meditation on First Philosophy* (1641), 5:8, in *Discourse on Method, and Meditations on First Philosophy*, 4th ed., trans. Donald A. Cress (Indianapolis: Hackett, 1998).

it is, he reasons, then none of the witnesses can be trusted. For that matter, neither can the accused; he may have only dreamed the whole murder. True, Descartes concludes that the world is not an illusion after all. But the juryman votes for acquittal anyway, reflecting that philosophers sometimes err.

Now the way that the juryman reasons about philosophers is very much like how Cardinal Dulles reasons about juries. The cardinal holds that because even honest courts can err, we must not trust any verdict, irrespective of the weight of evidence which supports it. But a doubt which cannot be affected by any possible evidence is not a reasonable ground for letting a convict off the hook.

The Lust for Revenge

Of course it is true that the death penalty might whet the appetite for revenge. It is hard to see, though, why this should be more true of the death penalty than of "locking them up for life." Indeed it is hard to see why it should be more true of punishment than of the other aspects of criminal justice. Seeing policemen on the streets, hearing the testimony of witnesses in court, hearing the judge's solemn charge to the jury — all of these things might whet the appetite for revenge, and no doubt they often do. Should we then abolish policemen, testimony, and solemn charges? Moreover, not only can the love of justice be twisted toward the wrong, but every good impulse can be twisted toward it: love of country, love of family, compassion for those who suffer: The first may be distorted into fanaticism, the second into jingoism, the third into sentimentality. Even the love of God can be perverted, and when it is, it is a terrible thing indeed. Yet the fact that something right can be perverted does not stop it from being right.

The Cheapening of Life

This concern is closely associated with Joseph Cardinal Bernardin. As Cardinal Dulles paraphrases it, "By giving the impression that human beings sometimes have the right to kill, [capital punishment] fosters a casual attitude toward evils such as abortion, suicide, and euthanasia."[7] Not even Cardinal Dulles considers this argument strong. In particular, he observes that many earnest opponents of these other deeds are earnest supporters of capital punishment, for they realize

7. Dulles, McGinley Lecture.

that the rights of the guilty and innocent are not the same. The cardinal is quite right, and we can pair his observation with another. Many fervent *supporters* of these other deeds are also fervent *opponents* of capital punishment. The phenomenon is as common as it is strange. Perhaps it is a form of compensation; conscience demands its pay. Having approved the private execution of the weak and blameless, one now seeks absolution by denouncing the official execution of the strong and ruthless. Whether or not this explains it, two things at least are plain. First, it is *psychologically* possible to hold either of the following combinations of positions: That it is wrong to kill the innocent but may be right to kill the guilty, and that it is wrong to kill the guilty but may be right to kill the innocent. Second, the *normal moral reason* for upholding capital punishment is reverence for life itself. Indeed, this is the reason why Scripture and Christian tradition uphold it, a fact which suggests that if anything, it is the *abolition* of capital punishment which threatens to cheapen life.

Christ's Teaching on Forgiveness

It is true that Jesus taught to love those who hate us, forgive those who wrong us, and abstain from hypocritical comparisons between ourselves and those who offend us. These things we should do, however difficult they may be. But let us remember that the same Lord and God who commands his people to pardon their debtors also gave them Torah, which commands magistrates to call them to account. Cardinal Dulles speaks rightly when he says that "personal pardon does not absolve offenders from their obligations in justice." Indeed he considers this fourth objection "relatively weak" and "complex at best."[8] My only objection to these words is that they are too polite, for the supposition that personal forgiveness implies a requirement for universal amnesty is not merely weak, but mistaken. Taken seriously, it would destroy all public authority, for if punishment *as such* is incompatible with forgiveness, then why stop with capital punishment? Must we not abolish prisons, fines, and even reprimands as well?

I have heard it asked by fellow Christians, "How dare we play God? How dare we wrest into our own hands the divine prerogative of life and death?" It is a good question. My answer is that we dare not. We dare not wrest into our own hands *any* of the divine prerogatives of justice, whether the deprivation of life, of liberty, or of property. It is a dreadful matter to kill a man, but it is also dreadful to lock him in a hole, away from wife, children, parents, friends,

8. Dulles, McGinley Lecture.

120

and all that he held dear in life. It is a fearsome matter to imprison a man, but it is also fearsome to use fines and impoundments to confiscate his worldly goods, treasure which he may have accumulated by honest labor and counted on for the succor of his family and the support of his declining years. No, we dare not wrest into our hands any powers over our fellow men. But if God *puts* such powers into the hands of those who hold public authority — what then? Does this not alter the picture? How dare we jerk our hands away, hide them behind our backs, refuse the charge? For the teaching of Scripture is just as clear about public justice as it is about personal forgiveness, and the teaching of Christ is that "scripture cannot be annulled" (John 10:35). The magistrate is "sent," whether he knows it or not; he is "the servant of God to execute his wrath on the wrongdoer." Yes, we have seen that he is a servant of God's patience too, but the second charge does not obliterate the first. However tempered with mercy, public authority remains an augur or a portent of the wrath which will one day fall upon the unrepentant.

The story has another side as well. To remit deserved punishment too easily is a miscarriage not only of justice but of mercy. When a heart is very hard, it may sometimes be the case that deserved punishment is the only knock strong enough to break the husk and spill out the seeds of repentance. God himself is said to use this method: Those whom he loves, he chastens, even perhaps with the prospect of death. If we are to imitate his love, then we must sometimes imitate his chastening too.

Conclusion

Our brief review of the objections to capital punishment has left the interim conclusion unshaken.

1. In considering whether to grant clemency, the proper question is not whether juries ever err, but whether we have reasonable ground to think that *this* jury has erred in fact.
2. Any deserved punishment, indeed any element of justice, might whet the impulse for revenge. But when a good impulse is perverted, we should fight not the impulse but its perversion; and so with the impulse for justice.
3. Scripture and Christian tradition uphold capital punishment not in contempt for life but in reverence for it. It is *because* man is made in God's image that Torah decrees that whoever sheds the blood of man, by man shall his blood be shed.

4. Christ did teach personal forgiveness, but he never challenged the need for public justice. Official pardon rightly has conditions which personal forgiveness does not. Not only is punishment compatible with love, it is sometimes demanded by it as the only medicine strong enough to do the offender good.

Classically, the Church has held that the state has the authority to inflict capital punishment. It has also classically held that in certain cases a deserved punishment of death may be remitted, but the grounds for possible clemency are particular, not universal. Categorical remission of the penalty for all who deserve death contradicts revealed teaching on the duty of the magistrate and has no warrant in Christian tradition. It would weaken three of the four purposes of punishment, confuse the good counsels of compassion, and bring about more harm than good. What then of *Evangelium Vitae?* I accept the conclusion of John Paul II that "today," cases in which the death penalty are still necessary are "very rare, if not practically non-existent."[9] However, we must resist the tendency to exaggerate his conclusion by reading these six words as the single word "non-existent."

Some say that because there is a risk of error in both directions, we should prefer to err on the side of mercy. I agree. We should indeed prefer to err on the side of mercy, in individual cases. But to err *categorically* is no longer to make a mistake. It is to abdicate from judgment, and forsake our bounden duty.

9. Sec. 56.

7. Biblical Perspectives on the Death Penalty

MICHAEL L. WESTMORELAND-WHITE
AND GLEN H. STASSEN

Both advocates and opponents of capital punishment often use the Bible in a simplistic "prooftexting" fashion. This essay seeks to pay close attention to historical and literary contexts, and to check scriptural interpretations in light of the life, teachings, death and resurrection of Jesus Christ, which we take to be the hermeneutical Rosetta Stone for biblical interpretation.[1]

The Hebrew Scriptures and the Way of Deliverance

The Law Codes

Various authors have compiled lists ranging from fifteen to twenty-five different offenses that merit the death penalty in the Torah, or Pentateuch, the first five books of the Bible. They include:

---

1. Other interpretations of biblical teaching on capital punishment can be found in Stassen's essays in Glen Stassen and David Gushee, ed., *Kingdom Ethics: Following Jesus in Contemporary Context* (Downers Grove, Ill.: InterVarsity, 2003) and "Biblical Teaching and Capital Punishment," in Glen Stassen, ed., *Capital Punishment: A Reader* (Cleveland: Pilgrim Press, 1998). The very best study of justice and punishment from the perspective of careful New Testament exegesis is Christopher D. Marshall, *Beyond Retribution: A New Testament Vision for Justice, Crime, and Punishment* (Grand Rapids, Mich.: Eerdmans, 2001).

1. Anyone but the priests touching tabernacle furniture (Num. 1:51; 3:10, 38; 4:15; 18:7).
2. Priests drunk on duty (Lev. 10:8-11).
3. Blaspheming the Divine Name (Lev. 24:16).
4. Profaning the Sabbath (Exod. 31:14; 35:12).
5. False prophecy (Deut. 13:1ff.; 18:20).
6. Sacrifice to or worship of pagan gods (Exod. 20:1ff; 2:20; Deut. 13:1-19; 17:2-7).
7. Sorcery (Exod. 22:18; Lev. 20:6, 27).
8. Cursing either of one's parents (Exod. 21:17; Lev. 20:9).
9. Striking either of one's parents (Exod. 21:15).
10. Being an incorrigible son (Deut. 21:18ff.).
11. Murder (Exod. 21:12; Lev. 24:17; Num. 35:16ff.).
12. Kidnapping for ransom or to sell into slavery (Exod. 21:16; Deut. 24:7).
13. False testimony in a capital trial (Deut. 19:16-21).
14. Adultery (Lev. 20:10; Deut. 22:22ff.).
15. Male homosexual intercourse (Lev. 20:13).
16. Sexual intercourse during menstruation (Lev. 20:13).
17. Sexual intercourse between humans and animals (Exod. 22:19; Lev. 20:15-16).
18. Prostitution by a daughter still living in her father's house (Lev. 21:9; Deut. 22:13-21).
19. Rape (Deut. 22:25).
20. Ten other forbidden sexual relationships (Lev. 20:11-13, 17f., 19ff.).
21. Contempt for a court's decision (Deut. 17:8-13).
22. Keeping livestock known to be dangerous (Exod. 21:9).
23. Negligence resulting in loss of life (Exod. 21:8-9; Deut. 22:8).
24. Sacrificing one's child to Molech (Lev. 20:1-2).
25. A bride falsely claiming to be a virgin (Deut. 22:13-21).

Few Christian retentionists advocate the death penalty for all of the crimes carrying that penalty in the Torah. Most single out premeditated murder as the one crime continuing to merit death. What is not clear is their rationale for citing Mosaic Law when making this argument. Furthermore, all of the sources are found in the first five books of the Bible; none appears in the prophets, the writings, or the New Testament, which do not teach the death penalty.

Israel's law codes required that anyone accused of a capital offense could be convicted only on the basis of two or more eyewitnesses whose testimony must agree completely (Num. 35:30; Deut. 17:2-7; Deut. 19:15-20). This is more stringent than the modern American judicial system, which often convicts persons on circumstantial evidence alone. Several biblical scholars have argued that the overriding concern of enforcing the death penalty in these various laws is to maintain the "purity" or "holiness" of Israel as the people of God.[2] Various crimes in ancient Israel were viewed as so grave that they polluted the people and required some form of ritual cleansing or expiation in order to restore the people's holiness.[3] Leviticus 20:1-5 demands the death penalty for sacrificing one's child to the god Molech, defiling "my (i.e., God's) sanctuary and profaning my holy name."[4] Likewise, in verses 26-27, being a medium that consults with the dead or a wizard who works magic results in the death penalty: "You shall be holy to me; for I the LORD am holy, and I have separated you from the other peoples to be mine." The rest of the chapter is a series of regulations, where the same rationale is operative. In Deuteronomy 17:8-13, contempt for decisions of Israel's court results in the death penalty, with the explicit rationale that "you shall purge the evil." Purging is the language of ritual cleansing; this same wording is used to demand the death penalty for bearing false witness in a murder case (Deut. 19:16-21). Likewise, a daughter of a priest committing prostitution is said to "profane herself" (Lev. 21:9), rendering her unclean. She has to be killed so that she does not pollute the Israelite priesthood by marrying a priest.[5] James McBride argues persuasively that atonement by scapegoating is a major motivation behind the death penalty in present-day practice as well.[6] For Chris-

2. E.g., John E. Hartley, *Leviticus,* Word Biblical Commentary, vol. 4 (Dallas: Word Books, 1992), pp. lvi-lxiii, 63-72, 140-46; Martin Noth, *Leviticus,* Old Testament Library (Philadelphia: Westminster, 1965, 1977), pp. 144-57; Gary A. Anderson, "Introduction to Israelite Religion," in *The New Interpreter's Bible,* vol. 1, ed. Leander Keck (Nashville: Abingdon Press, 1994), pp. 280-83; Walter C. Kaiser, Jr., "The Book of Leviticus," in *The New Interpreter's Bible,* vol. 1, pp. 997-1000; John G. Gammie, *Holiness in Israel,* Overtures to Biblical Theology (Philadelphia: Fortress Press, 1989).

3. For the general sociological and anthropological investigation of this kind of thinking, see e.g., Mary Douglass, *Purity and Danger: An Analysis of the Concepts of Pollution and Taboo* (London: Routledge and Kegan Paul, 1966). Pages 41-58 deal specifically with "the abominations of Leviticus." René Girard, *Violence and the Sacred,* trans. Patrick Gregory (Baltimore: Johns Hopkins University Press, 1977), has developed a different anthropological explanatory model which various religious scholars, including biblical specialists, have found highly persuasive. Studies which show how the Bible participates in this worldview, yet ultimately overthrows the sanctioned violence of it include Raymond Schwager, S.J., *Must There Be Scapegoats?* trans. Maria L. Assad (San Francisco: Harper & Row, 1987); James G. Williams, *The Bible, Violence, and the Sacred: Liberation from the Myth of Sanctioned Violence* (San Francisco: Harper & Row, 1991).

4. Unless otherwise noted, all biblical quotations will be from the New Revised Standard Version.

5. Noth, *Leviticus,* p. 156.

6. James McBride in Stassen, ed., *Capital Punishment: A Reader,* pp. 182-204.

tians, for whom expiation has been accomplished once for all in Jesus Christ (Heb. 9:26ff.; 10:10), it would be blasphemous to argue that capital punishment is needed to atone for or expiate sin. That would deny the efficacy of Christ's expiatory death on the cross.

The Sixth Commandment

The Sixth Commandment (fifth in Catholic and Lutheran numbering) is "Thou shalt not kill" (Exod. 20:13; Deut. 5:17). Many translators render the text, "Thou shalt not murder." Yet, this is grammatically problematic. The Hebrew term used, *rasah*, is a general term for killing that is used at least once for capital punishment itself (Num. 35:30), and twice for accidental manslaughter (Deut. 4:41-43; Josh. 20:3). So in the history of Christian ethics the command has usually been given a much wider application, pertaining to many forms of killing, and not just murder. The Sixth Commandment by itself (in its original contexts) neither demands nor prohibits capital punishment.

Genesis 9:6

Most Christian retentionists rest their biblical case primarily on a single text, Genesis 9:6, which is structured as a chiasm (i.e., using an ABB'A' structure in which the second half is a mirror image of the first half):

A   "Whoever sheds the blood
 B   of a human,
 B'   by a human
A' will his blood be shed."[7]

Claus Westermann, who has written what is widely recognized as the most authoritative commentary on Genesis, explains that scholars do not

---

7. Authors' translation to show the chiastic order. The passage is equally well translated "will" or "shall." For retentionists basing their argument on this passage, see William H. Baker, *On Capital Punishment* (Chicago: Moody Press, 1973, 1985), chapter 4; John S. Feinberg and Paul D. Feinberg, *Ethics for a Brave New World* (Wheaton, Ill.: Crossway Books, 1993), pp. 143-47; H. Wayne House, "In Favor of the Death Penalty," in H. Wayne House and John Howard Yoder, *The Death Penalty Debate* (Waco, Tex.: Word, 1991), pp. 35-47; John Jefferson Davis, *Evangelical Ethics: Issues Facing the Church Today*, 2nd ed. (Phillipsburg, N.J.: Presbyterian and Reformed Publishing, 1993), pp. 179-80, 188.

agree whether Genesis 9:6 is a legal penalty, a prophetic admonition, or a proverb.[8] On the one hand, the passage shows the influence of ancient traditional laws of revenge; on the other hand, it is clearly formulated as a proverb and not as a law. As it stands in Genesis, the passage does not command the death penalty, but gives strong warning based on the likely consequence of one's action: if you kill, you will end up being killed. Westermann, in his commentary on Genesis, and Hagner, in his commentary on Matthew, say Jesus interprets the meaning of Genesis 9:6 in Matthew 26:52. Jesus clearly interprets it as a proverb, teaching "the generally true principle that violence begets violence."[9] Jesus' teaching is like Genesis 9:6 — both in chiastic order in the original biblical language — which indicates that Jesus is indeed repeating and showing the meaning of Genesis 9:6 as proverbial wisdom. Jesus says:

A   "For all
    B   who take a sword,
    B′   by a sword
A′   will die."

The text in Genesis 9:6 has very little pertinence to the question of the morality of capital punishment in modern legal systems. We cannot say, as most Christian retentionists do, that this is a divine mandate, part of the Noachic covenant and thus universally binding on all human societies.[10] First, this is not legislative language, nor is the context one of legislation. It is poetic recital: in Hebrew "man" *(adam)* and "blood" *(dam)* rhyme, and are related to each other etymologically. This verse offers wisdom, prediction, a description of the way things are in most ancient societies.[11]

Second, Genesis 9:1-7 constitutes a blessing as a prologue to God's covenant in verses 8-17. That covenant contains no requirements. It consists in God's promise to both humans and animals that the earth will never again be destroyed by flood, together with the sign of the rainbow as a symbol of God and reminder to the creatures of that divine promise.

Third, no mechanism is given for enacting the "mandate." The verses do not say who will shed the blood of the killers. No human government exists in the passage, simply one extended family. As other parts of the biblical writings show, Israelite readers would probably assume that the retribution would

8. Claus Westermann, *Genesis 1–11* (Minneapolis: Augsburg, 1984), p. 467.

9. Donald Hagner, *Matthew 14–28* (Waco, Tex.: Word, 1993), p. 789.

10. House, "In Favor," pp. 39-40; Feinberg and Feinberg, *Ethics*, p. 146; Baker, *On Capital Punishment*, pp. 31-37; Davis, *Ethics*, pp. 178, 179.

11. Yoder, "Against," in House and Yoder, p. 120.

be carried out by the "kinsman redeemer," a relative who would seek out and kill the killer. Seeing this verse as a "mandate" would not authorize state executions, but family-based vengeance that often escalated into long "blood-feuds." This we know to be contrary to Christian teachings.

Finally, Genesis 9:6 cannot be viewed as a universal mandate for capital punishment in modern societies unless one is willing to execute animals and accidental manslayers along with premeditated murderers. Since no distinction is given between adults and children, nor any allowance made for mental retardation, one would also have to be willing to execute minors and those mentally incapable of knowing good from evil.[12]

But most important for us is how Jesus interprets this passage — as a proverb, a prediction, not as a command, since he clearly teaches in Matthew 26:52 not to use a sword to kill.

This interpretation fits the fact that nowhere in the Old Testament do we see a case of what seem like prescriptions of the death penalty carried out by an Israelite criminal law system. The injunctions of death function more as declarations of the moral seriousness of these offenses than as binding criminal laws.[13]

The Lex Talionis

Some retentionists quote the rule "an eye for an eye, a tooth for a tooth," which scholars call the *lex talionis,* or "law of retaliation," as a primary justification for the death penalty. This rule is widely known in many ancient cultures, and is not unique to the biblical writings. In the Old Testament, it appears only three times, and never as a central part of Torah morality.

The first instance is Exodus 21:22-25, where it appears as an appendage to a case law. The law states that if two men are fighting and hit a pregnant woman, different penalties are to follow depending on the results — a monetary fine or life for life. The death penalty is imposed for an accidental killing; no distinction is made concerning motivation. In the following case (21:26-27), which protects slaves from abuse by masters, the penalty for the loss of the slave's eye or tooth is freedom for the slave. There is no suggestion of a removal of the master's eye or tooth.

12. Lewis Smedes underlines this problem very nicely. Smedes, *Mere Morality* (Grand Rapids, Mich.: Eerdmans, 1983), pp. 119-20.

13. Henry McKeating, "The Development of the Law on Homicide in Ancient Israel," *Vetus Testamentum* 25 (1975): 61-67; and McKeating, "Sanctions against Adultery in Ancient Israelite Society," *Journal for the Study of the Old Testament* 11 (1979): 58f. and 66f.

The second instance is Leviticus 24. A man of mixed Hebrew and Egyptian parentage is overheard cursing God. In verses 13-14 God tells the people through Moses to take the blasphemer outside the camp, to let all who heard the blasphemy lay hands on the culprit's head, and then have the people execute him by stoning. In verses 15-22, God gives general rules on such matters (with one set of laws for both resident aliens and Hebrew citizens) that include verse 19, "Anyone who maims another shall suffer the same injury in return: fracture for fracture, eye for eye, tooth for tooth; the injury inflicted is the injury to be suffered." Oddly, the specified penalty does not apply to the case at hand. The penalty for cursing God is stoning, not being cursed by God in turn.

The final occurrence is Deuteronomy 19:19-21, where the context is a trial and the rules of evidence demand two or three eyewitnesses whose stories all agree. In the case of a false witness, the *lex talionis* subjects the false witness to the penalty the accused would have received if found guilty. The language of purging the evil from your midst is invoked. Again, however, the penalty for false accusation is not being lied about in return, but the penalty intended for the accused.

In sum, the teaching seeks to satisfy the sense that punishment be appropriate and proportional to the crime, and is not meant as literal repetition of the crime. There is no command to lie to a liar, rape a rapist, or steal from a thief — a consistency that would be grotesque.[14] Further, the *lex talionis* is not a demand to force symmetrical justice on persons who would otherwise be inclined to be overly merciful, but rather limits escalating vengeance cycles. It is an important legal reform. It stops the escalating violence of Lamech's boast: "If Cain is avenged sevenfold, truly Lamech seventy-sevenfold" (Gen. 4:24).[15]

God's Actions toward Famous Biblical Murderers

The drama of Cain and Abel is the sad tale of the first murder. Notice the character of God displayed throughout this drama. God begins to intervene before the crisis is out of hand. He warns Cain of his danger, holding out hope that sin can be mastered. "[S]in is lurking at your door; its desire is for

14. Smedes, *Mere Morality*, p. 122.

15. John Howard Yoder, *The Christian and Capital Punishment* (Newton, Kans.: Faith and Life Press, 1961), pp. 6-7; John I. Durham, *Exodus* (Dallas: Word Publishing, 1987), p. 324; Nathaniel Micklem, "Exegesis of Leviticus," in *The Interpreter's Bible*, vol. II (Nashville: Abingdon, 1953), p. 119.

you, but you must master it." God's method of "crime prevention" focuses on correcting distorted relationships, taking transforming initiatives between brothers; not simply "laying down the law." Alas, Cain is mastered by his anger instead; he lures Abel to the fields and kills him (v. 8). After the crime has been committed, God continues to work for redemption, attempting to bring good out of evil. Cain is judged and punished, but God protects Cain, denying blood vengeance to others. God's answer to the first murder was neither a "liberal" excusing of Cain's actions, nor a "law and order" insistence that he be executed. God acted to punish in order that Cain would seek redemption. Should not the people of God act similarly in seeking to address violent crime and violent offenders?

In Moses, God's work of redemption bore better fruit than with Cain. The young Moses kills an Egyptian for beating a Hebrew (Exod. 2:1-12). Verse 12 depicts Moses' act of deliberate but unpremeditated murder. Realizing his danger, Moses flees to the desert (v. 15). Yet, in that desert, after some forty years of herding sheep, Moses comes face-to-face with God (unlike Cain who fled God's face). That encounter changes Moses and he becomes God's agent for Israel's redemption. A furtive murderer is transformed into a mighty leader for God, the human agent in the liberation and creation of God's covenant people. Surely Christians, who claim to be a part of God's new covenant people, should consider murderers with the redemptive possibilities of God firmly in mind. (As an aside, one of the authors knows a murderer who was spared the death sentence and is now devotedly and effectively counseling youth not to be violent.)

No biblical character so captivated the imagination of Israel as did King David.[16] Yet this model king in Israel's memory, the lens through which the messianic hope was envisioned, is also remembered as a murderer. With painful honesty the Bible records that David coerced the sexual favors of Bathsheba, wife of Uriah the Hittite, an officer in the king's army (2 Sam. 11–12:25). Then David arranged Uriah's death in battle. Through the prophet Nathan, God confronts David with his crime and leads him to pronounce sentence on himself: "The man deserves to die" (12:1-6). David repents and is forgiven (12:7-25) rather than killed. The consequences of David's sin are not annulled, but David is restored and allowed to continue to lead Israel.

How should we construe these stories of murderers pardoned and redeemed by God? Norman Geisler believes that they should be seen as exceptions of God's mercy that in no way qualify the normative character of God's

16. Walter Brueggemann, *David's Truth in Imagination and Memory* (Philadelphia: Fortress, 1985), p. 13.

retribution.[17] This misses the point that these narratives show God's dealing with murderers in ways that the Bible regards as revealing God's character. Repentance and renewal are possible precisely because God "is gracious and merciful, slow to anger and abounding in steadfast love" (Ps. 145:8). Jonah quotes these exact words to God when he claims that he fled to Tarshish precisely in order to keep God from sparing Nineveh (Jon. 4:1-3). This is what we, like Jonah, would expect from a God who spares the first murderer, and works redemptively with such onetime murderers as Moses and David. Contra Geisler, redemptive and merciful treatment of murderers, while still upholding justice, seems characteristic of God. This subverts the natural tendency of humans to look for retributive justice.

The New Testament and the Way of Jesus

The Sermon on the Mount

The Sermon on the Mount is the largest selection of Jesus' teachings contained in the New Testament. Four teachings in the Sermon shed much light on our subject, and have been used frequently in the death penalty debate. The first teaching is Matthew 5:17-20:

> Do not think that I have come to abolish the law or the prophets; I have come not to abolish but to fulfill. For truly I tell you, until heaven and earth pass away, not one letter, not one stroke of a letter, will pass from the law until all is accomplished. . . . For I tell you, unless your righteousness exceeds that of the scribes and Pharisees, you will never enter the kingdom of heaven.

Christian retentionists have used these verses to claim that the Torah is still in effect, and thus, that we must continue to execute murderers in order to be faithful to our Lord's words.[18] Therefore, they claim, Jesus will teach nothing new or different from what they have interpreted to be the meaning of the first five books of the Bible. However, such a reading of this passage would demand the continuing validity of the entire Torah, including all of the fifteen-to-twenty-five crimes demanding capital punishment. Employing this text so legalistically produces too much, including the Christian retention of Israelite dietary laws.

---

17. Geisler, *Ethics: Issues and Options* (Grand Rapids, Mich.: Zondervan, 1971), pp. 242-43.
18. E.g., Baker, *On Capital Punishment*, p. 4; Geisler, *Ethics*, p. 241.

In Matthew 15:14-20, Jesus radically relativizes all of the Mosaic food laws with his teaching that impurity comes from within a person, not from externals (like food). As the parallel passage, Mark 7:19, "Thus, he declared all foods clean," makes clear, the early Church abandoned Jewish food regulations. In Mark 7:20-23, Jesus explicitly gives a new moral definition of purity that accords with Isaiah 56 and other Isaiah passages.

A second passage of the Sermon on the Mount that is directly relevant to the death penalty is Matthew 5:21-26. It has a threefold or triadic form:

1. You have heard that it was said to those of ancient times, "You shall not murder"; and "whoever murders shall be liable to judgment."
2. But I say to you that if you are angry with a brother or sister, you will be liable to judgment; and if you insult a brother or sister, you will be liable to the council; and if you say, "You fool," you will be liable to the hell of fire.
3. So, when you are offering your gift at the altar, if you remember that your brother or sister has something against you, *leave* your gift on the altar and *go;* first *be reconciled* to your brother or sister, and then *come and offer* your gift. *Come to terms quickly* with your accuser while you are on your way to court.

The first part of the triad states the traditional teaching, "You shall not murder," and "whoever murders shall be liable to judgment." The second part names and diagnoses the vicious cycle that places us in systems in which we sin. Some incorrectly understand this as the "hard teachings" of Jesus' new command, but there are no imperatives here. Jesus does not command us not to be angry, but rather to make peace if and when we are angry. There are five imperatives in the third part, marked above with italics. Notice that they are "transforming initiatives" which lead us out of sin, change our character and habits, and potentially change much else, including institutional structures and relations with nonbelievers.[19] They are not "hard teachings," but are the way of deliverance from the vicious cycles of sin.

It is interesting that Jesus uses the term "brother" (made inclusive in the NRSV) in this passage. Does it not remind his hearers of the destructive sibling rivalry of Cain and Abel and all who followed them? This teaching is about murder; Cain's killing of his brother was the first murder. It is about causes of murder: anger, hostile name-calling, accusation and enmity; Cain was angry at

19. Stassen, *Just Peacemaking: Transforming Initiatives for Justice and Peace* (Louisville: Westminster/John Knox, 1993), pp. 33-52; Stassen, "The Fourteen Triads of the Sermon on the Mount," *Journal of Biblical Literature* (Summer 2003): 267-308.

his brother. It is about a brother offering a gift to God in worship; Cain was doing exactly that. Cain nursed anger against Abel, despite God's warning, and murder was the result. As God called Cain to do what is right, Jesus teaches clearly what it is to do right: engage in practices of reconciliation that break out of cycles of rivalry-jealousy-bitterness-hatred-violence. This is the pattern of working to redeem people who are headed for destruction that characterizes God's work in Jesus, who came to us to make peace where there is separation. The Son of God enfleshed the very pattern of redemption that he taught us.

Matthew 5:38-42 teaches similarly: do not retaliate, as in an eye for an eye and a life for a life, but take initiatives to transform the relationship of hostility into one of peace. The first part is the traditional teaching: "an eye for an eye and a tooth for a tooth." It is significant that Jesus quotes the traditional teaching concerning the eye and the tooth, but does not quote "life for life." He avoids quoting the part of the teaching that implies the death penalty. Similarly, in 5:21, Jesus quotes the prohibition of murder in the Ten Commandments, where no penalty is named. In all his teachings, he never quotes an Old Testament passage that calls for the death penalty or any other form of killing.

Many believe the second part of this teaching, Matthew 5:39, teaches nonresistance to evil, but the evidence is clear that this is a mistranslation. The mistranslation has led death penalty advocates to resist the teaching by suggesting it applies only to interpersonal encounters between Christians, thus making Jesus' teachings here irrelevant to the death penalty discussion. Since almost all relationships in life involve responsibility to more than one other person, this marginalizes the lordship of Jesus to a very small part of life. Nowhere in the New Testament does Jesus limit his teaching or his lordship only to individual relationships. That would contradict biblical monotheism, in which God is Lord over all and is revealed in Christ. An insight from Clarence Jordan can help us understand the teaching accurately. Jordan's insightful grammatical observation points out that "evil" in Matthew 5:39 is translated from the Greek word *ponero*. The translation can be either the instrumental "do not retaliate by evil means," or the dative "do not retaliate against an evildoer." The context determines the meaning. Jesus resisted evildoers throughout the Gospels, so it makes no sense for him to say, "do not resist an evildoer." But he never resisted evildoers by employing evil means. So the context indicates the correct translation: "Do not retaliate by evil means."[20] New Testa-

20. John Ferguson, *Politics of Love* (Cambridge: James Clarke & Co., 2000), pp. 4f.; Donald Hagner, *Matthew 1–13*, pp. 130f.; Pinchas Lapide, *Sermon on the Mount* (Maryknoll, N.Y.: Orbis, 1986), p. 134; and Willard Swartley, "War and Peace in the NT," in *Aufstieg und Niedergang der römischen Welt*, II.26.3, ed. Wolfgang Haase, p. 2338, argue similarly to Jordan.

ment scholar Walter Wink has provided additional evidence. The word here translated "resist" in verse 39 is the Greek word *antistenai*. This Greek word is used in the Greek translation of the Hebrew Scriptures (the Septuagint), and in the Greek sources of the time, usually to mean "revenge or armed resistance in military encounters." Therefore, combining the insights of Jordan and Wink, the verse should be translated: "Do not retaliate or resist violently or re-vengefully, by evil means."[21] This is how the apostle Paul reports the teaching in Romans 12:17ff.: "Do not repay anyone evil for evil. . . . Beloved, never avenge yourselves, but leave room for the wrath of God. . . . Do not overcome evil by evil means, but overcome evil with good." Paul also commands trans-forming initiatives of peacemaking: "If your enemies are hungry, feed them; if they are thirsty, give them something to drink." The teaching is also echoed in Luke 6:27-36; 1 Thessalonians 5:15; 1 Peter 2:21-23; and Didache 1:4-5. Not one of these passages refers to an evil person; not one of them speaks of not resisting evil; not one of them speaks of renouncing rights in a court of law. The pas-sages, to a one, teach against retaliation and emphasize the transforming ini-tiatives of returning good and not evil, of using good means and not evil means in order to overcome evil. The evidence is conclusive: Matthew 5:39 is not an impossible ideal of non-resistance to evil, but a naming of the vicious cycle of retaliation by violent, revengeful means — the "vicious cycle" that un-leashes the spiral of violence.

The third part of the teaching, Matthew 5:39b-42, is the transforming initiative: turn the other cheek, give your cloak, go the second mile, give to the beggar. These are nonviolent actions which seek to restrain violence and thwart retaliation. Wink calls these refrains "Jesus' third way."[22] We call them "transforming initiatives." They catch the adversary off-guard, not only con-fronting her or his unjust actions, but opening the way for reconciliation.[23] In sum: Jesus is teaching about retaliation — an eye for an eye. He teaches not to retaliate, but to take initiatives of deliverance. These are initiatives that partic-ipate in God's way of deliverance from vicious cycles of evil. Followers of Je-sus are to engage in practices that seek to break cycles of vengeance.

In Matthew 5:43-48, we see the same triadic pattern of breaking destruc-tive cycles of vengeance. (1) The traditional teaching, "You have heard it said, 'Love your neighbor and hate your enemy,'" is not a quotation from the Old

21. Wink, "Beyond Just War and Pacifism: Jesus' Nonviolent Way," *Review and Expositor* 89:2 (Spring 1992): 199.

22. Wink, "Beyond Just War," pp. 199-207, describes the concrete social settings of such counter-practices, without which they appear to us to be a "doormat strategy" that Jesus did not intend.

23. Stassen, *Just Peacemaking*, pp. 63-70.

Testament, nor the rabbinic writings, but from Qumran (1QS 1:10-11). (2) The vicious cycle is loving only those who love you and greeting only your brothers and sisters (i.e., fellow Jews). (3) The imperative, "love your enemies and pray for your persecutors" (Matt. 5:44), transforms the bondage of limiting love only to one's own community while hating outsiders that has led to devastating human conflict throughout history. If we are children of our heavenly Father, then we will love enemies and pray for persecutors as he sends sun and rain on the just and unjust alike. The further imperative, "Be *teleios* as your heavenly Father is *teleios*" (Matt. 5:48), should probably be translated "be whole," or "be complete" rather than "be perfect." That is, we are to be complete in our love, including all in that love just as God is complete in giving rain and sunshine to God's enemies. Thus the parallel teaching in Luke 6:36 says to be compassionate or merciful, as God is. People who regularly emulate the merciful, compassionate character of God have moral characters that are highly suspicious of executing societal enemies. Criminals, even murderers, are persons whom Christians are commanded to love and pray for, working for their redemption.

John 7:53–8:11

There was no question in this passage of the woman's guilt of a crime — adultery — that the Mosaic law says deserves the death penalty. Jesus was being confronted with a test: If he forbade her execution they could claim that he denied the Torah. Christian ethicist Henlee Barnette rightly says that Jesus' adversaries would not have brought the woman to him unless they already suspected that he would not approve of executing her.[24] Jesus' answer, "Let the one of you without sin cast the first stone" (John 8:7b), radically undermines Christian support for capital punishment. He teaches that only the sinless are morally qualified to execute others.

We see once again the biblical pattern of God working to bring good out of cycles of sin. Jesus does not imply that adultery is not sinful; he tells the woman to "sin no more." Yet Jesus forgives her, and confronts her would-be executioners with their own self-righteousness.

Retentionists have claimed that Jesus was not speaking about absolute sinlessness, but referring only to the scribes and Pharisees' guilt in failing to bring the man, too (Deut. 22:22-24), or failing to bring the witnesses.[25] If they

24. Henlee H. Barnette, *Crucial Problems in Christian Perspective* (Philadelphia: Westminster, 1970), p. 129.
25. Davis, *Evangelical Ethics*, p. 182; Feinberg and Feinberg, *Ethics*, pp. 142-43.

had brought the man or the witnesses, according to the retentionists, Jesus would have said, "Go ahead and stone them both to death." However, nothing about the passage indicates such a restricted attitude.[26] Jesus says nothing about the need to stone the man, and nothing about the guilt of the scribes and Pharisees being failure to bring the man. Consistently in his confrontations with the scribes and Pharisees, he criticizes them for their hardheartedness, their excluding those they consider outcasts from the community, their violence and lack of compassion. Nowhere does he criticize them for not stoning enough people, or not being hardhearted enough to sinners. Had Jesus said "Bring the man, too, and go ahead and stone them both to death," we would be shocked. We would recognize it as completely out of character of our Lord who commanded us to "be merciful as your heavenly Father is merciful."

The Crucifixion of Jesus

Christians have the odd distinction of claiming to worship and follow one who was tried and convicted as a criminal and executed by the ruling authorities of the day. Christians, of course, contend that Jesus' series of trials before the Sanhedrin, Herod, and Pilate were unjust. Jesus was innocent of the contrived charges of threatening the temple and preaching sedition against Rome. Further, his admission to being the Son of God was not blasphemy because it was true.[27]

Christ's crucifixion should bias Christians against capital punishment. We follow one who was executed unjustly by legally sanctioned state violence. Every time we contemplate Christ's cross, or partake of the Lord's Supper, we are reminded that the death penalty allows the legal execution of innocent persons.[28] We should be biased against executing criminals, since our Lord was executed as one (Luke 22:37).

---

26. Claus Rengstorf, *"Anamartetos,"* in *Theological Dictionary of the New Testament,* vol. 1, ed. Gerhard Kittel (Grand Rapids, Mich.: Eerdmans, 1964), pp. 333-35, does not suggest that *anamartetos* can mean "without fault in the particulars of this case." Instead, in John 8:7 general sinlessness is implied. See also George R. Beasley-Murray, *John* (Dallas: Word, 1987), pp. 146-47; Yoder, *The Christian,* p. 4.

27. E.g., Martin Hengel, *Crucifixion* (Philadelphia: Fortress, 1977), pp. 33-50; Jürgen Moltmann, *The Crucified God* (San Francisco: Harper & Row, 1974), pp. 126-59; Richard A. Horsely, *Jesus and the Spiral of Violence: Popular Jewish Resistance in Roman Palestine* (San Francisco: Harper & Row, 1987), pp. 160-63.

28. So also Vernon W. Redekop, *A Life for a Life? The Death Penalty on Trial,* Peace and Justice Series 9 (Scottdale, Pa.: Herald, 1990), pp. 48-49.

Romans 13:1-7

Retentionists give more weight to Romans 13:1-7 than any other passage save Genesis 9:6. Here, they claim, the apostle Paul expressly validates government's right and duty to punish evildoers, even by lethal means.[29] The passage has been used in Christian history in ways that few find comfortable in this post-Holocaust era. German Christians under Hitler used it to support their cooperation with the state, in spite of the enormous injustices of that state. If we deny such authoritarian claims for this text, then we must be cautious about using it to argue for the rightness of the death penalty, something not even mentioned in the passage.

The most thorough study of the historical context of the passage by the German New Testament scholars Johannes Friedrich, Wolfgang Pöhlmann, and Peter Stuhlmacher says the first five verses are Paul's borrowings from common teachings in the Jewish and Roman culture to remind them of the widespread understanding that we need governments and should generally obey them. Nothing specifically Christian — such as Christ, grace, redemption, faith, love — is mentioned in these verses. Paul gets to his own language and the point he is driving at in verses 6-11, when he instructs Christians to pay their taxes. A few years previously there had been a tax revolt, which resulted in Christians like Priscilla and Aquila being kicked out of Rome, and now a new tax revolt was brewing under Nero. Paul's point is that we should not make insurrection, but pay our taxes: "Pay to all what is due them — taxes to whom taxes are due, revenue to whom revenue is due. . . . Owe no one anything except . . . love." Here is the Christian language and the point — pay your taxes. The sword that is mentioned in verse 4 is not the kind used in executions, but the kind worn by the policeman who accompanied tax collectors. The Greek word for "pay" or "render" dues in 13:7 is the same word Jesus uses in Luke 20:25, "render" to Caesar the taxes that are due. Paul is echoing Jesus: pay your taxes to Caesar. He is surely not echoing a teaching of Jesus that the sword should be used to kill people, since there is no such teaching of Jesus. The point of the passage is clearly to pay your taxes and not make a revolt, and has nothing to do with capital punishment.[30]

29. Davis, *Evangelical Ethics*, pp. 182-83; Feinberg and Feinberg, *Ethics*, pp. 139-40, 145; House, "In Favor," pp. 67-69; Baker, *On Capital Punishment*, pp. 64-69; Geisler, *Ethics*, p. 241. See also Antonin Scalia's essay in this volume.

30. Johannes Friedrich, Wolfgang Pöhlmann, and Peter Stuhlmacher, "Zur historischen Situation und Intention von Röm 13,1-7," *Zeitschrift für Theologie und Kirche* 73 (1976): 131-66; Klaus Wengst, *The Pax Romana and the Peace of Jesus Christ* (Philadelphia: Fortress, 1987), p. 82.

Conclusion

Christians who argue biblically for the death penalty base their arguments mostly on Genesis 9:6 and Romans 13 and argue that Jesus teaches nothing relevant or nothing new. Bypassing Jesus in this way is a historical hangover from the Middle Ages, when the church advocated putting heretics to death and ceased basing its teaching on the way of Jesus, adopting other rationalizations instead.[31] To argue that Jesus teaches nothing new, so that our obligation depends on a pro–death penalty interpretation of a verse from outside Jesus' teaching rather than anything Jesus said, seems systematically to block out the word of God that comes from Jesus. We have shown that these passages do not say what retentionists claim and that Jesus' teachings concerning these passages contradict what retentionists claim.

Christians who argue biblically against the death penalty usually base their arguments on the teachings and the cross of Christ. We believe this is right: Christian ethics needs to recover its basis in Christ as fully Lord and Savior. The recovery of ethics based on the way of Jesus is more prevalent now than it was in the Middle Ages, and this is one reason why almost every recent church pronouncement on the death penalty opposes it.[32]

31. James Megivern, *The Death Penalty: An Historical and Theological Survey* (New York: Paulist, 1997).

32. J. Gordon Melton, *The Churches Speak on Capital Punishment* (Detroit: Gale Research, 1989).

8. Christian Witness, Moral Anthropology, and the Death Penalty

RICHARD W. GARNETT

In this age of toleration, [no one] will ever try actively to interfere with our religious faith, provided we enjoy it quietly with our friends and do not make a public nuisance of it[.]

William James
The Will to Believe

Without witness, there is no argument.

Stanley Hauerwas
With the Grain of the Universe

"Are human beings different from meat?" A recent book review opens with the complaint that this is "[a]n example of the worst type of modern philosophical question"; a question that, "[f]or those among us who have never been invited into Socratic dialogue by, say, a porterhouse, . . . is dumb in ways

I am grateful to Robert Burt, Fr. John Coughlin, Rebecca D'arcy, Gilbert Meilaender, and Jay Tidmarsh for their comments and suggestions. I have addressed elsewhere several of the themes and points raised in this essay. See Richard W. Garnett, "Sectarian Reflections on Lawyers' Ethics and Death Row Volunteers," *Notre Dame Law Review* 77 (2002): 795; Richard W. Garnett, "A Quiet Faith? Taxes, Politics, and the Privatization of Religion," *Boston College Law Review* 42 (2001): 771.

rarely thought possible before."[1] The reviewer is right, of course — the question *is* "dumb." Then again, we might wonder if this "worst kind" question is really all that different from the psalmist's own: "Lord, what is man . . . that thou makest account of him?" (Ps. 143:3). The question, it turns out, is both perennial and profound: "What is a human being, and why and how does it matter?"

Now, because my contribution to this volume has been billed as a "theological" reflection on the death penalty, I should emphasize at the outset that I am not a "theologian." I am a Christian layman, lawyer, and law-teacher with, I suppose, some expertise in the areas of criminal justice and "law and religion." That said, my aim in this essay is to offer an answer — a Christian answer, I hope — to one of the several provocative questions posed by this symposium's hosts: "What role ought religious beliefs play in a pluralistic democratic society that often presumes strict boundaries between matters of private faith and political life?" More particularly, what should Christians *say* who are engaged in dialogue and debate with our fellow citizens in the public square of civil society? In Professor Jean Bethke Elshtain's words, "how should we talk?"[2]

Let me start where I want to end: I will argue, *first,* that we should resist, as distorting and even dishonest, the imposition of "strict boundaries" between "matters of private faith and political life"; and, *second,* that in the context of our public arguments about capital punishment, the task for faithful believers is not merely to baptize the policy analyses and preferences of abolitionist or other interest groups, but rather to bear authentic Christian witness to what Pope John Paul II has called the "moral truth about the human person."[3] To be sure, I will ask more questions than I answer, and I will offer not so much a resolution of, as a framework for, the death penalty debate. What is needed, I submit, is an "anthropological" argument about who we are, and why it matters. What is missing from the conversation, and what Christians can and should supply is not more data, but a different and better vocabulary. What our fellow citizens need to hear, and what is perfectly appropriate for us to offer, are distinctively Christian claims about the dignity and destiny of every person, and about why it might therefore be wrong to execute even those who have so cruelly wronged others.

1. Matthew Rose, "Things Fall Apart," *Weekly Standard,* 17 June 2002, p. 39 (reviewing John Lukacs, *At the End of an Age*).

2. Jean Bethke Elshtain, "How Should We Talk?" *Case Western Reserve Law Review* 49 (1999): 741.

3. John Paul II, *Ad Limina* "Address to the Bishops of Texas, Oklahoma, and Arkansas," *Origins* 28 (1998): 283. (The address was delivered 6 June 1998.)

Moral Anthropology

I believe that moral problems — and the death penalty poses, inescapably, such a problem — are *anthropological* problems, because moral arguments are built, for the most part, on *anthropological* presuppositions.[4] In other words, as one scholar put it, our attempts at moral judgment tend to reflect our "foundational assumptions about what it means to be human."[5] And these assumptions matter. If they are untruthful, there is little reason for confidence in the analysis that follows, or for surprise at unsound conclusions. My teacher and colleague Thomas Shaffer got it right: "Ethics" — or, "thinking about morals" — "is valid only to the extent that it truthfully describes what is going on."[6]

It strikes me that there is a crying need for anthropological truth-telling in the context of what passes today for public moral argument on the death penalty and similarly weighty matters. And my claim here is that religious believers not only may, but must, contribute what Shaffer might call a truthful description of "what is going on" to the public dialogue about capital punishment. We are called today to argue with our fellows about human nature, to provide our political communities what Cardinal Wojtyla of Krakow called a "kind of 'recapitulation' of the inviolable mystery of the person."[7] But not only to argue. I am convinced by Stanley Hauerwas's recently published Gifford Lectures that, in the end, "Christian argument rests on witness."[8] Indeed, "the life of the Christian cannot avoid becoming the life of a witness" — a witness, in this context, to the truth about who we are and why it matters.[9]

---

4. Jean Bethke Elshtain, "The Dignity of the Human Person and *The Idea of Human Rights: Four Inquiries," Journal of Law and Religion* 14 (1999-2000): 53.

5. Rev. John J. Coughlin, "Law and Theology: Reflections on What It Means to Be Human," *St. John's Law Review* 74 (2000): 609. Coughlin notes the "perennial nature" of the "anthropological question": "What does it mean to be a human being?"

6. "The norm of Christian social ethics is the obligation to see and speak truthfully." Thomas L. Shaffer, "The Legal Ethics of Radical Individualism," *Texas Law Review* 65 (1987): 965. See also H. Jefferson Powell, *The Moral Tradition of American Constitutionalism: A Theological Interpretation* (Durham, N.C.: Duke University Press, 1993), p. 264.

7. Letter from Cardinal Wojtyla to Henri de Lubac, quoted in George Weigel, "John Paul II and the Crisis of Humanism," in Richard John Neuhaus, ed., *The Second One Thousand Years: Ten People Who Defined a Millennium* (Grand Rapids, Mich.: Eerdmans, 2001), p. 116.

8. Stanley Hauerwas, *With the Grain of the Universe: The Church's Witness and Natural Theology* (London: SCM Press, 2002), p. 210. This argument is reinforced in Hauerwas's contribution to this volume; see Chapter 4.

9. Hauerwas, *With the Grain of the Universe*, pp. 229, 194. "[T]he truthfulness of Christian speech about God," he writes, "is a matter of truthful witness" (p. 194).

This might sound, I admit, like theology, not politics, policy, or law. But I understand Hauerwas's point to be that Christian theology, revealed by God and rightly understood, "makes claims on persons' lives"; true, Christian theology "begins with God," but in so doing, "it tells humans who they are and how they should be."[10] And, I submit, the moral anthropology that attends Christian theology "makes claims" as well on our arguments about capital punishment.

Of course, by framing the death-penalty problem in terms of moral anthropology — and "moral anthropology" is used here to mean *an account of what it is about the human person that does the work in moral arguments about what we ought or ought not to do and about how we ought or ought not to be treated*[11] — I do not mean to deny that the imposition of the death penalty raises a wide variety of challenging, provocative, important, and perhaps more practical questions. For example, does the death penalty deter crime? If so, do the "costs" of capital punishment justify its deterrence "benefits"? How much confidence should we have in the accuracy of the results of capital trials, and how might we increase that confidence? How much appellate and post-conviction review is necessary, appropriate, and feasible in capital cases? To what extent, if at all, should American constitutional and criminal law relating to the death penalty reflect developments in international law, and in the domestic laws of other countries? Are death-eligible defendants provided with adequate legal representation? Do prosecutors and jurors discriminate on the basis of race or sex in the imposition of the death penalty? Does the United States Constitution require that juries, not judges, make the decision for death,[12] or that some convicted murderers — say, those with severe developmental disabilities or teenagers — be exempted categorically from execution?[13] And so on.

10. Hauerwas, *With the Grain of the Universe*, p. 205.

11. Michael Perry, for example, argues that because "every human being is sacred," there are "some things that ought never . . . to be done to any human being." Michael J. Perry, *The Idea of Human Rights: Four Inquiries* (New York: Oxford University Press, 1998), p. 7. There are, I realize, other ways to use this term. See, e.g., Ronald Dworkin, "Darwin's New Bulldog," *Harvard Law Review* 111 (1998): 1719, where "moral anthropology" means the examination of "[w]hat best explains how human beings developed the disposition to make judgments of moral right and wrong."

12. See *Ring v. Arizona*, 536 U.S. 584, 122 S.Ct. 2428 (2002), in which the Sixth Amendment's jury-trial guarantee requires that juries, not judges, find facts legally necessary for the imposition of a death sentence.

13. See *Atkins v. Virginia*, 536 U.S. 304, 122 S.Ct. 2242 (2002), in which execution of "mentally retarded" offenders violates the Eighth Amendment's ban on "cruel and unusual" punishments.

Even this quick survey of the debate's landscape confirms that the disputants' attention is focused more on these issues than on abstract questions of moral anthropology. And certainly, these and other constitutional, empirical, administrative, and even fiscal problems deserve and require careful attention, thoughtful consideration, and even our engaged activism. The questions, and their answers, matter. (It would be strange if I thought otherwise, given that I teach courses in criminal law and have a client who until recently sat on death row but who was resentenced to life in prison.) Still, this volume aspires to serve as more than (yet) another policy-oriented "white paper." It purports instead to be the response of a group of faithful believers and engaged citizens to a "Call for Reckoning," a call that presumes and is intended to mine the "resources" — the "unique standpoints and important reflective dimensions" — that "religious voices" can and should provide to neighbors, voters, legislators, and civil society.[14] And so, what is asked of us, and what is needed from us, is not merely a "faith-based" echo of others' proposals and prescriptions, but something distinctive, authentic, unsettling, and even radical.[15]

Now, this is not to claim that faithful witness requires imprudence. We have, in any event, no guarantee, of course, that our neighbors and leaders will like what they hear; or that they will listen at all.[16] Still, what our public square needs, and what I believe in the death-penalty context is required of us, is a countercultural argument — a Story, perhaps[17] — about the dignity and destiny of the human person, "the noblest work of God — infinitely valuable, relentlessly unique, endlessly interesting."[18] As I explain in more de-

14. See the Introduction to this volume, as well as the "conference overview" for "A Call for Reckoning: Religion and the Death Penalty," available at http://pewforum.org/deathpenalty.

15. H. Jefferson Powell, for example, writes that "Christian theology . . . provides an intellectual and moral basis for a social criticism of American . . . law and politics that is both more radical and more truthful than that based upon secular leftist ideologies." Powell, *The Moral Tradition of American Constitutionalism*, p. 262 n. 10.

16. As Stanley Hauerwas has written, "I cannot help but appear impolite, since I must maintain that the God who moves the sun and the stars is the same God who was incarnate in Jesus of Nazareth. Given the politics of modernity, the humility required for those who worship the God revealed in the cross and resurrection of Christ cannot help but appear as arrogance." Hauerwas, *With the Grain of the Universe*, p. 16.

17. See Steven D. Smith, "The 'Secular,' the 'Religious,' and the 'Moral': What Are We Talking About?" *Wake Forest Law Review* 36 (2001): 498 (observing that many people believe that "this world and this life are part of an overarching Story" and that this Story is what provides the answer to the Socratic question, "How should I live?"); and Hauerwas, *With the Grain of the Universe*, p. 215 (observing that "Christianity is not a 'position,' just another set of beliefs, but a story").

18. Thomas L. Shaffer, "Human Nature and Moral Responsibility in Lawyer-Client Relationships," *American Journal of Jurisprudence* 40 (1995): 2.

tail below, I am convinced that we can best help our fellow citizens reach the right conclusion about what to do with convicted murderers not so much by sprinkling the usual policy arguments with God-talk as by challenging our culture to understand who these condemned persons *are*, what they were made to be, and why it should make a difference.

Religious Witness in the Public Square

I teach, study, and write about crime, punishment, and religious freedom at Notre Dame Law School. Ours is a relatively close-knit community, with a still-real sense of Christian mission. At the heart of that mission is inviting and (we hope) inspiring young lawyers to bring their faith with them to their studies, and then to carry it away with them into their lives in the law. Our view is that we should not expect young lawyers to think well about crime and punishment; about retribution, forgiveness, abuse of power, and the common good; about their clients' despair, fear, contrition, and hope; or about corruption, redemption, damnation, and beatitude, if we tell them to wall off their faith from their practices like a dangerous intruder or an unwelcome eccentric. We are encouraged to challenge our students with the suggestion that any purported resolution of a legal, moral, or public policy question that requires lawyers or citizens who are religious believers to hamstring their deliberations by dis-integrating their lives is really no resolution at all.

This volume, then, presents a welcome opportunity to reflect on the challenge that I pose regularly to myself and to my students of integrating our professional, political, intellectual, and religious lives. After all, it is the shared aim of the Pew Forum on Religion and Public Life, and of each of the contributors to this volume, to explore and encourage precisely this kind of integration. This shared aim proceeds, I suspect, from a shared premise: namely, the proposition that the claims, arguments, and expression of religious believers and communities not only have a place and a role in the "public square" of civil society, but are properly directed at its transformation.

We should recall at the outset, though, that this foundational premise cannot — at least, not in the context of contemporary elite opinion — be treated as given, or taken for granted. That religious believers should be speaking at all is, it turns out, hardly less contested than the substance of what we are called to say. After all, John Rawls became one of the most influential political philosophers of the twentieth century in no small part by making the case that public arguments must sound in "public reason" alone.[19] Religion and religious conviction, on the other hand, "are purely private matters that have no role or place" in the political arena.[20] Richard Rorty, another of our leading public intellectuals, put the matter more bluntly: in his view, what we are about in this volume is not civic-minded, but *gauche;* and it is not public-spirited, but in "bad taste to bring religion into discussions of public policy."[21] This is because for Rorty, as Stephen Carter memorably put it, religion is "like building model airplanes, just another hobby: something quiet, something trivial — not really a fit activity for intelligent . . . adults."[22]

Nor can these criticisms of religious expression be brushed aside as the views of a few ivory-tower luminaries; only a glance through the letters to newspaper editors or the Sunday morning talk shows is needed to confirm that such opinions are deeply rooted in both the popular culture and in the commentariat. Alan Wolfe's recent work would seem to confirm that contemporary Americans respect, value, and even cherish religious faith, but only so long as it stays in its place, and remains personal, private, and "non-judgmental."[23] It appears to be broadly — if not deeply — accepted that religious faith really is something that can be privatized, and cordoned off from civic and public life; and also that such a separation is somehow consistent with, if not required by, American constitutional law and the political morality of liberal democracy.

It is against this backdrop that a generation of writers and thinkers — lawyers and legal scholars in particular — have wrestled with the "religion in the public square" question, and with the extent to which the contemporary liberal state, or a modern constitutional democracy, can, may, and should allow religiously grounded arguments and expression in the public square of

19. In *Political Liberalism,* for example, Rawls defends an ethos of "public reason" that requires, *inter alia,* that arguments about public policy be couched in terms that are "accessible" to all citizens and that do not presuppose adherence to any religion or other "comprehensive" philosophy. John Rawls, *Political Liberalism* (New York: Columbia University Press, 1993), pp. 212-54.

20. William Marshall, "The Other Side of Religion," *Hastings Law Journal* 44 (1993): 844.

21. Richard Rorty, "Religion as Conversation-Stopper," *Common Knowledge* 3 (1994): 2.

22. Stephen L. Carter, *The Culture of Disbelief: How American Law and Politics Trivialize Religious Devotion* (New York: Basic Books, 1993), p. 22.

23. See generally Alan Wolfe, *One Nation, After All* (New York: Viking, 1998). In "How Should We Talk?" (pp. 743-44) Jean Bethke Elshtain argues that "Wolfe's middle-class respondents begin by viewing religion as a private matter to be discussed only reluctantly, a position that already cuts rather dramatically against the American grain. . . . The general view is this: If I am quiet about what I believe and everybody else is quiet about what he or she believes, then nobody interferes with the rights of anybody else."

civil society. Almost all of the leading lights have weighed in, and the conversation shows few signs of flagging.[24] I could not possibly do justice here either to the richness of the debate itself or to the care with which the participants have honed their arguments.[25] Still, before trying to make the case for a public and distinctively Christian argument about what it means to be human, it makes sense to say a few things in defense of public and distinctively Christian arguments generally.

As I see it, there are at least three different strands to the "religion in the public square" debate: The first has to do with constitutional law, the second with the political morality of secular democracies, and the third with faithfulness and theological authenticity. That is, in trying to determine the appropriate role and content of faith-based expression in public life, we might ask not only "What does the First Amendment Religion Clause permit?" and "In a liberal democracy, committed to equality and characterized by pluralism, how ought citizens to act and argue?" but also: "Can religious believers, institutions, and associations keep the faith as they engage the world, and if so, how?" Putting this last question differently, the faithful might wonder how we are to square our (understandable) desire for a voice in the dialogue and a "place at the table," with what we might regard as our obligation to speak truthfully and prophetically about God and humanity — in other words, to "build and set the table itself."[26]

I will start with the third, theological dimension of the debate, because before we tackle the question whether we may respond, in the idiom of faith, to the questions tendered in this symposium while remaining citizens, we

24. For a small, but still representative, sampling of the legal and political-theory literature, see, e.g., "Symposium: Religiously Based Morality: Its Proper Place in American Law and Public Policy?" *Wake Forest Law Review* 36 (2001): 217; "Symposium: Religion in the Public Square," *William and Mary Law Review* 42 (2001): 647; Paul J. Weithman, ed., *Religion and Contemporary Liberalism* (Notre Dame, Ind.: University of Notre Dame Press, 1997); Robert Audi and Nicholas Wolterstorff, eds., *Religion in the Public Square* (Lanham, Md.: Rowman & Littlefield, 1997), p. 147; "Symposium: The Role of Religion in Public Debate in Liberal Society," *University of San Diego Law Review* 30, no. 4 (1993): 643; Kent Greenawalt, *Religious Convictions and Political Choice* (New York: Oxford University Press, 1988); Richard John Neuhaus, *The Naked Public Square*, 2nd ed. (Grand Rapids, Mich.: Eerdmans, 1988).

25. But see Elshtain, "How Should We Talk?" pp. 732-33: "[A] powerful school, associated with the work of John Rawls . . . , holds that when religious persons enter the public sphere they are obliged to do so in a secular civic idiom, shorn of any explicit reference to religious commitment and belief. I will not rehearse this position yet again. It has been done over and over to the point of near tedium."

26. Hauerwas, *With the Grain of the Universe*, pp. 238-39 n. 77 (citing Michael J. Baxter, C.S.C., "Not Outrageous Enough," *First Things*, May 2001, pp. 14-16).

ought to ask — putting aside the Justices and John Rawls — whether and to what extent we may do so while remaining Christians.[27] We should ask, in other words, whether believers should enter the arena at all; and also, if they do, what they should say.

Meaning no disrespect to what my colleague Thomas Shaffer has described as the "Gathered Church" tradition — "[a]n ancient and sometimes inevitable tradition among Jews and Christians that teaches believers to get together and then get out of the way"[28] — my claim is that the answer to the first of these latter two questions is "yes." I believe that religious faith in general — and Christianity in particular — makes claims about the meaning and purpose of life and the universe that push the believer inexorably toward engagement in public life and with "political" matters. As the theologian Johannes Metz observed, the "eschatological promises of biblical tradition — liberty, peace, justice, reconciliation — cannot be made private. They force one ever anew into social responsibility."[29] To the extent that religion claims to "contain objectively true insights into human social existence" — and, generally speaking, it does — that "encompassing account of existence necessarily influences the *polis*."[30] The state should not banish faith to a "nonpublic ghetto," nor should the faithful retreat there.[31] And, in fact, they have not.

Turning back, then, to the debate's first, legal dimension, we are, I suspect, on familiar ground. The First Amendment to our nation's Constitution promises that "Congress shall make no law respecting an establishment of re-

27. See, e.g., Michael J. Perry, "Christians, the Bible, and Same-Sex Unions," *Wake Forest Law Review* 36 (2001): 449-85. Perry writes: "In deciding whether she should forgo or at least limit reliance on her biblically grounded moral belief, a citizen of a liberal democracy who is a Christian will want to consult the wisdom of her own religious tradition at least as much as she will want to consult either the morality of liberal democracy or . . . the American constitutional morality of religious freedom" (p. 451).

28. "The notion here is that the civil society in which each community of the faithful exists . . . is irrelevant to the communal business of believers. Believers are pilgrims in the world, passers-through, 'resident aliens.' At best, the civil society is irrelevant. At worst, the civil society is corrupting and destructive, and if the community of the faithful exists for anything it exists to protect itself from secular corruption, so that it can remember what it is, preserve its identity in teaching and in ritual observance, perpetuate itself through educating its children, and wait for the Lord to come back." Thomas L. Shaffer, "Review Essay: Stephen Carter and Religion in America," *University of Cincinnati Law Review* 62 (1994): 1609.

29. Johannes B. Metz, *Theology of the World*, trans. William Glen-Doepel (New York: Seabury Press, 1973 [1969]), p. 153.

30. Gerard V. Bradley, "Dogmatomachy: A 'Privatization' Theory of the Religion Clause Cases," *St. Louis University Law Journal* 30 (1986): 277, 329.

31. Bradley, "Dogmatomachy," p. 280.

ligion, or prohibiting the free exercise thereof." Few constitutional provisions have a comparable hold on the popular imagination, and fewer still have been so misunderstood and misrepresented.[32] For more than fifty years, judges, scholars, and citizens alike have confused Thomas Jefferson's "figure of speech"[33] about a "wall of separation between church and State" with a rule of constitutional law that would outlaw not only fairly obvious interferences with, and impositions upon, religious freedom, but also obligate the state and its courts to scrub clean the public square of all "sectarian" residue. Stanford Law School's Dean Kathleen Sullivan, for example, has argued forcefully and prominently that the First Amendment's Establishment Clause was designed not simply to end official sponsorship of churches but also to affirmatively establish a secular "civil order for the resolution of disputes."[34] In other words, she contends, the Constitution is not simply a charter for limited government and ordered liberty, it sets the ground rules for deliberation among citizens about the common good.

Dean Sullivan's view is, I think, mistaken. The First Amendment's "Establishment Clause" is directed at governments only; it neither mandates nor implies a duty of self-censorship by believers; it does not demand a naked public square; and active and engaged participation by the faithful is perfectly consistent with the institutional separation of church and state that the Constitution is understood to require. The Constitution imposes no "don't ask, don't tell" rule on religionists presumptuous enough to venture into public life.[35] True, it is not hard to find examples of judicial rhetoric and decisions that provide support for Sullivan's secular-order claims. Our courts and judges have at times seemed more worried about the "divisiveness"[36] and "coercion"[37] thought to attend public manifestations of religious commitment than about the threats posed to authentic religious freedom and pluralism by their own overreactions. As a result, their pronouncements have, on occasion,

32. I will not impose on the reader a catalogue of the flaws and failings of the Supreme Court's Religion Clause jurisprudence. For (just) one powerful critique, see Steven D. Smith, *Foreordained Failure: The Quest for a Constitutional Principle of Religious Freedom* (New York: Oxford University Press, 1995).

33. "A rule of law should not be drawn from a figure of speech." *McCollum v. Board of Education*, 333 U.S. 203, 247 (1948) (Reed, J., dissenting).

34. Kathleen Sullivan, "Religion and Liberal Democracy," *University of Chicago Law Review* 59 (1992): 197.

35. "To tell religious believers to keep quiet, else they interfere with my rights simply by speaking out is an intolerant idea. It is, in effect, to tell folks that they can not really believe what they believe or be who they are: Don't ask. Don't tell." Elshtain, "How Should We Talk?" p. 744.

36. See, e.g., *Lemon v. Kurtzman*, 403 U.S. 602 (1971).

37. See, e.g., *Lee v. Weisman*, 505 U.S. 577 (1992).

in Chief Justice Rehnquist's words, seemed to "bristle with hostility to all things religious in public life."[38]

The trend appears to be away from such ahistorical aversion, though, supplying good reason to believe that courts are abandoning the enterprise of monitoring the religiosity of public discourse. Demands that religious believers either muzzle themselves or retreat from civil society — i.e., that they take their faith and go home — are increasingly rejected. In *Mitchell v. Helms,* for example — a case involving loans of computers and other educational materials to public, private, and religious schools serving low-income students — Justice Clarence Thomas was joined by three of his colleagues in disclaiming a "most bizarre" reading of the First Amendment that would "reserve special hostility for those who take their religion seriously, [and] who think that their religion should affect the whole of their lives."[39] And Justice Antonin Scalia sounded a similar note not long ago, going out of his way in *Good News Club v. Milford Central School* to emphasize that the Establishment Clause imposes no special obligation on devout religious believers to "sterili[ze]" their speech before entering the public forum.[40] In that case, a comfortable majority of the Justices agreed that the Establishment Clause does not require — and, indeed, the First Amendment's free-speech guarantee does not permit — a small-town public school to exclude a Christian student club from otherwise-generally-available public facilities, simply because the club's activities were unabashedly religious. And finally, in *Zelman v. Simmons-Harris,* the recent decision upholding Ohio's landmark experiment in choice-based education reform, Chief Justice Rehnquist affirmed yet again that there is nothing constitutionally unworthy about the work and mission of religious schools, or about the decisions of parents who choose them.[41]

So, putting aside for present purposes the many difficult questions about what the Constitution allows governments to say and do with respect to religious belief, practice, and institutions; and notwithstanding the widespread misperceptions about the public-square implications of our "separation of church and state"; it should be quite clear that the First Amendment's Religion Clause erects no barrier to — in fact, it protects — the determination of religious believers to respond, in public debate and *as believers,* to the "Call for Reckoning." In Michael Perry's words, political reli-

38. *Santa Fe Indep. Sch. Dist. v. Doe,* 530 U.S. 290, 318 (2000) (Rehnquist, C.J., dissenting).

39. *Mitchell v. Helms,* 530 U.S. 793, 827-828 (2000) (plurality op.).

40. *Good News Club v. Milford Central School,* 533 U.S. 98, 124 (2001) (Scalia, J., concurring).

41. *Zelman v. Simmons-Harris,* 536 U.S. 639, 122 S.Ct. 2460 (2002).

ance on religiously grounded morality is both permitted and protected by the Constitution.[42]

But again, there is more — much more — to the problem of religious voices in the public square than constitutional law. One might insist that, whatever the positive law might permit, political morality and the "ethics of citizenship"[43] counsel that religious believers ought still to cabin their commitments and translate their claims when they deliberate with their fellows about the common good. One might ask, in other words, whether "political reliance on religiously grounded morality [is] illegitimate" — even if not unconstitutional — "in a liberal democracy like the United States."[44] One might wonder whether, even if expressing, and acting upon, one's faith in public life does not make me an outlaw, does it nonetheless make me a bad citizen, a bad democrat, or a bad liberal?

The answer, according to more than a few of our more prominent theorists, to these questions is "yes." John Rawls, again, has famously contended that the morality of political liberalism requires religious believers, when engaged in public discourse on public matters, to employ a secularized, "accessible" vocabulary, and to proceed in their arguments from similar premises. Stephen Macedo has sounded a similar note, writing that "[t]he liberal claim is that it is wrong to seek to coerce people on grounds that they cannot share without converting to one's faith."[45] Not that we should be surprised by the fact that many of our most gifted thinkers embrace these and similar views; after all, these positions follow from, and cohere nicely with, the "religion as a hobby" mind-set identified by Professor Carter. If religion really is a purely "private" idiosyncrasy, not only in terms of the scope of its influence but also in terms of the matters to which it speaks, then it would be strange, and perhaps not very responsible citizenship, to speak and act as though one's faith had consequences for state and society.

42. Michael J. Perry, "Why Political Reliance on Religiously Grounded Morality Does Not Violate the Establishment Clause," *William and Mary Law Review* 42 (2001): 663.

43. Paul Weithman, "Religious Reasons and the Duties of Membership," *Wake Forest Law Review* 36 (2001): 511.

44. Michael J. Perry, "Why Political Reliance on Religiously Grounded Morality Is Not Illegitimate in a Liberal Democracy," *Wake Forest Law Review* 36 (Summer 2001): 127.

45. Stephen Macedo, "Transformative Constitutionalism and the Case of Religion: Defending the Moderate Hegemony of Liberalism," *Political Theory* 26 (1998): 71. See also, e.g., Robert Audi, "Religious Values, Political Action, and Civil Discourse," *Indiana Law Journal* 75 (2000): 276 (arguing that "citizens in a liberal democracy have a prima facie obligation not to advocate or support any law or public policy that restricts human conduct, unless they have, and are willing to offer, an adequate secular reason for this advocacy or support").

I cannot do much more here than report that these thinkers are mistaken. The political morality of liberal democracy, rightly understood, does not require self-censorship on the part of persons who are believers *and* citizens. Nicholas Wolterstorff put it well:

> [T]he ethic of the citizen in a liberal democracy imposes no restrictions on the reasons people offer in their discussion of political issues in the public square. . . . If the position adopted, and the manner in which it is acted upon, are compatible with the concept of liberal democracy, and if the discussion concerning the issue is conducted with civility, then citizens are free to offer and act on whatever reasons they find compelling. I regard it as an important implication of the concept of liberal democracy that citizens should have this freedom — that in this regard they should be allowed to act as they see fit.[46]

In fact, it strikes me as unconvincing, and more than a little bit illiberal, to propose as a foundational tenet of political morality that this particular source (i.e., religious faith) of morality, "values," and commitment is especially unfit for public discourse.[47] To force religious believers to concede, as the price of admission to the political community, that they "recognize that religious reasons are not good reasons for political action," is, as my colleague Paul Weithman has observed, in effect to deny religious believers "full membership" in that community.[48] As Professor Carter put it, given "the ability of [religion] to fire the human imagination, . . . [religious people] should not be forced to disguise or remake themselves before they can legitimately be involved in public debate."[49] Professor Elshtain agrees: "If we push too far the notion that, in order to be acceptable public fare, all religious claims . . . must be secularized, we wind up de-pluralizing our polity and endangering our de-

46. Nicholas Wolterstorff, "Audi on Religion, Politics, and Liberal Democracy," Audi and Wolterstorff, *Religion in the Public Square*, p. 147.

47. See, e.g., Michael W. McConnell, "Five Reasons to Reject the Claim That Religious Arguments Should Be Excluded from Democratic Deliberation," *Utah Law Review* (1999): 654 n. 56 ("Some views — such as advocacy of slavery or cruelty — may be treated by a liberal society as beyond the pale. But to treat religious views, which have been, and are, entertained by a large majority of the people, including many people of eminent reasonableness and good sense, as within this category, is surely illiberal"); Michael J. Sandel, "Political Liberalism," *Harvard Law Review* 107 (1994): 1772-73 (reviewing John Rawls, *Political Liberalism*) ("Why must we 'bracket' . . . our moral and religious convictions, our conceptions of the good life? Why should we not base the principles of justice that govern the basic structure of society on our best understanding of the highest human ends?").

48. Weithman, "Religious Reasons and the Duties of Membership," p. 532.

49. Carter, *The Culture of Disbelief*, p. 232.

mocracy."[50] More particularly, as I discuss below, the secularization obligation proposed by some can serve only to hobble our efforts to think well — indeed, to think *reasonably* — about the death penalty.

Christian Witness and the Call for Reckoning

We can say, then, that neither a sound understanding of constitutional law, nor an attractive theory of democratic citizenship, requires the politically engaged religious believer to cabin, bracket, translate, or censor herself before entering the fray. The question remains, though: If Christian believers — *as* Christian believers — do elect to engage the world, what should we say? Having overcome the objections of those who would require, as the price of admission to the public square, that we dis-integrate our religious faith from our commitment to the common good, how should we talk, and to what should we speak as we engage the death-penalty debate?

Professor Elshtain asks whether "the full force of Christian witness [should] be brought to bear on every public policy question," or should instead be "reserved . . . to situations of unusual civic moment and moral challenge."[51] I suspect that the right answer falls somewhere in between these options. In any event, I am confident that the problem of the public authority's response to murderers is one to which we *should* speak. That said, it does seem wise to warn those who would unleash the "full force of Christian witness" in the death-penalty debate that they — that *we* — ought to take care, to make sure that prophecy is not watered down to punditry and that we not become so comfortable on the talk-show circuit that we lose the ability to challenge the world on its Creator's terms.[52] Such caution serves not only the integrity and authenticity of our religious traditions, but also the society and citizens with whom we are engaged in dialogue; even Camus could see that the world needs "Christians who remain Christians."[53] Our calling, again, is

50. Jean Bethke Elshtain, "State-Imposed Secularism as a Potential Pitfall of Liberal Democracy" (paper delivered at the Becket Fund conference, "Religious Liberty and the Ideology of the State," in Prague, Czech Republic, 9-11 August 2000, available at http://www.becketfund.org/other/Prague2000/ElshtainPaper.html).

51. Elshtain, "How Should We Talk?" p. 734.

52. Thomas L. Shaffer, "Faith Tends to Subvert Legal Order," *Fordham Law Review* 66 (1998): 1089, quoting John F. Kavanaugh, *The Word Encountered* (1996), p. 8. "Faith must always resist acculturation," Shaffer writes, "or it will have nothing to say to the world or to the culture."

53. Albert Camus, "The Unbeliever and the Christian," in *Resistance, Rebellion, and Death,* trans. Justin O'Brien (New York: Knopf, 1961), p. 70.

not to provide the death penalty debate with a chorus of church-based "me too's"; it is not to christen the bullet-point memos of consultants or even the causes of our political allies; nor is Christianity's task "to underwrite a politics external to itself."[54]

Which brings us back to the question raised at the outset: If, as faithful and engaged citizens, we resolve to answer the "Call for Reckoning" proclaimed in this volume in a way that is true to the traditions out of which we speak, what should our contribution be? Recall my opening assertion that moral problems are *anthropological* problems, in that moral arguments tend to boil down to arguments about "moral truth about the human person."[55] A recent example: Professor Michael Perry argues, in *The Idea of Human Rights,* that "[because] every human being is sacred" (his anthropological premise), it follows that there are "some things that ought *never* . . . to be done to any human being" (his moral claim).[56]

Now, I believe that, for the most part, our nation's moral vocabulary, constitutional law, and political discourse — including its debates about capital punishment — rest upon the unsteady foundation of a flawed moral anthropology. This superficially appealing, but in fact untruthful, unreliable, and ultimately unworthy account of what it means to be human is captured well in the now-infamous "mystery passage" of the joint opinion in *Planned Parenthood v. Casey,* the Supreme Court's 1992 decision that reaffirmed the constitutionally mandated abortion license: "At the heart of liberty is the right to define one's own concept of existence, of meaning, of the universe, and of the mystery of human life."[57] This account of human freedom states an anthropological as well as a legal claim. In fact, what the *Casey* opinion provides is not so much a workable constitutional principle, but a generalized and radical argument about moral self-sufficiency. Professor Elshtain is right that the anthropology offered in *Casey* is "impoverished," and that there is no getting around the fact that it is also "so deeply entrenched that . . . it is simply part of the cultural air we breathe."[58]

My claim is that this "deeply entrenched" *Casey* anthropology serves as the (shallow) foundation for, and does much of the "work" in, our communities' public arguments about moral questions. We — or, at least, many of us — think about the person, and about her rights and duties, and about her

54. Elshtain, "How Should We Talk?" p. 736.
55. John Paul II, "Address to the Bishops of Texas, Oklahoma, and Arkansas."
56. Perry, *The Idea of Human Rights,* p. 7.
57. *Planned Parenthood of Southeastern Pennsylvania v. Casey,* 505 U.S. 833, 851 (1992) (joint opinion).
58. Elshtain, "The Dignity of the Human Person," p. 58.

very nature, in *Casey's* terms, and the fact that *Casey's* anthropology provides the scaffolding for our arguments cannot help but affect the conclusions we reach and solutions we offer. We have, by and large, embraced an account in which the person is and should be regarded as untethered, unsituated, and alone. She is "autonomous," not simply in the obvious sense that her choices are not determined or crudely reducible, but in that the only standards against which those choices can be evaluated and judged are those that she generates or endorses. By this account, the autonomy of atomized and rootless individuals is not only given, but good in itself — its orientation cannot be judged. Agency is more a raw, pre-moral power than a fragile gift that permits and facilitates the authentic flourishing of the human person. Conduct is good because it is chosen, not chosen because it is good.[59]

"Well," one might ask, "so what?" Why shouldn't we, as both believers and citizens, embrace and celebrate the autonomy, and thus the dignity and worth, of the untethered self? Why not ground our faith-based case for the abolition (or retention) of the death penalty on the foundation of the *Casey* anthropology? The difficulty, in my view, is that the anthropology of the mystery passage is not capable of supporting and sustaining a Christian argument — i.e., the kind of argument that Christians should be making in this context — against (or for) the death penalty. This is not to say that *Casey's* vision does not spin off quite sincere talk about "human dignity"; of course it does. But such talk cannot, in the end, be sustained by its working anthropological premises.[60] The problem, as Fr. Neuhaus has noted, is "not that it is wrong about the awesome dignity of the individual," but that "it cuts the self off from the source of that dignity."[61] As a result, the "dignity" that emerges from the reigning anthropology is more Promethean than Christian. It is pos-

---

59. To be clear, the problem, in my view, with *Casey* is not that it emphasizes and celebrates our capacity to seek, choose, and embrace the good, but that it seems to define the good (for us) solely with reference to the fact of its having been chosen (by us). The opinion's weakness is not that it celebrates human autonomy, or even that it links the dignity of the person with his ability and right to engage in moral decision-making, but rather that it cannot supply any basis for situating and evaluating moral decisions.

60. See Wilfred M. McClay, "The Continuing Irony of American History," *First Things*, February 2002, p. 25 ("Without a broadly biblical understanding of the sources of the dignity of the human person, it is hard to see how that dignity can continue to have a plausible basis in the years to come"); and Alasdair MacIntyre, *After Virtue: A Study in Moral Theory*, 2nd ed. (Notre Dame, Ind.: University of Notre Dame Press, 1984), pp. 1-5 (offering the "disquieting suggestion" that "the language and the appearances of morality persist even though the integral substantive of morality has . . . been fragmented, and then in part destroyed").

61. Fr. Richard John Neuhaus, "The Liberalism of John Paul II," *First Things*, May 1997, pp. 16-21.

ited to consist precisely in our being self-governing choosers. It not only includes, but is utterly reducible to, the capacity to make, and the right to act upon, "autonomous" choices.

"Well then," one might respond, "why not put aside these abstract and probably irrelevant speculations about 'moral anthropology,' and simply join with those partisans in the death penalty debate who base their arguments on human fallibility, discrimination, rehabilitation, or cost?" The answer, I think, is that we cannot — and Christians should not — do so. Our public morality ought to be able to support an argument about why it is that a convicted murderer may not be executed. And it is not enough — though it might well be politically effective — for death-penalty opponents to argue that "capital punishment does not deter crime" or that "capital punishment costs too much." These are empirical, not religious, arguments, and it strikes me as unwise and unfaithful to pretend otherwise.[62] In any event, death-penalty supporters can simply respond by saying that "cost isn't the issue," or perhaps by showing that executions actually do deter some homicides. Nor is it even enough to point out the facts that our system of capital punishment is administered unfairly, and even discriminatorily; that the poor and racial minorities do not receive adequate representation; and that mistakes are inevitable. These observations do little to say why we should not execute a guilty, well-represented, white man like Timothy McVeigh.

Here is the challenge, then, for Christian witness: If the "cultural air that we breathe" cannot sustain a moral case against the death penalty, and cannot explain why, in Professor Perry's words, there are "some things that ought never . . . to be done to any human being," then perhaps this failure presents religious believers with the opportunity for truth-telling, with the chance to rebuild the debate on sturdier anthropological foundations? We have, remember, an alternative vision to propose, one that turns the received anthropology on its head, one that emphasizes not so much our autonomy and moral self-sufficiency as our dependence and incompletion.[63] After all, the fact that freedom of choice is a gift, and even that its value is "inestimable,"[64] does not make it the only valuable thing; that we are distinguished by our ca-

---

62. See Hauerwas, *With the Grain of the Universe*, p. 20 (noting the "platitudinous emptiness of liberal Christian moralizing in which the positions of secular liberalism reappear in various religious guises").

63. See, e.g., Alasdair MacIntyre, *Dependent Rational Animals: Why Human Beings Need the Virtues* (Chicago: Open Court, 1999).

64. *Faretta v. California*, 422 U.S. 806, 834 (1975) ("And whatever else may be said of those who wrote the Bill of Rights, surely there can be no doubt that they understood the inestimable worth of free choice").

pacity for choice does not mean that our dignity is reducible to that capacity. We are not merely agents who choose; we are people who belong, who exist in and are shaped by relationships. We live less in a state of self-sufficiency than in one of "reciprocal indebtedness";[65] this truth is both a point of pride and a call to humility.[66] A Christian anthropology acknowledges our limits. It recognizes, as Professor Gilbert Meilaender put it recently in a beautiful essay, that we occupy an "in between" place, "between the beasts and God."[67] It grounds our dignity not so much in claims of self-sovereignty as in our status as creatures.[68] That is, it proposes that "the greatness of human beings is founded precisely in their being creatures of a loving God,"[69] and not self-styled authors of their own destiny. Its fundamental proposition is that "the person is a good towards which the only proper and adequate attitude is love" and whose "proper due is to be treated as an object of love."[70] And, finally, a Christian anthropology directs our attention to the question that, in the end, must be the focus of our struggles with the difficult issue of capital punishment, namely: "Is the capital sanction 'in conformity with the dignity of the human person'?"[71]

*　　　*　　　*

It should be clear that this essay is offered more as a prolegomena than a resolution. I am not yet sure what all this might mean, or what a shift in our anthropological premises and idiom might yield, in the context of the death penalty debate. I do not yet know how our arguments would change if our

---

65. Gilbert Meilaender, "Still Waiting for Benedict," *First Things,* October 1999, pp. 47-55 (reviewing Alasdair MacIntyre, *Dependent Rational Animals: Why Human Beings Need the Virtues*).

66. See John Lukacs, *At the End of an Age* (New Haven, Conn.: Yale University Press, 2002), p. 204:

> We did not *create* the universe. But the universe is our invention; and, as are all human and mental inventions, time-bound, relative, and potentially fallible. Because of the recognition of the human limitations of theories, indeed, of knowledge, this assertion of our centrality — in other words: of a new, rather than a renewed, anthropocentric and geocentric view of the universe — is neither arrogant nor stupid. To the contrary: it is anxious and modest.

67. Gilbert Meilaender, "Between Beasts and God," *First Things,* January 2002, pp. 23-29.

68. See Coughlin, "What It Means to Be Human," at pp. 619-20.

69. John Paul II, "Address to the Bishops of Texas, Oklahoma, and Arkansas."

70. Fr. Thomas Williams, L.C., "Capital Punishment and the Just Society," *Catholic Dossier,* September-October 1998.

71. *The Catechism of the Catholic Church* ¶2267 (1994).

understanding of those who have been condemned to die — of their worth, respect-worthiness, and destinies — rested on different anthropological pre-suppositions. I am sure, though, that it would make a difference; that the debate would *sound* different; and that it would, in Professor Shaffer's words, more "truthfully describe what is going on" if our arguments reflected and explicitly proceeded from a "doctrine of human dignity that turns finally on the client's being a child of God."[72]

Certainly, as a Christian, I am confident that we are not diminished by a faith-inspired shift in focus from autonomy and choice to creaturehood and dependence. As C. S. Lewis once wrote, in his essay *The Weight of Glory:* "There are no ordinary people. You have never talked to a mere mortal. Nations, cultures, arts, civilisations — these are mortal, and their life is to ours as the life of a gnat. But it is immortals whom we joke with, work with, marry, snub, and exploit — immortal horrors or everlasting splendours."[73] Our challenge, then, is to frame the debate so that the death penalty stands or falls not so much on whether or not it is cost-effective, or deters, or is popular, or is imposed without respect to race, sex, or class — though all this certainly matters — but on whether it is consistent with the status, nature, and dignity of the people on whom it is applied. Our challenge is to propose a truthful vision of the human person as "the noblest work of God — infinitely valuable, relentlessly unique, endlessly interesting," and to propose that the question of the death penalty stand or fall on that. Such a vision — "truthful Christian speech" — is required "if we are to be faithful to the God we worship."[74]

72. Shaffer, "The Legal Ethics of Radical Individualism," p. 965; Thomas L. Shaffer, "The Unique, Novel, and Unsound Adversary Ethic," *Vanderbilt Law Review* 41 (1988): 699 n. 7.

73. C. S. Lewis, *The Weight of Glory, and Other Addresses,* revised and expanded edition, Walter Hooper, ed. (New York: Macmillan, 1980), p. 19.

74. Hauerwas, *With the Grain of the Universe,* p. 140.

9. Human Nature, Limited Justice, and the Irony of Capital Punishment

JOHN D. CARLSON

It was a year of new beginnings. Before starting my junior year in college, I moved into a new home, a stately old Victorian converted into a halfway house for ex-offenders. My new housemates included a handful of other students and a dozen or so former prisoners who were completing terms of their parole or reentering society following their sentences. The day I arrived was also Leslie's first day in his new home. A lanky African American man with a broad smile, partially obstructed by the drawn bill of his ball cap, Leslie was enjoying the comfort of the large parlor and the cool breeze coming from the ceiling fan overhead. As I joined him it was clear that we were both relieved to be settling in. We introduced ourselves, exchanging pleasantries, before curiosity finally got the best of me and I asked Leslie about his time in prison.

He had just completed a nineteen-year sentence in the state penitentiary. At age thirty-eight, he had spent half of his life in prison for the murder of a taxi driver. While this announcement gave me some pause, I was not alarmed by it; I knew entering this program that some of my housemates would be murderers, and they knew that we knew this too. What surprised me, however, was his self-professed innocence. According to Leslie, he and a friend were sharing a late-night cab ride when the so-called friend spontane-

---

I am grateful to Jean Bethke Elshtain, Robin Lovin, Richard Garnett, and John Witte, to my co-editors, and to members of my dissertation group for sharing with me their reactions and thoughtful suggestions to early drafts of this chapter.

ously produced a gun, demanded the cabdriver's money, then shot and killed the driver before fleeing. The police arriving on scene apprehended Leslie, who was later convicted for murder.

Leslie's story of mistaken guilt seemed plausible enough. Of course, it occurred to me at the time — and still does to this day — that he may have lied to me. There was no way for him to prove his story, and as his housemate, it was not my place to prod. It also occurred to me that if I had served on his jury, depending on the presentation of evidence, I, too, might have been persuaded of his guilt. Yet, I remained disconcerted. Even though criminals are not always known for their honesty, my other housemates, including other murderers, routinely — though not proudly — admitted their guilt. Even one lifelong resident who, rumor had it, poisoned his wife, did not deny his guilt (he just preferred not to talk about it). But at this point, what had Leslie or the other residents to lose in telling the truth? Their sentences were behind them; they had renounced their former ways and paid their debts to society. They had no reason to fear reprisal in the supportive environment of this group home.

Whether he was guilty or not, Leslie turned out to be a model resident and a highly decent, responsible housemate who went on to make a full transition back into society. His story has stuck with me, vexing me to this day. For the rest of my tenure at the halfway house, I oscillated, wondering whether I had been duped or whether Leslie had been unjustly incarcerated or whether the truth might be somewhere in between. I still don't know.

I offer this introductory vignette because it illustrates important themes to which I return later in this discussion of capital punishment and its ambivalent promise for justice.

*   *   *

Debates about the morality and fittingness of the death penalty readily trade on the currency of justice. There is no agreement, however, on what justice entails or which version of justice is to be preferred.[1] Restorative justice, retributive justice, and transformative justice are a few of the most common versions put forth. One need only look to the panoply of religious perspectives incorporated into death penalty arguments to recognize that religion lends scant clarity for adjudicating a true measure of justice. Religious arguments do, however, tend to share some common features that assist us in nar-

---

1. For a sophisticated tracing out of the philosophical and diachronic developments of rival versions of justice, see Alasdair MacIntyre, *Whose Justice? Which Rationality?* (Notre Dame, Ind.: University of Notre Dame Press, 1988).

rowing the range of "justice talk"; they sharpen our focus onto the moral dimensions of justice in ways that legal codes and public policies, when
pragmatically applied and divorced from deeper philosophical or theological
groundings, do not. Two such features worth lifting up are the anthropological and transcendent dimensions of justice: claims about human nature, on
one hand, and, on the other, appeals to God, the divine, or to transcendent
values not reducible to empirical affairs. Most forms of justice implicitly affirm some kind of assumptions about the human person (and perhaps about
a transcendent order as well), but religious arguments often locate these features as crucial moral axes of justice.

Before exploring these dimensions, it is propitious to offer at least a
working definition of justice itself: In a rough and ready fashion, we might
say that justice involves the proper ordering and balance of human relations
within a social and political community, including the right relations of citizens to one another and vis-à-vis the state. I mean to enlarge our understanding of justice beyond the offender's desert or the vindication of victims.
While justice involves these vital components, it also opens up a much
broader notion of political order that draws in other members of a community, implicating them and the values and relations in which they, too, find
meaning. The intent to *preserve* these right relations — or to deter the injuries
of injustice — is a mainstay, while another key feature concerns efforts to *restore* justice when human relations have been damaged or disordered and the
moral balance of a community disturbed. All forms of justice — whether
known as retributive, "restorative,"[2] transformative, or something else — essentially strive in some way to restore imbalanced human relations. These are
not so much different understandings of justice, it seems, but different conceptions of the *regulative principles* or means by which justice is best pursued.
Accordingly, deliberation over competing regulative principles becomes a
secondary, though crucial, question about which means promise the greatest
measure of communal order and harmony and the fullest restoration of balanced relations among citizens.

*My thesis is that attention to accounts of moral anthropology and notions
of transcendence illuminates deeper understanding about corresponding
construals of justice.* I am guided by the belief that politics is a nexus where
these two axes of interpretive vitality converge and play out. What follows is
an attempt to narrow the range of compelling and promising accounts of jus-

---

2. I refer here to the specific positions associated with "restorative justice," which I would
want to distinguish from a general aim, one shared by all forms of justice, to restore equilibrium
to disordered human relations and communities.

tice concerning the death penalty; to this end, examining the anthropological and transcendent dynamics of capital punishment arguments reveals certain upper and lower limits of debate about the pursuit of justice. These limits do not in themselves yield a precise formula for attaining justice, including if and when the death penalty should be applied. This approach does, however, refine the realm of relevant concerns about capital punishment by challenging us to consider the moral principles that underwrite its use; moreover, this approach can provide concrete guidelines and practical proposals regarding the implementation of capital justice.

Making this case entails first putting on display two religiously grounded positions on capital punishment that illustrate the upper and lower limits of justice. *Ultimate justice* and *nominal justice* are the respective names I give to these positions, examples of which will follow.[3] Bringing forward embedded claims about the human condition and the divine reveals both where these positions succeed and where they leave other concerns unresolved. With the limits of the debate delineated, an alternative or *via media* is offered, a position I call *limited justice,* so named for its explicit attempt to identify these moral limits and work within the boundaries of excess and deficiency that they represent. I plumb the moral depths of limited justice, along the same anthropological and transcendent channels of approach, through the work of the discerning philosopher-critic *cum* secular mystic Albert Camus. As well, the influence of Reformation theologian John Calvin permeates all three positions, sometimes for better, other times for worse. Where Calvin and Camus share common ground and become strange bedfellows, limited justice proffers a position that seeks to garner the sympathies of two stripes of religious seekers: the confessionally committed and the cautiously inquisitive.

Irony pervades capital punishment in a plurality of ways. By irony I mean the quite closely linked relationship between seemingly disparate elements, in which one element elicits its opposite. I allude here to the irony of how the debate itself often takes shape. Many treatments of capital punishment (whether abolitionist or retentionist statements) take either a practical, results-oriented approach (i.e., invoking arguments about deterrence, rehabilitation, or "closure") or a conceptual approach that aspires towards transcendent standards of fittingness or justice (including arguments about divine retribution, mercy, or forgiveness). If the former often fails to take

---

3. One might reasonably object that justice, if it errs to excess or deficiency, *prima facie* is not justice at all. Despite the labels, which I assign, I aim to treat these proposals on their own terms as honest political-ethical endeavors, variations of which many people find compelling.

seriously the conceptual depth needed to address sufficiently the practical considerations it raises, then the latter often lacks the practical rigor needed to ground adequately the implications and unintended consequences of its conceptual thinking. The irony is that these are not fortuitous, unrelated approaches to the issue as may be assumed; rather, they are dialectically linked. The irony of their mutual dependence must first be gleaned so more considered judgment on these concrete yet conceptually complex issues can be reached.[4] For this reason, identifying the conceptual limits of justice entails the need for practical limits. Hence limited justice takes concrete form through a casuistry of capital punishment that resolves the conceptual problems identified.

Upper Limits of Justice

Negotiating the gray middle ground of justice depends in part on demarcating its upper limits, so as to avoid transgressing this moral threshold. This ceiling sets apart a position I term *ultimate justice,* an ambitious pursuit of justice fueled by strenuous claims to transcendence that justify, if not mandate, specific political proposals and practices — for our purposes here, capital punishment. Ultimate justice is recognizable by a high doctrine of transcendence and a correlative — high or low — moral anthropology; together, they give rise to a political rejoinder that reconciles the relationship of human nature and human action to the divine. Schemes of ultimate justice may repair to religious perspectives that some would portray as rigid or literalist, particularly in their interpretation of sacred laws and texts. Certain strict adaptations of Islamic Shari'a law, which counsel violence as divine retribution for wicked behavior, come to mind. Some communities, for example, take quite seriously Qur'anic injunctions to punish "crimes against God" like theft or adultery with flogging, stoning, or amputation. Other views that approach ultimate justice, albeit less severe, can be found in democratic political cultures among faithful citizens of good will. While non-theocratic governments that uphold basic human and civil rights tend to mitigate the propensities for ultimate justice, when such a breach of this ultimate boundary does occur — even in a democracy — it can be cause for worry. Or, at least that is what I argue in this section.

Some strands of Reformed thought possess the elements from which an

4. I am indebted to Robin Lovin who, influenced by Reinhold Niebuhr, urged me to explore the ironic angle of the debate itself.

appeal to ultimate justice may emerge. A low or pessimistic view of human nature that emphasizes human corruption and sinfulness is compensated by a comparatively high doctrine of the divine that, in response, evokes God's sovereignty, omnipotence, and judgment. The theology of John Calvin provides a classic statement of such a view. Suspending judgment of Calvin for the time being, it is fair to say that some have found within his writings the resources and sentiments in which notions of ultimate justice can take root. Christian ethicist Daryl Charles, in his account of capital punishment, presents a more contemporary illustration of divine retribution. Charles rejects the optimistic Enlightenment view of humanity that he asserts many mainline Protestants have adopted today. In the rush to embrace values associated with psychology, secularization, cultural relativism, and deterministic views of human behavior, Charles argues, many Protestants (and other Christians) have lost sight of the "biblical understanding of sin, evil, and moral accountability."[5] The collective result is that the contemporary United States, as in the pre-diluvian world, is consumed by "[h]uman wickedness carried to an extreme . . . the reflection of a society whose social character is putrefied."[6]

While this pessimistic moral anthropology is crucial to this position, it does not reveal the full story, however. In fact, the strenuous doctrine of sin is actually coupled with a quite lofty account of human dignity, such that the murder of human beings, as sacred bearers of the *imago Dei*, tarnishes the God who gives human life its intrinsic worth: "An assault on human life is comparable, as it were, to an assault against God."[7] On this anthropological reasoning, it follows, "precisely *because* the human being is the image of God that one who purposely sheds the blood of another must die." Capital punishment, on this view, preserves and upholds human dignity; the story of the Flood, the biblical witness of Genesis 9:1-7, serves to support this contention. When extreme sins like murder undercut the high moral standing of the human person, the task of justice is to restore that standing: "desecration of life's sanctity should be — indeed must be — visited by divine judgment in the present life." Such judgment takes the form of stiff retribution in civil law and penal codes: "The core of the covenant with Noah is a moral imperative formulated in no uncertain terms, namely the institution of a life-for-life policy in the case of premeditated murder."[8]

5. Daryl Charles, "Outrageous Atrocity or Moral Imperative? The Ethics of Capital Punishment," *Studies in Christian Ethics* 6.2 (1993): 10 and "Crime, the Christian, and Capital Justice," *Journal of the Evangelical Theological Society* 38.3 (1995): 429-30.
6. Charles, "Outrageous Atrocity," p. 11.
7. Charles, "Crime, the Christian, and Capital Justice," p. 440.
8. Charles, "Outrageous Atrocity," p. 11.

In this design of justice, beliefs about our moral anthropology intersect with, and are complemented, if not compensated, by, revelations about the divine. Justice becomes the moral imperative, and politics the milieu, to reconcile human nature — in both its dignity and its depravity — with mandates of the divine. These interwoven anthropological and transcendent dimensions of justice illustrate the "tension between divine sovereignty on the one hand and human authority and accountability on the other."[9] Capital punishment is the moral-political mandate, carried out by specified human means, that resolves this tension: "Whoever sheds the blood of a human, *by a human* shall that person's blood be shed" (Gen. 9:6). And since human accountability refers not only to individuals' duties to accept responsibility for their crimes but also to society's collective responsibility to punish them, those who resist use of capital punishment risk violating sacred biblical injunctions. As in the pre-diluvian world, when a society refuses to stem wickedness in its midst, it invites the wrath of God who *will* requite justice.[10]

"Separationists" might wonder at this juncture whether ultimate justice could be achieved constitutionally, at least in the United States: Doesn't the so-called "separation of church and state" — or at least the First Amendment non-establishment clause — forbid such religious rationales for civil penalties? But there is no need here either to craft law out of sacred verse (as the Shari'a does) or to invoke scripture in legal parlance; secular legal vernacular will do just fine. Why? Because, the law is underwritten by divine fiat and is "inherently religious and theological" even when such fiats are not explicitly spelled out in public law or the Constitution. Again, though, the religious character of the law must be preserved in quite precise ways, especially where capital punishment is concerned. Ultimate justice is not served unless we safeguard the sacred trust revealed in Genesis 9 by heeding its command to execute those who murder with premeditation.

Justice, on this view, turns on a transcendent reference point that honors God's divine authority by putting to death those who besmirch God's image. Justice's stern and unyielding dependence on "something beyond itself . . . a foundation of transcendent moral truth" is essential to this account of justice.

> When law loses what only a conviction of ultimacy can bestow . . . it degenerates into pragmatic utilitarianism and a moral-cultural breakdown ensues. It follows that when the transcendent moral value is denied, com-

---

9. Charles, "Outrageous Atrocity," p. 5.
10. See Charles, "Crime, the Christian, and Capital Justice," p. 437.

mandments or laws become little more than opinions, since no compelling sanction can be invoked.[11]

Yet, what confers justice with its ultimate character, I would suggest, is the intimate and inflexible relationship between human political instruments and divine imperatives. That is, ultimate justice involves not simply the existence of some transcendent reference point nor even the belief that governmental authority possesses a divine mandate; human justice is rendered ultimate by embracing the belief that the divine will commands society to use specific political processes or practices in order to consummate and reify divine justice. Capital punishment as divine retribution transcends political judgment and necessity in that it also bears biblical witness "that murder cannot be atoned for, inasmuch as it is the ultimate crime against God: effacing the *imago Dei.*" For Charles, "atonement for capital crimes is not pushed off into the *eschaton.* Rather, criminal justice is to serve as a (present) shadow of eternal punishment."[12] *In short, human justice becomes ultimate neither by preserving earthly standards of justice nor by referencing the divine, but by establishing itself in such close relation to transcendent standards of justice that the distinction between the two quite easily becomes eclipsed.* The death penalty, so construed, accrues ultimate status because it grasps too tightly onto transcendent features of justice and punishment *at the expense of more limited earthly standards of justice.* It is one thing to justify the death penalty based upon standards of conduct or principles of justice that are gleaned in the dim light of worldly political conditions, whether or not rays of transcendence illumine them. It is something quite different when human justice seeks to mirror divine retribution and becomes an explicit agent of divine atonement, thus collapsing the moral space between infinite and finite, between the transcendent realm of ultimacy and the imperfect reign of polity.

How specifically does ultimate justice cling "too tightly" to the transcendent ambit of moral duty? First, it presumes an undiminished level of certainty regarding our discernment of "the ultimate," especially its prescriptions for justice and punishment in this world. Many citizens share a belief in God and an ultimate and sublime realm — of justice, goodness, and beauty — that stands in perfection or in judgment over the conditions of this life

---

11. Charles, "Outrageous Atrocity," p. 5.

12. Charles, "Crime, the Christian, and Capital Justice," p. 440. Charles elsewhere notes that through "the law of purification," human suffering prepares the executed individual "to meet his Maker" ("Outrageous Atrocity," p. 6). This does seem difficult to reconcile, however, with his earlier statement that "murder cannot be atoned for" unless he is sure that, at the time of final judgment, God will not pardon such sins.

and world. The variety of such contemplations — whether they augur punishment and pain or eternal pleasure and bliss — is staggering, as are the implications for political life. Within Christian thought alone, scholars differ sharply over notions of justice, both divine and earthly, and what that entails for human punishment. Charles provides one such interpretation. Consider another possible Christian interpretation of the transcendent imperative of capital justice. New Testament scholar Christopher Marshall puzzles over how the death penalty, when divinely ordained, purges or atones for the sins of murderers, as Charles maintains. For what reason then, Marshall wonders, did Christ die? In Marshall's view, "Charles ends up in a theological quagmire in which God requires dual atonement for murderers, once by their own death and once by Christ's." That is, if God means for society to execute criminals so they may atone for their crimes, then for what reason did Christ die upon the cross? Marshall goes on to state quite succinctly, "It is one thing to see capital punishment as a debt owed to human society; it is another to see it as an atonement offered to God for a sin already atoned for at the cross and freely forgiven by God."[13]

Whether one finds more compelling Charles's position, Marshall's rebuttal, or some other viewpoint will depend upon one's religious convictions and interpretation of scripture. I am pessimistic that this dispute could be settled with the level of certainty that political life in a democratic order requires. My own interpretation is that it would seem that belief in the ultimate makes possible one very important facet of earthly political life, namely, that we are relieved from having to agree upon the exact nature of divine judgment, forgiveness, or the life-yet-to-come. Nor are we obliged to resolve how precisely penultimate politics should reflect or foreshadow such movements of transcendence. Belief in a final judgment, moreover, would seem to alleviate some of the burden of human punishment: that is, we can take some solace in the knowledge that whatever punishment is not fully achieved now will ultimately be consummated later. In the meantime, though, careful attention to the conditions of the here and now, perhaps informed simply by the presence of larger transcendent horizons, can provide sufficient moral clarity to discern limited standards of justice and assign measures of punishment that are appropriate to our present circumstances.

Secondly, the overconfidence that accompanies a farsighted bedazzlement with ultimate justice may cause us to overlook certain essential and knowable features of penultimate existence, particularly pertaining to the

13. Christopher D. Marshall, *Beyond Retribution: A New Testament Vision for Justice, Crime, and Punishment* (Grand Rapids, Mich.: Eerdmans, 2001), p. 222.

ironic and tragic nature of politics. When we fail to prescind distinct realms of justice, merging those that are available to human means with those that are not, we risk elevating politics to a near-divine standing. This is both prideful and avoidable. By co-opting transcendent powers and unfathomable purposes, we increase the likelihood of turning earthly designs of justice into agents of injustice. This is true irony — transforming one thing into its opposite, turning virtue into vice — since the lofty drive for justice inures us to the risks of inflicting injustice. When ultimate justice makes strenuous appeals to the divine, it effectively claims an omniscience that overextends the epistemic limits of human creatures, at least in our efforts to shape wide-scale norms for political society. Overshooting justice in this way obscures a subtle limitation of the human condition: that we may be able to glimpse perfect justice — we can imagine what it looks like — yet we can never fully achieve it. And to strive for perfect justice ironically invites its opposite.

Such epistemological limitations should chasten, not embolden, us; they should alert us to the keen propensity for tragedy that ultimate justice conceals. (I'll say more in a moment about what "tragedy" entails.) Consider Charles's assertion, "If the argument based on the potential for an innocent execution is to proceed in all honesty, one will be forced to concede that innocent deaths resulting from released or paroled criminals are *far more frequent* (and *tragic*) than the rare instance of an innocent convict dying. . . . [W]hy not devise the system so as to place potential and convicted murderers, not society, at risk?"[14] Perhaps we should agree to devise the system so as not to extend parole to repeat offenders or to those believed to be a continued risk to society. But Charles's assertion is, nonetheless, worrisome on two other fronts. First, many would challenge the rarity of the occurrences in which the innocent are wrongly accused; we know that citizens and polities are not always in a position to achieve the certitude they claim for themselves.[15] Second, the sensitivity to tragedy in Charles's assertion is underdeveloped. Let's parse out more carefully the "tragic" element of capital punishment. The death of any innocent victim of murder is a *calamity* and a woeful loss. This kind of loss, however, should be distinguished from the *tragedy* in which the state, as an agent of justice, condemns as "guilty" and executes an innocent

14. Charles, "Outrageous Atrocity," p. 13.

15. In the past decade, observes federal judge Mark Wolf, "substantial evidence has emerged to demonstrate that innocent individuals are sentenced to death, and undoubtedly executed, much more often than previously understood." Adam Liptak, "Federal Judges Express Concern about Death Penalty," *New York Times*, August 11, 2003. Also, see George Ryan's chapter in this book for several harrowing examples of innocents who were sentenced to death by juries certain of their guilt.

person; classically understood, this is tragic because an innocent suffers unjustly for the sake of a contrary value, in this case justice. For Charles, the possibility (or inevitability) of unintentionally executing the innocent is outweighed by the increased safety to society that comes from executing the guilty. That itself is a supremely tragic statement: that a few innocents must die so that other innocents can enjoy a greater measure of safety. The irony is that Charles's drive for justice overshadows the tragic injustice of his view. It is doubly ironic (and perhaps doubly tragic as well) to note that society is still no safer when the innocent are executed. We can accept, albeit reluctantly, that living in an organized society entails the tragic possibility of imprisoning the innocent, perhaps for life. But must we also risk the additional step of irrevocably finalizing and consummating that tragedy?

I do not mean to question whether *any* kind of certainty — even certainty "beyond a reasonable doubt" — can ever be achieved. We know, for example, that there are numerous death row cases in which the offenders themselves do not contest their guilt. Let us return later to the cases where such certainty is available, and whether capital punishment might be appropriate or necessary. For the moment, though, having established a preliminary warrant for limited aspirations of justice, we descend to circumscribe further the terrain of this moral inquiry.

Lower Limits of Justice

Not all articulations of justice are as beholden to retributive theories of punishment as the previous account. In fact, accounts of "restorative justice" often seek to counter the perceived shortcomings of such retributive theories.[16] Recently, some theologians and ethicists have even challenged the notion of punishment itself. For example, in *The Protestant Ethic and the Spirit of Punishment*, T. Richard Snyder, a Protestant himself, defies what he takes to be Protestantism's unduly harsh influence on modern forms of penal theory. His inquiry is not an explicit treatment of the death penalty (though he rejects the practice outright).[17] It serves, nonetheless, as an illuminating counterweight to a divine punishment or ultimate justice position which, it is proba-

16. For an overview of restorative justice, see Howard Zehr, "Restoring Justice," in Glenn H. Stassen, ed., *Capital Punishment: A Reader* (Cleveland: Pilgrim Press, 1998), pp. 23-33; for more in-depth discussion, see Zehr's *Changing Lenses: A New Focus for Crime and Justice* (Scottdale, Pa.: Herald Press, 1990).

17. T. Richard Snyder, *The Protestant Ethic and the Spirit of Punishment* (Grand Rapids, Mich.: Eerdmans, 2001), p. 146.

bly safe to assume, represents the strenuous kind of theological-punitive vindication to which Snyder objects. Snyder's study is also salutary for our exploration of the anthropological, political, and transcendent features of justice.

Snyder's chief worry is the "punitive spirit" that, he argues, has permeated American culture and society. The desire to punish has become part of the air we breathe, reinforced by mandatory federal sentencing guidelines, by the media's coverage of criminals and their victims, and by the depiction of crime and crime-solving in film and television dramas. Where crime enrages, punishment appeases. Snyder even comments that executions have become public entertainment, comparing ancient gladiatorial spectacles to the modern-day celebrants who revel outside prisons while lethal sentences are administered inside.[18]

Religion bears its own unique responsibility for this cultural cancer, Snyder professes, especially "the heritage of a largely Protestant ethic and theology [that] gives rise to or provides support for the spirit of punishment." Specifically, two distortions in Protestant thought give way to the punitive ethos Snyder describes, and in each case, Calvin and other famed Protestant paragons are in part to blame. First, Protestantism's overemphasis on the fall, original sin, and total human depravity has strained other efforts to affirm the goodness of human creatures (including, Snyder contends, the worth of criminals).[19] Second, Protestant theories of grace have distorted and overemphasized God's gift of "redemption grace," which atones for the depravity of our fallen nature, thereby overshadowing "creation grace," which accentuates the inherent worth that one possesses by dint of being a creature of God. As well, redemption grace has overstressed its ahistorical and individualized character, outshining the more "social-historical" or collective dimensions of grace that can provide for the "holistic redemption" of societies and their citizens, including their institutions, laws, and public policies.[20]

These two distortions point up the anthropological and transcendent features of Snyder's analysis and function to set apart morally those who are set apart already by differences in social status. When "we believe that all persons are essentially corrupt save for the extraordinary intervention of God's [redemptive] grace in their lives, it is a simple step to think that those who are poor, or sick, or in trouble with the law, or different from us in anyway are

18. Snyder, *The Protestant Ethic,* p. 9.
19. Snyder, *The Protestant Ethic,* pp. 12, 36.
20. Snyder, *The Protestant Ethic,* p. 12.

somehow evil."[21] To be more theologically specific, when creation is divorced from grace, "it follows that some of creation stands outside the purview of grace, fallen from the image of God and therefore [seen to be] inferior in the order of things."[22] The embedded anthropology in our previous appraisal of ultimate justice seems to exemplify the "kind of superior/inferior ontology" that Snyder criticizes given that it extols the dignity of human persons writ large while deploring the depravity of murderous criminals. When this dichotomous anthropology is coupled with an individualized notion of transcendent grace, Snyder believes, "a spirit of punishment is inevitable" against those who we perceive to be unredeemed. Snyder bids us to consider that Protestant theology has facilitated the treatment of persons as "other," allowing them to be objectified as non-persons worthy only of judgment and punishment.[23] When this spirit of punishment enjoys free reign, justice is reduced to retribution or "payback." Capital punishment becomes the supreme form that such retribution takes.

For Snyder, a different vision of justice is clearly needed. His counterproposals for restorative and transformative justice begin by remaking the anthropological and transcendent foundations of justice, upon which a more suitable cultural edifice may be erected. To compensate for the anthropological distortion of traditional Protestantism, Snyder promotes a moral anthropology that downplays notions of evil and sin while highlighting the dignity and worth of all persons. A related task involves reclaiming the inherent grace of the created order, including human beings, by recognizing that "[b]ecause of the gracious gift of the creator God, we are beautiful and good."[24] This ap-

---

21. Snyder, *The Protestant Ethic,* p. 14. True, one of these groups is not like the other. But let us beg for the moment whether criminals should be distinguished from victims of poverty or illness.

22. Snyder, *The Protestant Ethic,* p. 43.

23. Snyder, *The Protestant Ethic,* p. 13. How precisely Snyder moves from judgment about human inferiority to punishment is not entirely clear. I am inclined to think that what Snyder understands to be punishment or retribution may, at times, be a matter of malicious treatment that stems from the objectification of persons. It is useful here to recall C. S. Lewis's argument that punishment, at least at its best, is intended to affirm human dignity, not to denigrate or dehumanize. See C. S. Lewis, "The Humanitarian Theory of Punishment," in *God in the Dock: Essays on Theology and Ethics* (Grand Rapids, Mich.: Wm. B. Eerdmans Publishing Co., 1972), pp. 287-300. Punishment acknowledges the moral capacities and choices available to humanity and pertains when such capacities are not exercised well. Because animals do not possess rational capacities or exercise moral choices, there is no defensible reason to punish them. (Of course, the ridiculous reality is that even some animals have been placed on trial and "punished" for killing.) In short, I might want to amend Snyder's point to say that punishment can wrongly serve as a pretense to justify cruelty and wickedness, especially the kind that flows from dehumanizing and objectifying others.

24. Snyder, *The Protestant Ethic,* p. 38.

plies to all creation including criminals who are, Snyder believes, the direct victims of social illnesses like poverty, racism, and social despair — maladies that must be combated through the collective redemptive power of God's grace. The transcendent features of Snyder's viewpoint invite into the workings of public institutions and social mores a comparatively subtler intervention than is present in divine retribution, such that redemptive grace, socially and historically construed, cures society and its citizens of their ills.

When crime is understood as a cultural sickness, then criminals become victims, and punishment becomes less vital. "Restorative justice" alternatives serve to "contribute to the health and healing of criminals" as well as their victims and the larger communal order, all of whom are injured or affected by crime.[25] In such an approach, punishing law-breaking and criminal conduct takes a backseat to reconciliation among victim, offender, and the wider community. The primary role of the state in this design is to facilitate the reparation of damaged relations though "non-punitive sanctions," mediation, and reparations. (Snyder reluctantly does admit that some cases may require incarceration.) The grace of God's forgiveness enters here to facilitate institutionally the restorative process of healing and regeneration so that offenders and victims of crimes may restore the relations that have been damaged. This "circle of justice" should be expanded as wide as possible: "Certainly the one who has committed a crime is in need of forgiveness. . . . But so too is the society in need of forgiveness for having created and permitted crime-generative communities to exist."[26] Furthermore, Snyder argues for "transformative justice," which includes the transformation of the offender as well as the transformation toward a more just and healthy society.

For reasons I shall attempt to make clear, the version of restorative justice that Snyder puts forward is inadequate. In staking out this claim, I argue, first, it presumes a moral anthropology that neglects the darker side of human nature. Correlatively, this optimistic view of humanity is complemented by transcendent categories of grace and forgiveness that turn out to be rather anemic. Unlike the high transcendent dimension of divine retribution — in which a sovereign, justice-seeking God uses political institutions to requite human sinfulness — Snyder's position puts forth a comparatively low and feeble vision of transcendence. Forgiveness runs amok in an arrangement that lacks a clear account of human sin in need of being forgiven. The sanative form of grace that Snyder extols is watery and thin, applied lavishly like a balm to cleanse "social illnesses" and heal the wounds they induce. This

---

25. Snyder, *The Protestant Ethic,* p. 74.
26. Snyder, *The Protestant Ethic,* pp. 110-11.

combination of anthropological and transcendent presuppositions enables Snyder to overlook the merits of punishment as well as crucial political measures of justice that are necessary for sustaining order and public safety and for preserving right relations among persons in political society. His vision of justice is hardly robust enough to warrant its namesake, for, in many ways, it abandons the grounds of justice altogether. It is justice in name only, or what we might call *nominal justice.*[27]

Recall that in Charles's anthropological scheme, he reserves his sternest statements about human sin for criminals convicted of murder; nonetheless, he bases his defense of capital punishment upon a rather lofty appraisal of humanity, given the dignity it owes to God. Snyder seeks an anthropological correction to this "divvying up" of people into discrete categories; Snyder seems to be saying that we all share a common condition of dignity and worth, by virtue of God's creative goodness. Neither position seems entirely correct to me, though there may be partial truth in each. Snyder rightly calls us to apply our anthropologies across the board. Charles's omission is that he discusses the sins of some, but not the universal sin of *all* that impairs each of us in *some* way, that pervades the structures of society and infects its institutions, including penal institutions. But Charles is also right that we need to develop a deeper anthropological comprehension for evil that lends insight into crime and punishment (and, I would add, how this form of sin differs from the sin which renders fallible institutions of justice). Snyder, like the Christians that Charles disparages, has forsaken Protestantism's theological heritage of sin.

In the move that nominal justice makes, sin becomes entirely dehumanized — withdrawn as a basic attribute of the human person. Put differently, sin becomes fully socialized, attributable to the forces and institutions of society. Of course, classically understood, sin has always had a collective or social component: Adam and Eve first sinned together; Augustine's supposed theft of the pears took place among friends. But, in Snyder's account, the classical language of sin, evil, and human wrongdoing gets morphed into the medical vernacular of sickness and healing — not just as metaphor, but as reality. If sin is reduced to societal illness, and if crime is nothing more than a symptom, then no one can be blamed or punished for being sick. In this effort to correct for an excessive Protestant punitive ethos, punishment ceases to have any meaning at all. There is no way to make sense

---

27. The term "nominal justice" sounds more pejorative to the colloquial ear than I intend. I would suggest, but do not have room to lay out here, that the roots of this position can be traced back to seeds planted centuries ago by the philosophical school of nominalism.

of our moral capacities or the choices we make when moral agency and accountability become socially determined. What can it mean to think of human freedom or the will in this kind of scheme? Should we *expect* the poor or disaffected to become criminals given that they are *merely* products of their environment? The upshot of nominal justice — perhaps as insulting to some as it is outrageous to others — is that we should express surprise or dismay when poor or minority populations do *not* commit crimes.

When Protestants lose touch with what their traditions have had to say about sin, we shed powerful resources for coming to terms with human freedom, the will, and the subjective dimension of human evil. Some in recent history have had little use for strenuous accounts of sin like those found in Calvin or Luther. Dietrich Bonhoeffer was incensed when classmates at Union Theological Seminary chortled during a lecture about Luther's conception of sin.[28] But might we retrieve and recoup from these theological ancestors some still germane lessons about the human condition? Consider Luther's famous account of the bondage of the will. Countering Erasmus's view of free choice, Luther implored that free choice belongs to God alone. Without God, the human will is enslaved and bound to sin. Worst of all, the will delights in sin: that is, we sin "with a ready will."[29] In a famous trope, Luther likens the human will to a horse bound to follow in whatever direction the rider — whether God or Satan — may take one. Silly talk and balderdash, many would claim today. We know we are free because we *feel* free, comes the usual rebuttal. But this was precisely Luther's point. Contra Snyder (who at one point compares a youth's decision to join a criminal gang to "Sophie's choice" to save only one of her children from the Nazis),[30] Luther reasoned that we sin not out of compulsion but from the necessity of the sinful self. That is, we do not feel compelled to sin, as though "taken by the scruff of the neck and forced" to do evil, to use Luther's locution. Rather, even when larger "causal" forces may be at work in these actions, we freely participate in and savor sin, subjectively speaking.

Theologically, then, we are not punished for the broader societal conditions that may contribute to human crime and malfeasance — anymore than

28. See Eberhard Bethge, *Dietrich Bonhoeffer: A Biography,* rev. ed. (Minneapolis: Fortress Press, 2000), p. 157.

29. Martin Luther, *The Bondage of the Will,* in F. Gordon Rupp and Philip S. Watson, eds., *Luther and Erasmus: Free Will and Salvation* (Philadelphia: The Westminster Press, 1969), p. 139.

30. The forces at work in the film *Sophie's Choice* are "different only in their stark clarity, but not in kind" to forces like poverty, a broken family, and lack of self-esteem that force young men to join criminal gangs. See Snyder, *The Protestant Ethic,* p. 70.

one is punished because "the devil made me do it" — but for the element of human participation in which the will freely participates and takes pleasure. Punishment entails a theological use of the law to convict one of one's *own* sin — not society's — in an effort to turn the individual will towards moral rectitude and lawful conduct. Conviction and sentencing under the law afford offenders a chance to repent, to take personal responsibility for their misdeeds, to seek forgiveness, and, if they desire, even to reconcile themselves to God. Legal scholars John Witte and Thomas Arthur note in their sophisticated survey that Protestant notions of punishment go well beyond retributive aspects to include deterrent and rehabilitative dimensions, too; they also note the relationship of punishment to maintaining and restoring justice.[31]

To be clear, defense of punishment does not relieve society from a responsibility to "the least among us." Affluent societies, particularly those with a Christian lineage, should expend greater resources to improve the living conditions of the poor; should craft more innovative legislation to combat poverty; and should implement more effective public policies that provide better opportunities for the disenfranchised. Such measures demonstrate a social and moral commitment to identify conditions and curb temptations related to crime. In this regard, Snyder, citing Calvin, judiciously draws from Protestant roots to show that the institutions of political society are instruments of "collective redemptive grace."[32] However, this ought not come at the expense of punishment, which reaches the sinner on the subjective or individual level. Interestingly, Snyder's critique of the prevailing punitive ethos proposes no countertheory of punishment of his own.

Wanting in the position of nominal justice is not only some account of punishment but also a discussion of key social features of justice such as the deterrence of future crimes, the creation of public order, or a community's public expression of deeds it finds unacceptable or abhorrent. These are usually considered minimal requisites of public justice, necessary for the preservation of civic well-being and ordered relations among citizens in a polity. Nominal justice expends little effort on such public considerations. Justice loses its status as a political (and moral) problem when it is overtaken by a therapeutic emphasis to rehabilitate offenders to "good health." According to Snyder, the state should even *habilitate* or transform those who have never enjoyed prior health or conditions worthy of rehabilitating. Moreover, restor-

31. John E. Witte, Jr., and Thomas C. Arthur, "The Three Uses of the Law: A Protestant Source of the Purposes of Criminal Punishment?" *Journal of Law and Religion* 10, no. 2 (1993-94): 454-55. These authors also cite the abandonment of traditional anthropological assumptions about human sin among contemporary discussions of crime, p. 461.

32. Snyder, *The Protestant Ethic*, pp. 62-63.

ative justice involves the creation of political space for injured parties to forgive their offenders and to commence their own healing process

Such transformative and restorative innovations in justice are worthy of deeper study, as they may prove effective in substantively setting aright relations that have been damaged by crime. Moreover, as classical Protestant theories of punishment suggest, there is no need to set them in opposition to retributive justice. But, in emphasizing these more maximal pursuits of justice, which are often associated with the *private* domain, nominal justice ignores the aforementioned minimal requisites of *public* justice. Ultimate justice alerted us that polities can be overly ambitious in their pursuits of justice. Nominal justice suggests, curiously enough, that it, too, can gesture towards a form of overreach by making state penal institutions responsible for duties traditionally reserved for parents, schools, or faith communities.

The question of the death penalty's legitimacy often bears directly upon these minimal social requisites of justice, which Snyder does not take up. So, it is not surprising that he devotes scant attention to capital punishment either.[33] However, he issues a fervent objection: the death penalty forecloses the possibility of redemption for perpetrators of crime as well as for the perpetrator's victims and the wider community. Empirically, the concern for reconciliation or redemption seems to motivate relatively few families of murder victims to reject capital punishment. Yet the human possibility for "new beginnings" seems to be a point worthy of more careful and sustained reflection. My concern, then, as we proceed, is whether one can reconcile redemptive encounters and overtures to transcendence with a compelling and attentive account of political justice.

Interlude with a Genevan: Protestant Intimations and Limitations of Justice

In charting out a *via media* that I will call *limited justice,* a modest course between the lofty cliffs of ultimate justice and the indeterminate shoals of nominal justice, it is instructive to dwell momentarily on some early Protestant adumbrations of this position. Having considered two candidate accounts by contemporary Protestant ethicists, we move now to classic Protestant resources that juxtapose anthropological and theological claims as part of the

---

33. Snyder assumes capital punishment amounts to vengeance or "getting even." On this point, Daryl Charles sagely distinguishes retribution from revenge by noting their different understandings of proportional punishment, public motives, and institutional legitimacy. See his "Thoughts on Retributions and Revenge," *Touchstone* (December 2001).

task of limiting ventures in political justice. The French-born Genevan and magisterial reformer John Calvin looms large in the background of this discussion. Calvin is often remembered for his austere doctrine of sin and human corruption; his apprehensive ruminations on an awesome, terrifying, and inscrutable God; and his controversial dabbling with theocratic ideas that ordered the lives of his fellow Genevans. All of these associations have left Calvin with an ambiguous legacy for the intersection of religion and politics. Let's ponder briefly such associations as they might pertain to questions about capital punishment, for the spirit of Calvin surfaces, as we have seen, amidst theological discussions both for and against the practice.

Let there be no doubt, Calvin, like most people of sixteenth-century Europe, supported capital punishment. The Schleitheim Confession of 1527 demonstrates that even Christian pacifists of his day took for granted the state's lawful and legitimate authority to "punish and put to death the wicked" in the service of the public good.[34] Calvin's rationale for the death penalty was not decidedly different from these early Anabaptists, though he never placed civil punishment or government "outside the perfection of Christ" as they did. For his part, Calvin is most distinctly remembered for his intense and anxious fretting over matters of public order and civic peace.[35] Fear of revolution, upheaval, crime, and general unrest — often theologically understood — led him to embrace the accepted civic practice of his day. Contemporary penal alternatives to execution would be quite foreign to the sixteenth-century mind.

Calvin's ardent belief in human depravity as well as the dignity of the *imago Dei* is partially in keeping with the premises of ultimate justice. He brooked no human malfeasance, especially violations of civic and moral order proscribed by the Ten Commandments, and demanded that Christians and the state actively resist evil. In both their public and private capacities, Christians are obliged to cooperate with civil government "to assist in protecting the lives of our neighbors . . . to procure those things which conduce to their tranquility; to be vigilant in shielding them from injuries; and in cases of danger to afford them our assistance."[36] This regard for fellow man and woman from Calvin's treatment of the sixth commandment extends as

34. "The Schleitheim Confession," in *Encyclopedia of American Religions: Religious Creeds*, 1st ed. (Wilmington, N.C.: McGrath Publishing, 1978), p. 418.
35. On the theological, cosmological, and political manifestations of Calvin's all-consuming anxiety and his perpetual yearnings for order, see generally William J. Bouwsma, *John Calvin: A Sixteenth Century Portrait* (Oxford: Oxford University Press, 1988), especially Chapters 2–4, 13.
36. John Calvin, *Institutes of the Christian Faith* (Philadelphia: Presbyterian Board of Christian Education, 1936), 2.8.39.

well to mollifying malicious inner dispositions of the will that could lead to injury or death. Care for the soul of the potential aggressor is as important as care for the body of one potentially aggressed.[37] Evasion of such duties is both a transgression of the civil law and a retreat from Christian responsibility to uphold the moral law. Interestingly, it is not only the image of God that we share with our neighbor, but also our common human flesh, both of which bind us to the law and to our neighbors' protection. Most telling is that Calvin's reverence for, and preservation of, the divine impression upon the human person is never treated abstractly, apart from physical protection of and "affectionate regard" for our corporeal well-being.[38]

Wanting in ultimate justice's treatment of depravity, though certainly not from Calvin's, is a sustained consideration not merely of the "fruits of sin" — murder, adultery, theft, hatred — but original sin itself, the inherited condition passed down to *all* of humanity that invites God's censure and condemnation.[39] Sin permeates every part of human nature, Calvin reproved: "from his head to his feet, man be entirely sin."[40] Sin fouls the mind and the will and surrounds the human condition with the most miserable of necessities; it extends to human institutions, infecting them with corruption and injustice.[41] We are wise to take heed of this institutional propensity for error when delimiting the scope of justice.

---

37. Calvin also counsels patience as he implores us to resist the desire for revenge, especially against the condemned. Always maintain charity towards the evildoer, Calvin advises, so his (or her) wickedness may be transformed to good (*Institutes*, 2.8.40; 4.20.19-20).

38. Calvin, *Institutes*, 2.8.40.

39. Calvin, *Institutes*, 2.1-2.3.

40. Calvin, *Institutes*, 2.2.8.

41. Calvin, through his own doing, has been tagged with the unfortunate legacy of promoting religiously inspired, state-sponsored violence. Civil magistrates, whom Calvin considers divinely appointed "ministers of God," possess special mandates to preserve public order and exercise God's vengeance. Perhaps no other passage in Calvin strikes such harsh notes to our modern democratic ears than when he declares that wicked magistrates just as rightfully possess the sacred majesty of civil government as the upright: even those "who rule in an unjust and tyrannical manner are raised up by him [God] to punish the iniquity of the people." We are inclined to think — and we would be right — that, through the smiting sword of an evil magistrate, a mighty and sovereign God is here requiting transcendent justice against iniquitous citizens. This conclusion becomes problematic, however, if one infers Calvin to mean that God is pleased with or indifferent to the unjust magistrate's conduct. Nothing could be further from the truth that God approves of corrupt political institutions, for Calvin notes the legitimacy of lower magistrates' rebellion against tyrannical rulers. Calvin goes on to remind us that the "correction of tyrannical domination is also the vengeance of God"; such vengeance is especially warranted against magistrates who betray the liberty of their subjects, undermine the divine office to which they have been called, and disappoint the God who has appointed them. See *Institutes*, 4.20.25, 31.

If sin impairs so pervasively, how can we rise above our fallen reason to achieve any knowledge or certainty about the affairs of this world, let alone the mysteries of God's transcendent order? Calvin prescinds two kinds of knowledge, an insight that reveals how the transcendent dimension of justice intersects with basic anthropological yearnings and capacities. He distinguishes human understanding about terrestrial things — civil polity, domestic economy, the arts and sciences — from understanding of celestial things — knowledge of the heavenly kingdom, true righteousness, God's divine will and "the rule for conformity to it in our lives." While our "celestial knowledge" is drastically impaired and limited, "terrestrial knowledge" is fully available; that is, we can — and must — act based upon penultimate certainty about our social natures, our desires to preserve society, and the laws and dispositions of civic order necessary to sustain our common life together. This basis knowledge is available by virtue of our nature. Reminiscent of natural law theory, Calvin avers, "The seeds of political order are sown in the minds of all."[42] For Calvin, we are, at root, not only social but political creatures.

Terrestrial knowledge, however, is also confined by limits set in part by celestial knowledge. To be sure, Calvin's encounter with scripture, especially the story of Job, gave him a glimpse into celestial knowledge and afforded him plenty to say in his commentary about God's multilayered and multivalent justice. But the provisional understanding of God's "double justice," which he developed, not only made Calvin tremble but also disclosed just how far off lies this ultimate dimension of justice and how limited is the human mind to appropriate it to penultimate affairs.[43]

Calvin's high doctrine of transcendent justice or God's "double justice" offsets his comparatively low theological anthropology. Within God's "double justice" are both "lower" and "upper" dimensions. The revealed portion of God's justice (or "lower justice") seeks to correct human sinfulness and demands conformance to the law of God; this "moral law," disclosed through scripture, is discernible to human reason in spite of its fallenness. In fact, it is knowable apart from scriptural revelation, for the moral law is also "natural law": social and political affinities intrinsic to all humans, including non-Christians, can recognize the need for such law. Yet, while humanity possesses the capacities to establish common civil laws, it is the divine backing of God's ordained justice that imbues the moral law with its transcendent, eternal

---

42. Calvin, *Institutes*, 2.2.13.

43. For a fascinating and lucid appraisal of the transcendent dimension of justice, especially Calvin's understanding of God's "double justice," see Chapter 3 of Susan Schreiner's *Where Shall Wisdom Be Found: Calvin's Exegesis of Job from Medieval and Modern Perspectives* (Chicago: University of Chicago Press, 1994), especially pp. 104-20.

character. God's "lower justice" provides us a transcendent reference point for the justice that governs human actions and affairs (witnessed, for example, in Calvin's sustained treatment of the Ten Commandments as the consummate decree of God's law).

Of course, this "lower justice" pales in comparison to the secret and terrifying realm of God's "upper" or "infinite" justice. For Calvin, we are graciously relieved from seeking out the instruction of God's perfect justice. To glimpse such celestial domains exposes "the deficiency of all human justice before God, including the justice of the Law."[44] That is to say, no matter how upright persons or polities may be, God could condemn them if he wished to impose his infinite justice. For our own good, we should leave hidden such ultimate horizons and be humbled by the knowledge of their hovering yet inscrutable presence. In the meantime, however, the penultimate conditions of the here and now provide sufficient clarity about terrestrial justice and the political exigencies to which we are obliged to respond — though we can take no comfort that such responses are measures of God's ultimate justice. This sets the metaphysical milieu in which capital punishment should be discussed.

Through what principles, then, does Calvin deliberate about earthly and limited justice? Equity, as both a theological and political principle, allows diverse nations and peoples to establish their own laws. The forms of *their* laws should be compatible with the particular circumstance of their cultural environs, that is, so long as they uphold the universal character and end of *God's* Law and "lower" justice. Depending on the local circumstances and political conditions, Calvin viewed the death penalty as a legitimate form of punishment to uphold the "equity of the end" or the moral law, including the Decalogue's various prohibitions against adultery, theft, murder, false witness, etc. At first blush, it seems for Calvin that execution is the only permissible punishment for murderers: "All laws agree in punishing murder with death, though in several different forms." But then Calvin goes on to explain:

> The punishments of adulterers in different countries have been attended with different degrees of severity. Yet we see how, amidst the diversity, they are all directed to the same end. For they all agree in denouncing punishment against those crimes which are condemned by the eternal law of God: such as murders, thefts, adulteries, false testimonies, *though there is not a uniformity in the mode of punishment; and indeed this is neither necessary, nor even expedient.*[45]

44. Schreiner, *Where Shall Wisdom Be Found?* p. 112.
45. Calvin, *Institutes*, 4.20.16 (italics added).

The end that equity demands is not execution per se but the upholding of God's moral law, including prohibition against murder; this may be achieved by any of a number of forms or modes of punishment depending upon the struggles or conditions facing a particular political community, the climate of the times, or the mores of the people. Times of great upheaval or elevated crime rates, for example, may call for more severe and frequent forms of punishment. But Calvin reveals nothing necessary about execution. What is morally and politically necessary is to protect the flesh and dignity of God's favorite creatures, to deter crime and to preserve public safety. Can this be achieved through any other means? Certainly Calvin could not have foreseen a world without capital punishment, but this condition was determined by the penultimate ambit of sixteenth-century political life,[46] not by a mandate of divine justice or retribution or any eternal injunction to atone, through civil execution, for crimes committed against the *imago Dei*.[47]

Does Justice Need Transcendence? An Unbeliever's Reply

How we understand the pursuit and limits of justice, I have tried to show, is intimately tied to how we construe human nature. Such pursuits also are often informed by religious notions of transcendence and may be complicated when there is disagreement about what transcendent principles of grace or retribution require or entail for political life. Is justice inherently religious? Can the case for limited justice be made in secular terms not explicitly premised on the divine? Turning to the thought of Albert Camus, the Algerian-born French philosopher, we take up how a self-styled "unbeliever" might assay both the need for, and limits of, justice. In this section and the next, I will attempt to illustrate how an ostensibly secular argument about justice invokes implicit religious categories concerning human nature — and even transcendence — to which both believers and unbelievers might appeal.

Challenging the communist and totalitarian political philosophies of his day, as well as intellectual precursors found in the French Revolution, Camus affirmed a pre-political view of human nature, independent of the

---

46. Calvin himself had observed that certain norms of Christian antiquity were hardly reliable guides for his own day. See Bouwsma, *John Calvin*, p. 148.

47. For a discussion of how Calvin's thinking on equity pertains to questions surrounding international war crimes tribunals, see my "Trials, Tribunals, and Tribulations of Sovereignty: Crimes against Humanity and the *Imago Dei*," in John D. Carlson and Erik C. Owens, *The Sacred and the Sovereign: Religion and International Politics* (Washington, D.C.: Georgetown University Press, 2003), pp. 219-20.

state's effort to shape it.[48] Camus's understanding of the self begins with what he takes to be an essential yearning, shared by all, for a unity that has been lost or shattered. This nostalgia hurls us into absurdity as we seek meaning amidst a silent universe that, offering none, fails to relieve our longing for wholeness.[49] Camus's notion of primordial unity approximates Christian conceptions of a pre-fallen state — John Calvin's "primeval dignity," Reinhold Niebuhr's "original righteousness," or Dietrich Bonhoeffer's "unbroken conscience" — the hovering memory of which reminds us that we are not the way we are supposed to be. Camus's response to disunity is rebellion — "a demand for clarity and unity . . . an aspiration to order"; rebellion serves as an anthropological analogue for the universal human urge to restore justice.[50] If justice is the endeavor to piece together human brokenness, then rebellion is the determination to seek justice, especially when it seems least attainable. The rebel is one who engages this tension between the "principle of justice which he finds in himself" and "the principle of injustice which he sees being applied in the world." The drive to "resolve this contradiction and establish the unitarian reign of justice" provides no guarantee of success.[51] Like Calvin's Job, "the rebel is a man who is on the verge of accepting or rejecting the sacred"; Job and the rebel are both "determined on laying claim to a human situation in which all the answers are human" — that is, they comport with human yearnings and expectations.[52] Unlike the faithful Job, though, the rebel is not surprised when, despite one's determination, the answers do not come; for, that is the burden of the absurd condition we bear. Like justice that is never fully realized, the primor-

48. Rulers must believe that they have the power to change human nature, Jean-Jacques Rousseau famously declared, "of altering man's constitution in order to strengthen it," *The Social Contract*, trans. Judith D. Masters in Roger D. Masters, ed. (New York: St. Martin's Press, 1978), p. 68. Camus objects to such a pliable account of the human person, which he traces through the yearnings of Robespierre and political revolutionaries back to the writings of Rousseau. Camus distinguishes revolution, a historical-political concept, from rebellion, a metaphysical-anthropological notion that lifts up essential, perduring features of human existence: "Absolute revolution, in fact, supposes the absolute malleability of human nature and its possible reduction to the condition of historical force. But rebellion, in man, is the refusal to be treated as an object and to be reduced to simple historical terms. It is the affirmation of a nature common to all men, which eludes the world of power." Albert Camus, *The Rebel: An Essay on Man in Revolt*, trans. Anthony Bower (New York: Vintage Books, 1956), p. 250.

49. Camus, *The Rebel*, p. 6.

50. Before Camus, Augustine, too, perceived that justice consists in order and the challenge of rightly ordering human pursuits, whether the individual will or the collective aspirations of society. See *City of God*, Book 19.

51. Camus, *The Rebel*, pp. 23-24.

52. Camus, *The Rebel*, p. 21.

dial longing for unity is never overcome; it is only sustained, Camus believes, like Sisyphus's enduring struggle with the mighty boulder.

Camus's philosophical inquiry into modern political history chronicles how efforts to reestablish justice and reclaim our lost unity and to overcome the metaphysical absurdity of our condition have turned violent and revolutionary, ending, ironically, in injustice and absolute negation. Witness the political drive for totality, which Camus termed "nothing more than the ancient dream of unity common to both believers and rebels, but projected horizontally onto an earth deprived of God."[53] Totality is the political quest for perfect justice and unity. Totality fueled the projects of Rousseau, Saint-Just, and Robespierre; the Romantics and Hitler; Marx and Stalin — all of whom ambitiously tried to create the political conditions for new human possibility, the eventual outcomes of which nihilistically destroyed the one value on which the human condition itself depends: life. Such overreaching efforts become the face of justice when transcendence is supplanted by totality. Absent some ultimate or transcendent standard, Camus believed, polities more readily adopt totalizing ideologies, inspired by the promise that violence will consummate their deluded schemes of absolute justice. To wit, France's revolutionary dream of a virtuous Republic, free from all faction and dissension, inevitably ended in terror; Germany's voracious craving for political unity and racial purity heralded holocaust; and Russia's utopian vision of a classless society gave birth to the gulags. If it is ironic that the drive for perfect justice has spawned the most loathsome and insufferable episodes of human injustice in modern history, then it is surprising that an unbeliever attributes this reality to politics collapsing the canopy of transcendence.

The longing for unity and justice must be more modest, limited, and supple, Camus cautions, than the engines of totality can supply. Rebellion as justice never creates. It never founds ideal societies or inspires revolutions in justice. It cannot usher in new life. Rebellion can only resist those forces that oppose it. Bruce Ward puts the matter quite nicely when he writes, "[I]t is precisely in the desire for justice that Camus himself discovers the intimation of a permanent meaning or 'value' in human life."[54] Rebellion upholds and affirms the *a priori* value of life and the "logic of creation" on which our unalterably imperfect condition depends.[55] Human justice does not require preeminence and grandeur. Simple decency will do: Political regard for, and pro-

---

53. Camus, *The Rebel*, p. 233.

54. Bruce K. Ward, "Prometheus or Cain? Albert Camus' Account of the Western Quest for Justice," *Faith and Philosophy* 8, no. 2 (April 1991): 199.

55. Camus, *The Rebel*, p. 285.

tection of, the humanly inviolable is plenty noble enough. We leave off the dream for total unity that brings destruction in tow in order that our modest yearnings for partial unity and justice might struggle and endure.

History and experience instruct us that the quest for total unity, often couched in absolute forms of justice, ends in violence and annihilation. Camus further deepens this understanding through another anthropological metaphor of a post-fallen condition, which bears likeness to the theological category of sin. Yet more evidence of Camus's inescapably religious thought. Plague is the metaphor Camus deploys to describe not only the evils of fascism and totalitarianism, not only the iniquity and suffering of the human condition, but also the moral affliction that indwells and unites us all, "the solidarity of all men in error and aberration."[56] Consider the line from his bracing novel *The Plague,* in which the character Tarrou poignantly admits "that each of us has the plague within him; no one on earth is free from it."[57] This plague or sin is resident in our nature, "a product of the human will" that requires vigilant resistance and restraint of each of us. Striking an Augustinian tenor, Camus suggests that plague is a deficiency, a lack of what we are called to be; plague is the way of death, against which we rebel when we choose life.

When we contentedly accept plague, it overtakes us and snuffs out life. Plague creates political necessities that we are obliged to resist in order to preserve life. When we retreat from political responsibility we complacently accept injustice, which imperils the value of life and the meaning it provides — no less than absolutist ventures do. The injustice of setting our sights too low, this, too, must be resisted and risen above. When we rebel against wretchedness in our world, we disclose vibrant human aspirations that bear modest fruits of hope. Rebellion against plague funds the sublime awareness that we are basically social and political creatures: in resisting evil, we find solidarity with one another. We transcend ourselves.

In spite of our solidarity, however, and because of sin and plague, certain features of human nature frustrate our endeavors to rebel and achieve justice. What Camus calls absurdity we might also dub irony. That is, we are essentially creatures who seek unity, meaning, and justice in a world that resists these yearnings. Carried too far, the desire for justice breeds its opposite. And it gets worse. The modest justice that is available to us is further threatened by defects of our condition, which often remain hidden or unknown to

---

56. Albert Camus, "Reflections on the Guillotine," in *Resistance, Rebellion, and Death,* trans. Justin O'Brien (New York: Vintage Books, 1960), p. 217.

57. Albert Camus, *The Plague,* trans. Stuart Gilbert (New York: Vintage Books, 1948), p. 235.

us. Consider, first, how our solidarity in error and aberration impairs our *moral disposition to justice*. Camus disconcertingly struggles with a trenchant question: If plague affects us all, who then is qualified to judge? "Without absolute innocence, there is no supreme judge . . . ," he warns. "There are no just people — merely hearts more or less lacking in justice."[58] Absent moral purity, Camus reasons, the task of human and limited justice is always to assess relative or comparable degrees of culpability and guiltlessness. Second, how do we come to terms with our *juridical ontology*, a term I assign to the fraught circumstances of being co-located in the world as both interested parties *within* — yet also judges and protectors *of* — society?[59] "I believe in justice, but I will defend my mother before justice," Camus famously pronounced.[60] That is to say, we are never impartial jurors who can rise above the connectedness of our earthly attachments to judge by transcendent ethical principles. Nor should we try. History is littered with murdered corpses from regimes that aspired to such triumphant moralistic and political ends. Rather, human justice is always finite and socially circumscribed: "It supposes a limit at which the community of man is established."[61] Finally, because plague enfeebles human knowledge, our *limited epistemology* precludes us from achieving the objective standards of certainty and culpability needed to attain perfect justice. Yet, Camus navigated between absolute truth and relativism to achieve a level of penultimate certainty, a sphere of facts and relative values: "If absolute truth belongs to anyone in this world, it certainly does not belong to the man or party that claims to possess it. . . . But facts are facts. And whoever says that the sky is blue when it is gray is prostituting words and paving the way for tyranny."[62] The preservation of the permanent value of which Camus is certain — the dignity of life itself — demands moral and political accountability: against tyrants who threaten life, rebels must seek to sustain it as best they can.

In spite of what I take to be a primordially religious understanding of human nature, Camus never renders an account of the divine or of transcendent prospects hovering above the realm of politics, soaring through the heavens to bid us along, or touching down with angelic grace to signal the perils as we approach the limits of our earthly mandates. As an unbeliever,

58. Camus, "Reflections," p. 221.

59. Camus, "Reflections," p. 220.

60. Cited in Michael Walzer, "Albert Camus' Algerian War," in *The Company of Critics: Social Criticism and Political Commitment in the Twentieth Century* (New York: Basic Books, 1988), p. 15.

61. Camus, *The Rebel*, p. 290

62. Albert Camus, "Socialism of the Gallows," in *Resistance, Rebellion, and Death*, p. 168.

Camus seems to have had little faith that such a realm, if it existed, afforded much clarity for rebels and justice-seekers. Clearly, though, he suggests that we would have been better served and history would have been less unjust (at least in the mid-twentieth century when Camus lived) had politics been humbled by the possibility of divine existence. Moreover, I suspect that Camus never ruled out altogether the possibility that supernal patterns of transcendence might be at work in the universe. Mostly, he seemed to challenge how such forces could be instructive to an age exiled in meaninglessness, alienated by its own nefarious success in destroying the very meaning for which it longed. How absurd; how ironic — like Job suffering *for* his righteousness. As an unconvinced unbeliever — a struggling seeker of sorts — Camus bore witness to the kinds of religious yearnings and inquiries that vex and daunt even the most faithful believers.[63] *Homo religiosus* is the idiom we might apply to one who makes use of broadly religious categories and instincts even when no theistic view is affirmed. In the end, it is not central to Camus's project and perhaps not to the task of limited justice that we achieve clarity about ultimacy, about transcendent imperatives of justice or the attendant character of divine mandates; provisional certainty about the dignity of human life and the political obligation to protect it, given the conditions of our age, sheds ample light upon earthly justice. However, through gestures towards transcendence — remaining open to unseen possibilities and refusing to collapse sacred horizons altogether — we keep absolutism at bay; we furnish the space needed for rebellion to flourish and the latitude required for human justice to work out its tentative formulations.

Limited Punishment, Limited Justice

It is perhaps ironic that Camus's ambivalence with the notion of punishment, nonetheless, affords such telling clarity about it and about justice as well. For Camus, punishment was a religious idea, which, as an unbeliever, he had trouble accepting. Religious notions of punishment seemed more ultimate to those who share no vision of divine punishment or rewards in the next life. He sympathized more with Prometheus who refused the right to punish because, after all, if no one is innocent enough to judge objectively or pro-

---

63. Howard Mumma, an American minister who preached in Paris during Camus's lifetime, recounts an illuminating series of encounters in which Camus sought him out to discuss on a quite personal level questions about theodicy, Christian anthropology, faith, and even Camus's own baptism. See Howard Mumma, *Albert Camus and the Minister* (Brewster, Mass.: Paraclete Press, 2000).

nounce guilt, who then can administer punishment? In the end, however, Camus did embrace, reluctantly perhaps, the necessity of punishment. It must have pained him to reach such a conclusion, to fathom that "[i]n his last incarnation, at the end of his exhausting journey, the rebel once more adopts the religious concept of punishment and places it at the center of his universe."[64] I would suggest that Camus's own introspective encounters with the force of history and its totalizing experiments in justice — many of which bypassed notions of punishment as they perpetuated violence, terror, and injustice — compelled him to conclude that punishment is an essential responsibility for any political community that seeks justice and affirms the dignity of the human person. This realization certainly places Camus back within striking distance of many religious accounts of punishment, including debates about the death penalty.[65]

Consider briefly one historical analysis in which punishment was eliminated from the quest for justice; interestingly, though, execution was not. Reflecting on the revolutionary "religion of virtue" and the Terror it inspired in France, Camus reminds us of Saint-Just and Robespierre (both of whom initially resisted the death penalty). Humankind is naturally good, the revolutionaries had pronounced, echoing famous Enlightenment refrains.[66] In the virtuous polity they espoused — founded on ultra-rationalism, a formal regard for moral purity, and remorseless conformance to law — citizens may be weak, but they are not guilty. For them, the ideal state for revolutionary France was a "republic of forgiveness" where the foibles of virtuous citizens would be tenderly overlooked, reformed perhaps, but certainly not punished. Yet, as Camus explains, the republic founded on forgiveness — and an unwillingness to punish — inexorably, "with implacable logic," devolved into a "republic of the guillotine," the defining symbol of the Terror.[67] How did this happen? I wager one reason was that crime was set out on rationalist and political grounds alone, without deeper moral or anthropological roots steeped in notions of human dignity or human depravity. The radical Jacobins never perceived criminal transgressions as violations of human sacredness or corruptions of the human will but as the seditious behavior of political factions that threatened the harmony of the republic. Thus, even the eventual decapitation of "enemies of the people" did not aim to punish immoral deeds so

64. See Camus, *The Rebel*, pp. 240-41. On the religious defense of capital punishment, see "Reflections," pp. 222-24.

65. Camus even references Cain and the Gospels as evidence for his position on capital punishment; see "Reflections," p. 232.

66. Camus, "Reflections," p. 222.

67. Camus, *The Rebel*, p. 124.

much as to purge civic impurity, using the blood that flowed to plug the cracks and harden the fissures of political unity.

In this continuum between the "republic of forgiveness" and "the republic of the guillotine," we see at work a dialectic that parallels the antithetical positioning of nominal justice and ultimate justice. Recall that the willingness in nominal justice to overlook human sinfulness and bypass attendant calls for accountability and punishment — instead providing comfort in a gauzy ethic of forgiveness — offsets, and perhaps even inspires, ultimate justice's efforts to reclaim the totality of the *imago Dei* by eliminating those whose very existence threatens the unity of the divine imprint. There is some overlap between contemporary American arguments about capital punishment and the ultra-rationalist ethic of eighteenth-century France that Camus studied. Camus perspicaciously gleaned how an "ethic of forgiveness," of endless compassion or runny sentimentalism, gives way to laxity, murder, and injustice. In an infrequently cited, though forceful passage near the end of his "Reflections on the Guillotine," Camus caustically challenges the belief "that there is no responsibility in this world and that we must give way to that modern tendency to absolve everything, victim and murderer, in the same confusion":

> Such purely sentimental confusion is made up of cowardice rather than of generosity and eventually justifies whatever is worst in this world. If you keep excusing, you eventually give your blessing to the slave camp, to cowardly force, to organized executioners, to the cynicism of great political monsters; you finally hand over your brothers.[68]

So, despite wrestling with the notion of punishment, Camus affirms, in the end, that we have no option but to rebel — *through punishment* — against the moral and political wretchedness that threatens life and the struggle for wholeness and meaning that gives life value. Yet this plea to preserve the nobility of life also drove Camus to oppose capital justice, which forecloses the possibility to rebel — to seek meaning and clarity from the universe, to search for unity and justice in a shattered world — because that defines and sustains the human condition. Society may be obliged to take away one's physical freedom in order to defend the lives of others, but when it keeps alive the most primordial yearning of every man and woman to rebel, society collectively affirms its "solidarity against death."

Capital punishment cuts a swifter path towards total justice when it seeks to restore the shattered unity of victims through the purgation of offend-

---

68. Camus, "Reflections," pp. 230-31.

ers. In our own culture, contemporary calls for execution in order to achieve "closure" — a full and final measure of justice for individuals and communities — can become totalizing yearnings. If closure became a totalizing aim, though, we would consider giving over murderers to families of victims — or in their stead, the state — to torture or inflict sufficient harm that a greater measure of justice might be felt.[69] Thankfully, justice is limited, in part because punishment is also limited. Punishment does not seek cleansing or "closure" but rather protects human life and preserves human dignity and agency by holding people accountable for their misdeeds. Such reckoning restores a symbolic balance to a disordered situation, even while sentencing limits prevent a totalizing drive for closure or brute justice from trumping all other concerns.

Taking together Camus's accounts of human nature, punishment, and justice, we arrive at what we might call *the principle of amends,* which underwrites his views on the death penalty. We know that human justice is necessary and that justice requires punishment. Yet we also know that human frailty places limits on our institutions such that when justice becomes absolute, it can participate in the very injustice it seeks to overcome.

> Must we therefore conclude that such frailty authorizes us to pronounce an absolute judgment and that, uncertain of ever achieving pure justice, society must rush headlong, through the greatest risks, toward supreme injustice? If justice admits that it is frail, would it not be better for justice to be modest and to allow its judgments sufficient latitude so that a mistake can be corrected?[70]

This principle, designed to give a state latitude to correct its errors, provides no hope for the state that unwittingly executes an innocent. This principle of amends cuts the other way, too. "Deciding that a man must have the definitive punishment imposed on him is tantamount to deciding that man has no chance of making amends."[71] For the convicted, capital punishment may eliminate the inkling of good that may come from publicly renouncing one's ways

---

69. Some families of murder victims lament the limits of punishment and justice, including the death penalty. Responding to the execution of Timothy McVeigh, a relative of one victim commented: "It seemed so little for so much pain that he gave us," while another declared, "Killing Timothy McVeigh 168 times [the number of his victims] wouldn't fill the void in my heart." See Lisa Anderson, "Some Felt Cheated by 'Easy' Death," *Chicago Tribune,* June 12, 2001, p. 1.

70. Camus, "Reflections," pp. 216-17.

71. Camus, "Reflections," p. 220. Camus poignantly defends his view by affirming the right of a convicted Gestapo agent to spend the rest of his life in prison reading the Bible, "Reflections," p. 222.

of nihilism and negation and joining others in the solidarity against death. Society, for its part, might challenge itself to consider the contribution to human justice that such lived contrition, when it affirms the moral and metaphysical conditions that authorize all of life, might provide over time. Capital punishment, which forecloses this possibility, should, on this reading, be forsworn. At least, *absent some exceptional warrant.* For, despite his heroic rebellion against capital punishment, even Camus counsels us to be wary of "monsters" who show no desire to repent or reform. Responding to retentionists who plead that such monsters "must merely be kept from doing it again, and [that] there is no other solution but to eliminate them," Camus concedes, "On this frontier, and it alone, discussion about the death penalty is legitimate."[72]

*　　*　　*

This argument for limited justice is premised on a view of human nature that affirms the nobility and worth of the human person while also acknowledging the corruption and fallibility resident in all humanity and human pursuits, including political aims and institutions. Limited justice, as taken up here, is not premised on a particular account of divinity or transcendence that obliges us to effectuate specific measures in order to achieve justice on earth. Belief in the divine may shape our understanding of justice, as was the case for Calvin; however, he also believed, along with Camus, that the necessities of earthly existence provide ample clarity for guiding political pursuits of justice. Moreover, if, like Camus, one never fully resolves the possibility that distant and divine horizons might be hovering above, then this gives credence to the belief that even a transcendent framework as ambivalent as this might be useful in limiting undertakings in justice and punishment. Limited justice presupposes that aspirations which reach for the heavens or collapse transcendent boundaries into earthly politics coincide with absolutist ventures that, at best, may foreclose more substantive realizations of justice and, at worst, may usher in supreme injustice. Three other key tenets flow from the case for limited justice.

First, justice is a primordial yearning fraught with irony. As justice-seekers, our infinite longing for unity, wholeness, and the proper harmony of relations in a social order is often frustrated by our finitude and inability to achieve a more suitable or perfect measure of justice. Limited knowledge, skewed moral dispositions, and the inability to achieve objective moral detachment all militate against efforts to redress injustices like murder that cry out for staunch response. Yet it is the unchecked human yearning for justice

72. Camus, "Reflections," p. 219.

that disposes us towards injustice. Recent examination of some capital systems of punishment reveals our inability to administer just capital judgments, the sole purpose of which is to achieve the robust measure of justice we seem to need. It is conceivable, however, that, under certain circumstances, eliminating the death penalty altogether risks allowing the state to become the ironic accomplice to violence and further injustice. Finally, consider the supreme irony of depriving a people from seeking justice for their own communities — citizens trying to restore balance and harmony following devastating crimes that have ripped apart the relational fabric of their collective lives — because the people of that community were perceived not to have a sufficiently robust sense of justice in that earlier they had prohibited the death penalty as a legal option.[73] The particular punishment — including death — is not the end itself, as Calvin said, but a mode of achieving justice; justice remains the eternal longing of a people to restore order and unity when they have been the victims of grave moral wrongs.

Second, because perfect and ultimate justice is always out of reach, the primary mandates of governments and polities are limited. Transformation or rehabilitation of criminal offenders may prove to be effective and worthy ends of public policy. Victims of crime may achieve a measure of healing or "closure" from their participation in the trials of accused criminals. Extra-civil efforts to restore damaged relations between aggrieved and offending parties may provide substantive and meaningful forms of reconciliation for certain victims, offenders, or members of a civic body. None of these goals, however, trump the primary mandates of government to preserve public safety, promote civic order, afford bodily protection to citizens, and render public judgment and censure on behavior that falls outside the bounds of a defined moral-political order that treasures human dignity. For these reasons alone, punishment remains an indispensable fulfillment of our most vital political responsibilities. The goods that government preserves are entirely secular, meaning that they pertain to the *saeculum* of earthly order and community — *under* God perhaps — but not *with, for,* or *alongside* God. *Pace* Calvin, such secular goods as quotidian peace and basic security may be divinely ordained; they need not be explicitly "divinized" in our political discourse, civil codes, or intimations of justice and punishment.

Finally, where feasible, limited justice leaves room for "new beginnings"

73. This seems to have been the case for many residents of Maryland who, perhaps even more than other Washington, D.C.–area residents, were terrorized by convicted snipers John Muhammad and seventeen-year-old Lee Malvo. Maryland's prohibition against executing minors was a central consideration in the U.S. attorney general's move to prosecute the snipers in Virginia where a capital sentence could be issued against Malvo (though, in the end, was not).

and human encounters with transcendence. That is to say, where forms of justice are available that are more substantive than criminal punishment — restorative efforts to repair relations damaged by criminal malfeasance — polities can provide some latitude on behalf of those who wish to pursue such measures, provided it does not undermine minimal commitments to public order and safety. Given their limited mandates as earthly arbiters of justice, governments are not obliged to facilitate contrition, exculpation, and other gestures toward the divine or to mediate divine and human forgiveness among criminals and their victims. But government can often refrain from closing off altogether such transcendent possibilities in which a greater measure of justice may be achievable, especially for those with religious commitments to repentance, forgiveness, and reconciliation and for those who seek the opportunity to make amends or new beginnings.

Of Casuistry and "Monsters"

Given the anthropological foundations of limited justice and the guiding ideals laid out above, can capital punishment ever be justified? And if so, under what circumstances? Reluctantly, we may come to accept certain exceptional circumstances that warrant execution. In proposing criteria surrounding the decision to impose the "ultimate punishment," as many see it, I accept the challenge of those who inquire why the relationship of capital judgment to just war reflection is not proposed more frequently. (See Stanley Hauerwas's chapter in this book.) For brevity's sake, I will only sketch the outlines of what a death penalty casuistry might entail.

The criterion of *necessity* is in keeping with the responsibilities of government to protect its citizens. If as a reasonable last resort, execution is the only way to ensure the safety of society, including corrections officials and other prisoners, then such extreme and exceptional measures might be warranted and indeed necessary. Inmates, especially, deserve the right to fulfill the terms of their sentences in safety; for among other reasons, the possibility for parole and to achieve new beginnings ceases to have any meaning if life in prison becomes so precarious. Furthermore, if the death penalty is eliminated altogether, what punishment is available to one who murders while sentenced to life in prison? Societies, of course, are free to expend their monetary resources to erect costly, extra-high security facilities (i.e., "supermax" prisons) if the very thought of execution is such anathema that a citizenry desires to avoid it at any expense. One would hardly be acting upon immoral instincts to suggest that such funds might also be put to good use elsewhere.

The criterion of *discrimination* asks whether society can adequately discriminate between those who are guilty and those whose guilt cannot be ascertained with moral certitude. The standard of guilt "beyond a reasonable doubt," we know, has proven to be inadequate in some capital settings. Rather, this standard has often lent so much doubt that citizens question the competence of their government. On this front — whether one supports or opposes the death penalty — current efforts to reform the practice must be heightened and accelerated to remove ambiguous elements like jail house informants and incompetent defense counsels that becloud the judicial process. Juries and state institutions tragically may condemn an innocent man to life in prison in the name of protecting society. But irreversible punishment requires a higher standard of "moral certainty," a standard that, if applied, would not only reduce significantly the number of executions carried out in the United States but would eliminate the chance of condemning the innocent to death row.[74]

Related to the category of discrimination, one dimension of the *principle of amends* calls our attention to the kind and quality of reparations society can feasibly make to one who is unjustly accused. While no public apology or financial restitution can give back to someone the years spent in prison, such public amends can seek to restore a symbolic modicum of justice to an unjust situation. Moreover, imposing death forecloses any opportunity to make amends or to seek a new beginning. And if we should seek punishment by death, it must be with the full moral certainty so as never to have occasion to question such an awesome decision, for which the state can never make adequate amends.

Public authority invites us to observe that the decision to impose death is never made on behalf of private motivations of vengeance, closure, or healing. To be sure, our civic sympathies should be most closely aligned to those who have experienced the terrible injuries associated with violent crime. Gilbert Meilaender, in his essay in this volume, suggests that one way to maintain the public character of capital judgment is to require randomly selected citizens to be official viewers of executions. Perhaps certain members of the convicting jury itself would be the appropriate body. Requiring that those who condemn a person to death be willing to witness the sentence they pronounce obliges individual citizens to evaluate in a personal, concrete, and unmediated way the political practice they legitimate.

The classical casuistic principle of *proportionality,* applied in this context, compares the death penalty to life in prison without the possibility for parole; it asks whether the "added" good that one believes comes *only* from execution is

---

74. The clearest cases involving "moral certainty" often involve those cases in which offenders or their counsels do not even contest criminal guilt.

compelling and whether it outweighs the harm committed by executing a member of one's society. This gets rather murky for, among other things, it requires us to take stock of all the many parties who are harmed or "helped" by the decision to execute — including the families of victims *and* offenders as well as members of the community who may feel vindicated by execution or disgusted by it. This is ultimately a decision that juries and voters will determine for themselves, but ensuring that juries consider the option to choose life imprisonment with no chance of parole will ensure that they first assess the "inadequacy" of this sentence before they go further in sentencing death.

Finally, the principle of *retributive equality* raises the consideration of the most hideous kinds of crimes that one may commit. "Monsters" — mass murderers, terrorists, architects of genocide, and other villains of humanity — come to mind here. If death is the appropriate sentence for evildoers responsible for the lives of tens, hundreds, or even thousands, are we right to wonder, Can the same sentence be equitable for "common murderers" who kill just one or even two people? The magnitude of some atrocities suggests perhaps that death, if it is to be applied, should be reserved increasingly for the very worst crimes. We might call this the Eichmann principle or, in the United States, the McVeigh principle. But this finds us on a slippery slope indeed: How many must one kill in order to be sentenced to death? Death penalty supporters might go so far as to suggest that this standard invites more harm than it censures: perhaps lesser criminals would be undeterred, or the lives lost by random murder would be deemed to count for less than those killed by terrorists. Certainly, these objections must be reckoned with, but we must also attend to realities that, in an age of terror and genocide, give new meaning to the notion of mass murder.

Casuistries are never black and white. They provide no easy answers to difficult questions of who should live and who should die. I will not try to answer this question either and will close instead in a Camusian vein, reminded of the first two federal executions committed in the United States after a twenty-seven-year hiatus. Terrorist Timothy McVeigh, in a widely celebrated execution, calmly walked to his death without a hint of remorse for the scheming and misdeeds that resulted in the loss of 168 lives in Oklahoma City. His nihilistic dreams of mass death and absolute negation were consummated the day he blankly welcomed the poison into his veins and proclaimed himself the unconquered master of his fate. A few days later, Raoul Garza, a drug lord charged with killing or ordering the deaths of three people, was dragged screaming to the lethal injection room. Pleading for his life and crying out for forgiveness, in his resistance, he joined the rest of the human community in solidarity against death. Perhaps one who renounces his comparatively lesser crimes and sins and seems to reconcile himself to his fellow man and who publicly expresses his contrition can restore a minute enough measure of justice to tip the scales against execution.

Epilogue

Many readers will note the similarity of this death penalty casuistry to the principles set out in just war thought.[75] Both forms of casuistry recognize the obligations of the state to protect its citizens and the state's mandate to pursue more than a nominal measure of justice; when necessary to preserve such ends, the use of coercion or force, while rueful, is considered justifiable. Both casuistries, however, also set limits concerning when and how such force may be applied. To that extent, casuistries of limited justice implicitly acknowledge that states may seek to overextend their influence; hence, for the protection of its own citizens and others, states' powers must be carefully circumscribed or restrained. Moreover, given that states often collectively possess formidable resources of power, they pose a greater political danger than ordinary citizens of misusing their powers, perhaps even as agents operating under the mantle of ultimate justice or divine retribution.

Finally, both forms of casuistry, despite their formulation in concrete and practical terms, rely upon a conceptual framework undergirded by strong assertions about human nature and even about the divine.[76] These anthropological and transcendent dimensions purport certain limits about the proper ambits and aims of political activity; such conceptual limits are entirely interconnected with those practical measures which not only legitimize the political pursuit of justice but also confine it. However, when the intellectual framework and its supporting theological, philosophical, and political traditions are bracketed, the accompanying casuistry gets reduced to a pocket-size tick-list in which the practical dimensions of limited justice lose much of their vigor. Hence the irony of limited justice involves the practical need that casuistry has for the conceptual framework from which it stems, however fortuitously unrelated the one, at first glance, may seem to the other.

75. For a rigorous treatment of, and constructive proposals for, modern uses of casuistry, see Richard Miller's *Casuistry and Modern Ethics: A Poetics of Practical Reasoning* (Chicago: University of Chicago Press, 1996), especially pp. 154-72 for his adaptation of just war principles to the debate about transplanting human fetal tissue.

76. For ways in which understandings of the human person and the divine give shape to a just war ethic, see Chapter 5 of Jean Bethke Elshtain's *Augustine and the Limits of Politics* (Notre Dame, Ind.: University of Notre Dame Press, 1995).

10. Responsibility, Vengeance, and the Death Penalty

VICTOR ANDERSON

In the fallen world, the center is at the same time the boundary. Man stands between law and fulfillment. He has the law, but he cannot fulfill it. Now Christ stands where man fails towards the law. Christ as the center means that he is the fulfillment of the law. So he is in turn the boundary and the judgment of man, but at the same time the beginning of his new existence, its center. Christ as the center of human existence means that he is man's judgment and his justification.

Dietrich Bonhoeffer
Christ the Center

While a student at Calvin Theological Seminary in Grand Rapids, Michigan, I became deeply immersed in the theologies of Karl Barth and H. Richard Niebuhr. Twenty years later, I find myself still turning to these Christian thinkers. I find in their ethics not only powerful vocabularies that help me to reflect clearly on the morality of the death penalty. They also offer two models of moral reflection that theologically crystallize the ethical question. With Barth, the ethical question is framed by the freedom and command of God in Jesus Christ. With Niebuhr, the ethical question is framed by the responsible self discerning the fitting response to the action of God upon us in all action. Moreover, in their accounts of the human condition, they attend to the ways that deeply sedimented human motives also act upon us in all things. They

195

provide a stereoscopic view of the Christian moral life. Such a point of view is what I want to develop in this essay.

I develop this short essay on Christian ethics and the death penalty in three moves. First, I discuss the divine command ethics of Barth in relation to capital punishment. I turn to Barth in particular because he provides a theological vocabulary that I find convincing for taking up the death penalty question in distinctive Christian terms. I am fully aware that Barth himself maintained a place for capital punishment in his ethics — albeit a highly mitigated place. However, I use Barth's theological insights to position Christian witness against the death penalty. The second move involves a turn into the human condition of vengeance as a "dark symbol" within the human-to-human encounter. I will argue that co-present with social symbols that reflect the freedom and command of God, symbols such as beauty, right, obligation, and justice, are dark social symbols such as violence and vengeance that act upon us. The power of these dark symbols may occasion moral ambivalence on the death penalty, even as Christian witness opposes it. Here, I will briefly turn to Edward Farley's discussion of deep symbols in his book, *Deep Symbols: Their Postmodern Effacement and Reclamation*.

In the third move, I take up the question of the death penalty under the responsibilist approach to Christian ethics and the deep symbols of grace and mercy in Christian social witness. The responsibilist approach shifts Christian categories from the language of obedience and command to the fitting response to God's action upon us in all action. I also employ the responsibilist approach because I find Barth's rejection of general ethics unhelpful for opening dialogue on a complex social issue such as the death penalty beyond the narrow parochialism of Christian answers. Dialogue is possible because both the Christian and society stand as responsible selves discerning out of their life together the fitting response to the death penalty. I will propose that where society may not be compelled to answer the question of the death penalty in terms of grace and mercy, these symbols nevertheless compel our Christian witness against it.

Divine Command and the Christian Moral Life

From Albrecht Ritschl in the nineteenth century and Karl Barth in the twentieth century to much of contemporary liberation and narrative theologies, the connection between theology and ethics is a matter of communal identification.[1] The connection involves theological consistency and coher-

---

1. I must say from the beginning that I do not hold that there is a necessary relation between

ence within a peculiar religious belief system. For instance, if God is supreme over all areas of human life, as a matter of internal consistency the moral life must be construed in theological terms. Again, the correlation of theology and ethics in such a case is a matter of the internal coherence between the teachings and actions of believers. In the divine command ethics of Karl Barth,[2] the identification of theology and ethics is made possible by his rejection of general ethics or what is usually called philosophical ethics. Barth suggests that typical general moral questions such as "What is the Good?" and "What ought I to do to be virtuous?" are simply false questions that give rise to what he called a general human ethics that is philosophically universalizable.[3]

For Barth, the moral question is the question of being. For him, the question "What am I?" or "Who am I?" is prior to the question "What ought I to do?" or "How shall I act?" Whether the question at hand is suicide or the death penalty, the fundamental ethical problem is that human beings want to know — independently of divine wisdom — what is right and good for them. Therefore, according to Barth, philosophical ethics is a human attempt to regulate good and evil, and the various systems of ethics are human answers to general ethical questions such as "What is the Good?" or "What does Justice require?" The very idea of a philosophical basis for ethics strikes against the theological recognition that "the grace of God protests against all man-made ethics as such."[4] For Barth, God's own being is both the norm of what is good and the answer to the ethical question.

God's grace through Jesus Christ puts to rest human answers to the ethical question, because the ethical question is settled in relation to the gracious action of God in Jesus Christ and Christ's obedience to God's action. Therefore, Christ's decision and obedience to God's action upon him is paradigmatic of the whole of the Christian moral life. Christian ethics is grounded in the Good, and Barth construes the Good theologically.

> [Jesus Christ] could not possibly regard as the good that which he had chosen for himself as such. No, it is as He is elected by the grace of God that the good is done. As the elect, quite apart from any choice of His own between good and evil, He is concerned only with obedience. He does not

---

ethics and theology. I think that the flowering of ethics throughout the professional and scientific discourses as well as its comfortable position in philosophy and social sciences suggest that ethics and, hence, ethical questions may be taken up under a wide spectrum of critical discourses.

2. Karl Barth, *Church Dogmatics* (Edinburgh: T&T Clark, 1957), II:2, §36-39; pp. 509-764.
3. Barth, *Church Dogmatics*, pp. 513ff.
4. Barth, *Church Dogmatics*, p. 517.

crave to be good of and for Himself. And so in all acts He is subject only to the will and command of God who alone is good. This is how the good is done here — in Jesus Christ. What has taken place in this way — in antithesis and contrast to all human ethics — is divine ethics.[5]

Barth crystallized the coherence of the Christian moral life in what has been called "divine command ethics." The divine command is (1) a correlate of the attributes of God's omnipotence, will, and goodness; (2) a function of divine liberty and grace in Jesus Christ; (3) a logical function of human radical dependence on God the creator; and (4) consistent with a God-centered faith that stands opposed to a human-centered faith. God alone is the ultimate center of the moral life.

Like Barth, I also think of Christian ethics as a response to God's acts toward humanity. For Barth, the manner of God's action toward humanity is disclosed in the "One" command to all of creation. "Be!" or "Live!" is the one command of God. In other words, God commands the flourishing of the creation, including the human creature. For Barth, the Christian life is a life of obedience to the command of God. As he describes the relationship between God and the human, it is one that subordinates the human to the creator. We ought not to think of subordination here as domination. Rather, the relationship of subordination is ontological. The relationship constitutes human existence before God, the creator of all life. This ontological relationship is morally framed under the command of God. The divine command is not a negative command. It is not absolutely determined by a negative imperative such as "No — you may not!" It is a positive imperative placed on the whole of humanity. It is the divine "Yes — you may live! Yes — you may flourish and thrive!" This divine "yes" establishes God's claim on humanity. Revealed in this one command is the character of God's action toward us all.

What, then, does the priority of the divine yes over the divine no mean for Christian ethics? It suggests that the God who commands favors the being, flourishing, thriving, and fulfillment of the creature's life. This is the divine yes. Death and vengeance are the divine no. For Christian ethics, this priority of the divine yes over no suggests that God acts for humanity as the gracious God who commands the creature to live and be. In other words, God's regulative disposition toward humanity is disclosed in the divine yes, which according to Barth is greater than God's no. On this point, Barth is worth quoting at length.

5. Barth, *Church Dogmatics,* p. 517.

The unredeemed mind of man, splits off from the mind of the Creator, denies its origin, denies itself. Now how does it happen that there is no resolving of this contradiction? The no from the earliest days has had on its side much greater power to convince than the yes has had; what is the reason it cannot once for all submerge the yes? Why is it that we never break through to the clear and final conclusion that our senses of being inside are mistaken? The answer is hinted at in the very inevitableness of our continued asking for knowledge of God; we belong to the yes and not the no.[6]

In Barth's divine command ethics, Jesus Christ is the "Ethical Man [*sic*]." In Jesus' person and works are shown the pattern of God's action toward all humanity. From this perspective, the ethical question is always the theological question: "How is God disposed toward humanity?" The answer is as the gracious God who commands being, life, and human flourishing as norms of human actions toward others. To summarize Barth's position: (1) the one command of God is ontologically entailed in the creature-to-creator subordination that structures the human and divine relationship; and (2) God's yes prioritizes the human-to-human encounter as it does the divine and human encounter in Jesus Christ.

When Barth takes up the question of capital punishment, he does so to test its compatibility with the command of God. He has no doubt that killing another person in self-defense is compatible with the command "Thou shalt not kill." Killing in self-defense is done in obedience to the law of life. Such a death results from a person protecting his or her own life from arbitrary and wanton disregard by an assailant. For Barth, however, the question is whether such a rationale holds when the state takes the life of an individual member. He argues that the state's interest in protecting life enters into internal contradiction when it punishes its members by death. As a regular, instituted practice of society, Barth regards capital punishment as incompatible with the divine command. It calls into doubt the character of society and it makes the death sentence a routine practice in punishing its members. Such a society oversteps its temporal responsibility for protecting life when it positions itself as ultimate judge and executioner. In an important passage Barth says:

> For is it not the case that, when organized society puts to death one of its members, it entangles itself in several serious self-contradictions? It belongs to its nature as an orderly society that its measures can have only a

---

6. Karl Barth, *The Word of God and the Word of Man* (Gloucester, Mass.: Peter Smith, 1957, 1978), p. 54.

provisional, relative and limited character, that they must always be in a position to transcend and correct. But in punishing by death, it does something unlimited, irrevocable, and irrepeatable. Again, it belongs to its nature as an orderly society that its actions must be designed to secure and maintain the life of its people. But to punish by death is to destroy life. Again, it belongs to its nature as an orderly society that it should affirm and protect the right of all its members along with its own right. But when it punishes by death, it does not merely limit the right of a culpable member, which is the essence of all punishment, but it takes away his right altogether. What is to become of self-defense from all these various angles? Punishing by death, it attacks the very thing which it prefers to defend. It renounces its very being as an orderly society. It returns to the level of anarchical self-defense. But all this means that it throws far more serious doubt upon its own position than it could ever do by allowing the criminal to live and rendering him innocuous in some other way. (pp. 444-45)

Barth does not affirm the death penalty as a regular institution in civil society. It should not be established punishment for crimes that fall under a nation's penal code. Nevertheless, there are two extraordinary occasions where, on Barth's divine command theory, God may command capital punishment. They are high treason in war and tyranny. His argument is based on the analogy that state-sanctioned capital punishment is analogous to a death that results from an individual defending his or her own life. The analogy is based on the body politic. Here, the state is the amalgam of all individuals constituting civil society. Barth reasons that God ordained civil society and endowed it with the gift of life which God gives to every human being. High treason in war and tyranny are understood as heinous assaults on society's life. Therefore, capital punishment is society's means of defending its life and righting the assault on its life.

Barth concedes that these two cases are exceptional. In high treason, the traitor joins his or her life to that of the enemy. Therefore, in wartime, society regards the traitor's life as co-joined to the enemy's life. The traitor's death ought rightly to fall under the nation's military code. In the second exceptional case, the tyrant seizes total authority over a nation's structures of justice and all legislative systems. All social systems for protecting the life of society, including the military, are corrupted by the absolute authority of one. Therefore, individual members of civil society have a duty to preserve the life of society by taking the life of a grievous tyrant. Duty, therefore, is the objective determinant of the divine command. However, as Barth reflects on these exceptional cases to capital punishment, his position is mitigated by the subjective determinant of the command, which is respect for life. Neither the traitor nor the tyrant ceases to fall under the grace, mercy, and judgment of God in Jesus Christ. Although as the state is constituted a body politic, it may be commanded by God to put to death those who threaten our social life with mass destruction, out of respect for life, the Christian citizen has a spiritual duty to proclaim the grace and mercy of God to the traitor and tyrant.

Barth's attempt to hold together the objective and subjective determinant of the command results in a paradox. We are commanded to kill the traitor and the tyrant, while ministering to each the grace and mercy of God. Barth reconciles the paradox, suggesting in effect that both the traitor and the tyrant have so isolated themselves from any means of security and safety in society that their deaths can be understood as an act of mercy (the strictest mercy) as opposed to their living in perpetual remorse, threat, fear of vengeance and vendettas. With their deaths, the temporal and relative gift of life is concluded, but they may anticipate eternal grace as each falls under the judgment of God in Christ. Capital punishment in these exceptional cases imposes humility on those who kill out of duty to the command (the objective determinant of the command) because respect for life (the subjective determinant of the command) — even the lives of the traitor and the tyrant — is also divinely commanded.

To conclude this section on divine command ethics and capital punishment, Barth's position of capital punishment is a mitigated one. It is mitigated by his view of the body politic. The state ought not to make capital punishment a regulative institution of civil society. However, insofar as it is constituted a body politic, the state may be commanded by God to execute the traitor whose action threatens the life of society. In this case, the death is analogous to self-defense. Moreover, where society and its apparatuses for protecting itself against internal threat are corrupted by dictatorial power, individual members of society may be commanded by God to kill the tyrant out of duty and respect for the life of society.

Barth's position is moreover mitigated on an anthropological basis. While standing under the grace of God, humanity nevertheless lives by the no of death, violence, and vengeance wherein one feels himself or herself irreparably harmed by another. Without the grace of justice, these human motives would so poison the human-to-human relation that society itself would die. Given the body politic, individuals transfer to the state their claims of harm, leaving to the state the power to act on their behalf to exact payment for the harm inflicted upon them. In turn, their human motives for vengeance and vendettas are transferred to the justice of the state and the peace and life of society are preserved. As I read Barth, vengeance is the underside of justice. And both are transformed by the grace, mercy, and judgment of God in Christ. In the next section, I want to discuss vengeance as a "dark social symbol" that is co-present with justice.

Vengeance as Dark Symbol

I am in great agreement with Barth's analysis of the human condition. I also hold the view that behind the justice of capital punishment lies the human motive of vengeance. However, in this section, I want to develop this line of thought by examining the human motive of vengeance as a "dark social symbol" that is co-present with the social symbol of justice. To guide my thinking on this mater, I turn to an essay entitled *Deep Symbols: Their Postmodern Effacement and Reclamation* by the North American systematic theologian Edward Farley.[7] By deep symbols, Farley means words of power that "constrain and guide" persons in their various negotiations with postmodern life.[8] Farley is aware that such words or symbols are not the conventions of any one institution such as religion, law, politics, or science. Nevertheless, they are human conventions. They arise from the intersubjective depth structures of human communities.

They function as deeply rooted categories of social meaning within our increasing, changing, and developing stock of knowledge about the earth and its relation to the sky, stars, and other planets. Such symbols as cosmos, universe, and chaos meet each generation's understanding of the world as each comes into the world. Social symbols such as family, love, and friend shape how each generation comes to terms with aspects of our social and moral world. Social symbols such as male and female, time and space are so sedimented that their meanings are taken for granted in the everyday ordinary activities of human communities. This sedimentation of symbols is what Farley means by the depth structure of intersubjective understanding and meaning within the human-to-human encounter.

Deep symbols are so basic that one almost always feels them to be *a priori,* or at least one is tempted to regard them as such. But they are historical constructs. As Farley warns, their "taken-for-granted" qualities often conceal their elusive ambiguities. Deep symbols function normatively insofar as they

---

7. Edward Farley, *Deep Symbols: Their Postmodern Effacement and Reclamation* (Valley Forge: Trinity Press International, 1996).

8. Farley, *Deep Symbols,* p. x.

are regulative ideals such as justice, equality, and freedom. They enchant insofar as they keep society open to mystery. In our society, for example, notions of the beautiful may keep us from ever turning our natural environment into mere utilities for consumption. However, deep symbols are fallible insofar as they are vulnerable to historical change and corruptibility. They are located in a master narrative that reflexively identifies and defines social actions in human communities. Deep symbols "can rise and empower, and they can lose their power and disappear."[9] In our postmodern context, Farley worries most about the erosion of agreement we have on symbols that make social life meaningful, mysterious, open to beauty, while cognizant of others that destroy cooperation and social peace. Such symbols I call dark symbols.

Among Farley's candidates for deep symbols are education, beauty, reality, rights, nature, freedom, community, and justice. To qualify as a deep symbol, the word must formally have the quality of signifying a value or a set of values "by which a community understands itself, from which it takes its aims, and to which it appeals as canons of cultural criticism."[10] Farley however brackets other symbols that signify dark motives, actions and social possibilities in the human-to-human relation. Where beauty is foreground, the ugly and repulsive are intersubjectively understood. We embrace the one and ridicule or hide away from the other. Reality and nature have social meaning against the absurd, false, freakish, and the mad. It takes no intellectual sophistication to imagine what we have done to each other as we act on such symbols. Right and freedom arise as powerful social symbols against the brute domination of some over others in the social world. Community rises as a powerful social symbol where lives are fragmented, isolated, and disempowered by alienating social systems. And justice appears in our human-to-human encounter, where we violate each other's lives and flourishing. Where violation seems irreparable the dark symbol of vengeance is co-present with the social symbol of justice. And with Barth, vengeance seems a "natural" condition of the human-to-human relation.

I am not suggesting that the dark symbol of vengeance is more basic or prior to the deep symbol of justice. My point is that it appears to be as basic as justice and other social symbols that Farley commends. The power of vengeance to socially shape our human encounters and open our imaginations to forms of cruelty and violence exhibits vulnerability to the transformative norms of justice. Justice limits this dark symbol from absolutely defining the human-to-human encounter. Vengeance is duplicitous. It may signify cultural

9. Farley, *Deep Symbols,* p. 3.
10. Farley, *Deep Symbols,* p. 3.

solidarity among groups of people, provide conceptual possibilities for social self-definition, and elicit possibilities for individual status within the community. Gang and paramilitary culture are examples of these possibilities. Yet it is fallible and unable to sustain itself as a regulative ideal in social life. Farley himself is quite aware of the potency of what I have called dark symbols to sustain, enchant, and empower forms of community that often rival the best intentions of Christian community. He sees such symbols as dangerously oriented toward forms of totality in which "death camps, genocidal policies and events, malicious torture, and cynical nihilism" cut off the interhuman appeal.[11] It is Farley's commitment to a set of regulative ideals such as self, personhood, justice, obligation, truth, and beauty that prohibits the dark symbol of vengeance from functioning for him as a deep social symbol.[12]

I have great sympathy with Farley's judgment about such a dark symbol as vengeance. However, given his emphasis on the fallibility and vulnerability of all our deep symbols, even the ones he wants to bring to the foreground, each of our social symbols may be oriented toward forms of totality. Farley himself seems to recognize the dark duplicity of his own deep symbols when he says:

> As instruments of corrupted power, deep symbols can mirror the society's stratification of privilege. . . . Thus, the deep symbols can be so framed as to advance the privileged members and suppress the voice of the unprivileged. They still may function as deep values and ideals, but in those ideas lurk racism, the disenfranchising of women, and the maintenance of social policies that favor an existing social elite.[13]

To be sure, vengeance is a poisonous symbol within the human-to-human encounter. And it has great power to distort and even destroy possibilities for reconciliation within the interhuman encounter. Yet, the condition that gives rise to this dark symbol remains human — all too human. With vengeance, the victim seeks an action of equal force upon the one or many who perpetrated irreparable harm on the victim. Scripture is replete with such responses, from the story of Cain and Abel (Gen. 4:1-15) and the rape of Dinah and the massacre of the Shechemites (Gen. 34:1-31) to the killing of the innocents by King Herod (Matt. 2:13-23). In these stories, vengeance guides to exact satisfaction.

Thus far my discussion of vengeance as a dark symbol that is co-present

11. Farley, *Deep Symbols*, p. 24.
12. Farley, *Deep Symbols*, p. 23.
13. Farley, *Deep Symbols*, p. 8.

with justice has been formal. But as I reflexively think about the association of vengeance to capital punishment, I can relate to vengeance as a deeply sedimented human motive and possibility when I consider the atrocities that people perpetrate on others. For me, there are many cases in which I feel the desire for exact satisfaction. There is the murder of James Byrd Jr. in Jasper, Texas. Byrd was beaten to death and dragged to pieces while chained to a pickup truck on June 7, 1998. Matthew Shepard, twenty-one, was left to die tied to a fence on a freezing night in Wyoming after being pistol-whipped because of his homosexual preference on October 19 of the same year. When I consider the victims of the Oklahoma City bombing of April 19, 1995, and the World Trade Center massacre of September 11, 2001, the dark symbol of vengeance meets me. I want exact satisfaction on the assailants. In these instances of killing, the violation is so arbitrary and wanton in its disregard for the life and flourishing of others that a "killing rage" wells up in me and cries for exact satisfaction.

To bring this section to a close, my initial discussion of vengeance as a dark symbol is formal. My point is that this dark social symbol is not prior to or more basic than the social symbol of justice. Rather, the two symbols are co-present to each other. Foregrounding the one, justice, as a regulative ideal limits the power of the other, vengeance, from totalization within the social order. However, while the dark symbol of vengeance recedes into the background of justice, it nevertheless enters into our social meaning of justice. This is the formal aspect of my discussion. But in the reflexive discussion of vengeance in the latter part of this discussion, I become morally ambivalent about the morality of the death penalty. I find myself standing where Barth stood. Barth sought consistency in his Christian interpretation of the divine command and called into question capital punishment as a regulative institution of civil society. He also recognized that there are some human acts so heinous and destructive of human life and flourishing that ethical absolutism against the death penalty appeared morally absurd. Squaring capital punishment with the divine command, he admitted two cases as exceptional to his moral injunction against the death penalty.

I hold that the manner of God's actions toward us in Jesus Christ issues in the divine no against capital punishment, for God's yes to life is greater than God's no. Reflexively, however, the human condition that seeks exact satisfaction wrestles against my theological convictions about the triumph of grace over death and vengeance. Barth reconciled his ambivalence by interpreting civil society and the state as abstract subjects, a body politic, that stands under the command of God. When its life is threatened by treachery and tyranny, the death of the tyrant and the traitor is the body politic killing in self-defense. I, like Barth, interpret civil society and the state to be a body politic. Unlike Barth, I do not interpret them theologically to stand under the command of God. Therefore, I shall have no need to reconcile by way of his self-defense argument the centrality of grace in Christian ethics with capital punishment. In making clear my own position, I will draw on the responsibilist approach to Christian ethics where the question of ethics shifts from "divine command" to the "fitting response."

The Responsibilist Approach to the Death Penalty

In *The Responsible Self,* H. Richard Niebuhr does not treat Christian ethics in the language of command or obedience. Rather, he evokes the symbol of responsibility. For him, when human existence is construed under the symbol of responsibility humans are seen as "answerers" to action upon them. Human moral life is framed by dialogue, acting in response to another's action upon one's self. He says:

> [W]e think of all our actions as having the pattern of what we do when we answer another who addresses us. To be engaged in dialogue, to answer questions addressed to us, to defend ourselves against attacks, to reply to injunctions, to meet challenges — this is our common experience. And now we try to think of all our actions as having this character of being responses, answers, to actions upon us.[14]

I take Niebuhr to suggest that all human institutions, civil society and the state, are responsible subjects, even if they are not Christian subjects. However, from the point of view of Christian ethics, our actions are responses or answers to God's action upon us. For the question in Christian ethics is "How is God acting upon us?" Here, Niebuhr follows Barth. "When we say that the power by which we are is God, we may express our interpretation in trust, for to say 'God' is to say 'good' in our common speech; the word 'God' means the affirmer of our being, not its denier. . . ."[15] Christian morality is an answer to God's gracious action upon us. Niebuhr writes:

> The responsible self we see in Christ and which we believe is being elicited in all our race is a universally and eternally responsive I, answering in universal society and in time without end, in all actions upon it, to the ac-

14. H. Richard Niebuhr, *The Responsible Self* (New York: Harper & Row, 1963), p. 56.
15. Niebuhr, *Responsible Self,* p. 119.

tion of the One who heals all our diseases, forgives our incquities, saves our lives from destruction, and crowns us with everlasting mercy. The action we see in such life is obedient to law, but goes beyond all laws; it is form-giving but even more form-receiving; it is fitting action. It is action which is fitted into the context of universal, eternal, life-giving action by the One. It is infinitely responsible in an infinite universe to the hidden yet manifest principle of its being and its salvation.[16]

From the responsibilist approach, the moral question of the death penalty is not framed by obedience to the divine command. Rather, the question of the death penalty is framed as the question of whether such an action as capital punishment is the fitting response to God's acts of grace, forgiveness, salvation, and mercy toward us. For the responsible self, the death penalty is understood theologically as the action of God upon us. From the responsibilist point of view, the relevant moral question is: What is the fitting Christian answer to state-sanctioned execution? However the question is answered, the responsibilist approach requires that the answer witnesses to the general pattern of God's action toward us in Christ. I hold that the pattern of God's actions toward us is framed in Christian faith by the deep symbols of judgment, grace, and mercy.

I recognize that as the question is particular (What is the fitting Christian response to the action of God in the death penalty?) so is the answer (God meets us in Jesus Christ as the God of grace and mercy). By centering the Christian response to the death penalty on grace and mercy, I am not suggesting that either society or the state is of necessity to be compelled by this Christian response. While my point of view is Christian enough, it is not theocratic. I do not hold the state or society to be divine institutions. I hold that when society and the state are construed formally as a body politic, as responsible selves, they no less than I struggle to discern the fitting response to the death penalty. However, neither are compelled to answer in Christian terms. Formally, I take the state to be an abstract rational subject and agent that is entrusted by its citizens to satisfy our claims of violation and harm. Its actions are to be guided by neither malice nor vengeance. Through its determinations of justice, it seeks to preserve the peace and life of society. And as it administers its duties (while in dialogue with Christian responses), its responses to punishment may be incompatible with the priority of grace and mercy in Christian ethics.

From the responsibilist approach, even if society and the state are ab-

16. Niebuhr, *Responsible Self,* pp. 144-45.

stract subjects formally, citizens are not; they have faces. As responsible citizens wrestle with the death penalty question, they are bound on every side by traditions and communities defined by racial, ethnic, gender, class, and sexual differences. As human beings seeking to resolve irreparable harm done against each other, we are finite in our judgments. Being human, the possibility of error hovers over all our judgments. This possibility is no less real when it is we who bring about the death of another. We are confronted by the sheer reality that as limited subjects with limited reason, understanding, judgment, and will, we are also limited in our ability to determine the fitting response to the social necessity of retributive justice. However, fallibilism in exacting justice warrants extreme caution about our practice of sentencing persons to death.

From the responsibilist perspective, as judges, we need to ask whether our having high probability — absent the guarantee of certainty — in our judicial determination of guilt is an adequate warrant for issuing the death penalty. This is especially the case when our judgments may bring about the execution of innocent persons based on probability alone and not certainty, for killing an innocent person is non-correctable. As a nation, we participate in the political and moral concerns of other global communities of justice. The responsible citizen asks whether our practice of sentencing persons to death reflects the moral character of the kind of people we want other nations to emulate in their practice of justice. Niebuhr says, "The responsible self is driven as it were by the movement of the social process to respond and be accountable in nothing less than a universal community."[17] As Christian citizens, we are to ask whether our practice of issuing the death penalty reflects the best moral insight and intent of the gospel of reconciliation, grace, and mercy.

Some Christian moralists justify the death penalty by appealing to scriptural warrants in Romans that entrust to the government the administration of justice;[18] my point of view is not opposed to our interpreting the state and society as divinely instituted. I do not hold such an interpretation, but I understand why others might. I ask instead whether the administration of death is the fitting response to the action of God upon us. With this question in mind, I quoted Dietrich Bonhoeffer at the head of this essay. "Christ as the center means that he is the fulfillment of the law. So he is in turn the boundary and the judgment of man, but at the same time the beginning of his new existence, its center. Christ as the center of human existence means

17. Niebuhr, *Responsible Self*, p. 88.
18. Romans 13:1-7.

that he is man's judgment and his justification."[19] I take this to mean that Christ has already stood both in the judgment of every person and in the justification of all. As I understand the gospel, this judgment is unrepeatable, for it was once and for all a judgment of death.

My appeal to the unrepeatable action of God in Christ's judgment for all does not negate the authority of the state to administer punishment. I agree with Barth here that the death penalty ought not to be a regulative institution of civil society for punishment. Rather, my appeal to the judgment of God in Christ centers reflection on the death penalty on God's action toward all persons — even the criminal, the traitor, and the tyrant. Christ's obedience and gracious response to the action of God upon him on the cross means that the penalty of death for sin is superseded by the resurrected life of Christ. Moreover, the penalty of death for sin is also superseded by a new manner of being in the world that was inaugurated by Christ's victory over death. The new is framed by two deep symbols of Christian faith: Grace and Mercy. I hold these symbols to be constitutive of our new being in Christ. They fundamentally guide our responses not only to God's action upon us but also our actions upon each other.

Where the death penalty remains the ultimate punishment by the state, Christian witness requires a fitting response to the action of the state upon us. Recognizing that our judgments in issuing justice are fallible, the responsible Christian citizen appeals to the state and its authorities for grace and mercy in its administration of justice. Notwithstanding my own reflexive moral ambivalence toward the death penalty when I consider both the atrocities we commit against each other and the human desire for vengeance, I am nevertheless compelled theologically to answer the ethical question of the death penalty in terms of God's actions upon us in Christ. In Christ, where there is hate, we are met with love. Where there is dread, we are met with hope. Where we appear fated, we are met with transcendence. Where we are wronged, we are met with forgiveness. And where we are guilty, we are met with grace and mercy.

To conclude, I look at the ethics of the death penalty from a responsibilist approach to Christian ethics. With Barth, I understand the divine command to be one that prioritizes life, being, existence, and the flourishing of the creature. This is the divine yes, which is over the no of death and vengeance. In agreement with Niebuhr, I believe that the God who commands is the God who meets us in all action upon us as the gracious and merciful God. I have proposed that in our Christian moral reflection on the death penalty,

---

19. Dietrich Bonhoeffer, *Christ the Center* (New York: Harper & Row, 1960), p. 63.

mercy and grace remain vitally relevant deep symbols of our Christian witness to and engagement with social life. While Christians may entrust to the state the administration of justice, I am fully aware that neither the state nor society may be persuaded by Christian responses that witness against the death penalty. Still, our response to the death penalty compels us to ask what is the fitting response to God's gracious action in Jesus Christ upon us all. In answering this question, I have evoked the deep symbols of Christian social witness, grace and mercy. These symbols constitute our Christian witness to those who administer the death penalty in the name of justice.

III Personal Commitments and
Public Responsibilities

11. The Death Penalty:
What's All the Debate About?

FRANK KEATING

I offer these thoughts and reflections on the death penalty from a public policy perspective and from a governor's perspective. State governors have direct roles to play in capital punishment administration: we are sworn to uphold the law in our states and we participate in the debate as well.

Before I begin, let me make a few personal remarks. I am a Catholic, but I come from a very diverse, ecumenical background. Of my four grandparents, one was a Methodist, one was a Presbyterian, one was a Quaker, and the other was a Catholic. My mother was not a Catholic, but later became one. My wife and I were not married in the Catholic Church since she was not a Catholic, though she later became one. I should probably also note that only 3 percent of the people in my state of Oklahoma are Catholic.

As governor, I was invited to University College in Dublin, Ireland — the place where John Henry Newman held forth with such extraordinary wisdom. I had never been to the Republic of Ireland and I arrived as a guest to participate in a debate on the subject of capital punishment. My name, Keating, is Irish, so of course while I was there I had to look up the Keatings. I didn't realize it was a rather common name, but we found some Keatings, went to lunch, and toured Dublin. One of my hosts asked, "Why are you here?"

I told her, "Oh, I've been invited to debate capital punishment."

This essay is adapted from Governor Keating's address, delivered on 25 January 2002 at the University of Chicago Divinity School.

Then she said, "Well, there's no debate; we're against it."

And I said, "Well, I realize you're opposed to it here, but you mean there's really no disagreement on the issue?"

"That's correct, I mean no one's for it," she replied. "Where are you debating capital punishment?"

"At University College, Dublin," I responded.

And she said, "Well, they're all against it there, too. You really should not have even come. This is a waste of your time."

Those who have ever been to those university classrooms in Ireland can visualize the scene: the amphitheater environments, filled with perhaps two or three hundred students, where everybody is smoking. The chief justice of the Irish Supreme Court was to be the moderator of the debate and there were to be two barristers against capital punishment and two barristers for. I was one of the barristers for. The problem was my fellow barrister didn't show up, so I was a lone ranger; I was all by myself.

But several of the things I said that day came as somewhat of a surprise to my Irish listeners. The impression they had was that the United States is a killing field, that we execute everyone for everything, and that it is a killing field largely focused on minorities. I explained to them that the United States' problem is its incredible violence: our problem as a country is that we — in many cities and in many rural areas, too — treat life cheaply. For example, it came as a big shock to me when the prime minister of Ireland said that, in the previous year, they had forty homicides in Ireland — a nation of 3.8 million or so, a little larger than the state of Oklahoma. In Oklahoma City alone last year, we had sixty homicides, and a total of 180 in the entire state.

When some Catholics in my audience pointed out that the Pope felt that capital punishment should be rare if not nonexistent, I told them, "In the United States, believe it or not, that is practically true." Between 1977 and the time of my speech (and the number of homicides has increased, unfortunately, since then) there were something like 480,000 homicides and 629 executions in the United States. In the state of Oklahoma, in the heartland of America, right in the middle of the United States, we had 8,000 homicides in the years since 1977 and thirty executions; something like one-half of 1 percent of the killings in our state resulted in executions. So for 480,000 deaths, the United States executed 629 people — something like one-twelfth of 1 percent of the killings resulted in executions; if one applied that same standard to the Republic of Ireland, the Irish wouldn't execute anybody either, because one-twelfth of 1 percent of forty people is zero.

The Irish listeners were also surprised that there was anguish on the part of those of us who consider ourselves conservative. As a pro-life conservative, I believe in the quality of each individual life, in the goodness of every human being, and in the right of everyone to stand tall, to do that which he or she can do in this magnificent free society in which we live. But again, my audience was surprised that there was anguish and debate, that in our religiously pluralistic environment we have a very vigorous debate on capital punishment. I think that debate is a good thing and that is why it's very important that we are taking up the subject in this volume.

My friends in Ireland were also surprised that, in my state, the average time between conviction and execution was ten years. They thought that if somebody committed a crime, that person was quickly executed. They were also surprised to learn that, nationwide, an average of nearly ten years passes between the time of a person's conviction and subsequent execution.

It is true, I said, that we have offenses at the federal level to which the death sentence can be applied — for trafficking large amounts of narcotics and for treason. But for all practical purposes, certainly at the state level, capital punishment is reserved for people who kill other human beings.

The Irish audience was also surprised that a life sentence was not a life sentence per se. In my career of public service, I have been an FBI agent, a state prosecutor, and a United States attorney. I have supervised all the federal prosecutions in the United States and most federal law enforcement agencies in the country, including the U.S. Bureau of Prisons. It came as a surprise to them that we had situations in which people were sentenced to life in prison without parole and yet people were released, people escaped, people killed other people while in prison — and that happens, by the way, far more frequently than we think.

Our moral challenge as a people not only is to continue debating this subject but also to try to make us a better people. We kill too many people and we have far too much violence — far, far too much violence.

My background is law enforcement, not the academy or divinity. I remember as an FBI agent in Seattle, Washington, I went to Seattle-Tacoma Airport during Christmas week and opened the door of a van, and out tumbled a man who had been shot in the temple. He was the driver of that van and in the course of robbing him, his assailants had killed him. I remember going to the home of his widow and his children. They had decorated a Christmas tree with tinsel and lights — it was a very moving, wonderful, and very special seasonal scene. And there I was telling them about the father and the husband that they would never see again; it just broke my heart that someone could do this to somebody else. I would guess that some of the most ardent capital punishment advocates are people like me who have seen up close and personally dealt with those who horribly, cruelly treat other people.

During my talk in Ireland I asked the audience, "What would you do with someone like Roger Dale Stafford, who was the first person executed on my watch as governor?" Tell me what you do with a Roger Dale Stafford who, south of Interstate 35 in Oklahoma City, waved down a car with a staff sergeant of the Air Force and his wife and their eight-year-old son inside. Stafford took the staff sergeant over the hill and shot him in the face, killing him. This was a robbery, yet he also took his wife over the same berm and shot and killed her. Then he came down to the truck, and, whimpering in the back of the cab of the truck, wrapped up in blankets trying to get away from it all, was the eight-year-old son; Stafford fired until he was out of bullets into the back of the truck to make the whimpering stop. Then he went to a steakhouse in Oklahoma City, a family restaurant. As it was closing up, he herded four fifteen-year-olds and two adults into the freezer and killed them execution-style while taking money from the cash register. Now, what do you do with someone like that?

According to my sense of ethics, my sense of morals, my sense of right and wrong, you don't chop off someone's hand for bouncing a check, but somebody who kills nine human beings forfeits the right to live. That is my sense of values, my sense of ethics. I look at someone like that and I think to myself that this good earth, this wonderful land, is too good for that person. I honestly believe that. Now, obviously if the state of Oklahoma, or the United States, were to move in another direction, I would uphold the law — not necessarily with a smile but I would do so — because I took an oath to uphold the law.

Timothy McVeigh killed 168 of our neighbors and friends in Oklahoma City, including nineteen children. Many people say the death penalty debate shouldn't get into emotions; you shouldn't talk about individuals. But you have to because that's what it is all about — people doing horrible, incredibly sick, evil things to other people. Timothy McVeigh made a political statement by blowing up a building — knowing that there was a daycare center inside. When I saw the wreckage, the carnage that resulted, the anguish, the agony, the destruction of lives and livelihoods and happiness and future that resulted, I was unforgiving.

Now, for those who say, "But isn't there a chance that you would execute the innocent?" there's no evidence of that. Even Barry Scheck, attorney and co-founder of the Innocence Project, admitted that, as far as he knows, that has never occurred; there's no evidence of it. But, yes, that is something that all of us have to be very concerned about. I would like to think that it's enough that ten to twelve years pass between conviction and execution, during which time in both the state and the federal systems the average number of appeals is about twelve. No governor, no pardon or parole board wants to execute an innocent person. Why? Because the guilty person would still be free. Why would any of us want an individual responsible for what Timothy McVeigh did or Roger Dale Stafford did to be walking the street? We want the right person identified and removed from society. That is our responsibility. We want to make sure we have the right person. Every individual has the rights and the full panoply of protections available through the criminal justice system, including a first-rate defense. But, in my view, once a judge or jury makes a decision, the law should be carried out. That does not cause me much disquiet; it does not give me sleepless nights.

Another common objection concerns deterrence. What do the numbers tell us about capital punishment's deterrent effectiveness? Well, I'm not sure they tell us a whole lot. They certainly tell us that the United States is a far more violent place than the Republic of Ireland. Maybe that's the result of our dysfunctional family life. Maybe that's the result of out-of-wedlock births and divorce and all of the various breakdowns that we experience in society. I will say this, however: in law enforcement, when there was a liquor store shooting, during which the police would shoot an individual involved in an armed robbery, there wasn't another robbery for several days. I do know that. Maybe potential criminals decided to sit it out for a while. The cops used to muse about it — that whenever you would catch a very bad guy, you would have at least several days of peace. I'm not saying that's universally the case; it probably isn't. Now as to *individual deterrence,* I can guarantee you Roger Dale Stafford has quite definitely — as has Timothy McVeigh — been deterred. Neither of those guys will ever do what they did again — and that's a pretty compelling fact.

Still another argument against the death penalty is that life imprisonment protects society equally well. Let me say this: if we could assure ourselves that an individual who did something horrific — who killed another human being — could, in fact, be segregated forever, I would be open to that. But, as a practical matter that simply wasn't, isn't, nor ever will be the case. At the federal prison in Marion, Illinois — the only Level Six prison when the federal prison system was under my supervision — we built a special building for an individual who killed three guards — a special building! How many more does he have to kill before we decide this individual isn't deserving of the building? And then there is the question, "Who in the world is going to work in a correctional facility with someone like that?" That is beyond comprehension to me. As a result, I would err on the side of public safety and not on the side of the guy who wants his own building.

On the issue of reforming capital punishment, consider what Governor

George Ryan of Illinois did when faced with the evidence and the likely prospect of an innocent person being executed. He imposed a temporary moratorium on all executions in his state. If I were in George Ryan's situation, I would have done exactly the same thing. When you have evidence that there is suborned perjury or fabricated evidence, then certainly you must stop the wheels, you must get to the bottom of things, you must clean out the stable.

We did one thing in Oklahoma that I would recommend to other states, and we debated a second issue that also has some merit. First, in Oklahoma we required that every felony case and certainly every capital case conduct DNA testing at the state's expense. And I think that's a very sound policy. (Although I should add that many cases do not involve DNA testing because there is no evidence available to test.)

Some death penalty reformers want to reform the practice out of existence. As a public policy person, I believe that any time a life-and-death issue arises, we should debate it with goodwill and with as much intelligence and sensitivity as we can muster. Just because the motive of some may be different than my motive, reform is still worth debating. I've learned a lot in this process. I think some of those opposed to capital punishment were responsible for moving us as a state in the direction of the DNA initiative, which has been very successful. For example, we have identified several individuals who were wrongfully convicted as a result of DNA testing, and we're still testing. It's a very expensive proposition but we are doing it.

The second issue involves pardon and parole boards. There are some governors that don't have the pardon power, who don't have the authority to commute or to grant clemency, and Oklahoma's is one of them. In Oklahoma, that power has to come from the Pardon and Parole Board. If they recommended clemency, then I decided yes or no. But the power to pardon is not something that I possessed on my own as some other governors do, particularly in the northeastern states, who on their own can decide whether to grant clemency. I have stated before that if the Pardon and Parole Board recommends clemency to the governor — which I granted in some cases — I think "proof beyond a reasonable doubt" with respect to capital cases is too low a standard. Moreover, state systems, including Oklahoma's, generally don't define this standard. If the governor is asked to determine yes or no on a particular capital event, there is no written guidance. This is unlike the federal system which, as United States Supreme Court Justice Antonin Scalia notes, defines "proof beyond a reasonable doubt": it is proof of such a convincing character that you would rely up on it unhesitatingly in the most important of your affairs.

Is that a high enough standard when you're taking another person's life?

I think there should be a "moral certainty standard," that is, an even higher standard *above* what "proof beyond a reasonable doubt" demands. I applied this moral certainty standard in cases I decided. In these cases, if I didn't have a confession or physical evidence, if I didn't have moral certainty, I was willing to, and did, commute a capital sentence. But once that standard was established in my own mind — which was not easy, because you're dealing with another human being — and once that standard was applied, I could deny clemency with no hesitation. The reason for that is that I believe if we love and elevate human life — *innocent* human life — then that means those who would intentionally, with malice, with violence, take such a life forfeit the right to live. That is my value system. Obviously I'm only one citizen, but I feel as a result of my own life experience this system is the right one.

Let me close with some comments on the role I think religion plays in this debate, first from the point of view of my own religious beliefs and then of the way religions figure more generally in public life. As I said, I am Catholic, and in an overwhelmingly non-Catholic state I was a something of a curiosity. I was occasionally in the battle on this issue with our archbishop in Oklahoma City and the bishop in Tulsa. I kind of hid under the bed when they started firing the big guns. I could find myself waiting to go to Mass on Sunday to be denounced from the pulpit. That never happened, but it's no fun being at odds with church leaders.

I think the Catholic Church's position on abortion is far more mature than its position on capital punishment. The Pope's position on capital punishment is one thing; the Church's position is quite something else, and I think the catechism and the historic teachings of the church have been supportive of capital punishment in rare instances. Certainly, the one-twelfth of 1 percent of killings resulting in capital punishment represents the warranted rare instance. When I was taught by Augustinians in middle school and Jesuits in college, quite truthfully the debate wasn't really a debate. Everybody assumed capital punishment was acceptable. That was the consensus in our academic circles among the schools and the scholars that we talked to. Now the situation has changed, and there is no question that the church is moving in the opposite direction. The abortion situation has been pretty well rock solid for a long, long time. The minute *Roe v. Wade* was decided there was an overnight eruption in the Church, but when capital punishment was legalized by the U.S. Supreme Court, there was not that same kind of overnight eruption.

Today, the public dimension of religious belief is far more complex given the religious diversity of the society in which we live. I think most citizens would like to elect people of integrity and vision and courage who are willing to speak their minds, but on subjects in which religion is an issue we need to have a consensus. If I were to have stood up and said, "I've got this great idea, my fellow citizens; we're going to make a flute and a basket and a cobra the official religious symbols of Oklahoma," I would have been quickly impeached. Why? Because that is not a consensus view of what religion should entail. When you have a huge diverse population with many different cultural and religious backgrounds, you have to try to pick your way through to find a civic and moral consensus. We all believe, I think, that your property is yours and your life is yours. There are religious and moral reasons for believing that, and they are basic concepts to many of the major religions of the world. In my state, to give just one example, we have some restrictions on abortion but not a wholesale ban on the practice. Why? Because there is no consensus on the issue, and we must try to wind our way through it.

As an elected political official, I always said what I thought and what I believed, but I honored those who disagreed with me. You have a right in this society to express your views, but that doesn't mean I don't also have a right to express my view or have an obligation to make an argument for my position and the values it represents. That is what I have tried to do here, because this is an extremely important discussion for all of us, as Americans, to engage in.

12. Reflections on the Death Penalty and the Moratorium

GEORGE H. RYAN

There are those who have asked how my religious and personal views bear upon the positions I have taken on the death penalty, particularly in light of an interview I did with the *Chicago Sun-Times* in which the religion editor inquired about my religious faith and political decisions I have made.[1] I was raised as a Methodist in a small town in Illinois called Kankakee. My family was not the kind to wear religion on its sleeve. But we did go to church when we could. What I said in that interview is that I have prayed over this issue. In the end, all of us who believe, who pray, who have faith, are taught certain precepts from the time we are young. We are taught what's right and what's wrong, whether we are Christians, Muslims, or Jews. We are taught about eternal life and celebration in the hereafter.

One of the most fundamental of those religious beliefs is to protect the innocent. As God told Moses in the book of Exodus, it is up to us to show justice and mercy:

> You shall not pervert the justice due to your poor in their lawsuits. Keep far from a false charge, and do not kill the innocent and those in the right, for I will not acquit the guilty. (Exod. 23:6-7)

---

1. Cathleen Falsani, "Ryan's Faith a Factor in Death Penalty," *Chicago Sun-Times*, 15 March 2002.

This essay is adapted from Governor Ryan's address, delivered on 3 June 2002 at the University of Chicago Divinity School and hosted by the Pew Forum on Religion and Public Life.

We weren't doing a very good job of protecting the innocent in Illinois until January of 2000, when I declared what is, in effect, a moratorium on executions. Up until then I had resisted calls to issue such an order. I had always supported the death penalty. I had always thought that only the guilty were punished and sent to death row for committing the most unspeakable crimes.

We in Kankakee always prided ourselves on trying to keep our small-town feel. Kankakee was not immune to crime, but there was always a sense of community outrage over it. We always wanted to see the bad guys put behind bars. Catch them, convict them, and throw away the key. That was the sentiment I heard growing up while working in my father's pharmacy. Why wouldn't I feel this way?

In 1976, after the U.S. Supreme Court ruled the death penalty was constitutional, I voted as a member of the Illinois House of Representatives to put the death penalty back on the books. I believed the ultimate punishment played a role in our society for crimes so horrendous that death was the only fitting penalty. During the floor debate on the capital punishment bill, an opponent of the death penalty said to those of us supporting the bill, "How many of you would like to throw the switch?" That was a sobering thought. I would never want to be the executioner (in those days, it was the electric chair), to "throw the switch," to be responsible for that. But as a legislator, I was far removed from making that kind of life-or-death decision. By reinstating the death penalty, my colleagues and I in the General Assembly were demonstrating that we were "tough on crime" — a good political stance to campaign on. It was up to prosecutors, judges, and juries to determine who was guilty of a capital offense; I just helped provide the tool for it. I never questioned the system.

But looking back, it is clear that I only dealt with the issue in the abstract. In those days, my opinion was just that: my opinion. I had no say on how the capital punishment system would be administered and applied. I was a pharmacist and then a legislator — not a judge or a lawyer. I had no idea that more than twenty-five years later, I would have the good fortune to be elected governor. And then I would, in effect, be the one to throw the switch. In most of the thirty-seven states that have the death penalty, the governor makes the final decision about whether to grant a stay of execution. That is an awesome responsibility — the most difficult faced by a governor. Should they live? Should they die? Imagine having that decision on your shoulders. I must admit, I didn't realize the enormity of it until I was faced with it. It has been a long, sometimes strange trip for me on the death penalty. I went from being the lawmaker from Kankakee who voted to reinstate the death penalty, to the governor who declared the country's only moratorium.[2]

We reinstated the death penalty in 1977 in Illinois, and since that time we have executed twelve death row inmates. But, thirteen times, judges and juries convicted innocent men of capital crimes based on evidence they thought was beyond a reasonable doubt. On thirteen occasions, innocent men were condemned to die. And thirteen times, innocent men were exonerated after rotting for years on death row. For that to happen even once is unjust. For that to happen thirteen times is shameful and beyond belief.

The first nine exonerations took place over several years, going back to 1987. In my first eleven months in office, four men were freed from death row after being cleared by the courts. That included Anthony Porter, a man with an IQ of less than sixty who spent sixteen years on death row for a crime he did not commit — sixteen years on death row, all the time knowing he was innocent while the state was trying to kill him and while the real killer was free. That must have been hell on earth. The state almost killed him: he had ordered his last meal and been fitted for his burial suit. And if not for the students at Northwestern University — journalism students! — who found the real killer, Mr. Porter would be dead. Killed by the state!

When the thirteenth death row inmate was exonerated, I did the only thing I could do, the only thing any governor could do under these circumstances — I halted all executions in the state. That was the easy part; the hard part was to find out what had gone so terribly wrong. How had our system of justice become so fraught with error, especially when it came to imposing the ultimate, irreversible penalty?

So I appointed some of the smartest, most dedicated citizens I could find to a commission to study what had gone so terribly awry. It was chaired by former federal judge Frank McGarr and co-chaired by former Senator Paul Simon and former U.S. Attorney for the Northern District of Illinois Thomas Sullivan. They led a panel that included former prosecutors, some defense lawyers, and non-lawyers, as well as famed author and Harvard Law School graduate Scott Turow.[3] The backgrounds of my commission members were different but they shared one thing in common: a passion and commitment

2. On 9 May 2002, Maryland governor Paris Glendening also instituted a moratorium in his state. His decision was based on a concern about racial disparity among death row inmates rather than about the kinds of flaws in the criminal justice system that Illinois was experiencing. But for whatever reason, I am glad that he imposed the moratorium because it highlights the problem and brings it to the fore.

3. For an extensive article detailing Turow's thoughts on capital punishment, see his essay, "To Kill or Not to Kill," *New Yorker*, 6 January 2003, pp. 40-47.

for justice. I thank them for their service. They put together a tremendous document.[4] The report itself is 207 pages and there are hundreds more containing technical analysis, including a study on race and sentencing.

These dedicated and brilliant citizens developed eighty-five recommendations to improve the caliber of justice in our state system. I took from the report everything that required legislation and introduced it to the Illinois General Assembly. My bill proposed barring the execution of the mentally retarded; mandating that "natural life" is given as a sentencing option to juries; reducing death penalty eligibility factors from twenty to five; and barring the death penalty when a conviction is based solely on a "jailhouse snitch." It was imperative to move forward on all of the commission's recommendations to fix our broken justice system. My wish was for the General Assembly to hold hearings and meetings with all of the key parties — the prosecutors, defense attorneys, victims, and the wrongfully convicted.

Yet I remain deeply concerned. I have said before that the more I learn about the justice system, the more troubled I become. My commission's report seems to confirm my worst fears about our capital punishment system: that it was error-ridden at every painful step of the process. The report reviews, at some level, every capital case that we have ever had in Illinois, but it looks most closely at the thirteen inmates freed from death row and exonerated. Most of them were not convicted based on solid evidence.

A perfect example is the case of a remarkable man, Gary Gauger. Mr. Gauger was from McHenry County, Illinois. In 1994 he was convicted and sentenced to die for brutally killing his parents. There was no physical evidence against him, and prosecutors presented no motive. The primary evidence against Mr. Gauger were statements he allegedly made to police; my commission reported that those statements were *never* put in writing. Mr. Gauger denied the statements, but prosecutors won the conviction anyway and sent him to death row. Case closed — until a few years later when federal authorities investigating a Wisconsin motorcycle gang (on a totally unrelated case) caught gang members on tape confessing to the brutal crime. Gary Gauger sat on death row for nearly three years. Not only was he grieving the brutal murder of his parents, he grieved for himself as well, for being accused of taking his parents' lives. His freedom and his dignity stripped from him, he was caught in a nightmare too painful to imagine. He never gave up hope, though; he knew he was innocent.

4. The State of Illinois, *Report of the Governor's Commission on Capital Punishment*, 15 April 2002, http://www.idoc.state.il.us/ccp/ccp/reports/commission_report/index.html. Accessed 21 September 2002.

At least one case involved a false confession. Ronald Jones confessed to police to a rape and murder. He later said that confession was coerced and, years later, DNA cleared him.

My commission reported that several cases involved prosecutors relying on the testimony of a witness with something to gain like a jailhouse informant or an accomplice. Verneal Jimerson and Dennis Williams were two of the so-called "Ford Heights Four," named after a south suburb in Cook County. The primary testimony against them came from a seventeen-year-old girl with an IQ of less than sixty, who police said was an accomplice in the murder of a couple. Seventeen years later, Jimerson, Williams, and two others serving lesser sentences were released after new DNA tests revealed that none of them were linked to the crime. Seventeen years. *Seventeen years.* Can you imagine serving even one day on death row for a crime you did not commit? Later that year, two other men confessed to the crime and were sent to prison. When my commission released its report, Thomas Sullivan noted that in the Ford Heights Four case, the police were given the names of the four actual killers and rapists within a few days after the event, but they failed to follow up. Meanwhile the four defendants collectively served over seventy years in jail.

Illinois had one inmate, Steven Smith, convicted and sentenced to die based solely on the testimony of one drug-addicted witness. The case of Anthony Porter that I mentioned earlier also highlights the unreliability of some eyewitness testimony. Two eyewitnesses had said they saw Porter kill a couple in a South Side Chicago park. Sixteen years later, journalism students working with a private investigator found those witnesses, who then recanted their testimony; afterwards, the students tracked down the real killer, who confessed to the crime. Sullivan said, and I agree wholeheartedly, "A system that is so fragile that a journalism student has to do the police work is obviously badly flawed."[5] Where in the Illinois criminal code does it say that journalism students are part of the system to ensure that only the guilty are convicted and executed?

There are ten more death row cases — known as the "Burge Ten," named after the police detective commander who handled their investigations — all of which involve allegations of police abuse and excessive force. They raise serious questions.

The commission co-chair, Thomas Sullivan, very eloquently summarizes the report's findings: "In medical terms, our report calls for triage, an at-

---

5. Remarks delivered at a press conference, 15 April 2002. Story covered by the Online News Hour, 10 June 2002, available at http://www.pbs.org/newshour/bb/law/jan-june02/ deathpenalty_6-10.html^. Accessed 21 September 2002.

tempt to stanch the extraordinary rate of errors, reversals and mistaken convictions in capital cases."[6] And he is right. If you look at the reversal rate in capital cases in Illinois, it exceeds 50 percent. In fact, the chance of executing the wrong person in Illinois was like the flip of a coin. That's not justice. Then, in perhaps in the most scathing indictment of our system, Sullivan noted the following:

> The police who conducted the investigations in these cases remain on the force. The prosecutors who overstepped the bounds of fairness and the defense lawyers who gave incompetent defense remain in practice. The judges who permitted or caused the errors remain on the bench.[7]

Now, when I was a pharmacist, I couldn't have stayed in business if I only got it right 50 percent of the time. There is virtually no other profession in which that level of mistakes would be tolerated. Yet that is the situation that we have with the police, prosecutors, defense lawyers, and the courts in capital cases in Illinois. Tom Sullivan says the message from the commission and of this report is clear: "Repair or repeal; fix the capital punishment system or abolish it. There is no other principled course."[8]

And these capital cases are just a small percentage of all of the criminal cases handled by the courts. What is happening in the rest of the system? If we have this level of error in cases where the ultimate penalty is at stake, what is happening with lesser crimes? How many more innocent people are sitting in jails today — not on death row, but in jails nonetheless for crimes they didn't commit — because of some poor prosecutor, some poor defense attorney, or some unreliable witnesses? I am concerned about that too, for the sake of the innocent.

Some of the critics of this report claimed the commission was stacked with death penalty opponents. As I mentioned earlier, Thomas Sullivan is the former U.S. Attorney for the Northern District of Illinois. He was a tough prosecutor, now in private practice. I would also point out that nine of the fourteen members are current or former prosecutors; yet, when I appointed them, those opposed to capital punishment accused me of stacking the commission with death penalty *supporters*. This commission is made up of some of the most conscientious, dedicated people ever to enter public service. I am proud of the work they've done. But, even before the report was officially released, it was being criticized. I cannot understand that. Why would anyone

6. Press conference, 15 April 2002.
7. Press conference, 15 April 2002.
8. Press conference, 15 April 2002.

prefer the status quo? I don't know of any crime victim, police officer, prosecutor, or politician who wants to see an innocent person executed. I don't know of any citizen who wants to see that.

My commission concluded that Illinois's twenty factors that could make one eligible for the death penalty were too many and ought to be reduced to five. Some critics at the time pointed out that it was an election year and, therefore, a bad time to suggest reducing the number of eligibility factors for the death penalty. I was well aware that it was an election year, but matters of life and death and justice and fairness are more important than getting elected. Political leaders have an obligation to study this report before they jump to conclusions.

Current and former prosecutors also found fault with the report. Some predicted that Illinois would become the new murder-for-hire capital of the world because participating in a murder-for-hire plot would no longer make one eligible for the death penalty. That's ridiculous. I proposed eliminating this factor in large part because these sentences rarely, if ever, withstand appeal. Other prosecutors and police officers said the recommendations are a slap in the face to police. I don't understand that either.

Throughout this review process, I always pointed out that there is enough blame to go around for everyone. The commission highlights the need for better-trained defense attorneys and judges. It even suggests the state has not pulled its weight by providing enough money for things like DNA labs and a DNA database, things that will help to protect the innocent and to convict only the guilty. No one is spared from accountability because we are all accountable: our system is riddled with errors and omissions from top to bottom. That is why I believe it is so vitally important that hearings be held. We must have an honest debate about our system and whether or not it can be repaired.

It is easy to support the death penalty in the abstract, like I did in my earlier days. But until you sit where I sit, until you have to throw the switch or be the executioner, you don't know just how difficult that decision can be. When I made my decision to declare a moratorium, I never consulted the opinion polls. Only since my decision did I begin to notice them. A recent Gallup poll was interesting.[9] Only 53 percent of those polled believe the death penalty is applied fairly, while 40 percent say it is applied unfairly. Among non-whites, 54 percent believe the death penalty is applied unfairly. When given the sentencing alternative of life without the possibility of parole, 52 percent of Americans support the death penalty and 43 percent fa-

9. Gallup poll taken on 2 May 2002.

vor life imprisonment. Eighty-two percent of respondents oppose the death penalty for the mentally retarded. Seventy-three percent oppose the death penalty for those who are mentally ill. Sixty-nine percent of Americans oppose capital punishment for juvenile offenders. While that same poll still showed strong support (72 percent) for capital punishment in principle, it is clear the American people are as concerned with fairness now as they have ever been.

Some worry that we are one of the few developed countries that still use the death penalty. The United States is in company with China, Iraq, Iran, as well as some African and other Middle Eastern countries that also have the death penalty. Castro's Cuba is among the nations still executing criminals and on the watch list of every human rights organization. I had an opportunity while I was in Cuba to meet with President Castro, and we talked a little bit about the death penalty and executions. I told him we have a moratorium on them in Illinois. Castro told me Cuba has a "de facto moratorium" that has been in effect for a couple of years. He indicated that he had some concerns about the death penalty but that he believed the people of Cuba still supported it for heinous crimes. Sound familiar? (That conversation was just one of many, many surreal moments that I had in Cuba during my two humanitarian missions there.) There must be something going on if even Cuba's longtime dictator is reconsidering the death penalty.

Is retribution or revenge reason enough for capital punishment? Can this impulse blind the eyes of those pursuing justice? In the wake of September 11, many say the American people support the death penalty now more than ever. This country is now at war, and the terrorists who attacked it, who used passenger jets as missiles, killing thousands of innocent men, women, and children, were deranged. They were on a suicide mission and the crime they committed was already a capital offense. It was no deterrent. If Osama bin Laden or his co-conspirators are caught, there is no question they would face the death penalty, and perhaps that is appropriate.

But, as a governor, my concern was the system in Illinois, fraught with error and convicting and condemning the innocent along with the guilty. At the beginning of my term, after Anthony Porter was freed, I sat in judgment of an inmate convicted of a brutal murder of a young woman. He was also involved in torturing and killing other women. After the Porter case I agonized: I personally reviewed the case files of convicted murderer Andrew Kokoraleis. I had veteran lawyers review them as well. I talked to victims and investigators. I left no stone unturned. In the end I was convinced Kokoraleis committed a monstrous, unspeakable crime, and he was executed.

Then the *Chicago Tribune* did a chilling report on the fact that the whole system was flawed. Their findings were later echoed in my commission's report. *Half* of the nearly *three hundred* capital cases in Illinois had been reversed for a new trial or resentencing. Over half! Thirty-three of the death row inmates were represented at trial by an attorney who had later been disbarred or at some point suspended from practicing law. Of the more than 160 death row inmates, thirty-five were African-American defendants who had been convicted or condemned to die by all-white juries. More than two-thirds of the inmates on death row are African-American. Forty-six inmates were convicted on the basis of testimony from jailhouse informants.

After Porter and Kokoraleis, I was already starting to question what I believed about capital punishment. The *Tribune* series left me reeling. And then two more inmates were exonerated. I had to act. After seeing, again and again, how close we came to the ultimate nightmare, I did the only thing I could do. Thirteen times we almost strapped innocent men to a gurney, wheeled them to the state's death chamber and injected fatal doses of poison in their veins. I knew I had to act. I said after issuing the moratorium in 2000, and I say again now: *Until I can be sure that everyone sentenced to death in Illinois is truly guilty, until I can be sure with moral certainty that no innocent man or woman is facing a lethal injection, no one will meet that fate.* A lot of people have called my stand courageous. Those are nice words, but they are nonsense. What I did was just the right thing to do.

I have also had to decide what to do with the 160 death row inmates who were convicted under our current broken system. There is no question that there are guilty criminals on death row in Illinois. But, at a rate of thirteen exonerations for every twenty-five death row inmates, and a 50 percent reversal rate by the courts, the odds are as good as the flip of a coin that there are also innocent men languishing behind bars.

My commission concluded that its recommendations would significantly improve the fairness and accuracy of the Illinois death penalty system. But it also concluded, and I quote, "No system, given human nature and frailties, could ever be devised or constructed that would work perfectly and guarantee absolutely that no . . . innocent person is ever again sentenced to death."[10] That's a powerful statement and one that I continue to ponder.

How has my faith influenced how I have faced this difficult issue? How do I deal with fundamental questions of justice and fairness and morality? I just try to follow my heart and my conscience. I have tried to remember what I've learned from my religious upbringing and my family. And, perhaps like

---

10. *Report of the Governor's Commission on Capital Punishment*, p. 207.

you, I might reflect upon what God told the Israelites in Isaiah, "Maintain justice, and do what is right" (56:1). That, I pray, is what we will do.

EDITORS' NOTE: On 10 January 2003, Governor Ryan pardoned four death row inmates. On 11 January 2003, three days before leaving office, Governor Ryan commuted the death sentences of the remaining 167 Illinois inmates (most to life imprisonment without the possibility of parole), effectively emptying Illinois's death row. The move garnered national and international attention and was considered "unprecedented" by supporters and critics alike. During his speech at Northwestern Law School, Gov. Ryan remarked, "Our capital system is haunted by the demon of error, error in determining guilt, and error in determining who among the guilty deserves to die. Because of all of these reasons today I am commuting the death sentences of all death row inmates." He went on to state:

> As I said when I declared the moratorium, it is time for a rational discussion of the death penalty. While our experience in Illinois has indeed sparked a debate, we have fallen short of a rational discussion. Yet if I did not take this action, I feared that there would be no comprehensive and thorough inquiry into the guilt of the individuals on death row or of the fairness of the sentences applied.
>
> To say it plainly one more time, the Illinois capital punishment system is broken. It has taken innocent men to a hair's breadth from their unjust execution. Legislatures past have refused to fix it. Our new legislature and our new governor must act to rid our state of the shame of threatening the innocent with execution and the guilty with unfairness.
>
> In the days ahead, I will pray that we can open our hearts and provide something for victims' families other than the hope of revenge. Lincoln once said: "I have always found that mercy bears richer fruits than strict justice." I can only hope that will be so. God bless you. And God bless the people of Illinois.[11]

---

11. From the text of Governor Ryan's 11 January 2003 speech at Northwestern University College of Law, as printed in the *New York Times*, 12 January 2003.

13. God's Justice and Ours:
The Morality of Judicial Participation
in the Death Penalty

ANTONIN SCALIA

Before discussing the morality of capital punishment, I want to make clear at the outset that what I will have to say — or, for that matter, what appears elsewhere in this very interesting book — has nothing to do with how I vote in capital cases that come before the Supreme Court. That statement would not be true if I subscribed to the conventional fallacy that the Constitution is a "living document" — that is, a text that means from age to age whatever the society (or perhaps the Court) thinks it ought to mean.

In recent years, that philosophy has been particularly well enshrined in our Eighth Amendment jurisprudence, our case law dealing with the prohibition of "cruel and unusual punishments." Several of our opinions have said that what falls within this prohibition is not static, but changes from generation to generation, to comport with "the evolving standards of decency that mark the progress of a maturing society."[1] Applying that principle, the Court came close, in 1972, to abolishing the death penalty entirely. It ultimately did not do so, but it has imposed, under color of the Constitution, procedural and substantive limitations that did not exist when the Eighth Amendment was adopted — some of which had not even been adopted by a majority of the states at the time they were judicially decreed. For example, the Court has prohibited the death penalty for all crimes except murder, and indeed even for what might be called run-of-the-mill murders, as opposed to those that are somehow characterized by a high degree of brutality or depravity. It has

1. *Trop v. Dulles*, 356 U.S. 86, 101 (1958).

prohibited the mandatory imposition of the death penalty for any crime, insisting that in all cases the jury be permitted to consider all mitigating factors and to impose, if it wishes, a lesser sentence. It has imposed an age limit at the time of the offense (it is currently seventeen) that is well above what existed at common law. And recently the Court ruled that the death penalty cannot be imposed upon those found to be mentally retarded.

If I subscribed to the proposition that I am authorized (indeed, I suppose, compelled) to intuit and impose our "maturing" society's "evolving standards of decency," this book and the Pew Forum conference that preceded it would be for me a sort of continuing judicial education, a preparation for my next vote in a death-penalty case. As it is, however, the Constitution that I interpret and apply is not living but dead — or, as I prefer to put it, enduring. It means today not what current society (much less the Court) thinks it ought to mean, but what it meant when it was adopted. For me, therefore, the constitutionality of the death penalty is not a difficult, soul-wrenching question. Capital punishment was clearly permitted when the Eighth Amendment was adopted (not merely for murder, by the way, but for all felonies, including for example horse-thievery — as anyone can verify by watching a western movie). And so it is clearly permitted today. There is plenty of room within this system for "evolving standards of decency," but the instrument of evolution (or, if you are more tolerant of the Court's approach, the herald that evolution has occurred) is not the nine lawyers who sit on the Supreme Court of the United States, but the Congress of the United States and the legislatures of the fifty states, which may, within their own jurisdictions, restrict or abolish the death penalty as they wish.

But while this book's discussions have nothing to do with how I *vote* as a judge, they — or at least that portion of them that pertains to the morality, as opposed to the policy desirability, of the death penalty — have a lot to do with whether I can or should be a judge at all. To put the point in the blunt terms employed by Justice Blackmun towards the end of his career on the bench — when he announced that he would henceforth vote (as William Brennan and Thurgood Marshall had previously done) to overturn all death sentences — when I sit on a Court that reviews and affirms capital convictions, I am part of "the machinery of death."[2] My vote, when joined with at least four others, is, in most cases, the last step that permits an execution to proceed. I could not take part in that process if I believed what was being done to be immoral. Preservation of the death penalty is not at the top of my list of moral concerns. But what *is* at the top, or close to it, is the question whether the death penalty that I take part in administering is morally wrong.

2. *Callins v. Collins*, 510 U.S. 1141, 1145 (1994), Blackmun, J., dissenting.

Capital cases are much different from the other life-and-death issues that my Court sometimes faces: abortion, for example, or legalized suicide. There it is not the state (of which I am in a sense the last instrument) that is decreeing death, but rather private individuals whom the state has decided not to restrain. One may argue (as many do) that the society has a moral obligation to restrain. That moral obligation may weigh heavily upon the voter, and upon the legislator who enacts the laws; but a judge, I think, bears no moral guilt for the laws society has failed to enact. Thus, my difficulty with *Roe v. Wade* is a legal rather than a moral one: I do not believe (and no one believed, for two hundred years) that the Constitution contains a right to abortion. And if a state were to permit abortion on demand, I would — and could in good conscience — vote against an attempt to invalidate that law, for the same reason that I vote against the invalidation of laws that forbid abortion on demand: because the Constitution gives the federal government (and hence me) no power over the matter. With the death penalty, on the other hand, I am part of the criminal-law machinery that imposes death — which extends from the indictment, to the jury conviction, to rejection of the last appeal.

I am aware of the ethical principle that one can be in "material cooperation" with the immoral act of another when the evil that would attend failure to cooperate is even greater. (For example, helping a burglar tie up a householder where the alternative is that the burglar would kill the householder.) I doubt whether that doctrine is even applicable to the trial judges and jurors who must themselves determine that the death sentence will be imposed. It seems to me these individuals are not merely engaged in "material cooperation" with someone else's action, but are themselves decreeing (on behalf of the state) death. The same is true of appellate judges in those states where they are charged with "reweighing" the mitigating and aggravating factors and determining *de novo* whether the death penalty should be imposed: they are themselves decreeing death. Where (as is the case in the federal system) the appellate judge merely determines that the sentence pronounced by the trial court is in accordance with law, perhaps the principle of material cooperation could be applied. But as I have said, that principle demands that the good deriving from the cooperation exceed the evil which is assisted. I find it hard to see how any appellate judge could find this condition to be met, unless that judge believes retaining a seat on the bench (rather than resigning) is somehow essential to preservation of the society — which is of course absurd. (As Charles de Gaulle is reputed to have remarked when his aides told him he could not resign as president of France because he was the indispensable man: "Mon ami, the cemeteries are full of indispensable men.")

I pause at this point to call attention to the fact that, in my view, the choice for the judge who believes the death penalty to be immoral is resignation, rather than simply ignoring duly enacted, constitutional laws and sabotaging death cases. He has, after all, taken an oath to apply the laws, and has been given no power to supplant them with rules of his own. Of course if he feels strongly enough, he can go beyond mere resignation and lead a political campaign to abolish the death penalty — and if that fails, lead a revolution. But rewrite the laws he cannot do. This dilemma, of course, need not be confronted by the proponent of the "living Constitution," who believes that it means what it somehow ought to mean: If the death penalty is (in his view) immoral, then it is (presto!) automatically unconstitutional, and he can continue to sit while nullifying a sanction that has been imposed, with no suggestion of its unconstitutionality, since the beginning of the Republic. (You can see why the "living Constitution" is so attractive for us judges.)

It is a matter of great consequence to me, therefore, whether the death penalty is morally acceptable, and I want to say a few words about why I believe it is. Being a Roman Catholic, and being unable to jump out of my skin, I cannot discuss that issue without reference to Christian tradition and the Church's magisterium discussed in Cardinal Dulles's chapter of this book.

The death penalty is undoubtedly wrong unless one accords to the state a scope of moral action that goes beyond what is permitted to the individual. In my view, the major impetus behind modern aversion to the death penalty is the equation of private morality with governmental morality, which is a predictable (though I believe erroneous and regrettable) reaction to modern, democratic self-government.

Few doubted the morality of the death penalty in the age that believed in the divine right of kings, or even in earlier times. St. Paul had this to say (I am quoting, as you might expect, the King James version):

> Let every soul be subject unto the higher powers. For there is no power but of God: the powers that be are ordained of God. Whosoever therefore resisteth the power, resisteth the ordinance of God: and they that resist shall receive to themselves damnation. For rulers are not a terror to good works, but to the evil. Wilt thou then not be afraid of the power? Do that which is good, and thou shalt have praise of the same: For he is the minister of God to thee for good. But if thou do that which is evil, be afraid; for he beareth not the sword in vain: for he is the minister of God, a revenger to execute wrath upon him that doeth evil. Wherefore ye must needs be subject, not only for wrath, but also for conscience sake. (Rom. 13:1-5)

This is not the Old Testament, I emphasize, but St. Paul. One can understand his words as referring only to lawfully constituted authority, or even only to lawfully constituted authority that rules justly. But the *core* of his message is that government — however you want to limit that concept — derives its moral authority from God. It is the "minister of God" with powers to "revenge," to "execute wrath," including even wrath by the sword (which is unmistakably a reference to the death penalty). Paul of course did not believe that the *individual* possessed any such powers. Only a few lines before the passage from the letter to the Romans that I quoted, he says "Dearly beloved, avenge not yourselves, but rather give place unto wrath: for it is written, Vengeance is mine; I will repay, saith the Lord." And in this world the Lord repaid — did justice — through his minister, the state.

These passages from Romans represent the consensus of Western thought until very recent times. Not just of Christian or religious thought, but of secular thought regarding the powers of the state. That consensus has been upset, I think, by the emergence of democracy. It is easy to see the hand of the Almighty behind rulers whose forbears, in the dim mists of history, were supposedly anointed by God, or who at least obtained their thrones in awful and unpredictable battles whose outcome was determined by the Lord of Hosts, that is, the Lord of Armies. It is much more difficult to see the hand of God — or any higher moral authority — behind the fools and rogues (as the losers would have it) whom we ourselves elect to do our own will. How can their power to avenge — to vindicate the "public order" — be any greater than our own?

So it is no accident, I think, that the modern view that the death penalty is immoral is centered in the West. That has little to do with the fact that the West has a Christian tradition, and everything to do with the fact that the West is the home of democracy. Indeed, it seems to me that the more Christian a country is the *less* likely it is to regard the death penalty as immoral. Abolition has taken its firmest hold in post-Christian Europe, and has least support in the churchgoing United States. I attribute that to the fact that, for the believing Christian, death is no big deal. Intentionally killing an innocent person is a big deal: it is a grave sin, which causes one to lose his soul. But losing this life, in exchange for the next? The Christian attitude is reflected in the words Robert Bolt's play, *A Man for All Seasons,* has Thomas More saying to the headsman: "Friend, be not afraid of your office. You send me to God." And when Cranmer, the archbishop of Canterbury, asks whether he is sure of that, More replies "He will not refuse one who is so blithe to go to Him."[3] For

3. Robert Bolt, *A Man for All Seasons* (New York: Random House, 1962), p. 162.

the nonbeliever, on the other hand, to deprive a man of life is to end his existence. What a horrible act!

Besides being *less* likely to regard death as an utterly cataclysmic punishment, the Christian is also *more* likely to regard punishment in general as deserved. The doctrine of free will — the ability of man to resist temptations to evil, which God will not permit beyond man's capacity to resist — is central to the Christian doctrine of salvation and damnation, heaven and hell. The post-Freudian secularist, on the other hand, is more inclined to think that people are what their history and circumstances have made them, and there is little sense in assigning blame.

Of course those who deny the authority of a government to exact vengeance, to punish, and to impose justice are not entirely logical: Many crimes — for example, domestic murder in the heat of passion — are neither deterred by punishment meted out to others nor likely to be committed a second time by the same offender. Yet capital punishment opponents do not object to sending those who commit such crimes to prison, perhaps for life. Because they *deserve* punishment. Because it is *just*.

The mistaken tendency to believe that a democratic government, being nothing more than the composite will of its individual citizens, has no more moral power or authority than they do has adverse effects in other ways as well. It fosters civil disobedience, for example, which proceeds on the assumption that what the individual citizen considers an unjust law — even if it does not compel him to act unjustly — need not be obeyed. St. Paul would not agree. "[Y]e must needs be subject," he says, "not only for wrath, but also for conscience sake." For conscience sake. The reaction of people of faith to this tendency of democracy to obscure the divine authority behind government should be not resignation to it, but resolution to combat it as effectively as possible. We have done that in this country (though continental Europe has not) by preserving in our public life many visible reminders that — in the words of a Supreme Court opinion from the 1950s — "we are a religious people, whose institutions presuppose a Supreme Being"[4]: "In God we trust" on our coins; "one nation, under God" in our Pledge of Allegiance; the opening of sessions of our legislatures with a prayer; the opening of sessions of my Court with "God save the United States and this Honorable Court"; annual Thanksgiving proclamations issued by our president at the direction of Congress; and constant reminders of divine support in the speeches of our political leaders, which often conclude with "God bless America" — all this is most un-European, and helps

---

4. *Zorach v. Clauson,* 343 U.S. 306, 313 (1952).

explain why our people are more inclined to understand, as St. Paul did, that government carries the sword as "the minister of God," to "execute wrath" upon the evildoer.[5]

You will gather from what I have said that I do not agree with the encyclical *Evangelium vitae* and the new Catholic catechism (or the very latest version of the new Catholic catechism).[6] Both state that the death penalty can only be imposed to protect rather than avenge, and that since it is not necessary for the former purpose in most modern societies, it is wrong. That, by the way, is how I read those documents, and not as Cardinal Dulles would read them, as simply an affirmation of two millennia of Christian teaching that retribution is a proper purpose (indeed, the principal purpose) of criminal punishment but adding the "prudential judgment" that, in modern circumstances, condign retribution "rarely, if ever" justifies death.[7] I cannot square that interpretation with the following passage from the encyclical:

> It is clear that, for these [permissible purposes of penal justice] to be achieved, the nature and extent of the punishment must be carefully evaluated and decided upon, and ought not go to the extreme of executing the offender except in cases of absolute necessity: *in other words, when it would not be possible otherwise to defend society. Today, however, as a result of steady improvements in the organization of the penal system, such cases are very rare, if not practically non-existent.*[8]

It is true enough that the paragraph of the encyclical which precedes this passage acknowledges (in accord with traditional Catholic teaching) that "[t]he primary purpose of the punishment which society inflicts is 'to redress the disorder caused by the offence,'" by "imposing on the offender an adequate punishment for the crime. . . ."[9] But it seems to me quite impossible to

5. A brief story about the aftermath of September 11 suggests how different things are in secularized Europe. I was at a conference of European and American lawyers and jurists in Rome when the planes struck the twin towers. All in attendance were transfixed by the horror of the event, and listened with rapt attention to the president's ensuing address to the nation. When the speech had concluded, one of the European conferees — a religious man — confided in me how envious he was that the leader of my nation could conclude his address with the words "God bless the United States." Such invocation of the deity, he assured me, was absolutely unthinkable in his country, with the Napoleonic tradition of extirpating religion from public life.

6. Pope John Paul II, *Evangelium Vitae* (1986); *Catechism of the Catholic Church* (1992), par. 2267. Both are available on the Vatican website, http://www.vatican.va.

7. Avery Cardinal Dulles, "Catholicism and Capital Punishment," *First Things* 112 (April 2001): 30-35. Also available at http://www.firstthings.com/ftissues/ft0104/articles/dulles.html.

8. *Evangelium Vitae*, par. 56, emphases deleted and added.

9. *Evangelium Vitae*, par. 56.

interpret the later passage's phrase "when it would not be possible otherwise to defend society" as including "defense" through the redress of disorder achieved by adequate punishment. Not only does the word "defense" not readily lend itself to that strange interpretation, but the immediately following explanation of why, in modern times, "defense" rarely if ever requires capital punishment *has no bearing whatever upon the adequacy of retribution*. In fact, one might say that it has an *inverse* bearing.

How in the world can modernity's "steady improvements in the organization of the penal system" render the death penalty less condign for a particularly heinous crime? One might think that commitment to a really horrible penal system (Devil's Island, for example) might be almost as bad as death. But nice clean cells with television sets, exercise rooms, meals designed by nutritionists, and conjugal visits? That would seem to render the death penalty more, rather than less, necessary. So also would the greatly increased capacity for evil — the greatly increased power to produce moral "disorder" — placed in individual hands by modern technology. Could St. Paul or St. Thomas even have envisioned a crime by an individual (as opposed to one by a ruler, such as Herod's slaughter of the innocents) as enormous as that of Timothy McVeigh or of the men who destroyed three thousand innocents in the World Trade Center? If just retribution is a legitimate purpose — indeed, the principal legitimate purpose — of capital punishment, can one possibly say with a straight face that nowadays death would "rarely if ever" be appropriate?

So I take the encyclical and the latest, hot-off-the-presses version of the catechism (a supposed encapsulation of the "deposit" of faith and the Church's infallible teaching regarding a moral order that does not change) to mean that retribution is not a valid purpose of capital punishment. Unlike such other hard Catholic doctrines as the prohibition of birth control and of abortion, this is not a moral position that the Church has always — or indeed *ever before* — maintained. There have been Christian opponents of the death penalty, just as there have been Christian pacifists, but neither of those positions has ever been that of the Church. The current predominance of opposition to the death penalty is the legacy of Napoleon, Hegel, and Freud rather than St. Paul, St. Augustine, and St. Thomas. I mentioned earlier Thomas More, who has long been regarded in this country as the patron saint of lawyers, and whom the Vatican has recently declared the patron saint of politicians (I am not sure that is a promotion). One of the charges leveled by that canonized saint's detractors was that, as lord chancellor, he was too quick to impose the death penalty.

I am therefore happy to learn from the canonical experts whom I have consulted that the statement contained in *Evangelium vitae* does not represent *ex cathedra* teaching — that is, it need not be accepted by practicing Catholics, though they must give it thoughtful and respectful consideration. It would be remarkable to think otherwise — that a couple of paragraphs in an encyclical almost entirely devoted not to crime and punishment but to abortion and euthanasia was intended authoritatively to sweep aside (if one could) two thousand years of Christian teaching. (And as for the very latest, hot-off-the-presses version of the Catholic catechism, I assume that is just the phenomenon of the clerical bureaucracy saying "yes, boss.")

So I have given this new position thoughtful and careful consideration — and I have rejected it. That is not to say I favor the death penalty (I am judicially and judiciously neutral on that point); it is only to say that I do not find the death penalty immoral. I am happy to have reached that conclusion, because I like my job, and would rather not resign. And I am happy because I do not think it would be a good thing if American Catholics running for legislative office had to oppose the death penalty (most of them would not be elected); if American Catholics running for governor had to promise commutation of all death sentences (most of them would never reach the governor's mansion); if American Catholics were ineligible to go on the bench in all jurisdictions imposing the death penalty; or if American Catholics were subject to recusal when called for jury duty in capital cases. I find it ironic that the Church's new (albeit non-binding) position on the death penalty — which, if accepted would have these *disastrous* consequences — is said to rest upon "prudential considerations." Is it prudent, when one is not certain enough about the point to proclaim it *ex cathedra* (and with good reason, given the long and consistent Christian tradition to the contrary) to urge, in effect, the retirement of Catholics from public life in a country where the federal government and thirty-eight of the states (comprising about 85 percent of the population) uphold the death penalty as sometimes just and appropriate? Is it prudent to imperil acceptance of the Church's hard but traditional teachings on birth control and abortion and euthanasia — teachings that *are ex cathedra,* a distinction that the average Catholic layman is unlikely to grasp — by packaging them under the wrapper "respect for life" along with another uncongenial doctrine *that everyone knows does not represent the traditional Christian view?* Perhaps, one is invited to conclude, all four teachings are recently made up. We need some new staffers at the Congregation of Prudence in the Vatican. At least the new doctrine should have been urged only upon secular Europe, where it is at home.

14. Why I Oppose Capital Punishment

MARIO M. CUOMO

I have spoken and written my opposition to the death penalty for nearly fifty years. During that time I have studied it and debated it hundreds of times. I have heard all the arguments, analyzed all the evidence I could find, and measured public opinion when it was opposed to the practice, when it was indifferent, when it was passionately in favor. Always I have concluded the death penalty is wrong. It lowers us all; it is a surrender to the worst that is in us; it uses a power — the official power to kill by execution — that has never elevated a society, never brought back a life, never inspired anything but hate.

For twelve years as governor I prevented the death penalty from becoming law in New York through my vetoes. But for all that time there was a disconcertingly strong preference for the death penalty in the general public. Recently, the events of September 11, 2001, and their tragic aftermath have inspired a new willingness to support capital punishment. Our passions were inflamed by the terrorist acts of that day as they have been by each new terrible headline announcing another atrocity and disturbance of domestic order.

People have a right to demand a civilized level of law and peace. They have a right to expect it, and when it appears to them that crime is rampant yet criminals seem almost immune from apprehension and adequate punishment, then no one should be surprised if the people demand the ultimate penalty. To a great extent the public call for death is a terrible cry of anger and anguish born of frustration and fear.

I understand that feeling. I have felt the anger myself, more than once. Like too many other citizens, I know what it is like to be violated and even to have one's closest family violated through criminal behavior in the most despicable ways. Even today, I tremble at the thought of how I might react to a killer who took the life of someone in my own family. I know that I might not be able to suppress my anger or put down a desire for revenge. But I also know this society should strive for something better than what we become during our worst moments.

Our society should try to reason its way to a better solution. We know we need to respond more effectively to violence, but there is absolutely no good reason to believe that using death as a punishment is any better an answer now than it was in the past when we had it, used it, regretted it, and discarded it. Dozens of studies demonstrate that there is simply no persuasive evidence that official state killing can make any police officer, or other citizen, safer.[1] There is, in fact, considerable evidence to the contrary. One sad statistic from New York that illustrates the point: in the decade before 1977, when we had the death penalty in New York State, eighty police officers were slain; in the decade after 1977, without the death penalty, fifty-four police officers were killed.[2]

The argument for deterrence is further weakened by realization of how rarely and unpredictably it is applied. For hundreds of years we have known that the effectiveness of the law is determined not by its harshness, but by its sureness. And the death penalty has always been terribly uncertain punishment. Experts in New York and the rest of the nation have come out strongly against the death penalty after hundreds of years of lawyers' cumulative experiences and studies revealed that the death penalty is ineffective as a deterrent — if for no other reason than because its application is so inconsistent. For example, the perpetrators of a miniscule fraction of 1 percent of all the homicides committed in America in the 1980s and 90s were executed.[3] How could such miniscule odds of facing execution deter a would-be murderer?

---

1. For a recent example, see Raymond Bonner and Ford Fessenden, "States with No Death Penalty Share Lower Homicide Rates," *New York Times*, 22 September 2000, available at http://www.nlg.org/death_penalty/lower_homicide.html. On the ineffectiveness of the death penalty as a deterrent to the murder of police officers, see W. Bailey and R. Peterson, "Murder, Capital Punishment, and Deterrence: A Review of the Evidence and an Examination of Police Killings," *Journal of Social Issues* 50 (1994): 53, 71. For several other studies that challenge the deterrence hypothesis, see http://www.deathpenaltyinfo.org/deter.html and http://www.deathpenaltyinfo. Org/dpic.ro3.html. Sites accessed 1 March 2003.

2. Based on official statistics obtained by the Office of the Governor of the State of New York.

3. Consider that, according to the Death Penalty Information Center, there were 595 executions between 1980 and 1999 (see http://www.deathpenaltyinfo.org/dpicexec.html) and according to the Bureau of Justice Statistics, there were 418,110 murders in the United States between 1980 and 1999 (see http://www.ojp.usdoj.gov/bjs). Sites accessed 1 March 2003.

Furthermore, notwithstanding the executions of Ted Bundy and Timothy McVeigh, capital punishment appears to threaten white drug dealers, white rapists, and white killers less frequently than those of other races. Of the last eighteen people in New York State to be executed, thirteen were black and one was Hispanic.[4] That racial makeup seems an extraordinary improbability for a system operating with any kind of objectivity and consistency.

There's more. Some of the most notorious recent murders occurred in the face of existing death penalty statutes. Psychiatrists will tell you there is reason to believe that some madmen, like Ted Bundy, may even be tempted to murder because of a perverse desire to take on and face the ultimate penalty. Clearly in such cases, capital punishment is no deterrent.

For many years deterrence was the principal argument for the death penalty. Because death penalty proponents have never been able to make the case for deterrence convincingly, they cling, unabashedly, to the blunt simplicity of the ancient impulse that has always spurred the call for death: the desire for revenge. That was the bottom line of many debates on the floor of the New York State Senate and Assembly I listened to and read with great care during my tenure as governor. It came down, in the end, to "an eye for an eye, a tooth for a tooth."

If we adopted this maxim, where would it end? "You kill my son; I kill yours." "You rape my daughter; I rape yours." "You mutilate my body; I mutilate yours." And we will pursue this course, despite the lack of any reason to believe that the death penalty protects us — even when it is clear, almost with certainty, that occasionally the victim of our official barbarism will be innocent.

It is believed that at least twenty-three people have been wrongfully executed in the United States during the twentieth century. Twenty-three innocent people were killed by the official workings of the state, but it is not called murder. Tragically, New York State holds the record for the greatest number of innocents put to death over the years. According to some, New York leads all the states in the nation with at least six (perhaps more) wrongful executions since 1905.[5]

---

4. The source of the original statistic is unavailable, though it refers to executions that took place on or before 15 June 1963, which was, as of March 2003, the date of the last execution in the state of New York. See http://www.deathpenaltyinfo.org/newyork.html.

5. See these studies, for example: Michael L. Radelet, Hugo Adam Bedau, and Constance Putnam, *In Spite of Innocence: Erroneous Convictions in Capital Cases* (Boston: Northeastern University Press, 1992); and Bedau and Radelet, "Miscarriages of Justice in Potentially Capital Cases," *Stanford Law Review* 40 (1987): 21-179. Excerpts of these studies have been compiled and are available at http://archive.aclu.org/issues/death/23executed.html. For a list

Proponents of the death penalty continue to assume that the criminal justice system will not make a mistake. Most are unconcerned about the overly ambitious prosecutor, the sloppy detective, the incompetent defense counsel, the witness with an ax to grind, or the judge who keeps courthouse conviction box scores. But these imperfections and the horrible and irreversible injustice they can produce are inevitable. In this country, a defendant is convicted on proof beyond a reasonable doubt — not proof that can be known with absolute certainty. There's no such thing as absolute certainty in our law. And with the increased use of DNA tests, evidence grows daily of the number of innocent people we have condemned to death in the past.

A young man named Bobby McLaughlin of Marine Park, Brooklyn, was convicted of the robbery and murder of another young man in 1980. This was a one-witness identification case — the least reliable and most frightening kind. In July of 1986, McLaughlin was released after serving six years for a murder he did not commit. The great State of New York wrongly convicted him — by intention or mistake (take your pick). It began when a detective picked up one wrong photograph. One wrong photograph and one mistake led to one date with the electric chair. It could have been one more tragically lost life. Thankfully, the execution didn't happen. But it took an almost superhuman effort by McLaughlin's foster father and some aggressive members of the media to keep the case from falling between the cracks of the justice system. Bobby McLaughlin had this to say after he was released: "If there was a death penalty in this state, I would now be ashes in an urn on my mother's mantel."[6] (See Governor Ryan's chapter in this book for stories of other innocent men who were condemned to die.)

Since I was governor, New York has reinstated the death penalty and with it the threat to take an innocent life. And it will take innocent life over and over again if we allow it to. When it happens, what will the governor tell the wife, or husband, or children, or parents of the innocent victim whom we had killed in our official rage? Will the governor say, "We had to do it"?

That governor would be asked, "But why, if you were not sure it would deter anyone else, why did you have to do it?" Then what would be the answer?

"Because we were angry. Because the people demanded an eye for an eye."

---

of people from other states who were executed despite significant doubts about their guilt, see also http://www.deathpenaltyinfo.org/article.php?scid=6&did=111#executed and http://www.macarthurjusticecenter.com/wrong.html. All websites accessed March 2003.

6. Jack Newfield, "Abolish the Death Penalty," *Local 100 Express*, February 2003, p. 19; available at http://www.twulocal100.org/news/express/february03/pdfs/page19.pdf. Accessed March 2003.

Even if it proved to be an innocent eye? Should the state tell the people that we had to kill, because, as a society, we have come to believe that the only way to punish the most despicable among us is to lie down in the muck and mire that spawned them?

I hear all around me that the violence and killing have become so frequent that we need to send a clearer message to the criminals and to citizens alike that the government knows how bad things are and will do something about it. I agree, and, of course, we must make clear that we intend to fight the terrible epidemics of illegal drugs, violence and crime, and terrorism that plague us. But the death penalty is no more effective a way to fight them than the angry cries that inspire our efforts.

We need to continue to do the things that will control crime by making the apprehension and punishment of criminals more likely. We need adequate police and prisons and alternatives to incarceration. We should also have a tough, effective punishment for deliberate murder. There is one: one that is much better than the death penalty; one that juries will not be reluctant to impose; one that is so menacing to a potential killer, that it could actually deter; one that does not require us to be infallible so as to avoid taking an innocent life; and one that does not require us to stoop to the level of the killers. There is a penalty that is, for those who insist on measuring this question in terms of financial cost, millions of dollars less expensive than the death penalty: true life imprisonment, with no possibility of parole under any circumstances.

True life imprisonment is a more effective deterrent than capital punishment. To most inmates, the thought of living a whole lifetime behind bars only to die in a prison cell, is worse than the quick, final termination of the electric chair or lethal injection. Anecdotal evidence is, of course, limited, but it can give you an insight into the mentality of criminal deterrence. In one article in the *New York Times Magazine,* a young man on death row named Heath Wilkins was asked whether people underestimated the deterrent power of life without parole. "Absolutely," Wilkins responded. "Death isn't a scary thing to someone who's hurting inside so bad that they're hurting other people. People like that are looking for death as a way out."[7] Twice in my life I've personally heard the same thing, and the second time it came from a man on the way to his execution in Oklahoma.

I was saddened when, after my departure as governor in 1995, the State of New York adopted the death penalty. That marked forever in the pages of

7. Ron Rosenbaum, "Too Young to Die?" *New York Times Magazine,* 12 March 1989, pp. 32-35.

our state's history the time we were driven back to one of the vestiges of our primitive condition because we were not willing to find a better answer to violence than more violence. I hope my state and my country will soon return to a higher level of civility.

My remarks thus far intentionally have not centered on the religious dimension of capital punishment. Let me briefly address the religious question, which is the topic of this book. I have spoken elsewhere about the hopeful possibilities that religious convictions and beliefs contribute to our civic faith as a pluralistic people. Many, if not all, religions share a commitment to treat one another with respect and charity and to come together to improve the world that we inhabit.[8] Certainly criminals are guilty of betraying these religious ideals, but society, too, can fail to honor them through the forms of punishment it seeks out.

Religion also bears upon this conversation in ways that can be unfortunate. In debating the death penalty against Ed Koch, which I did for years and years, he loved to get up and say, "Well, Mario is against the death penalty because he thinks it's a sin." This was kind of a deprecating way to characterize my position, invoking religious overtones to do so. I have been against the death penalty all of my adult life. Yet, for most of my adult life the Catholic Church did not express an opinion against the death penalty. I actually wrote to the Vatican when I was governor and said, "Please, please, speak out on this subject." Yet since my views on the death penalty predate *Evangelium vitae* and the new catechism, my position has not always been sanctioned by the magisterium.

My opposition to the death penalty did not originally emerge out of religious reasoning — at least not identifiably Catholic thinking. Nor, when I spoke out against the death penalty, did I identify it as a moral issue. Someone like Justice Scalia (who disagrees with the Pope regarding capital punishment) will label an issue as moral or immoral; he does not consider the death penalty immoral. But I don't know exactly what counts as a "moral issue" to him or to others who share this approach. It is because "morality talk" as such often gives rise to confusion that I very seldom speak of issues in terms that are explicitly "moral." When it comes to the death penalty, I am willing to talk about religious issues, but not about "morality" per se.

So, on what grounds, then, do I oppose capital punishment? As I have said, I am against the death penalty because I think it is bad and unfair for so-

---

8. See my remarks from a Pew Forum address, 2 October 2002, at http://pewforum.org/events/index.php?EventID=34 (accessed 1 March 2003). Also, see Mario Cuomo, "Faith and Government: What Religion Demands and Pluralism Requires," *Commonweal,* 6 December 2002, pp. 11-12.

ciety. I think it is debasing. I think it is degenerate. I think it kills innocent people. I think it eclipses other more significant issues that we should be addressing when we're talking about murder and how to do away with it. For these political and democratic reasons and others, I oppose capital punishment. Some might contend that these are moral reasons, but clearly, my position is based, in large part, on reasons that you could fairly say were not questions of religion or morality. These are basic civic issues that are appropriate to raise in a pluralistic society; they seek out what is good for citizens and society, what is fair, what is reasonable, what works, and what does not.

Now there are also those who believe that invoking religion makes public issues more divisive; instead, they say, we should strive for harmony by leaving religion out of the conversation altogether. I do not think this is a good reason to avoid discussing religion. In fact, at times, it is important to risk division and alienation by taking a stand on contentious issues. Capital punishment is one such example, and it is a divisive issue regardless of whether religion is invoked.

During my election campaigns, I made a very strong case against capital punishment, and — pardon the expression — I got murdered for it, especially in the 1994 gubernatorial election when the exit polls showed that I lost 7.5 percent of the votes. (Considering that I actually only lost the election by two and a half or three points, that was a lot.) During and after the campaign, many asked why I spoke out on the death penalty. When I brought up the subject with my political handlers, they had resisted; making the death penalty such a central issue, they said, was bad for my campaign. Why then, they asked, would I do it? Well, at the risk of sounding noble, it was more important to state my case against the death penalty than to win the campaign. It was better to make my points and to make them as loudly and insistently as I could than to walk away from the issue simply because it was divisive, unpopular, or strategically questionable for winning an election.

I pushed this issue into the center of public dialogue because I believed the stakes went far beyond the death penalty itself. Then, as now, capital punishment was an issue that went beyond the decision whether to execute somebody at Sing Sing.[9] It raised important questions of how, as a society, we view life. It was a question of how we view human beings. And it was a question of how we deal with our anger as a society, since many death penalty proponents

---

9. I was in Sing Sing and saw the death house. I represented the second-to-last person ever to occupy that building. Before I was a governor I did *pro bono* work on three murder cases that were capital cases, where the defendants were sentenced to death. After much effort on their behalf, all three defendants' sentences were commuted during the Rockefeller years.

support the practice because they are angry and want revenge. I thought at the time I was governor, and I still think, that the practice and support for capital punishment was corrosive, that it was bad for a democratic citizenry and that it had to be objected to — and so I did.

There are issues on which it is important to go forward and take a stand; I think the death penalty is one of them. Such issues do not need to be explicitly religious. You don't even have to call them "moral." But this does not make them insignificant. And it may be our religious commitments that give us the courage to push divisive issues, even ones that could backfire on us politically. There are some things that we believe in our hearts are absolutely wrong. Some choose not to say anything about it. Why? Maybe in order to win elections or stay in office. These people might reassure themselves by saying, "Look, it's more important that I serve here, because in the long run I will do more good things — and weightier things — in office than any good that may come from staking out some courageous position that will cost me an election." Or they may just think that they can't accomplish anything on a particular issue: "I'm doomed, and so as a matter of prudence and pragmatism, I decide to sit back and not make the point."

Is it a sin to do that? Well, the God I trust and believe in, I hope, is more supple than that. I am not sure I would call it a sin. But the question of when to take a stand on a controversial issue comes up all the time, and you have to decide it by your own lights, your own conscience, and maybe even your own faith. I chose to take a stand against capital punishment; then, as now, I think it was the right thing to do.

15. Capital Punishment: Is It Wise?

PAUL SIMON

I would like to depart somewhat from the approach taken by most of the other contributors to this volume, by asking not whether the death penalty is permissible on moral or theological grounds, but rather whether capital punishment is a wise public policy. In so doing, I do not intend to suggest that religious beliefs ought to play no role in our deliberations about public policies. As a former legislator, I know that we cannot totally separate our backgrounds from the decisions we make when writing laws. For example, my religious background influenced me when as a United States senator I voted for the Civil Liberties Act of 1988, which provided reparations to those who suffered when the U.S. government forcibly interned more than 115,000 law-abiding Japanese-Americans in February 1942. My decision was deeply influenced by the memory of my father, a Lutheran minister in Oregon who took a vocal and public stand against the internments. I remember the hate mail and phone calls he received, and I remember the terrible *Korematsu* decision of 1944, in which the Supreme Court said the president had acted lawfully when he ordered the internment.[1] My background influenced my decision to support reparations, but on that issue in 1988, as with the death penalty today, I had to be careful that I didn't impose my Lutheran background on others. In areas like these, where personal moral questions blur into the public policy questions, we have to be very careful as we apply our faith to public life.

This is not to say that church and state should somehow be completely

1. *Toyosaburo Korematsu v. United States*, 323 U.S. 214 (1944).

separated. The "wall of separation" that many people argue ought to exist between church and state is not part of the Constitution; it is merely a phrase coined by Thomas Jefferson in a letter to a Baptist conference. In fact, church and the state *must* interact in many ways. If the local Methodist church is on fire, you call out the fire department — you don't say that separation of church and state prohibits it. No one is suggesting we ought to change the name of St. Louis or St. Paul to avoid religious affiliation with those city governments. More people attend religious services on a Friday, Saturday, or Sunday in the United States than in almost any country in the world. State accommodation of religion has been good both for government and for religious communities in the United States, but we have to be very cautious about the relationship. That is why avoiding "excessive entanglement" between church and state should continue to be the policy of the U.S. government and its courts.

Each of us must come to terms with the moral and theological questions surrounding capital punishment, but *as a democratic society,* the central question we face is: *Is it wise?* Our sense of what policies are wise evolves over time, as we learn from mistakes and acquire new knowledge and renew old insights. The Bible does not advocate the abolition of slavery — as defenders of slavery in this country regularly noted — but gradually we came to appreciate that slavery is incompatible with its teachings. On the question of racial segregation, *Plessy v. Ferguson* said in 1896 that "separate but equal" doesn't violate the Constitution, but we gradually came to realize that "equal protection" precluded discrimination in school attendance and many other activities. We don't want to move away from the fundamental tenets of the Constitution, but we do acquire more knowledge over time, and by 1954 (when *Brown v. Board of Education* was handed down), we had learned enough about what segregation was doing in our society to know that it was unjust. If we are to be a society that seeks the common good of *all* Americans, our public policies must reflect the wisdom that comes from careful deliberation. Let us then consider some facts about the death penalty.

Canada, Mexico, and all of Western Europe have abandoned the practice. Turkey's reluctance to eliminate its death penalty has contributed to the long delay in its acceptance into full membership in the European Union.[2] An internationally circulated magazine put the matter succinctly: "Throughout

---

2. Turkey insituted a moratorium on executions in 1984, three years before applying for full EU membership. It retained legislation authorizing the death penalty, however, until January 2004, when it signed the second of two protocols of the European Convention on Human rights that bans the practice in all circumstances.

Europe in particular, the death penalty is thought of as simply uncivilized."[3] In accord with this sentiment, the European Parliament passed a resolution in 2000 urging the United States to abandon the death penalty.[4]

Which nations utilize capital punishment the most? The best estimates for 2001 are that China (with nearly two thousand executions) and Iran (at least 139 executions) led the world in the use of the death penalty, though accurate statistics are not available for either country. Saudi Arabia was third (with seventy-nine executions), and the United States was fourth (with sixty-six executions, down from eighty-five the previous year). Together, these four countries accounted for 90 percent of all known executions in 2001.[5] Since 1990, only seven countries in the world are known to have executed child offenders (people convicted of crimes committed when they were under the age of eighteen): the Democratic Republic of Congo, Iran, Nigeria, Pakistan, Saudi Arabia, Yemen, and — the nation that has executed more than any other — the United States.[6] At least thirty-five people with some degree of mental retardation (defined as having an IQ below seventy) were executed in the United States from 1976 to 2002, when the practice was ruled unconstitutional by the Supreme Court in *Atkins v. Virginia.*[7]

Capital punishment costs more than sentencing a convicted killer to life in prison. I am not suggesting that economics ought to dictate our decision on this, but the Timothy McVeigh defense, for example, cost $13.8 million. For 10 percent of that amount, we could have held him in prison for the rest of his life. One study determined that over the last twenty-five years, it has cost the state of

3. Mary Dudziak, "Giving Capital Offense," *Civilization,* October-November 2000.

4. "EU Memorandum on the Death Penalty," 25 February 2000. http://www.eurunion.org/legislat/DeathPenalty/eumemorandum.htm.

5. In 2002, 81 percent of known executions worldwide took place in just three of those countries: China, Iran, and the USA. Amnesty International. http://web.amnesty.org/deathpenalty (accessed 6 February 2004).

6. Between 1985 and 2001, the United States executed eighteen child offenders. Yemen has since outlawed the practice (as did China in 1997); in 2001, the President of Pakistan announced that he would commute the death sentences of all young offenders on death row in his country, in line with legislation passed in 2000 that abolished the juvenile death penalty. Only the U.S. and Somalia have failed to ratify the United Nations Convention on the Rights of the Child Article 37 (a), 1995, which states that "Neither Capital punishment nor life imprisonment without possibility of release shall be imposed for offenses committed by persons below 18 years of age." For these and other statistics, see the Amnesty International USA web site (http://www.amnestyusa.org/abolish/juveniles.html [accessed 6 February 2004]).

7. Amnesty International, http://www.amnestyusa.org/abolish/mental_retardation.html (accessed 15 April 2003). In *Atkins v. Virginia,* 122 S.Ct. 2242 (2002), the Court held that it is a violation of the Eighth Amendment ban on cruel and unusual punishment to execute death row inmates with mental retardation.

Illinois $800 million more to execute people than to put people in prison for life. But the greatest cost is a moral one: desensitizing us to death and to the use of violence as a legitimate penal instrument in a civilized society.

The death penalty also makes heroes out of criminals. Shortly after Timothy McVeigh's execution I was in central Illinois, where I saw someone wearing a T-shirt with McVeigh's picture on it. Maybe that would have happened if he had been sentenced to life in prison, but I doubt it. This is the kind of perverse effect that Supreme Court Justice Felix Frankfurter had in mind when he wrote, "I am strongly against capital punishment for reasons that are not related to concern for the murderer or the risk of convicting the innocent. When life is at hazard in a trial, it sensationalizes the whole thing almost unwittingly. The effect on juries, the bar, the public, the judiciary, I regard as very bad."[8]

Who actually receives capital punishment? With rare exceptions, those who face and receive the death penalty in this country are poor and non-white. If you have enough money, you generally won't face capital punishment. (Timothy McVeigh's situation was exceptional. The nature of his crime set him apart from others who faced the death penalty, and they convicted and executed him despite having an unlimited defense budget and excellent counsel.) Since 1977, the overwhelming majority of death row defendants (over 80 percent) have been executed for killing white victims, although only 50 percent of all homicide victims are white.[9] In Kentucky, more than a thousand African-Americans have been murdered since 1975, but all thirty-nine death row inmates there in early 2002 — and both of those who have been executed since then — were sent there for killing a white person.[10] Furthermore, according to a 1990 report by the U.S. General Accounting Office which reviewed twenty-eight statistical studies of death penalty sentencing:

> In 82% of the studies, race of the victim was found to influence the likelihood of being charged with capital murder or receiving the death penalty, i.e., those who murdered whites were more likely to be sentenced to death

8. Felix Frankfurter, *Of Law and Men: Papers and Addresses, 1939-1956*, Philip Elman, ed. (New York: Harcourt Brace, 1956), p. 81.

9. Amnesty International Program to Abolish the Death Penalty. Statistics available at http://www.amnestyusa.org/abolish/racialprejudices.html (accessed 14 April 2003).

10. "Racial Justice Act Passes Senate," *The Advocate*, 20, no. 4 (July 1998): 5. Available online at http://dpa.state.ky.us/library/advocate/july98/Racial.html (accessed 14 April 2003). It should be noted that Kentucky remains the only state to have passed legislation (in 1998) directly addressing the racial disparity in capital sentencing. The U.S. House of Representatives has passed a similar bill on two occasions, but it has been defeated in the Senate.

than those who murdered blacks. This finding was remarkably consistent across data sets, states, data collection methods, and analytic techniques. The finding held for high, medium, and low quality studies.[11]

Is the death penalty a deterrent against future murders? Does it make our communities safer? Of the twelve states that do not have capital punishment, ten have below-average murder rates. Of the seven states with the lowest murder rates, five don't have capital punishment. All but two of the twenty-seven states with the highest murder rate have the death penalty on the books. To take an example from another country, England used to have capital punishment for pickpocketing (among other things). What do you think happened while crowds gathered in the town common to witness the public executions? Other thieves worked the crowd, pickpocketing. I'm not suggesting that the way to reduce the murder rate or eliminate pickpocketing is to eliminate capital punishment, but rather that the death penalty is simply not a factor. Do you feel safer in Texas (which has the death penalty) than in Iowa (which doesn't)? Are you more secure in South Dakota than in North Dakota? Is Connecticut less threatening than Massachusetts? To ask the question is to answer it.

Perhaps most importantly, we must admit that innocent people have been put to death in our country. As co-chair of Governor George Ryan's Commission on Capital Punishment, I have taken a very careful look at the situation in Illinois.[12] We had the case of Anthony Porter, two days away from execution when he was granted a temporary reprieve by the courts, during which time new information surfaced that exonerated him. He was freed sixteen years after being convicted for a crime he did not commit. Since 1976 the state of Illinois has executed twelve people, while thirteen people were released from death row because evidence ultimately proved that they were not guilty. As shocking as this is, I think there are more mistakes that have yet to be uncovered. There is no question in my mind that some people currently on Illinois's death row shouldn't be there, and that some people who were executed by the state in the past were in fact innocent. It is clearly immoral to send innocent people to prison for the rest of their lives, but even this travesty of justice pales in comparison to executing an innocent person. If new evidence appears that exonerates someone with a life sentence, society can free

11. U.S. General Accounting Office, "Death Penalty Sentencing: Research Indicates Pattern of Racial Disparities" (1990), p. 5.

12. For more information about the Governor's Commission on Capital Punishment, or to read the Commission's final report and recommendations for reform, see http://www.idoc.state.il.us/ccp/index.html.

that person and even provide some compensation. That won't remove the injustice of false imprisonment, but at least prisoners can be set free again; the death penalty doesn't admit the possibility of error.

Finally, I think we have to learn the lesson — not just in our country but everywhere around the world — that violence breeds violence. From time to time, the state has to use force, but that force should not be excessive. When it is excessive, we do harm to society. Given all these considerations, is it wise to have capital punishment in the United States today? The evidence is overwhelming that it is not wise.

16. Facing the Jury: The Moral Trials of a Prosecutor in a Capital Case

BETH WILKINSON

I served as a prosecutor for the Timothy McVeigh case in the 1995 bombing of the Murrah Federal Building in Oklahoma City. Before discussing some of my experiences from that trial, let me open with a brief story, which is relevant given this book's focus on religion and the death penalty. Just a few months after the Timothy McVeigh and Terry Nichols cases ended, while I was contemplating the next step in my career, I was asked by one of the judicial circuits to participate on a panel entitled "Handling a High Profile Case." They also asked me to attend a luncheon beforehand, at which I would meet the judges and other participants on my panel. Of course I agreed to attend. I arrived to find that the speaker was none other than Sister Helen Prejean, the celebrated anti–death penalty activist whose story was most famously told in her book and in the film *Dead Man Walking*. As many know, she is unbelievable — a magnificent speaker. She uses all the great rhetoric of a Southern Baptist preacher: she has the Louisiana accent, and, most importantly, she tells a story from her heart. She presents a very compelling discussion about sitting and waiting for death with a death row inmate. As she began her speech, she brought in the entire audience immediately; meanwhile, I was shrinking back in my chair. She spoke of the people who participate in the "death machine" and how it was beyond her comprehension how one could participate in it. I shrank back a little further. The luncheon ended and she received a standing ovation while I went with my colleagues to my panel. I doubted that Sister Helen would attend. My fellow panelists and I spoke and responded to several questions, and at one point, someone asked me about delivering the death argument to the jury in the McVeigh case. I looked down into the audience and I saw Sister Helen, and she looked up at me and smiled. And as I started to speak, I saw her cross herself. I saw grace that afternoon, and it is grace that I seek whenever I reflect on the death penalty.

In this essay, I would like to discuss my experiences of being a public servant and juxtapose my public duties with my religious views in a personal way, because I think that marks both the beginning and the end of my soul-searching over the death penalty. As a lawyer, when I appear before a judge and am asked a question, I am told to get immediately to the answer. So let me begin with my answer and then describe how I got there.

I describe myself as a struggling supporter of the death penalty, a stance I adopted very early in my life and one that I continue to hold today both as a supporter and a critic of the death penalty. Back in June of 1997, when I sat down to write the death penalty argument in the McVeigh case, I thought carefully and extensively about what I should say. I realized that what I said probably was not going to matter one bit because once the jury had decided that Mr. McVeigh was guilty of the crimes, most of those jurors, I was sure, would believe that death was the proper sentence. Nevertheless, I wanted to say something that was appropriate — not just on my part, of course, but on behalf of the U.S. government that brought the suit and which I represented as Special Attorney to the Attorney General. I realized that I was confronting moral and religious questions regarding the death penalty in the most personal way that I had ever experienced.

So I sat down and did what some people do: I called my dad. I spoke with him about some of my views, some of the historical references that I wanted to use in my closing argument of the sentencing phase, and also about my surprise at my comfort and ability to write and deliver the closing argument. I wrote the entire closing argument in probably about three hours (the closing was just thirty-five minutes long) with almost no problem. I wrote it two days before the argument. I went to a baseball game with my prosecution team the day before the argument and slept well that night. The next day I stood up and delivered my statement in front of the twelve jurors and four alternates. Here are some of the words that I wrote and delivered to the jury during the closing argument of the sentencing phase, after Timothy McVeigh had already been found guilty:

> The enormity of the impact of this crime cannot be overstated. It can barely be comprehended. It is not just the immediate families that have suffered loss; but communities, churches, employers, schools across this country have endured the repercussions of Timothy McVeigh's crimes.

You heard Pam Whicher when she told the story of her daughter. Mrs. Whicher, a widow of a Secret Service agent [who was killed in the bombing], Alan Whicher told you about the paper her daughter wrote about the day that changed her life. In that paper, her daughter told of a struggle to deal with her father's murder. She said, "I never knew such a dark, horrible place existed until I had to claw my way out of there." She could have just as well been speaking for the entire nation, which had never before had to endure such monstrous crimes as Timothy McVeigh's. We never knew that such a dark and horrible place could exist in America until Timothy McVeigh sent us there.

In his opening statement to you, [defense attorney] Mr. Jones recognized that the bombing at Oklahoma City was seared into the memory of our generation like the attack on Pearl Harbor was to the generation before us. Mr. Jones was right. Like the attack on Pearl Harbor, the bombing in Oklahoma City threatened our sense of security within our own borders; and this threat to our security came from and was caused by Timothy McVeigh. He betrayed every American. He betrayed his fellow soldiers from the Persian Gulf. He betrayed his family, and he betrayed you. He is a traitor who chose of his own volition to betray his country by murdering as many United States citizens as he could. No person, no government action, no second or third reality that [defense attorney] Mr. Burr mentioned, made Timothy McVeigh murder 168 of his own people.

As the moral conscience of the community, you must speak on behalf of all Americans who rightly refuse to accept any justification for this horrible crime. It is time for justice. It is time to impose the ultimate sanction on the man responsible for this terror. Serve justice. Speak as the moral conscience of the community, and sentence Timothy McVeigh to death.

I was rather surprised that it was so easy for me to make those strong statements. They certainly do not seem to come from someone who considered herself then — and still considers herself — to be struggling with her views on the death penalty. Like Justice Scalia, I have very little difficulty believing capital punishment is moral; my question, like Senator Simon's, is whether it is wise. Let me describe how I arrived at this ambivalent position that I hold today.

I grew up in a household with two public servants: a submarine captain and a total pacifist. I think that probably speaks volumes about why I am a struggling supporter of the death penalty. I come from a very religious household: a New England Methodist family. We practiced religion every day by watching my mother who lived and still lives according to her values in every-thing that she does. But as we sat down at the dinner table to discuss issues like the death penalty and other weighty issues of the day, I had the subma-rine captain on my right, who believed in his religious views just as strongly as my mother, the public servant and pacifist on my left. Those struggles, those discussions that we had as I grew up, gave me, I think, a rather nuanced view of this issue and many others. I was also forced to figure out how my fa-ther was able to put his finger on that nuclear button and press it if it was nec-essary to defend our country, while believing in the religious teachings of the Methodist Church; and how my mother could be married to a man like my father when she believed that there was no justification for war or any other type of violence.

After growing up in that environment I had faith that I could reconcile my views and my responsibilities as a public servant because of two things: first, because I was brought up in a strong religious household where we dis-cussed our views and were allowed to have differing views; and second, be-cause I actually watched my parents live and get along together when they shared such diametrically opposed views on moral issues yet shared the same fundamental religious values that structured our household. If they could stay married for forty years, I could certainly reconcile my views on the death penalty.

As I started college, like many others, I was typically opposed to the death penalty. Then I read Reinhold Niebuhr's *Moral Man and Immoral Soci-ety*,[1] which gave me an entirely new perspective on how to reconcile individ-ual morality with governmental policies and collective morality and behavior. It was there, looking back, where I first started transforming my views about whether I could personally participate in a system that sanctioned the death penalty. As public servants, there is no moral dilemma for attorneys to partic-ipate in capital cases so long as they support the practice of capital punish-ment. Those who do not either choose to participate anyway — because as lawyers or other public servants it is their obligation — or choose not to par-ticipate and find another vocation. For many years as a federal prosecutor, I had the luxury to be able to participate in the system without having to take on death cases. I learned how to be a prosecutor while serving in the Eastern District of New York; the U.S. attorney there allowed people to choose whether or not they would participate in capital cases. Unlike many other ju-rists who have no choice to participate in death cases as they come across

---

1. Reinhold Niebuhr, *Moral Man and Immoral Society* (New York: Simon & Schuster, 1932).

their desk, I could prosecute non-capital types of cases, and for many years I did. In fact, I never participated in any death cases as a prosecutor in New York.

But as I developed as a prosecutor and ascended in my career, I started to witness true evil. I started prosecuting people who had been involved with things that were well beyond my personal experience or knowledge, growing up in my protected world in Connecticut. I saw people whose crimes I thought justified the death penalty from a moral perspective, from a retributive perspective. Yet I struggled with this because I also thought the system was so flawed — in that an innocent person might be executed — that there could be no way to justify the death penalty in any instance.

Without addressing those issues directly in New York, I left for Washington, D.C., to the Justice Department. To make a long story short, I was asked one day whether I would participate in the prosecution of Timothy McVeigh. One can imagine what a privilege it was for me, as a prosecutor and a government servant, to be asked to participate in something that was so important to our country. From a personal and religious perspective, it was my first time confronting the question of whether my ambition and public service would be able to accommodate participation in a death penalty case and the possible executions of Timothy McVeigh and Terry Nichols.

I am not sure whether I can identify a particular moment in time when I transformed my position and said that I personally could participate, but if there was such a moment, I believe it was when, as a federal prosecutor, I saw the vast evil perpetrated by Timothy McVeigh. And so I took on my responsibilities in the McVeigh case alongside other members of the prosecution team. We had between seven and nine lawyers on the team at any one time. It is worth noting that not one of them had ever participated in a death case before we prosecuted Timothy McVeigh, so we had absolutely no prior experience in capital cases. Nor did anyone who had any direct role in the prosecution consider him- or herself to be an outspoken supporter of the death penalty.

As a public servant involved with a death case, every day one considers how to reconcile participating in a process where the goal is to execute the defendant and simultaneously provide that person a fair trial. That means participating in discovery by deciding which documentation should be turned over, what type of motion should be made, what kinds of arguments should be directed at the court, and what kinds of arguments should be directed at the public and the jury.

We struggled with those issues every day as we prepared during the pretrial phase and the trial phase of the Timothy McVeigh and Terry Nichols cases. But not until January 10, 1997, when I sat down to draft the argument for the sentencing phase, did I fully confront my own moral compass about standing in front of twelve people to ask them to execute another individual.

The actual delivery of my closing argument was significantly more difficult than writing it had been. As I reviewed the script that I had prepared to argue in front of the jury, I tried to reassure myself that I was not the one making the decision. I am just an advocate and it is up to those twelve jurors to make the decision. That worked for about five minutes, for I realized that I was indeed part of the "machinery of death," that I was using my skills, whatever they were, to advocate on behalf of the government's position. I believed it was a lawful and justified position, but there was no evading that my goal was to give the jury the arguments they needed to go back into the jury room and persuade each other that execution was the appropriate punishment.

As I stood in front of the jury, I looked each member in the eye and I thought, if I am asking these twelve people to do something that I believe is morally just — and not only just, but necessary in this case — I have to be able to do what I'm asking them to do. I have to be able to look Timothy McVeigh in the eye and say that he deserves to die. So, as I was going through my closing argument, I turned to him and told the jury to take a moment to look at him, to call him a coward and to tell him that he had committed treason and an act of terrorism. Tell him that the use of violence to further political goals is something we reject in this country, especially when it involves innocent civilians. Our country is premised upon the notion that we admit almost anything into our debate and our democracy, other than taking human life — especially when it is taken to perpetuate or achieve someone's political ideals. At a certain point it is appropriate for society to speak out and say, "We will not tolerate as a member of our organized society one who murders 168 innocent people because he feels, in his personal analysis, that there has been some wrong done by the United States government or by anyone else." Then I asked the jury to sentence him to death. That was, for me, perhaps the most difficult moment in the case, not because I did not believe it, but because I found myself looking into the eyes of the person that I thought should receive the ultimate punishment.

I had a very important responsibility during the pre-trial phase to put Jennifer McVeigh, Timothy McVeigh's sister, on the stand as a witness for the government. As you might imagine, she loved her brother and was politically aligned with him in that she shared an anti-government perspective. She did not want to be a witness, but for a variety of reasons had made statements early in the investigation about some of his activities, so she could be commanded to testify and impeached with her statements if she was not forthcoming. I recall having had a discussion with her as we were preparing for the "guilt phase," the first phase of a death penalty trial before the sentencing phase (also called the "death phase"). It was not a friendly conversation, as you might guess — respectful, but never friendly. She was struggling with the fact that she was going to be testifying in a few months. I told her that she was going to have to testify one way or the other and that she was going to have to tell the truth. But I thought if she wanted to find some comfort, being candid and truthful in front of the jury during the guilt phase would give her some credibility if she wanted to argue during the death phase to save her brother's life.

I am not sure whether that advice was sound, but it spoke to how I felt at the time and it seemed to give her some comfort as she was called to the witness stand to make some very incriminating statements about her brother. During the closing argument, as I turned from Mr. McVeigh and the jury towards the podium, my eyes met those of Jennifer McVeigh, who was sitting in the front row. I could see tears in her eyes, listening to the arguments I was making about why her brother should be executed.

It didn't take the jury very long to return the death sentence for Mr. McVeigh, and afterward I felt no regret about participating in that process. In fact, on the day of the execution, June 11, 2001, I wondered how I would feel as I watched the media announce Mr. McVeigh's death. Even as a Christian, I felt nothing for Mr. McVeigh. I felt a lot for the victims and I felt, obviously, a deep sadness for the country having suffered so much. I felt especially sad for having to participate in this death machine in order to vindicate our moral principles and our rule of law. But I felt nothing for Mr. McVeigh.

*   *   *

Let me now turn to another dimension of my thinking about the death penalty. The Constitution Project is a commission that seeks to develop bipartisan solutions to constitutional and governance issues. The Project, through the work of its Death Penalty Initiative, decided to bring together both sides of the death penalty debate — those who support and those who oppose it — to focus on how to reform the current system and address the issues that all persons, whether retentionists or abolitionists, believe are problematic. I was very comfortable participating as co-chair of the Death Penalty Initiative, since I had just participated in a unique death penalty prosecution. Many people, however, have asked me not to use the McVeigh case as an example of whether we should have the death penalty because, they say, it is too easy to see why you would have the death penalty for a Timothy McVeigh. I couldn't disagree more. If you want to have a moral and religious debate about the death penalty, then start with a case in which the system works properly. In the Oklahoma City bombing trials, there were excellent government lawyers, a fabulous judge, and very, very capable defense attorneys. I don't think there was any question whether Timothy McVeigh or Terry Nichols received a fair trial, and I don't think there is any question about their guilt.

Of course, we're all opposed to capital punishment when the system doesn't work, when we convict innocent people. From a practical standpoint, I don't know anyone who supports the death penalty when an innocent person is incarcerated or put to death. The question from a theoretical perspective involves how one feels about execution when all the rights of the defendant have been protected. When someone has committed the most heinous crime imaginable, then we are left with the moral question: Is capital punishment right, is it just? I have always resisted discussing the morality of the death penalty in relation to the flaws of the system, because that debate asks whether the death penalty is wise and being administered properly, not whether it is just and right.

I want to point out that everyone takes this debate very seriously, especially people who participate in the process directly. But if one looks at the federal system as an example, at least as of January 2002, not one of the defendants on death row in the federal system is claiming actual innocence. So despite the press attention and the debate about this issue, which I think is crucial as a matter of public policy, there are very few people on death row who claim they are innocent. That doesn't mean that they aren't entitled to a rigorous appeal, good counsel, and a habeas review of their cases. It just means that, by and large, those cases are not being discussed in terms of whether the accused actually committed the crimes but whether they received a fair trial, and whether there was some error that amounts, under certain jurisprudence, to an error of either constitutional or statutory magnitude such that the case has to be reversed, at least for the sentencing phase.

As strongly as I feel about my participation in the McVeigh case, I still continue to struggle with the death penalty. Furthermore, by working on the death penalty reforms, like those suggested in "Mandatory Justice,"[2] I feel that I am able to carry through on what I think is my consistent philosophy about trying to balance my viewpoints on the death penalty where public policy and morality intersect. That is, even if the law has been complied with, is it wise?

2. Thirty members of the Constitution Project's Death Penalty Initiative produced the "Mandatory Justice" document. Their names and the full text of this document are available at: http://www.constitutionproject.org/dpi/index.html (accessed 15 January 2002).

Is it being exercised judiciously and appropriately? Here is where questions of race, true innocence, and representation come into play and where our reforms are aimed: Where, for example, are the problems in the system that don't rise to the level of constitutionality but are still problematic and lead many to believe that the death penalty should not, as a policy matter, be implemented in our country at all?

Those of us who avidly seek to reform the death penalty know that the argument over actual innocence is not going to get us very far. Of the people who really know about the death penalty debate — especially those who have been opposing it for many years — they fear this line of argument, because in 99 percent of the cases, there is no question about the guilt of the defendant.

The crucial question is did he or she (and mostly he) get a fair trial and a fair sentencing hearing? Was the jury informed about the alternative of life without parole? And did the jury consider fully the possible sentence of life without parole, understanding that the offender would be secure in prison and that they need not feel forced to choose death just to eliminate a future security risk. We, at the Constitution Project, have tried to move the debate in these directions where the reforms take place.

I close where I began, which is that I think my viewpoints are a product of my religious training, my genetic material, and my personal experience in participating in the system as a public servant. As imperfect as my reasoning may be for my justification of the death penalty, I have found a comfortable place as a struggling supporter. But let me also be clear that prosecutorial discretion is not an invitation to admit my personal beliefs. This is sometimes hard for people to understand. Just because I had the discretion of the state to decide whether to charge someone for a capital offense does not mean that it can be done because I personally feel a particular way about a particular case. Even within a prosecutor's office, there are standards for bringing a case. There is review by supervisors; there is a presentation to the grand jury so that citizens have a chance to make a determination about bringing those charges; and ultimately, the jury makes the decisions. All of these factors ultimately limit prosecutorial discretion, even if one thinks the defendant is guilty of the crimes with which he or she is charged.

Do I think our system is perfect, or that anyone can perfectly separate their individual views from their prosecutorial responsibilities? Of course not. But I do see people trying to do that every day by upholding standards, by having discussions, by requiring proof. All these kinds of pre-trial requirements for proving cases limit prosecutorial discretion in certain ways. But ultimately in a death case, prosecutorial discretion has an impact on a community level on whether certain prosecutors bring certain cases. Would I bring a death case involving a murder that was committed during a holdup of a convenience store? No, I would not. Personally I don't think that felony murder should ever be a death-eligible offense. But if I worked in a prosecutor's office, I would not get to make that personal decision. That decision would involve a policy discussion within the office, and I think that is appropriate. So, unless someone canonizes me as the person who gets to make those decisions based on my own personal beliefs, I still have a duty as a public servant to my community.

17. The Problem of Forgiveness: Reflections of a Public Defender and a Murder Victim's Family Member

JEANNE BISHOP

The death penalty debate demands that we bring our truest selves — informed by our work, our beliefs, and our experience — to the table. The death penalty is not purely a political, academic, or religious issue. Many people debate state-sanctioned executions from a single perspective — for example, as a prosecutor, a judge, a social activist, a grieving family member, a religious leader, or as a concerned citizen. I come to this debate with a clarity born of defending accused murderers; with a sorrow sprung from the deep and still-open wound of having lost family members to murder; and with a commitment to follow Christ. For some people, this may be a startling juxtaposition of perspectives that raises challenging questions. How do I honor my beloved dead while also defending those accused — and often guilty — of like crimes? Where and how does my Christian faith fit in?

Experiencing Murder in My Family

My younger sister Nancy was murdered in 1990 when she was twenty-five years old. She and her husband Richard were moving into their first home, and she was three months pregnant with their first child. With so much to look forward to, they were happy and brimming over with dreams. But, one warm April night, when they returned home to their suburban home outside Chicago, they found a killer inside waiting for them. Entering through the patio sliding glass door, the intruder had used a glasscutter, silently stacking the pieces on the ground. Police surmised later that he positioned a chair in the middle of the living room to better view all possible entries as he sat with his gun and waited for Nancy and Richard to return home.

As soon as they entered, the intruder forced them to lie down on the floor, where he handcuffed Richard. They both begged for their lives, and Nancy pleaded for their baby's life. They offered the intruder money and belongings, which were later found rejected and scattered around the room. Those things were not what he wanted. He had come for something else.

He was probably nervous as he squeezed the trigger, for when the gun went off, he fired a bullet into the wall. Rattled, he then forced them into the basement, where he assured them he would lock them in but then leave. But he didn't leave. Instead, he shot Richard once in the back of the head, execution style. I know witnessing her husband's murder shattered Nancy; her dream of growing old with her love and raising a family was literally blown to pieces in front of her.

After her husband slumped to the floor, the killer turned the gun on her. He pointed it at her swollen belly and fired twice. I remember how much Nancy had prayed and cared for that baby. She had shunned anything she thought might endanger it: cigarette smoke, even junk food. More than anything she wanted to be a mom. Somehow the cruel mind of this killer must have known those shots would wound not just her body but also her heart. It would have been more merciful to shoot her in the head, like Richard had been killed, like an animal is killed when put out of its misery.

But the killer left my little sister to bleed to death on the cold concrete floor. Blood and marks on her body revealed her final moments: she tried unsuccessfully to crawl upstairs for help. She banged on a metal shelf in a futile attempt to summon aid. Finally, when she must have understood that she was dying, she dragged herself back to her husband's body and wrote in her own blood a heart symbol and the letter "U." Love you. It was how Nancy had closed her letters through the years.

The killer was arrested six months later, upon which time all these grisly details came to light. In his spacious suburban bedroom, police found the gun, burglary tools, handcuffs, and a trophy album filled with press clippings about the murders and his own poems about the killing. We learned that he had even attended Nancy and Richard's funeral.

A jury convicted him of the first-degree murders of Nancy and Richard and the intentional homicide of an unborn child. The court sentenced him to life imprisonment without parole on all three charges. Because he was sixteen at the time of the murders, he was ineligible for the death penalty in Illinois (unlike a number of other states which do not spare juveniles). The killer has never shown remorse; he has never asked my family or me for forgiveness.

Defending Murderers

My work as a criminal defense lawyer who has represented alleged killers is irrevocably tied to both Nancy's murder and to my Christian faith. At the time Nancy was killed, I was a corporate attorney for one of the country's largest law firms. Single and childless, I worked long hours with no passion for my work except for the few *pro bono* cases I took on. When Nancy died, I realized how happy she had been. She had lived exactly as God intended and, until her death, exactly the life she had wanted to lead. In more ways than one, her murder was a wake-up call which forced me to confront my own life.

Soon after Nancy's death, the unthinkable occurred: I became the target of the police and the FBI in my own sister's murder investigation. Until the killer was eventually arrested, my life was an open book: my telephone calls were monitored, apartment searched, mail opened, friends interrogated and even subpoenaed. FBI leaks to reporters resulted in front page stories and nightly news updates. I needed a criminal lawyer, and because I could afford it, I hired a very good one.

Those hellish months taught me an unforgettable lesson about the power of government over the individual. I began to wonder what happened to innocent people under investigation who did not have the educational, emotional, and financial resources I possessed. This experience prompted me to become a public defender within months after Nancy's murder. Since that time, I have defended accused murderers, some of them guilty. Of course, I have also met the families of the victims, and I know firsthand what it feels like to be one of those family members, sitting in the courtroom day after day, staring at the jurors, begging them silently to convict. But now, sitting across the courtroom at the defense table, I also see the other side of a death penalty case as it unfolds.

In short, it is ugly. These are the cases where mistakes shouldn't happen. Yet preventable mistakes occur consistently and repeatedly. Evidence appears at the last minute; audiotapes contain inexplicable gaps; witnesses misrepresent facts; defense attorneys underprepare their cases; prosecutors spew inflammatory arguments; and judges issue rulings that stray from the law.

United States Supreme Court Associate Justice Antonin Scalia has referred to errors arising in death penalty cases as "foot faults," a tennis term describing the error when a player unintentionally steps over the line while serving.[1] But the many incidents of prosecutorial misconduct that I have witnessed in murder cases are not "foot faults." They are neither minor nor unintended mistakes. In a proceeding where human life is at stake, this use of a sports metaphor is inaccurate at best, callous at worst. In court, as I stand next to my client — a living, breathing human being — it is impossible to forget that the intended result of these messy proceedings is to strap him down on a table and snuff out his life.

The Death Penalty's False Promises

In addition to my work as a public defender, I am a public advocate for justice for the family members of murder victims. From firsthand experience I know that the death penalty hurts, not helps, victims' families. Moreover, it desecrates the memory of the victims. In short, capital punishment is an untrustworthy, ineffective, and expensive attempt to dispense criminal justice, which holds out a series of false promises.

Closure

Death penalty proponents often promise "closure" for families. But, from my experience, I am certain of this: executions do not and cannot deliver closure. Capital punishment does not heal or put an end to the grief that comes from losing a loved one. Nor perhaps should it. Why? Because that kind of grief never ends. As the culmination of sweet memories and the bitter loss of possibilities, grief lives on, as it should. My grief over Nancy's murder is not "closed"; it dwells within me today, albeit differently than in those first few months after her death. At first grief numbed and paralyzed me. Today grief energizes me to love more passionately; to share more generously; to live more fearlessly; to work to prevent the violence that could inflict upon another family the suffering mine has endured.

Grief also instructs me. I have learned not to hold back love, because I understand, in the core of my being, that those whom we cherish can be snatched from us at any moment. You don't waste time being afraid when you

---

1. Remarks made during a question and answer period at the conference *A Call for Reckoning: Religion and the Death Penalty* on 25 January 2002 at the University of Chicago Divinity School and sponsored by the Pew Forum on Religion and Public Life. See http://pewforum.org/deathpenalty/resources/transcript3.php3 for transcript.

realize how brief life is. Every day that I have lived since Nancy and Richard's murder is one day they never enjoyed. So I try to live in a way that honors them and the God who gives the gifts of life and love.

In the play *Shadowlands*, the writer C. S. Lewis tries to avoid the painful prospect of life without his wife, Joy Gresham, who is dying of cancer. Yet she forces him to confront the imminent reality: "Pain, then, is part of the happiness now. That's the deal."[2] So it is with Nancy and me. The pain now is part of the happiness of when she lived. Why would I "close" that, even if I could? The notion that killing another human being — no matter how despicable his act — could somehow honor someone's memory or heal someone else's grief, is untrue.

Closure, it is true, also involves a measure of psychological resolution and peace, which, unlike the overcoming of grief, is possible. But that inner peace, I hope to demonstrate here, does not come from killing someone else, however cruel and guilty that person may be. That form of closure, rather, comes from introspection, faith, forgiveness, and renewal.

Justice

The death penalty also holds out a false promise of justice. Victims' families are often told that "justice" demands a life for a life, which is an insulting assertion. Imagine if all my sister's killer could give me in return for my loved ones were his life. His life is not worth theirs. His death could never begin to pay for theirs, nor could his suffering ever make up for theirs. To suggest that a murderer's death can requite that of his victim is hardly justice.

Some years ago, the *New Yorker* ran an essay by a judge who stated that he voted for death in murder cases because he heard the tortured voices of the victims crying out for "vindication."[3] Not this victim, surely. My sister does not require the death of another to vindicate her life; it stands unassisted in its beauty and integrity. Killing contradicts everything she stood for. How is justice served through a process that effaces the ideals she embodied?

Furthermore, is justice achieved if the system under which the killer is convicted is unfair? Former American Bar Association president John C. Curtin Jr. persuasively pronounced that "A system that will take life must first give justice."[4] Webster defines justice as "the principle of ideal or moral right-

2. William Nicholson, *Shadowlands* (New York: Plume, 1991), p. 90.
3. Alex Kozinski, "Tinkering with Death," *New Yorker* (10 February 1997), p. 48.
4. John C. Curtin, quoted from the Death Penalty Moratorium Implementation Project

ness . . . the upholding of what is right: fairness."[5] It defines vengeance as "the act of causing harm to another in retribution for wrong or injury."[6] So which is the death penalty as applied in the United States?

In "Anatomy of a Verdict," a *New York Times* Sunday magazine cover story, D. Graham Burnett chronicles his experience serving on a murder jury. He relates the twelve jurors' dilemma: they sensed the defendant had committed a crime, yet they also believed the prosecution had not met its legal burden of proof. Would the jury hew to the law and acquit? Or would its members follow their gut instincts and convict? Burnett recalls the pivotal moment:

> Then Juror Nine rose to speak. "I've been listening," he began, "to these things people are saying, and I have tried to pray about all this. Now I've decided what I have to do. I believe this young man did something very, very wrong in that room. But I also believe that nobody has asked me to play God. I've been asked to apply the law. Justice belongs to God; men only have the law. Justice is perfect, but the law can only be careful."[7]

The law — or its enforcement, at least — has not been very careful in death penalty cases, particularly in my state, Illinois. Since 1977, Illinois has executed twelve people yet released thirteen death row prisoners who were proven to be innocent. The mistakes in these wrongful convictions were so appalling that Governor George Ryan established a commission to study how to eliminate the possibility of error. As Governor Ryan discusses in his chapter in this volume, the commission concluded that the State of Illinois needed eighty-five reforms to reduce mistakes to apply the death penalty fairly.[8] But even with these changes, human error could not be ruled out completely. And when mistakes occur in this process, the result is not only the death of a human being, but also the death of justice.

Reverend Dale Turner, religion columnist for the *Seattle Times*, links the term "justice" inextricably with Micah 6:8: "He has told you what is good; and what does the Lord require but to do justice, and to love kindness,

---

of the American Bar Association, Section of Individual Rights and Responsibilities, http://www.abanet.org/irr/deathpenalty (accessed 30 January 2003).

5. *Webster's II New Riverside Dictionary,* (New York: Houghton Mifflin Co., 1996), p. 378.

6. *New Riverside Dictionary,* p. 749.

7. D. Graham Burnett, "Anatomy of a Verdict," *New York Times Sunday Magazine* (26 August 2001), p. 50.

8. Office of the Governor of the State of Illinois, *Report of the Governor's Commission on Capital Punishment,* April 2002.

and to walk humbly with your God?" Turner goes on to write, "Justice is love distributed."[9]

The death penalty in twenty-first-century America is the antithesis of mercy. We have the capacity to keep ourselves safe from murderers without killing them. Yet, we choose to kill. It is also the antithesis of the humility God demands of us when, with all our imperfections, we still insist we can reach a perfectly certain decision regarding life and carry out an irreversible sentence.

The only sliver of justice I could receive after Nancy's death is an apology from her killer — for him to recognize the value of what he destroyed and to show remorse for that destruction. He hasn't yet; perhaps he never will. But as long as he lives, I can hope.

My friend Bud Welch's hope for an apology is gone, however. His only daughter, Julie Marie, a vibrant young woman who worked as a translator in the federal building in Oklahoma City, died at the hands of Timothy McVeigh. Like many family members of the bombing victims, Bud wanted to hear McVeigh say he was sorry. He befriended Timothy McVeigh's father and sister and tried unsuccessfully to arrange a meeting with his daughter's killer. Bud speaks of the hole in his heart since the execution, a hole that can never be filled. Has he received justice? Bud and I have decided our grief is too great to waste on something as small as revenge paraded as justice.

Deterrence

Deterrence is a particularly alluring but empty promise. Death penalty advocates argue that people will think twice about killing if they know they may face execution. Abner Mikva, former congressman and federal judge, once commented on the inanity of assuming that the least rational members of society — first-degree murderers — will stop to ponder their fates, act rationally, and decide against killing someone because they are deterred by the possibility of execution.[10]

I learned long before September 11, 2001, that a person's hate can supply sufficient reason to kill, even if that reason makes no sense to anyone else. The phrase "senseless killing" became real to me in the wake of Nancy's murder. It long ago ceased to bother me that Nancy's killer never said why he did it. Af-

9. Dale Turner, "How to Follow Jesus' Path? With Justice, Kindness, Humility," *Seattle Times* (23 March 2002).

10. Abner Mikva, "Crime and Punishment in Politics" (Howard J. Trienens Lecture delivered at Northwestern University School of Law on 5 November 2001).

ter all, what reason could he possibly give that would be comprehensible enough to be deterred? And yet in the face of this senselessness, some propose the death penalty as a response.

The Cost

Finally, the death penalty is not just a false promise but also a terrible allocation of precious financial resources. About the only thing actually deterred by the death penalty is financial assistance for victims' families to put toward the costs of the healing process. The death penalty is a colossal waste of money. Lengthy trials (including aggravation and mitigation proceedings), appeals, and executions squander the resources that should go to the victims' families. Millions of dollars were spent to execute McVeigh; countless more millions were spent publicizing his death — and him. Yet, we are no safer now that he is dead than if he had been incarcerated for life. But we are certainly poorer. Money desperately needed for police, crime prevention, hospitals, damage restitution, and counseling for victims' families all went instead to death row personnel, security, lethal injection drugs, court costs, and lawyers' fees.

The bipartisan commission which studied the Illinois death penalty for two years took pains to note that victims' families do not receive the services they need, that the horrific effects of their loved ones' murder plague them years after the event.[11] Such services cost money. A minority of the commission felt that if the death penalty were justified for a particular defendant, the costs associated with executing him were "not relevant."[12] But the costs *are* relevant to victims' families, who are largely left to themselves, to hate or to heal. I chose to heal, but many others do not. This choice should not be bound by financial constraints when the state holds in its power the resources needed for healing.

Overcoming Hatred with Forgiveness

Does healing require forgiveness? As a Christian, I believe that it does. Let me be clear: I forgive Nancy's killer not because he had an excuse — he had none whatsoever. I forgive not because he asked for it — he has not. I do not forgive for *him*. Rather, I forgive for the One who asked and taught me to — for God. I forgive for the author and perfecter of my faith, Jesus Christ.

11. Office of the Governor, p. 10.
12. Office of the Governor, p. 11.

I do not see that God gives me a choice other than to forgive. Consider the title of Kathleen Norris's poem "Imperatives."[13]

> Look at the birds
> Consider the lilies
> Drink ye all of it
>
> Ask
> Seek
> Knock
> Enter by the narrow gate . . .
>
> Love
> Forgive
> Remember me.

How can Christians ignore these imperatives? "For if you forgive others their trespasses, your heavenly Father will also forgive you; but if you do not forgive others, neither will your Father forgive your trespasses" (Matt. 6:14-15). "Forgive your brother or sister from your heart" (Matt. 18:35).

I also forgive for myself. It is said that living with hate is like drinking poison and expecting the other person to die. Hating my sister's killer would not affect him at all, but I believe it would devour me. Perhaps for that reason, Desmond Tutu views forgiveness as an act of self-interest since it releases us from bonds that would otherwise eternally link us to those who have hurt us.[14] I was heartsick over the testimony of murder victims' family members in Illinois's recent clemency hearings for death row inmates. The sister of one victim, angrily demanding death for the killers, testified that she can no longer bring herself to say the Lord's Prayer because she cannot utter the words about forgiving others.[15]

Sometimes I think Nancy's killer wants my hate. He shall not have it. Like Bud Welch, I want something bigger than revenge. Bud and I both seek the overcoming of hate that forgiveness makes possible *for victims*. We belong to Murder Victims' Families for Reconciliation, an organization of people who have relinquished any attempt to avenge a wrong that can never be

13. Kathleen Norris, "Imperatives," in *Little Girls in Church* (Pittsburgh: University of Pittsburgh Press, 1995), p 62.

14. Dean E. Murphy, "Beyond Justice: The Eternal Struggle to Forgive," *New York Times* (26 May 2002), sec. 4, p. 1.

15. Remarks made in opposition to clemency of defendants Reginald and Jerry Mahaffey before the Illinois Prisoner Review Board in Chicago, Illinois, on 15 October 2002.

righted. We will never get our loved ones back, whether their killers live or die. We want to remove the burden of hate from our hearts. On this point, I am inspired by Roger W. Wilkins, the civil rights activist and historian at George Mason University who spoke about murders committed during the civil rights era: "After a while you figure it out for yourself: you can't be consumed by this stuff because then your oppressors have won. If you are consumed by rage, even at a terrible wrong, you have been reduced."[16]

Finally, I forgive for Nancy because she never would have wanted her memorial to involve the killing of another. A woman told me once that I must not have loved my sister very much if I could forgive her murderer. Precisely the opposite is true.

A Moral Question

After giving a speech entitled "The Moral State of the Nation," historian Garry Wills was asked what the death penalty says about the United States. Wills responded with this story. During the 2000 presidential campaign, George W. Bush was asked what philosopher most influenced him. Bush answered, "Jesus Christ." Wills then asked his audience, "What do we know about Jesus and executions? He stopped one."[17]

He did indeed: "Let anyone among you who is without sin be the first to throw a stone at her," he said in John 8:7. Jesus then forgave the sinner (v. 11). And, interestingly, he never said, "Spare her, she may be innocent." She was not: she was guilty, "caught in the very act of adultery" (v. 4). Nor did Jesus say, "Adulterers don't merit death." He never said she didn't deserve to die; he suggested instead that those standing in judgment didn't deserve to kill her.

Here's what I know about this Jesus Christ, whose name I bear when I call myself "Christian." In his dying moments, Jesus, himself a victim of crucifixion, the Roman empire's particularly ghastly brand of state execution, requested forgiveness for his executioners (Luke 23:34) and welcomed into heaven one of the criminals hanging beside him (Luke 23:43). He rejected violence as a solution (Matt. 26:52) and urged mercy (Luke 6:36).

The question "What would Jesus do?" is sometimes derided as simplistic (although Christians including St. Augustine have pondered this through two millennia). In a *Newsweek* cover story, Jon Meachem examined the question:

16. Murphy, sec. 4, p. 1.

17. Garry Wills, "The Moral State of the Nation" (address delivered at a *Christian Century* dinner meeting, Chicago, Illinois, 22 June 2000).

Though it is hard, Christians are called to bear the Gospels' central message in mind when confronting the challenges of our time. Facing a decision, evangelicals like to ask: "What would Jesus do?" As a believing, middle-of-the-road, churchgoing Episcopalian, I am, in thinking and in temperament, about as far from an evangelical as you can get. But they do have a point: it helps to be reminded that the Christian story is one of revolution, of rethinking assumptions, of overturning, as Jesus did the tables in the temple, the order of the world as we find it. In the Sermon on the Mount, Christ says, "But I say to you that listen, Love your enemies, do good to those who hate you, bless those who curse you, pray for those who abuse you. If anyone strikes you on the cheek, offer the other also. . . . Do to others as you would have them do to you."[18]

I take the question one step further and ask: "What would Jesus have *me* do?" He has already told me: *Follow me* (Matt. 10:38). *Follow me to the outcast, to the poor, to the prisoner, to the cross.* I do not believe that Jesus would have picked up the hammer to drive nails between flesh and a cross, or that he would want me to today.

This is why I am baffled by arguments that Christian faith is compatible with, even supportive of, the death penalty. Justice Scalia, in his chapter in this book, bases this view on the words of St. Paul, from Romans 13:1-4:

Let every person be subject to the governing authorities; for there is no authority except from God, and those authorities that exist have been instituted by God. Therefore whoever resists authority resists what God has appointed, and those who resist will incur judgment. For rulers are not a terror to good conduct, but to bad. Do you wish to have no fear of the authority? Then do what is good, and you will receive its approval; for it is God's servant for your good. But if you do what is wrong, you should be afraid, for the authority does not bear the sword in vain! It is the servant of God to execute wrath on the wrongdoer.

Claiming that this passage supports modern capital punishment is not new. Mark Lewis Taylor of Princeton Theological Seminary notes its use by many others. He also notes the irony of finding support for the death penalty in the writing of St. Paul, a man who preached Christ crucified and who himself is thought to have been executed by Rome.[19] There is also good reason to be-

18. Jon Meachem, "What Would Jesus Do?" *Newsweek* (6 May 2002), p. 25.
19. Mark Lewis Taylor, *The Executed God: The Way of the Cross in Lockdown America* (Minneapolis: Fortress Press, 2001), p. 81, 5, 9.

lieve, several biblical scholars note, that "the sword" here represents the general authority and coercive power of the state rather than the divine mandate of the state to execute. Scholars argue that this passage illustrates Paul's counsel to Christians to respect the authority of the state — in particular, by paying their taxes, the collection of which was enforced by Roman soldiers who bore swords. In Paul's time, execution by the sword was reserved for Roman citizens (which would have excluded most Christians); thus, it seems quite unlikely that Paul was offering to Christians an account of divine authorization for capital punishment.[20]

Justice Scalia also says in his chapter that "long and consistent Christian tradition" supports the death penalty. But, as the distinguished preacher and editor of the *Christian Century,* John M. Buchanan, remarked: "We obey Jesus Christ, our Lord, and interpret all of scripture in light of Him, what He said and what He did."[21] Support for a great many evils can be found in "Christian tradition," but not in Christ. *Newsweek's* Meachem, pointing out that churches change their minds about things which once seemed certain, sums it up:

> Asking the hard questions, even about our most basic assumptions, is to be true to our origins. Christianity was never supposed to be easy. The contradictions in Jesus' legacy are thick, and epic. In defeat there is victory; in humility, strength; in surrender, gain; in darkness, light. All counterintuitive ideas, and all promise rewards later, not now — beyond time and space. It is not a creed of comfort.[22]

Yet hate continues to be the "creed of comfort" for too many in our world. Consider the message painted on a house just after September 11 — "God forgives but we don't." One of the relatives of Texas killer Karla Faye Tucker's victims loudly resented the fact that Tucker, a woman who became a Christian on death row, could go to heaven after her execution. He said he hoped the victim would "kick Tucker's ass" when she arrived. What to make of the hordes I witnessed celebrating outside the prison where serial killer John Wayne Gacy was executed at midnight? The macabre group tailgated in the

20. For an excellent discussion of Romans 13:4 as questionable justification for capital punishment, see New Testament scholar Christopher Marshall's *Beyond Retribution: A New Testament Vision for Justice, Crime, and Punishment* (Grand Rapids, Mich.: Eerdmans Publishing Co.; Auckland, New Zealand: Lime Grove House Publishing Ltd., 2001), pp. 234-39.
21. John M Buchanan, "What Wondrous Love Is This?" (sermon delivered at Fourth Presbyterian Church, Chicago, Illinois, 24 February 2002).
22. Meachem, p. 32.

darkness, their young children in strollers beside them. The daughter of a Tennessee murder victim said of the killer's impending execution, "I can't wait to be there. We think he should be put in a wood-chipper."[23]

Contrast these instances of debilitating bitterness to which others cling so desperately with profound moments of Christian compassion: Pope John Paul II forgiving his would-be assassin; the late Joseph Cardinal Bernardin of Chicago forgiving the man who falsely accused Bernardin of sexual abuse. Hatred sounds tough; it always will. But being hateful and being tough are not the same as being strong. Strength is entirely different. And strength, true strength begotten of love, not of killing, will always have the last word.

About a week after my father found Nancy and Richard's bodies in the basement where they died, the police told us about Nancy's final message of love, written in her blood. That was the moment, finally, when my mother cried in front of me. "It's true, isn't it?" she asked. "Love is stronger than death."

23. John Shiffman, "Sunquist Denies Clemency: Abdur'Rahman Faces Execution," *The Tennessean*, 6 April 2002.

Lifting New Voices against the Death Penalty: Religious Americans and the Debate on Capital Punishment

E. J. DIONNE JR.

Revolving prison doors. Willie Horton. An announcer with a dark, sonorous voice accusing some politician of being "soft on criminals." These are the images of the politics of the death penalty, circa 1988. From the 1970s to the beginning of the 1990s, the debate over the death penalty was as stale as it was predictable. Rising crime rates in the 1960s had produced an understandable revulsion in the electorate against street violence. The government's failure to stem the criminal tide produced widespread mistrust of the criminal justice system. Support for the death penalty rose steadily in the polls as voters demanded some certainty of justice in the face of what they saw as chaos. If the police and the courts could not be trusted to make the streets safe, perhaps the ultimate punishment would at least instill the fear of God, and the fear of public vengeance, in criminals.

Even opponents of the death penalty understood why the public was angry. And many liberal politicians feared that anger would be turned against them. Slowly but steadily, liberals who had long opposed capital punishment began voting for it. In some cases the politicians made a principled re-evaluation of their views, but in virtually all such conversions, there was an undercurrent of fear that a few devastating political advertisements from more conservative opponents would successfully paint them as friends to criminals (or, as one colorful New York City politician once put it, "members of the hoodlum lobby"). A few politicians resisted the tide in favor of executions and remained opposed to the death penalty. But many of them — for example, Massachusetts governor Michael Dukakis and New York governor Mario

Cuomo — were eventually swept away. Dukakis was defeated in the 1988 presidential election. Cuomo was defeated for re-election as governor of New York in 1994. Many factors besides capital punishment were at work in these contests, but their opposition to the death penalty certainly played a role in their defeat.

For a sense of how much the country changed its mind on capital punishment, consider that only 42 percent of Americans supported the death penalty in 1966, according to Gallup. In 1994, support for the death penalty reached its peak, at 80 percent.[1]

But in the late 1990s, something happened. Support for the death penalty began declining, dropping from that 80 percent in 1994 to 66 percent in 2000.[2] What was going on? What can account for the change?

Undoubtedly, the decline of the crime rate in the 1990s (including huge declines during Rudolph Giuliani's tenure as New York City's mayor) had a reassuring effect on the public. If the criminal justice system was still far from perfect, it was working better. If worries about crime persisted, the sweeping fears bred by the crime wave years ebbed. The combination of more faith in the authorities and less fear of the criminals created an opening: Americans could reconsider whether the death penalty was as essential as they had thought. They could ponder alternatives and have some hope that the alternatives might work. They could begin to examine the problems with the death penalty itself.

The new opening was widened by new evidence. Illinois governor George Ryan assumed leadership among those rethinking the death penalty when he called a halt to executions in his state until he could be sure the death penalty was being administered fairly. A longtime capital punishment supporter, Ryan said there was too much evidence of past mistakes. He called for a bold reexamination of how the system worked. He was influenced by a group of Northwestern University journalism students led by Professor David Protess. They provided startling evidence of flaws in the system and errors in particular capital trials. A *Chicago Tribune* investigative series by Ken Armstrong and Steve Mills studied the state's 285 capital cases; among many glaring shortcomings, they discovered that thirty-three death-row inmates were represented by lawyers who had at some point been disbarred or suspended.[3]

1. ABCNEWS/*Washington Post* poll, reported on 2 May 2001. (This poll was conducted by telephone 20-24 April 2001 among a random national sample of 1,003 adults. The results have a three-point error margin. Data collection and tabulation by ICR — International Communications Research of Media, Pa.)

2. ABCNEWS/*Washington Post* poll, 2 May 2001.

3. Ken Armstrong and Steve Mills, "The Death Penalty in Illinois," *Chicago Tribune*, 14-18 November 1999. The five-part series is archived online at http://www.chicagotribune.com/news/nationworld/chi-dpdpillinois-special.special (accessed 6 August 2003).

Ryan helped death penalty opponents create a safe zone for capital punishment supporters who harbored doubts. Few death penalty supporters were willing to accept the execution of the innocent. As Senator Pat Leahy, a Vermont Democrat and death penalty reformer, put it, "Even those who are for the death penalty are more willing to admit that it's not foolproof and can be capricious."[4] In the battle for hearts and minds, it was far more persuasive to talk about innocent people whose lives might be taken at the gallows than to argue about whether those clearly guilty of heinous crimes should be executed. The new movement for "death penalty reform" was based on the simple principle that if the death penalty were to continue, it needed to be administered with more care and more concern for justice. Inevitably, the reform movement cast doubts upon the death penalty itself.

The role of Ryan and those Northwestern students is well known. But a third large element in the new death penalty debate is often overlooked: the voices of religious Americans, including religious conservatives. Some of these voices were always there as were part of the hardy 20 percent who opposed capital punishment at its high tide. The Roman Catholic bishops and many Protestant and Jewish leaders had long taken stands against the death penalty. African American clergy were especially outspoken. These messages seemed to have little effect until the late 1990s, when members of the religious rank-and-file began developing doubts of their own — and when critics of the death penalty were joined by new voices among evangelical Christians.

A watershed moment was the 1998 execution of Karla Faye Tucker, a convicted double-murderer — and born-again Christian. Foes of capital punishment are often perceived to be defending people who not only did awful things but seem to have done them without remorse. They are hard-pressed to answer the families of murder victims shouting for just vengeance. The power of the Tucker case came from the challenge her execution posed to Christian conservatives who supported the death penalty in principle. During her incarceration on Texas's death row, Tucker experienced a religious rebirth and repented of her sins; a dramatic change in both her outlook and her behavior followed. She impressed all those around her with the completeness of her conversion. Many Christian conservatives came to believe that she had earned clemency through sincere repentance, and because of her apparent rehabilitation. The Revs. Pat Robertson and Jerry Falwell rose to her defense, using language that echoed arguments long made (albeit ineffectually) by opponents of the death

---

4. E. J. Dionne Jr., "Challenging the Death Penalty," *Washington Post*, 16 April 2002. Interview with the author in April 2002.

penalty. As Robertson put it: "Mercy trumps justice."[5] Tucker's gender may have played a role in increasing the public's sympathy. Until Tucker was put to death, Texas had not executed a woman prisoner since 1863, when Chipita Rodriguez was hanged for the ax murder of a man. Governor George W. Bush, however, was not swayed, and he refused to grant a thirty-day reprieve of the execution. He draped his decision in religious language of his own. "I have concluded [that] judgments about the heart and soul of an individual on death row are best left to a higher authority," Bush said.

The alternative religious view was stated powerfully by Ron Carlson, the brother of one of Tucker's victims. "The reason I think that Karla should live is that I don't think that we, as human beings, have the right to take a life, whether it is for justice or whether it is in vengeance or revenge. We, human beings, did not create life. God creates this life. Therefore, I believe that only God should take the life."[6]

This view reverberated around the nation. Jennifer Morgan, a twenty-five-year-old accountant in Boston, told *New York Times* reporter Sam Howe Verhovek: "Before this, I was for the death penalty. But when you come to know someone through these television shows, it makes you think: Is that what they deserve?"[7]

"The real question we should ask ourselves is why so many people saw Tucker's humanity but refuse to see it in others," said David R. Dow, a University of Houston law professor who has represented more than twenty death row prisoners. "Because the truth is that almost all execution victims are like Tucker. Most come to regret that they killed. Most have families who love them. Many find religion. Many are articulate. Some are even physically attractive."

Dow told Verhovek that Tucker had five characteristics that combined to make her a media sensation. "She was a woman, white, attractive, articulate and a Christian," he said. "A lot of people on death row have three of those characteristics; some have four. But very few have all five, and I simply don't see another case commanding this amount of attention."[8]

But Tucker did command attention. In doing so, she made it easier for political conservatives who had long harbored doubts about capital punishment. Vin Weber, a former Republican congressman from Minnesota, spoke of once being lonely in his wing of the party when he cast his votes on capital punishment. "I was one of only five or six Republicans to vote against the death pen-

5. *Larry King Live*, CNN, 15 January 1998.

6. *Larry King Live*, 15 January 1998.

7. E. J. Dionne Jr., "Conservatives against the Death Penalty," *Washington Post*, 27 June 2000. Interview with the author in June 2000.

8. Dionne, "Conservatives against the Death Penalty."

alty," he said.[9] He is less lonely now because many on the right who have made "limited government" the cause of a lifetime have begun to question how the death penalty advances that goal.[10] Referring to the complaints of militia members against government intrusion, conservative writer Kate O'Beirne says: "We conservatives don't have to be marching around with those folks in the woods of Minnesota to fear the power of government, a well-armed government."[11]

Make no mistake: Most conservatives, including most conservative evangelicals, still support the death penalty. In particular, few conservative politicians have joined their colleague Weber in his view. For now, outright opposition is being expressed more by conservative writers such as O'Beirne, Carl Cannon, and Paul Craig Roberts than by active politicians.

The welfare reform debate may offer the best metaphor to the shift on the right on the death penalty. Over the years, even liberals who strongly supported government aid to the poor acknowledged that the welfare system was working badly. "A lot of people who didn't want to repeal welfare 'as we knew it' were willing to talk about the problems," Weber says, referring to liberals who began criticizing the welfare system in the 1980s. By admitting the problems, liberals opened the way for change — even if they opposed the actual reform passed by Congress in 1996. Conservatives now raising doubts about the capital punishment system, Weber says, could play a similar role in spurring death-penalty reform and, perhaps eventually, even repeal.

The moral impulse behind the movement for reform and repeal is brought home by the nature of who is switching sides — many are religious conservatives — and by the reasons they advance for doing so. For abortion opponents such as Rep. Chris Smith, a New Jersey Republican, opposition to capital punishment has always been part of a "consistent ethic of life." O'Beirne thinks that Pope John Paul II's strong statements against the death penalty have pushed more Catholic conservatives in Smith's direction. Opinion is also shifting among conservative evangelical Protestants. Pat Robertson's support for a death-penalty moratorium is only one of many unexpected developments.

The conventional view of American politics sees religious activists as pushing the debate consistently toward the right, especially on abortion and matters related to sexuality. The death penalty is the large exception to that conventional wisdom. A survey conducted in March 2001 by the Pew Forum

9. Dionne, "Conservatives against the Death Penalty."

10. Vin Weber now serves as a member of the Constitution Project's Death Penalty Initiative, a commission made up of retentionists and abolitionists dedicated to reforming the American capital justice system.

11. Dionne, "Conservatives against the Death Penalty."

on Religion and Public Life and the Pew Research Center for the People and the Press found (in line with other surveys) that 65 percent of Americans favored the death penalty, while 28 percent opposed it. But when supporters and opponents were asked what had most influenced their view on the issue — they were given a list of options that included personal experience, the views of family and friends, their religious beliefs, their educational experiences, or something else — opponents of the death penalty were far more likely to cite their religious beliefs than supporters. Fully 42 percent of death penalty opponents cited their religious beliefs as the most important influence on their opposition, while only 15 percent of supporters said their view was mostly shaped by their religious convictions.

Further overturning the conventional view, white evangelical Protestants with a high degree of religious commitment were significantly more likely to oppose the death penalty than white evangelicals with less of a religious commitment. According to the survey, 23 percent of white evangelicals with a high level of religious commitment opposed the death penalty, compared with 13 percent among those of low commitment. A similar relationship was found among white Catholics — 36 percent of Catholics with a high level of religious commitment opposed the death penalty, compared with only 20 percent among those with low religious commitment levels. It should be noted that African Americans in these categories opposed the death penalty more strongly than their white counterparts in either of these groups, but the role of religiosity among whites in encouraging opposition to the death penalty remains striking. Among high-commitment white evangelicals, for example, fully 62 percent of death penalty opponents cited their religious beliefs as the main influence on their view; among high-commitment Catholics, that figure reached 71 percent.[12]

If the death penalty is ever repealed or scaled back in a significant way, it will happen in part because liberal politicians who were intimidated by those "soft on crime" ads in the 1980s find their voices again. But it will also happen because a growing band of courageous conservatives is taking what was once a toxic political question and allowing it to be seen as the serious moral, theological, and philosophical problem it always has been. And the shift within conservatism — if it happens — will be led largely by the movement's religious voices.

---

12. "Faith-Based Funding Backed, But Church-State Doubts Abound," the Pew Forum on Religion and Public Life, and the Pew Research Center for the People and the Press (10 April 2001). Available online at http://people-press.org/reports/display.php3?ReportID=15 (accessed 30 July 2003).

Index

Abel, 46, 79-85, 129-30, 132-33, 204
abortion, 26, 29, 153, 219-20, 233, 238-39, 281
Abou El Fadl, Khaled, 16, 18, 73-105
Abravanel, Don Isaac, 42-43
Abu Bakr, caliphate of, 101
Abu Zahrah, Muhammad, 95n.49, 99n.58, 100n.62, 101n.66, 102nn.71,73, 103n.76
Adam, 88, 172
adultery: as capital crime in Islam, 96n.53, 99-102, 103n.76, 162; as capital crime in Judaism, 124, 179; Jesus' forgiveness of, 135-36, 273
Afghanistan, 16, 44, 104n.76
African Americans, and the death penalty, 69n.28, 229, 251, 279, 282
Agag, 44-45
Akivah, Rabbi, 36-38-40, 47
Al-Qaeda, 32-33
Amalekites, 44-45
Ambrose, 65
Amnesty International, 250nn.5-7, 251n.9
Anabaptists, 176
"Anatomy of a Verdict" (Burnett), 269
Anaya, Toney, 2n.3
Anderson, Gary A., 125n.2

Anderson, Lisa, 188n.69
Anderson, Victor, 16-18, 195-210
anthropological understanding: of the death penalty, 141-44, 153-57, 163; of justice, 160-64, 170-72, 175, 178, 180-83, 186, 191, 194
apostasy, as capital crime in Islam, 96n.53, 99-102
'Arabi, Abu Bakr Muhammad b. 'Abd Allah b. al-, 103n.75
Arendt, Hannah, 15, 33-34, 41n.24
Armstrong, Ken, 278
Arthur, Thomas, 174
'Asqalani, Shihab al-Din Ibn Hajar al-, 104n.78
Atkins v. Virginia, 13n.33, 142n.13, 250
atonement, 112, 125, 166
Atonement, Day of, 47
Audi, Robert, 146n.24, 150n.45
Augustine, St., 23, 172, 181n.50, 183, 238, 273
authorities. *See* state

Babylonian Talmud: Baba Metsia, 46n.43; Gittin, 38n.16; Kiddushin, 36n.6, 41-42nn.25,27-29; Makkot, 36n.7, 46n.46;

Postawko, Robert, 76n.10, 77n.12, 99n.59, 102n.69
Powell, H. Jefferson, 141n.6, 143n.15
Prejean, Helen, 254-55
premeditation, Talmud on, 45-46
Princeton Theological Seminary, 274
Prometheus, 185
proof "beyond reasonable doubt," 118, 168, 192, 218-19, 223, 243
protection of society, and the death penalty, 5, 24, 27-28, 60, 111, 113-14, 117, 190-91, 217, 237-38, 241-42
Protess, David, 278
Protestant Ethic and the Spirit of Punishment, The (Snyder), 168-75
Protestant tradition: on the death penalty, 15-16, 48-56, 279, 282; on penal theory, 168-75. *See also* Catholic tradition; Christian tradition
Psalms, 43n.34, 112, 131, 140
public order, and the death penalty, 54, 62-63, 176-77, 180, 240-41, 277
punishment: Camus on, 185-89; Christian understanding of, 58-62, 67, 69-72, 168-75, 236; purposes of, 18, 28, 49-56, 59-65, 110-16, 121-22, 179, 188, 237-38
Putnam, Constance, 242n.5

Qumran, 135
Qur'an: Cain and Abel in, 79-85, 88; on corruption of the earth, 80-82, 87-90, 97, 99; on forgiveness, 82-86, 92-93, 96-97; Khidr and Moses in, 74n.7; and law of talion, 84-86; on mercy and compassion, 91-92, 96-99; power delegated to victims by, 84, 93-98; on punishment, 85-86, 162; on retribution, 84, 92-93, 162; on sanctity of human life, 87-88; and terrorism, 80, 82n.20; on vengeance, 84, 86n.29, 87, 96-98
Qurtubi, Abd Allah Muhammad b. Ahmad al-, 103n.75

racial bias in the death penalty, 6, 13n.32, 29, 77n.12, 142, 223n.2, 229, 242, 251-52
Radelet, Michael L., 242n.5

Rahman, S. A., 101n.67
Rawls, John, 144-45, 146n.25, 150
rebellion (Camus on), 181-87
Redekop, Vernon W., 136n.28
redemption of God, 130-33, 169-71, 174-75
"Reflections on the Guillotine" (Camus), 187
reform of the death penalty, 4, 6, 12, 192, 217-18, 252n.12, 260-62, 269, 278-79, 281
rehabilitation, as purpose of punishment, 24, 60, 64, 111, 113, 117, 190
Rehnquist, William H., 149
Reid, Richard, 9
"religion in the public square," 15, 144-53, 219-20, 236-37, 245-46, 249
Rengstorf, Claus, 136n.26
repentance, 72, 82, 102, 131, 193-94
Responsible Self, The (H. R. Niebuhr), 206-8
retribution: and the death penalty, 4-5, 23, 27-28, 63-64, 117, 228, 237-38, 258; as different from vengeance, 50-51, 64, 110, 112, 115, 175n.33, 269; and just punishment, 50, 64, 110-13, 115-16, 160, 163, 165, 170-71, 237-38; Qur'an on, 84, 92-93, 162. *See also* vengeance
Reu, J. M., 50
revenge. *See* vengeance
Rice, Charles E., 27n.5
Richardson, William, 14n.35
Ring v. Arizona, 13n.33, 142n.12
Ritschl, Albrecht, 196
Roberts, Paul Craig, 281
Robertson, Pat, 9, 279, 281
Robespierre, 181n.48, 182, 186
Rockefeller, Winthrop L., 1n.3
Rodriguez, Chipita, 280
Roe v. Wade, 219, 233
Roman government, 38, 116, 137, 273-75
Romans, Epistle to the, 116, 134; on role of government, 23, 50, 53, 109, 137-38, 208, 234-37, 274-75
Romantics, 182
Roper v. Simmons, 13n.34
Rorty, Richard, 145